Y0-DUD-191

Federal Copyright Records 1790 - 1800

Federal Copyright Records 1790 - 1800

edited and with an introduction by
James Gilreath

compiled by
Elizabeth Carter Wills

Library of Congress Washington 1987

Library of Congress Cataloging-in-Publication Data

Federal copyright records, 1790–1800.

Bibliography: p.
Includes index.
Supt. of Docs. no. : LC 23.2:C79/790–800
1. Copyright—United States—Catalogs.
2. Bibliography, National—United States.
I. Gilreath, James, 1947– . II. Wills, Elizabeth
Carter. III. Library of Congress. Rare Book and
Special Collections Division.
Z642.L53 1986 015.73 86–600334
ISBN 0–8444–0540–X (alk. paper)

This book is printed on acid-free paper.

For sale by the Superintendent of Documents, U.S. Government Printing Office
Washington, D.C. 20402

CONTENTS

Foreword

In a report to the Center for the Book eight years ago, bibliographer and historian G. Thomas Tanselle pointed out that one of the basic sources of information about the intellectual activity of our country—the records produced by the operation of the U. S. copyright law between 1790 and 1870—was largely neglected. The reason was the complexity of form of these records, which are large, bulky, and often incomplete and include record books compiled by different district court clerks throughout the country. Tanselle thought that a project to make the information in these records more widely and easily accessible "would be one of the most valuable conceivable projects for the study of intellectual history in this country." This publication, we hope, is the first step in such a project, for it makes the records for the first decade (1790–1800) widely available and usable. It is sponsored by the Center for the Book in the Library of Congress in cooperation with the Library's Rare Book and Special Collections Division, where most of the records are housed. Our goal is to stimulate interest in the early copyright records and in a large-scale, cooperative project that would cover the entire 1790–1870 period.

Encouraging the study of the history of books is one of the principal aims of the Center for the Book. Created by an Act of Congress to stimulate public interest in books, reading, and the printed word, the center is an informal organization funded primarily by contributions from individuals and corporations. Its symposia, projects, events, and publications are of interest to both scholars and the general public.

Many people have assisted in this project. For their encouragement, the Center for the Book is grateful to G. Thomas Tanselle, vice president of the Guggenheim Memorial Foundation, and to William Matheson, chief of the Library's Rare Book and Special Collections Division. Special thanks go to the compiler, consultant Elizabeth Carter Wills, and to James Gilreath, American history specialist in the Rare Book and Special Collections Division, who supervised the project, edited the manuscript, and wrote the preface and introduction.

The early copyright records are a basic source for those attempting to understand the development of almost any aspect of American life. We know this volume will interest historians, biographers, and bibliographers and trust many others will find it useful too.

John Y. Cole
Director
The Center for the Book

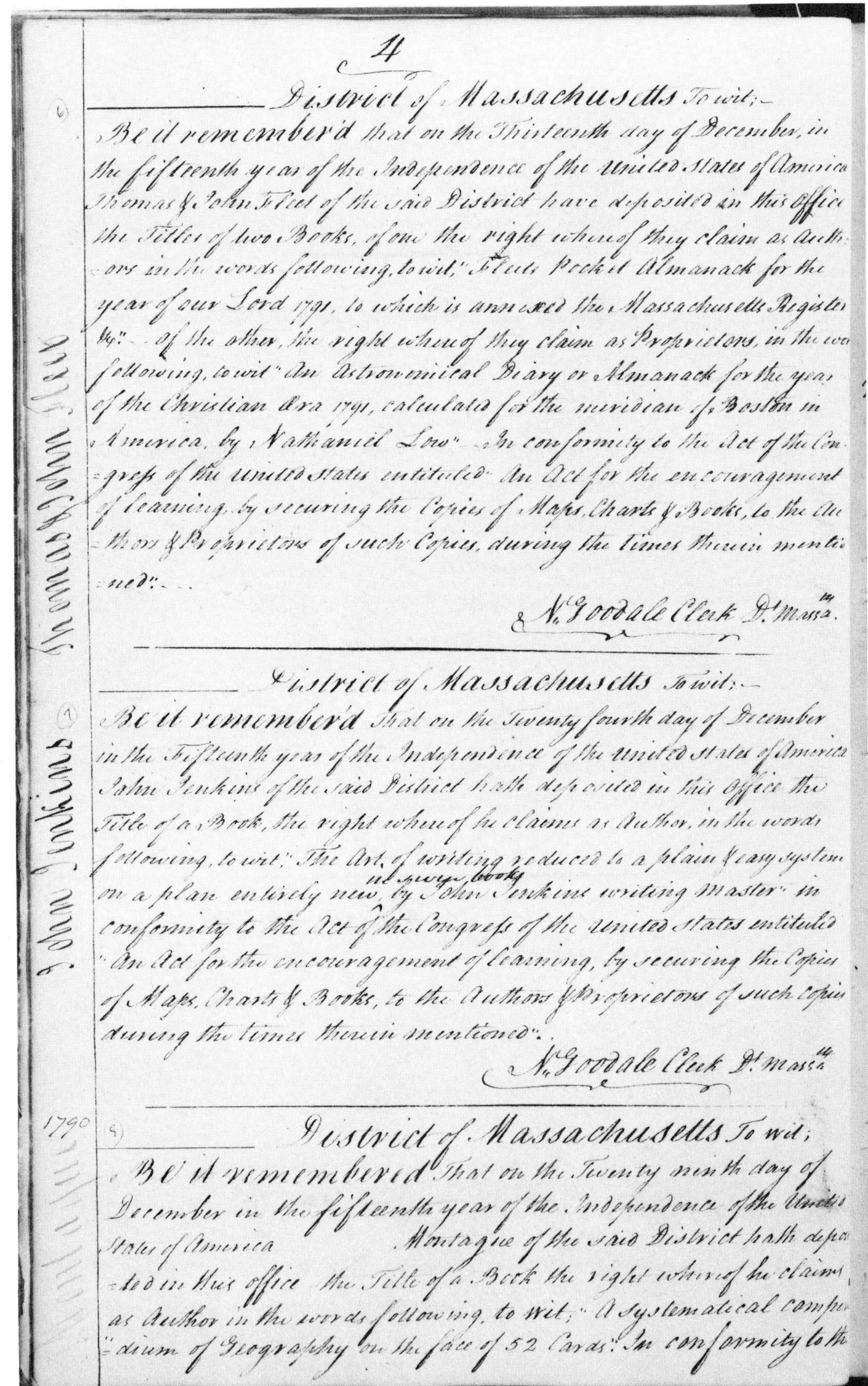

4

(6) District of Massachusetts To wit;—

Be it remember'd that on the Thirteenth day of December, in the fifteenth year of the Independence of the United States of America Thomas & John Fleet of the said District have deposited in this Office the Titles of two Books, of one the right whereof they claim as Authors in the words following, to wit," Fleets Pocket Almanack for the year of our Lord 1791, to which is annexed the Massachusetts Register &c." — of the other, the right whereof they claim as Proprietors, in the words following, to wit" An Astronomical Diary or Almanack for the year of the Christian Æra 1791, calculated for the meridian of Boston in America, by Nathaniel Low" — In conformity to the Act of the Congress of the United States entituled " An Act for the encouragement of learning, by securing the Copies of Maps, Charts & Books, to the Authors & Proprietors of such Copies, during the times therein mentioned". —

N. Goodale Clerk Dt. Massa.

Thomas & John Fleet

(7) District of Massachusetts To wit;—

Be it remember'd That on the Twenty fourth day of December in the Fifteenth year of the Independence of the United States of America John Jenkins of the said District hath deposited in this Office the Title of a Book, the right whereof he claims as Author, in the words following, to wit;" The Art of writing reduced to a plain & easy system on a plan entirely new, in seven books, by John Jenkins writing master" in conformity to the Act of the Congress of the United States entituled " An Act for the encouragement of learning, by securing the Copies of Maps, Charts & Books, to the Authors & Proprietors of such Copies during the times therein mentioned".

N. Goodale Clerk Dt. Massa.

John Jenkins

1790 (8) District of Massachusetts To wit;

Be it remembered That on the Twenty ninth day of December in the fifteenth year of the Independence of the United States of America Montague of the said District hath deposited in this office the Title of a Book the right whereof he claims, as Author in the words following, to wit;" A Systematical compendium of Geography on the face of 52 Cards". In conformity to the

Figure 1. Registrations recorded in chronological order on a page of the copyright ledger of the District Court of Massachusetts

Editor's Preface

The Library of Congress copyright collection for the period between 1790, the date of the first federal copyright law, and 1870 consists of 615 court registration ledgers, more than 44,000 deposited title pages, about 23,000 deposit copies, and ledgers from the Patent Office and the State Department that indicate that a copy of a published work had been deposited with them. Before 1870, these records were held by the federal district courts and the Patent Office, which in 1854 had assumed the State Department's duty of recording copy deposits. The copyright act of 1870 consolidated in the Library of Congress all copyright registration activity and all the extant records for the pre-1870 period. Most documents held by the district courts were sent to the Library, but some title pages and ledgers do exist in institutions other than the Library of Congress. Documents of many states for certain time periods are lost, and only partial information for a few of them can be found in secondary sources.[1] Almost all the Library's ledgers and title pages are in the custody of the Rare Book and Special Collections Division, though two groups of title pages were separated from the collection and are now kept in the Music Division and the Geography and Map Division.

There were more than fifteen thousand American imprints between 1790 and 1800, but only 779 copyright registrations could be found for that period. In six states—Connecticut, Georgia, Delaware, Tennessee, Maryland, and New Jersey—no copyright records could be located for those years. Among those states, only Connecticut could rival Pennsylvania and Massachusetts as a publishing center. Few copyright deposit copies of books and maps for the period 1790 to 1800 survive.[2]

At a joint meeting of the American Historical Association and the Bibliographical Society of America in 1937, Chief Assistant Librarian of Congress Martin A. Roberts called the copyright archives "basic sources for a history of our literary and typographic arts for the period which saw those arts spring from the swaddling clothes of the eighteenth century to the great stature of the nineteenth."[3] In 1969, G. Thomas Tanselle remarked that "the publication of these entries would facilitate and stimulate bibliographical and historical research into the Anglo-American cultural heritage; it would also insure the preservation of the most detailed official record ever produced of the nation's literary and artistic product."[4] Bibliographers and historians can benefit from the copyright information about claimants, the identification of authors of pseudonymous or anonymous works, and the exact dates of registration. The deposited title pages help document the pre-publication history of these works and often offer significant bibliographical details.[5] Some registrations refer to books no longer extant or never published.

All commentators agree that the research potential of the copyright records has not been realized. The lack of an index has made the records frustrating to use. Ideally, the data recorded in all 150,000 copyright entries in the Rare Book and Special Collections Division should be indexed and published, but the money for such a massive project does not at this time exist. The purpose of publishing the present compilation of the registrations for the first decade of the federal copyright law is to bring these records to the attention of many more scholars and investigators and to demonstrate the kind of information available in the research material. The project brings the bibliographical record of pre-1801 American imprints closer to completion. Use of this volume will make clear the desirability of having all the records from 1800 to 1870 fully accessible and will serve as a guide to show which parts of the copyright records are most valuable to researchers.

Until 1870, American copyright claimants were required to submit a proposed title page when making their applications to a federal district court. The clerk in the court wrote out the registrations in the ledgers in the order they were received (fig. 1) and filed the title pages (see fig. 2). The registration included a standard legal phrase common to all claims, the name of the author, the title of the work, and the name of the claimant of the copyright (see fig. 3). Before 1831, the claimant was also required to insert a notice of each claim in a newspaper for a period of four weeks. A copy of the copyrighted work was to be sent to the State Department before 1853 and to the Patent Office between 1854 and 1870.

To gather information about title pages, ledger registrations, and copy deposits for the time period covered by this volume, I have used sources from all locations except the newspaper notices referred to above. Whenever data in this book are taken from a source other than an original document in the Rare Book and Special Collections Division, the authority is given in a note in the entry. Though newspaper notices would be particularly valuable for those states that do not have extant title pages and ledgers, this project's funding could not support the time and travel necessary to consult them, and these states are therefore not included here.

Historians and bibliographers expressed different preferences about the presentation of the entries in this volume. Whereas bibliographers thought that the differences between the ledgers and the title pages in capitalization, punctuation, title page design, and other bibliographical elements should be preserved, historians showed little interest in these aspects of the claims and saw an accurate breakdown of the records into logical elements like author, title, and imprint as important. Neither group thought it necessary to transcribe the legal formula surrounding the entries in the ledgers. Both expressed the hope that the index would provide the comprehensive access the records so desperately need.

The form of entry devised for this publication is an attempt to satisfy these many needs. The title page and the registration for the same work are joined in one entry. The code for each ledger entry indicates the volume's place in the collection, gives an abbreviation for the state, and supplies the number of the page in the volume on which the registration can be found. Thus, District Court Ledger 262 PA 7 shows that this Pennsylvania entry appears on page 7 of volume 262. This code would serve as a unique control number were all the data one day entered in a computer database. In those instances where the dates in the ledger and on the title page are identical, the date is entered only in the ledger portion of the entry. The claimant's name is exactly as it appears, with an "A" indicating that he is claiming the work as its author, a "P" as proprietor, or an "A, P" as both.

Transcribing the author's name was particularly difficult. Giving the author a separate line in the entry altered the original order of the wording of the title page. To avoid repetion, I entered the phrase "<author statement>" at the place in the title where the author's name occurs. When the author's name is the same in the author and claimant portion of the entry, an ellipsis is inserted in place of the name on the author line. Any additional information in the author statement that does not appear in the claimant segment, such as his honorary degrees, is retained after the ellipsis. Entry 1 is an example of this method of description.

To enable the user to visualize the deposited title pages, all punctuation, spelling, and capitalization are reproduced exactly, though smaller or larger capitals are not distinguished. Illustrations or type ornaments are described within angle brackets in the entry. Line endings are shown by a slash. When a line of transcription in an entry ends in the middle of a word before a line ending occurs on the title page, the word is divided but no hyphen is inserted at the break. An example can be found on the fourth line of the title page description of entry 1. Roman and italic type are used here as they were used on the title page. Other typefaces, such as black letter or script, are described within angle brackets. Such a description applies to a single line unless otherwise indicated. For example, "<black letter> Modern Chivalry:/ CONTAINING THE/ ADVENTURES/ OF/ Captain John Farrago/" indicates that only the words *Modern Chivalry* are in black letter on the title page. Space considerations dictate that literary or classical quotations, which appear frequently on eighteenth-century title pages, be described within angle brackets rather than transcribed. The lengthy tables of contents that appeared on a few title pages are omitted, and ellipses inserted in their place. Manuscript notations made by the printer or author are given within angle brackets (fig. 4). Information printed on a title page that does not relate to the author, title, or imprint is included in the note field of the entry. In the New York ledger, manuscript registrations are arranged on the page in the form of title pages (see fig. 5), and therefore all conventions for transcribing printed title pages are followed for the New York ledger registrations.

All titles, authors, printers, booksellers, publishers, and important names in titles are indexed. Publishing partnerships are indexed with cross-references to each partner's name. Titles are given as they appear in the entry. The variety of spellings of names in the records made it necessary to standardize personal names in the index.

This book was entered on a floppy disk using a Compucorp 675. A Compugraphic MCS composing unit with an 8400 typesetter was used to produce the photoready copy.

I would like to thank John Y. Cole, director of the Center for the Book, sponsor of this publication, and William Matheson, chief of the Rare Book and Special Collections Division, who made the division's resources available. Ellen Bryant was indefatigable in entering this work on the Compucorp. Peggy Pixley and the staff of the Library's Composing Unit were patient in handling our numerous revisions during the proofreading process. G. Thomas Tanselle of the John Simon Guggenheim Foundation, Roger Stoddard of Harvard University, and Alice Schreyer of The University of Delaware were generous with their advice about the form of the entries. I benefited from the reactions of Robert Winans of Wayne State University to a draft of the introduction. As compiler, Carter Wills, consultant to the Center for the Book, was tireless in filling out forms, indexing, and helping to proofread. Her constant good cheer brightened each day of this project for all involved.

---

[1] G. Thomas Tanselle's "Copyright Records and the Bibliographer," *Studies in Bibliography* 22 (1969), gives a list of extant records and their locations.

[2] Roger Stoddard, "United States Copyright Deposit Copies of Books and Pamphlets Printed before 1820," *Publishing History* 13 (1983), pp. 5–21.

[3] Martin A. Roberts, *Records in the Copyright Office Deposited by the United States District Courts Covering the Period 1790–1870* (Washington: Government Printing Office), p. 13.

[4] Tanselle, "Copyright Records," p. 121.

[5] Frederick R. Goff, "The First Decade of the Federal Act for Copyright, 1790–1800," in *Essays Honoring Lawrence Wroth* (Portland, Maine: Printed by The Athoensen Press, 1951), pp. 101–28.

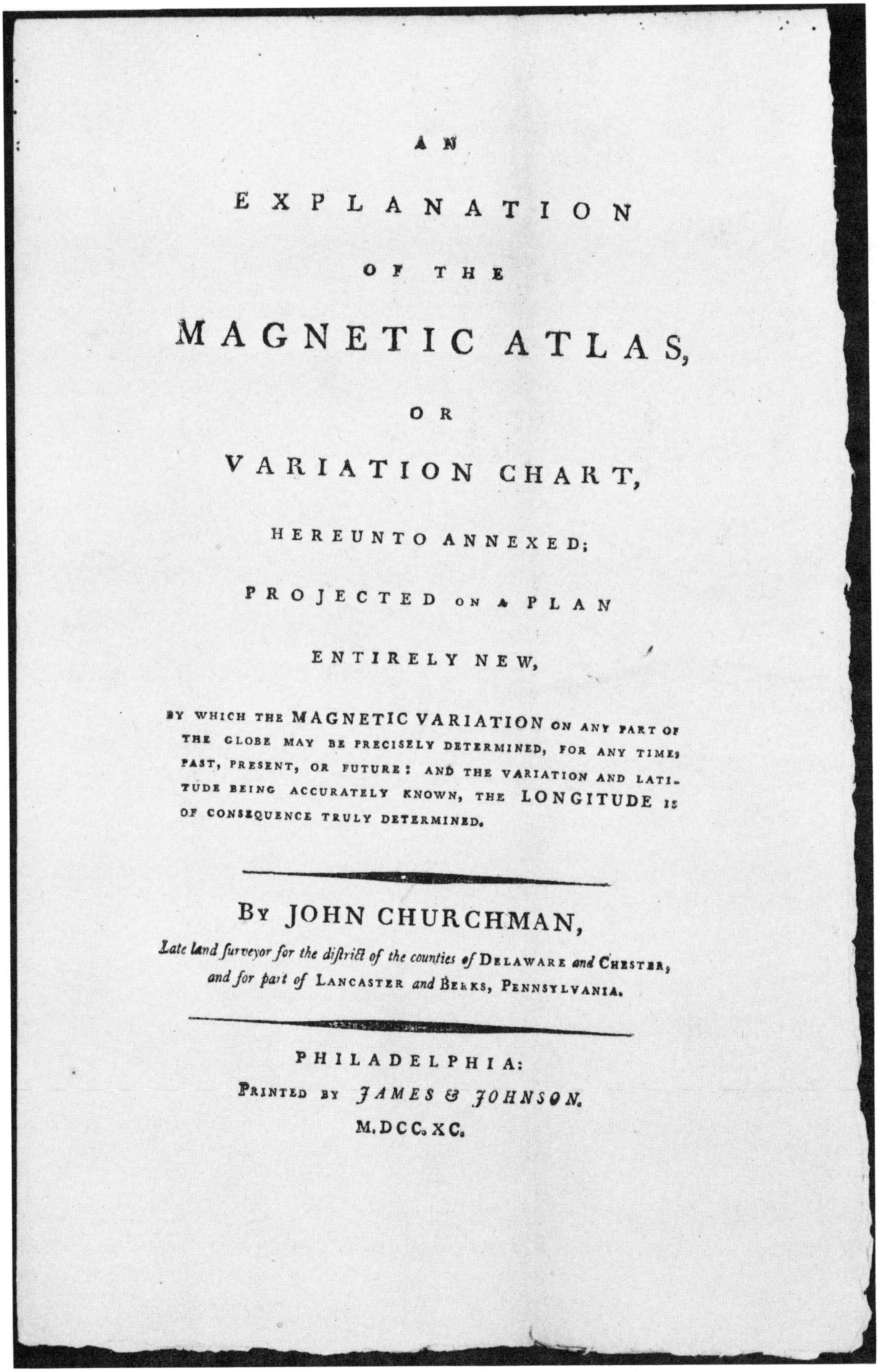

AN

EXPLANATION

OF THE

MAGNETIC ATLAS,

OR

VARIATION CHART,

HEREUNTO ANNEXED;

PROJECTED ON A PLAN

ENTIRELY NEW,

BY WHICH THE MAGNETIC VARIATION ON ANY PART OF THE GLOBE MAY BE PRECISELY DETERMINED, FOR ANY TIME, PAST, PRESENT, OR FUTURE: AND THE VARIATION AND LATITUDE BEING ACCURATELY KNOWN, THE LONGITUDE IS OF CONSEQUENCE TRULY DETERMINED.

BY JOHN CHURCHMAN,

Late land surveyor for the district of the counties of DELAWARE *and* CHESTER, *and for part of* LANCASTER *and* BERKS, PENNSYLVANIA.

PHILADELPHIA:

PRINTED BY *JAMES & JOHNSON.*

M.DCC.XC.

Figure 2. Title page of John Churchman's *An Explanation of the Magnetic Atlas,* deposited to secure copyright in the District Court of Pennsylvania (entry no. 3)

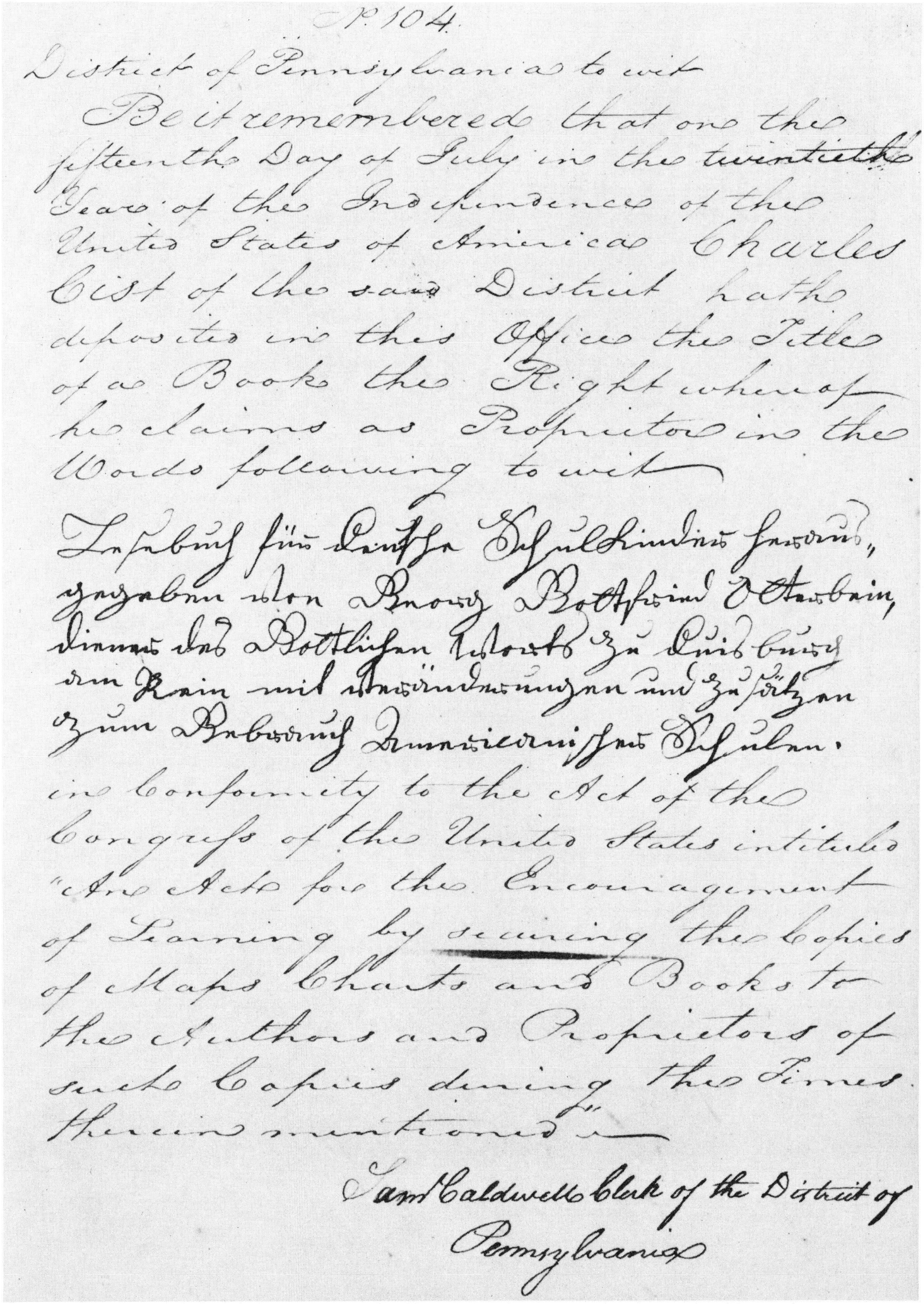

N.° 104.

District of Pennsylvania to wit

Be it remembered that on the fifteenth Day of July in the twentieth Year of the Independence of the United States of America Charles Cist of the said District hath deposited in this Office the Title of a Book the Right whereof he claims as Proprietor in the Words following to wit

Lesebuch für deutsche Schulkinder herausgegeben von Georg Gottfried Otterbein, Diener des Göttlichen Worts zu Duisburg am Rhein mit Veränderungen und Zusätzen zum Gebrauch Americanischer Schulen.

in Conformity to the Act of the Congress of the United States intituled "An Act for the Encouragement of Learning by securing the Copies of Maps Charts and Books to the Authors and Proprietors of such Copies during the Times therein mentioned."

Saml Caldwell Clerk of the District of Pennsylvania

Figure 3. Copyright registration for a German-language book in the ledger of the District Court of Pennsylvania (entry no. 105)

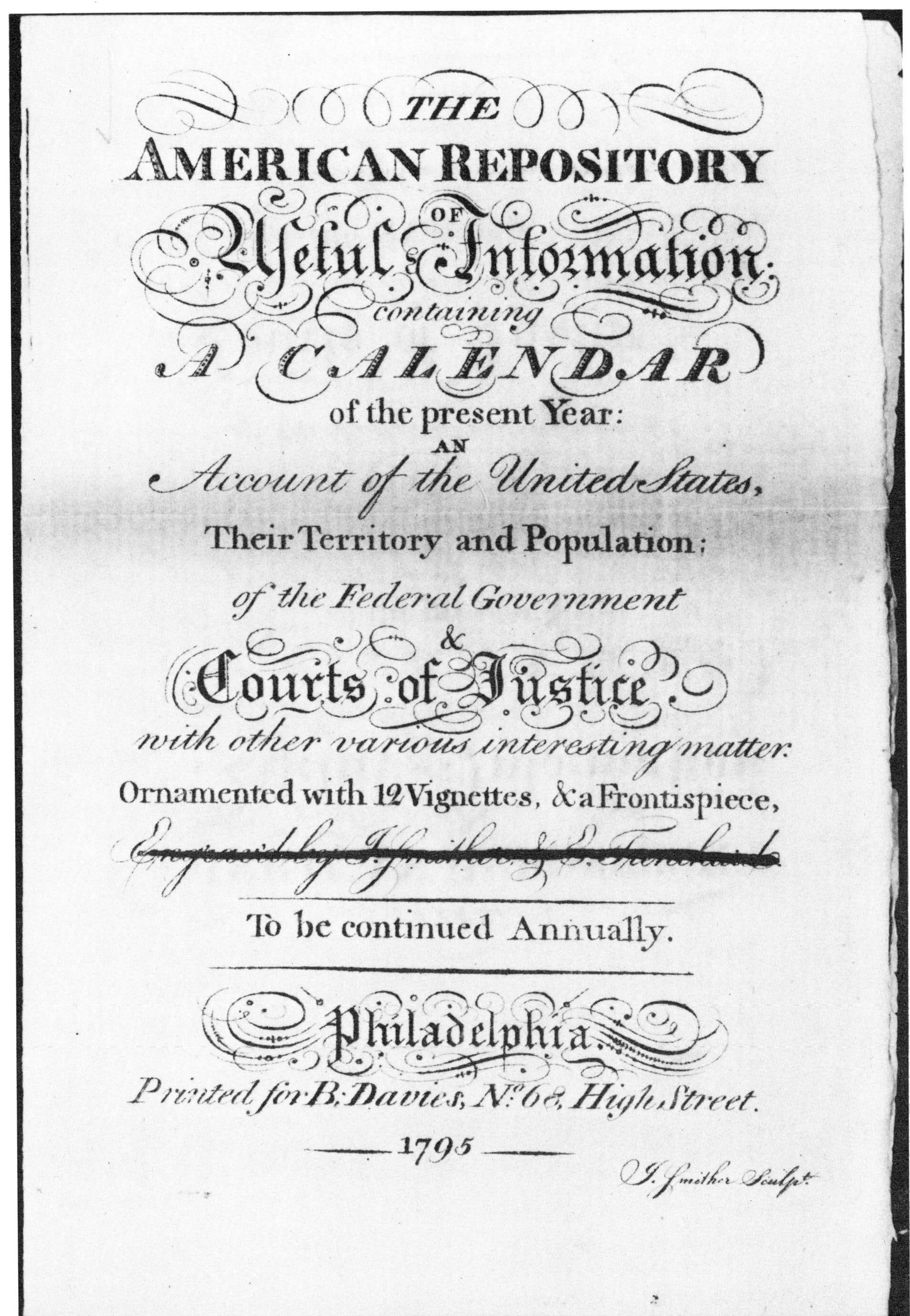

THE
AMERICAN REPOSITORY
OF
Useful Information
containing
A CALENDAR
of the present Year:
AN
Account of the United States,
Their Territory and Population;
of the Federal Government
&
Courts of Justice
with other various interesting matter.
Ornamented with 12 Vignettes, & a Frontispiece,
~~Engrav'd by I. Smither & J. Trenchard~~

To be continued Annually.

Philadelphia.
Printed for B: Davies, No. 68, High Street.
—— 1795 ——
I. Smither Sculpt.

Figure 4. An annotated title page deposited for copyright (entry no. 88)

District of New York ss. Be it remembered that on the thirtieth day of April in the Fifteenth Year of the Independence of the United States of America Donald Fraser of the said District hath deposited in this Office the title of a Book the right whereof he claims as Author in the words following to wit

The
Young Gentleman and Lady's
Assistant;
Partly Original
But chiefly compiled from the works of
the most celebrated Modern Authors;
Calculated
To instruct Youth in the principles of
Useful Knowledge:
In five Parts viz,
Geography
Natural History
Elocution,
Poetry — and
Miscellany
To which is annexed — A short System of
Practical Arithmetic;
Wherein every example is wrought at large,
and the whole
Including the Money of the United States,
rendered easy to the meanest capacity.
This Work, is divided into small Sections
for the convenience of Schools.
By Donald Fraser,
School-Master, New-York.—

Figure 5. Copyright registration for *The Young Gentleman and Lady's Assistant* recorded in the ledger of the District Court of New York (entry no. 463)

American Literature, Public Policy, and the Copyright Laws before 1800

Article 1, Section 8, of the United States Constitution, adopted by the Constitutional Convention on September 17, 1787, gives Congress the power "to promote the progress of science and the useful arts, by securing, for limited time, to authors and inventors, the exclusive right to their respective writings and discoveries." In 1790 An Act for the Encouragement of Learning enumerated the specific powers and responsibilities reserved for Congress in the Constitution to guarantee to authors and proprietors the legal rights for literary works they had created, purchased, or been assigned.

Before 1770 there was little activity relating to copyright in the colonies. Cultural conditions and attitudes about the relationship among writers, publishers, and the state hindered any legal agreement. Between 1770 and 1783 there were several individuals who for various reasons petitioned for private laws to protect their works. A resolution passed by the Continental Congress under the Articles of Confederation offered citizens the opportunity to secure their intellectual property, but few took advantage of the chance. The United States Constitution and the Copyright Act of 1790 were revolutionary changes for authors and publishers.

Colonial culture is often seen as gradually evolving, slowly and subtly adapting to new experiences forced on it by an environment shaped by its isolation from Europe and the difficult conditions of the frontier. The evolution culminated in an American society with a new system of values and institutions. There are many descriptions of this kind of social change in historical literature, but none so dramatic or so well-defined as Perry Miller's in his two-volume history of colonial New England. In *The New England Mind: The Seventeenth Century*, Miller outlined "the architecture," to use his word, of the Puritan intellect at the time of the founding of the Massachusetts Bay Colony. The following volume, *The New England Mind: From Colony to Province*, traced the changes in the ideological foundation of New England culture. Each movement away from founding principles was barely perceptible, especially to participants, but, in the aggregate over a century, the end effects were significant. According to Miller, "a hundred years after the landings . . . [the Puritans] were forced to look upon themselves with amazement, hardly capable of understanding how they had come to be what they were."[1]

Though such gradual trends may be apparent in the general contours of the entire culture, a whole society never moves uniformly at the same pace, and copyright law was an area that made few advances in prerevolutionary America. For most of the period before the ratification of the Constitution, and especially before 1770, the most fitting historical model is not an evolutionary one but rather that proposed by James Hurst in "Legal Elements in United States History," which emphasized "the influence of uncalculated drift and human inertia."[2] The only instance of copyright activity in seventeenth-century America occurred in Massachusetts in 1672. The Massachusetts General Court, the colony's legislative body, regretting the lack of law books and hoping to encourage periodic codification of the laws, formed a committee to collate and edit the colony's laws prior to publication. Little was done until John Usher became involved. Usher arranged for Samuel Green, the Cambridge, Massachusetts, printer, to produce copies of the compilation of Massachusetts laws.

Usher was afraid, however, that his investment in the books would be endangered if Green or Marmaduke Johnson, Green's Boston competitor, were to reprint the work and undersell the copies being offered in Usher's bookstore. When John Usher petitioned the General Court to give him a monopoly for the book, he was received sympathetically. The General Court ruled in 1672:

> In answer to the petition of John Usher, the Court Judgeth it meete to order, and be it by this Court ordered and Enacted, That no Printer shall print any more Coppies than are agreed and paid for by the owner of the Coppie or Coppies, nor shall he nor any other reprint or make Sale of any of the same without the said Owner's consent upon the forfeiture and penalty of treble the whole charges of Printing and paper of the quantity paid for by the owner of the Coppie, to the said owner or his Assigns.

At the time of this ruling, the British booktrade was dominated by the Stationers' Company, a royally chartered corporation of booksellers, printers, and bookbinders. The company regulated relationships in the trade by offering a copyright that gave its members protection from printers publishing works that were registered with the company in another's name.[3] The Massachusetts General Court could not offer to Usher such security since there was no branch of the Stationers' Company in the colonies. The Massachusetts Bay Company was itself a royally chartered corporation, not unlike the Stationers' Company, and the colony's General Court skirted the problem of protecting Usher's interest in the books without access to the Stationers' copyright by granting him a printing patent. The English printing patent was the exclusive right given to an individual as a royal prerogative. In the case of John Usher's petition, the Massachusetts General Court, as the ruling body of the Massachusetts Bay Corporation, issued the patent for *The Book of the General Lawes and Libertyes* as a way of regulating its internal affairs.

The absence of copyright activity during the seventeenth century contrasted sharply with the steady number of patents granted during the same period. As early as 1641 the Massachusetts General Court passed a law making it possible for individuals to hold monopolies for practices or procedures that benefited the colony. This action was based on the English Statute of Monopolies passed only seventeen years before. The Massachusetts authorities did not take long to apply the legislation. In the same year they granted a monopoly of ten years to Samuel Winslow to protect his method of making salt. Other patents were soon given to entrepreneurs producing firewood, linen, and iron. There was continued widespread interest in practical and even experimental science during the colonial period.[4] Americans were a practical people, and they held in high regard innovations that might control the hostile elements in nature and make daily life more comfortable.

There were reasons for the difference in emphasis between copyright and patent activity in early America other than the preference for applied science and technology. First, printers and publishers were few and supplies of ink, paper, and type scarce. The booktrade was still a long way from the cutthroat competition of the late nineteenth century. Marmaduke Johnson's edition of John Eliot's *Indian Dialogues, for Their Instruction in that Great Service of Christ, in Calling Home Their Countrymen to the Knowledge of God and of Themselves, and of Jesus Christ* published in Cambridge in 1671, to use only one example, was an act of piety rather than a profitable publishing venture in need of protection from greedy rivals. With few exceptions, notably Michael Wigglesworth's best-seller, *The Day of Doom,* most American imprints before 1771 can be similarly characterized. Printers made a living selling almanacs, newspapers, writing supplies, and imported books. American books were distributed locally, and Massachusetts printers had little to fear from their counterparts in Philadelphia and Charleston, South Carolina.

Second, the emaciated book industry in early America was further starved by the assumption among American writers that the primary audience for their most ambitious works was in England rather than in the colonies. Cotton Mather sent his monumental *Magnalia Christi Americana* to London in 1702 rather than consign it to a local printer. Bostonian John Cotton carried on a debate with Londoner Daniel Cawdry in a series of pamphlets issued by British publishers. Cotton wrote *The Keyes of the Kingdom of Heaven* in 1644 to be answered by Cawdry in *Vindiciae Clavium* the following year. In 1648 Cotton refuted *Vindiciae Clavium* with *The Way of Congregational Churches,* to which Cawdry replied in *The Inconsistencie of the Independent Way*, prompting Cotton to strike back with *A Defence of Mr. John Cotton from the Imputation of Selfe Contradiction*.

Lastly, the Puritan conception of the relationship among God, man, and ideas differed substantially from today's. Contemporary culture glorifies artistic genius as the secular articulation of an artist's perception of the world. The twentieth century sees artists as standing apart from ordinary individuals, and feels that alienation from conventional society is necessary for the creative imagination. In contrast, seventeenth-century Americans considered an idea to be revealed truth and the creative act a moment of clear understanding of the pattern of God's will rather than a flash of subjective human vision. The Puritan historian's tasks were to discover in past events the chronology of God's providence and to establish the links between an individual's spiritual development and the community's moral progress. Larzer Ziff observed that colonial Americans shifted "the glory of literature from the form and content of the work which, of necessity, speaks through respected convention, to the alleged inspiration of the writer who insists that the glory of his work is that it is the product of the Holy Ghost speaking through him."[5] To have copyrighted an early American theological book would have been a presumptuous act.

It was not until the last third of the eighteenth century that copyright became an active concern of the American world of letters. American music masters felt the need for copyright protection from pirate publishers before other writers. Their lessons were based on manuscript musical books of instruction, some created by the instructor, others purchased or borrowed from other composers. When a musician's work became popular and his services eagerly sought, he capitalized on his popularity by publishing a book of instructions, usually consisting of compositions for both voices and instruments. In eighteenth-century America, musical type was not widely available, and each page of a music book was engraved on a copperplate, an expensive and time-consuming process.[6] Eighteenth-century authors often had to shoulder production expenses that in the twentieth century are paid by publishers. For this reason, an author might risk his personal fortune by venturing to publish his works. Andrew Law, a well-known Connecticut singing master, complained that he had spent 500 pounds in hard money, not depreciated Continental currency, to publish one of his music books, and if it were pirated he would be financially ruined.

In 1770, William Billings, a celebrated New England music instructor and composer, petitioned the Massachusetts General Court to give him the "exclusive privilege" of printing and selling his book of church music, *The New-England Psalm-Singer,* because he feared that another publisher was soon to publish a part of it under a different title. The privilege Billings sought was much like that given John Usher more than a century before. His request was refused on the grounds that the court could not decide with certainty that Billings was the true author of the work. The following year Billings again approached the court. He tried to strengthen his argument by documenting his authorship of the book, again reiterating the threat of someone else pirating his work to "reap the Fruit of his great labor & cost." This time the Massachusetts General Court ruled in Billings' favor, and in 1772 he was given the exclusive right to print and sell his book. In spite of this initial success, Billings was again disappointed. The Massachusetts royal governor, Thomas Hutchinson, refused to sign the law giving *The New-England Psalm-Singer* protection. Hutchinson did not comment on the merit of the case and may have taken this action because of the difficulties he then was having with the Massachusetts legislators on the eve of the Revolution.[7]

Andrew Law found local authorities more sympathetic to his plight. In 1781 Law was given by the Connecticut General Assembly the "exclusive patent" for a period of five years for printing and distributing his 1778 book of musical compositions, *The Singing Master's Assistant*. Law sought legal protection for a work published three years earlier when he heard that Daniel Bayley of Newburyport, Massachusetts, planned to use some of his compositions from it.[8]

John Ledyard was the next to request a private bill to protect his literary efforts. Ledyard, who had accompanied Capt. John Cook on his third and last voyage around the world, returned to America at the voyage's conclusion to write *A Journal of Captain Cook's Last Voyage to the Pacific Ocean*. Anticipating that his work would profit from the widespread curiosity about Cook's exploits, Ledyard followed Law's lead in petitioning the Connecticut General Assembly to give him the exclusive privilege to print and sell his work. The pattern of repeated requests had alerted the Connecticut legislators to the growing discontent of authors and publishers with their status. The General Assembly therefore referred Ledyard's petition to a committee with the observation that "it appears that several Gentlemen of Genius & reputation are also about to make similar Applications."[9]

The campaign to enact a general copyright law in Connecticut continued with an anonymous editorial in the January 7, 1783, issue of Hartford's *Connecticut Courant*.[10] This was a brilliant strategic piece that eschewed aesthetics while effectively mixing national antagonism to Great Britain and Connecticut state pride. The editorialist began by declaring that the encouragement of literature has been an aim of all great civilized nations and that foreign countries would base their opinion of the United States not only on its conduct of military maneuvers but also on the character of the American people as expressed in their literature. Not to encourage writing would be to run the risk of being branded "stupid and illiterate," a characterization that would have international political consequences. This was an effective opening argument to make to political leaders looking to European alliances for support during their bitter war with Great Britain. The article continued by flattering local officials. Connecticut, it observed, must carry the fight for the national literature because "there is no one of the united states, in which knowledge, and a good taste are more generally diffused, or polite literature has been more successfully pursued, or better encouraged by the public favor, than the State of Connecticut."

The *Connecticut Courant* writer then depicted the difficulties facing anyone who attempted to make a literary contribution to the national struggle with England. An author was forced to face two unhappy consequences after publication. On the one hand, if his book was not well received by critics or by the general public, he "stands forth the butt at which all the arrows of criticism and censure are aimed . . . loses all hope of profits by the sale, the edition lies on his hands, his expenses in the impression are lost, and he stands on the record, as a dull writer the object of ridicule for a mistake of his abilities." On the other hand, if his book was successful and popular with the public, his fate was equally unappealing. The editorial continued: "If [the writer] succeeds, the world immediately divides into parties, and while one part purchase, admire and applaud, the other will be equally virulent in opposing him by censure and misrepresentation." Whatever critical success or popular acclaim he may receive will never benefit him financially because unscrupulous printers will immediately pirate his book in a cheaper edition.

Almost simultaneously, Noah Webster decided that his textbook *A Grammatical Institute of the English Language* required Connecticut's legal protection. Webster, a Connecticut schoolteacher who was convinced that Americans needed textbooks for their new school system, composed his speller, the first part of *A Grammatical Institute of the English Language*, to fill that need. Webster anticipated the American desire for educational tools without an English accent, and by his own estimate approximately 15 million copies of his various spellers had been sold by 1837, about one for every person in the United States at that time. As early as August 1782, Webster brought his manuscript to Pennsylvania, New York, and New Jersey to persuade their state legislatures to provide some form of copyright protection.[11] In January 1783, Webster widened his effort on behalf of *A Grammatical Institute of the English Language* by petitioning the Connecticut legislators for a private law in his behalf.

Webster's contribution to the copyright debate was to add a democratic dimension to its terms. Throughout his career Webster argued that democracy was based on an educated citizenry well enough informed to make the choices previously made for them by the aristocracy. For Webster, books like *A Grammatical Institute of the English Language* would mean the difference between a successful democratic republic and a failed experiment in self-government. Whereas Ledyard, Billings, Law, and Usher might base their requests for exclusive printing privileges on the expenses they incurred, Webster took a different approach in soliciting the government's support. He wrote in his letter to the Connecticut Assembly, "A folio upon some abstract philosophical subject might, at first thought, appear to be the work of some consequence and attract the public attention. But this would be read by a few and its utility seldom reach further than the philosopher's head. While a little fifteen penny volume, which may convey much useful knowledge to the remote, obscure recesses of honest poverty, is overlooked as a matter of trivial notice. The former, like a taper, gives light only in the chambers of study. The latter, like a star, casts its beams equally upon the peasant and monarch."[12] This combination of nationalism, egalitarian democracy, and social utilitarianism has been a persuasive mix throughout American history.

The Ledyard, Law, and Webster memorials supported by the *Connecticut Courant* editorial showed that a general law was necessary to ensure copyright protection in Connecticut. During the January session the General Assembly passed the first general copyright statute, which was a remarkable initiative considering that the country was still at war with Great Britain. The statute was very sympathetic to authors' rights, stating that it was because of "principles of natural equity and justice that every author should be secured in receiving the profits that may arise from the sale of his works." The act did not permit printers to issue an edition of a book without the consent of the holder of its copyright and also held booksellers liable for any illegal copies they distributed. The term of the copyright was set at fourteen years, and was renewable for another fourteen if the author was still alive at the term's expiration. The Connecticut General Assembly tried to ensure observance of the act by setting damages for any violation at twice the cost of unauthorized books.

Within days of the *Connecticut Courant* editorial, Joel Barlow carried the struggle for copyright protection beyond the boundaries of Connecticut to the harassed Continental Congress. Barlow wrote to Elias Boudinot, president of the Congress, requesting that he introduce a bill encouraging each of the thirteen states to enact its own guarantee of authors' rights to literary property.[13] Barlow's varied career included being minister to France, newspaperman, poet, lawyer, army chaplain, and businessman, but he is best remembered by those interested in American literature as the author of the epic nationalistic poem *The Vision of Columbus*. He was one of the leading lights of the Hartford Wits, a small literary group in Connecticut whose poetry satirized Jeffersonian democracy and extolled Federalist principles.

In his letter to Boudinot, Barlow broadened the argument for a copyright act in important ways. First, he indicated that he was not asking for a private bill, as other writers in the past had done, but was offering himself as a representative of American authors, a member of a fledgling literary establishment. Previously, the country had no individuals who thought of themselves primarily as men of letters. American writers were politicians, scientists, or religious leaders who wrote books and pamphlets as one duty among many. Barlow reported to Boudinot that two members of this new class of authors had suffered from the lack of copyright protection, Timothy Dwight of Massachusetts, author of the epic poem *The Conquest of Canaan*, and John Trumbull of Connecticut, author of *M'Fingal*. Barlow showed how Trumbull's literary reputation and therefore his livelihood were damaged by printers who issued without his consent cheap editions that contained "typographical errors, a bad paper, a mean letter & an uncouth page." Timothy Dwight had learned from Trumbull's problems and had resisted publishing his work for fear of a similar fate.

The second part of Barlow's letter presented his thinking about the effect of political events on American literature. For Barlow, the Revolution created a new literary order with entirely different rules. This new order required that authors rely for a livelihood solely on the sale of their works rather than on the generosity of a wealthy patron. A democracy could not support the life-styles enjoyed by the European aristocracy. Democratic institutions in America required wide support among the country's citizens, and the national literature must be based on a broad cross section of middle-class readers.

William Charvat missed this aspect of Barlow's reasoning when commenting on this letter in *The Profession of Authorship in America, 1800–1870* and *Literary Publishing in America, 1790–1850*. Charvat rightly cited Barlow's letter to Boudinot as central in the history of American authorship but concluded that the profession was dominated by cultural elitism. Barlow's use of words such as *gentleman* and *vulgar* were, for Charvat, symptomatic of his identification with the upper class. Though it is indisputable that eighteenth-century American authors might have preferred a society which supported their efforts by patronage, the overriding importance of this letter was Barlow's recognition that such a society no longer was a widely held ideal in the United States. Barlow wrote: "As we have few Gentlemen of fortune sufficient to enable them to spend a whole life in study, or induce others to do it by their patronage, it is more necessary, in this country than in any other, that the rights of authors be secured by law."

One other important idea in Barlow's letter deserves highlighting. Recognizing that the new American writer must be more self-reliant than his European counterpart, Barlow believed that this independence would result in a decline in the quality of American literature. Pointing out that literature in the new Republic had fallen to an embarrassing state, Barlow remarked that "this embarrassment is natural to every free government." A national literature founded on popularity must compromise its commitment to excellence in this view. Fine art and popular art are incompatible. Barlow's observations began a debate that has continued throughout the history of American critical thought. In the mid-nineteenth century Alexis de Tocqueville in *Democracy in America* seconded Barlow's thinking. Tocqueville thought that the majority of readers in democratic countries preferred easily accessible books that could be quickly read and contained chapters of vivid dramatic quality with rapidly changing scenes. For Tocqueville, democracy not only changed the role of readers and writers but also the nature of literature itself. Tocqueville concluded: "Democracy not only infuses a taste for letters among the trading classes, but introduces a trading spirit into the literature."[14]

During March 1783, the Continental Congress received a copy of the Connecticut Copyright Act and quickly referred it to the committee that was considering Barlow's proposal. The interests of the publishing community and the nation were advanced by the quality of the members of this committee—Ralph Izard (South Carolina), Hugh Williamson (North Carolina), and James Madison (Virginia). All three were educated men. Williamson's intellectual contributions entitled him to membership in the American Philosophical Society. Izard was later elected president pro tempore of the Senate and founded the College of Charleston. Madison, the principal architect of the United States Constitution, was widely read and, like his close friend Thomas Jefferson, one of Virginia's cultural leaders. After his retirement, Madison was associated with both the University of Virginia and the College of William and Mary. Individuals other than Barlow must have written to Congress on behalf of the copyright law, because the records indicated that "sundry papers and memoirs on the subject of literary property" were referred to the committee. Only Barlow's letter is known today, however.

There is no record of the committee's deliberations, but on the basis of its favorable recommendation the Congress passed an act on May 2, 1783, encouraging all states

> to secure to the authors or publishers of any new books not hitherto printed, being citizens of the United States, and to their executors, administrators and assigns, the copy right of such books for a certain time not less than fourteen years from the first publication; and to secure to the said authors, if they shall survive the term first mentioned, and to their executors, administrators, and assigns, the copy right of such books for another term of time not less than fourteen years, such copy or exclusive right of printing, publishing, and vending the same, to be secured to the original authors, or publishers, their executors, administrator's and assigns, by such laws under such restrictions as to the several States may seem proper.[15]

Maryland and Massachusetts had anticipated the Continental Congress' action and already followed Connecticut's example, the former on March 17 and the latter on April 21. The Massachusetts legislators sought to improve the Connecticut act. Whereas Connecticut declared that its law was intended simply to "encourage men of learning and genius to publish their writings; which may do honor to their country, and service to mankind," the Massachusetts leaders proclaimed that their purpose was the "improvement of knowledge, the progress of civilization, the public weal of the community, and the advancement of human happiness." Two features of the Massachusetts law were unusual among state copyright statutes. To claim copyright protection for a book, the writer had to acknowledge in the book that he was the author. This requirement eliminating the possibility of protecting anonymous or pseudonymous works was later adopted in the laws passed in New Hampshire and Rhode Island. Massachusetts also made a legal claim dependent on the deposit of a copy of the book, as did North Carolina. In the case of Massachusetts, the librarian of Harvard College issued certificates of receipt that served as proof of a valid claim.

By 1786, all states except Delaware had passed a copyright law. Several general features were common to most of the laws passed by state assemblies. In all states, copyright protection was available only to citizens of the United States and only for texts that had not been previously published. The states adopting Connecticut's term of protection of fourteen years included Maryland, New Jersey, Pennsylvania, South Carolina, North Carolina, Georgia, and New York. This length of time was borrowed from the Statute of Anne, the copyright law in force in Great Britain since 1710. Massachusetts,

Rhode Island, and Virginia chose a twenty-one year period, and New Hampshire decided on twenty years. Connecticut, Maryland, New Jersey, Pennsylvania, South Carolina, Georgia, and New York granted authors or proprietors the right to renew their copyright for one additional term when the first expired.

All states assigned penalties for those violating the law. The most common sanction, that adopted by Connecticut, New Jersey, Pennsylvania, Virginia, North Carolina, Georgia, and New York, was the forfeiture of all illegal books and a monetary fine of double their value. Other penalties were set at two pence per printed sheet in Maryland, and one penny per sheet in South Carolina. Massachusetts and Rhode Island established a fine of not more than 3,000 pounds and not less than 5 pounds. New Hampshire set the range of damages as not more than 1,000 pounds and not less than 5. A majority of states required authors or proprietors to register their works with various public officials: Connecticut (secretary of state), Maryland (clerk of the general court), Massachusetts (librarian of Harvard College), Pennsylvania (prothonotary in Philadelphia), South Carolina (secretary of state), Virginia (clerk of the council), North Carolina (secretary of state), Georgia (secretary of state), and New York (secretary of state). South Carolina, North Carolina, Georgia, and New York followed Connecticut by including an anti-monopoly section in their copyright laws, which required that claimants guarantee that they would provide for an adequate number of copies to be available in the state at a reasonable price to have a lawful claim.

Few authors and publishers took advantage of the protection offered by the Massachusetts law. Among the works deposited at Harvard for copyright registration were Noah Webster's *A Grammatical Institute of the English Language, Part I* (1783), Andrew Law's *A Collection of Hymn Tunes* (1783), Noah Webster's *A Grammatical Institute of the English Language, Part II* (1784), Joel Barlow's *A Translation of Sundry Psalms* (1785), William Billings' *The Suffolk Harmony* (1786), and Caleb Bingham's *The Young Lady's Accidence* (1790).[16] Even if the records are grossly incomplete, only a small percentage of the total number of books produced in Massachusetts were copyrighted. This pattern was repeated in all the states with existing records. Most books registered were literary books, musical works, and a few expensive titles, such as *A New and Correct Map of the United States of North America*, by Abel Buel, published in New Haven in 1783 and registered in Connecticut. There were occasional claims for political works such as Noah Webster's *Sketches of American Policy*, entered in Massachusetts in 1785.[17]

The difficulty facing an author or publisher under the system of state copyrights was almost insurmountable. Though the general features of the various copyright laws were clear, they differed in numerous details. To give only one example, a claimant would be hard pressed to keep in mind when the copyright terms expired in various states and in which of these he was able to reapply. Communication between distant states was difficult and added to the problems with which a claimant contended. Noah Webster's odyssey on behalf of *A Grammatical Institute of the English Language* during 1785 and 1786 is an example of the great lengths to which one author went to ensure that he had a national claim to his book.

Having registered his work in Connecticut and Massachusetts, Webster left Connecticut during the spring of 1785 to visit the southern and middle Atlantic states. He made the trip to deliver a series of lectures to influential political and cultural leaders on the English language. While on his travels, he applied for copyright in those states that had an existing law, and he lobbied legislators to pass a law in those states that had none. Webster's first stops were Philadelphia and Alexandria, Virginia, where he took the opportunity to acquaint powerful people with his case for the benefits of copyright protection, among them George Washington. He next sailed for Charleston, South Carolina, visiting the mayor and registering his speller in the secretary of state's office. After returning to Baltimore by ship, he left for Virginia to lecture in Richmond and had the satisfaction of learning that his efforts had helped to pass the Virginia copyright act. Leaving Richmond, Webster next gave his lectures at Williamsburg and Annapolis, where he registered his work in Maryland. After his Maryland stop, he visited the state legislatures of New York and Delaware to discuss the advantages of passing a copyright act. In total, Webster had spent thirteen months on the road.[18]

Webster's use of the state copyright laws led to legal snares. The publishers Hudson and Goodwin of Hartford, Connecticut, issued the first edition of *A Grammatical Institute of the English Language* in 1783. Hudson and Goodwin assumed the printing costs in return for sole rights for the book for an indeterminate number of years. When the contract was renegotiated, the publishers retained printing rights for the New England states but returned those for other parts of the United States to Webster. Webster sold the printing rights for New York, New Jersey, North Carolina, South Carolina, and Georgia to Samuel Campbell for $200.[19] Later, Nathaniel Patten of Hartford bought 1,500 copies of Webster's speller from Campbell and offered them for sale in his Connecticut store. Hudson and Goodwin petitioned the Connecticut Supreme Court arguing that Patten had violated their copyright for the book in New England. Patten pointed out that he had acquired copies of the book from one legally able to sell it. Because Patten was offering copies of the book for sale at a lower price than Hudson and Goodwin, the competition was injuring their sales.

Isaiah Thomas, as the leader of the New England publishing trade, tried to negotiate between the two publishers. He successfully got Patten to agree to raise his price but could not prevent his selling the books. The entire matter was complicated by the fact that Campbell had not actually printed the speller in his shop but had contracted with Hudson and Goodwin for 2,000 copies.

In 1789, the Connecticut Supreme Court ruled for Hudson and Goodwin. The court thought that because Campbell had commissioned these copies of the book from his residence in New York, they were under the authority of his New York printing right, even though the book was actually printed in Connecticut. The decision raised many questions about the distinction between printing and distribution rights that certainly would have caused further legal action. Thomas wrote to Hudson and Goodwin: "All these matters, which are continually shewing themselves in disagreeable forms, shew the necessity of a regulation in our business."[20]

Webster's difficulties demonstrated the need for a national copyright law, but copyright was not a major concern among the delegates who gathered in Philadelphia during May 1787 for a constitutional convention. Government under the Articles of the Confederation had stumbled over divisive questions. Individual states seemed determined to go their own way. The first printed draft of the Constitution as reported by the Committee on Detail on August 6, 1787, contained no mention of the central government's role in questions concerning literary property or patent rights. As the month's debate continued, the weak governmental role proposed in the August 6 document was considerably strengthened, though its power was tempered by those who argued that the national government should have specific enumerated powers rather than operate under the sweeping authority of a general welfare clause. On August 18, James Madison and Thomas Pinckney proposed on the floor a number of amendments giving certain responsibilities to the proposed federal government. Both men included copyright among the central authority's duties. Madison advocated that the new government "encourage by premiums & provisions, the advancement of useful knowledge and discoveries." Pinckney thought that the central authorities should "secure to authors exclusive rights for a . . . certain time." Madison's proposals came from his experience in forming the Copyright Act passed during the rule of the Articles of the Confederation and from his belief that a national government should exercise a strong positive influence in shaping the American society.

The proposals by Pinckney and Madison were referred to the Committee on Detail along with amendments by Elbridge Gerry and others. At the end of August, the Committee of Eleven considered all clauses and amendments that had been proposed but not yet decided, including copyright. This powerful committee consisted of Madison, Gouverneur Morris, Rufus King, Roger Sherman, David Brearly, John Dickinson, Nicholas Gilman, Daniel Carroll, Hugh Williamson, Pierce Butler, and Abraham Baldwin. We know nothing about the committee's discussion. The committee's spokesman, David Brearly of New Jersey, reported on September 5 to the entire Congress the proposed copyright and patent sections for the Constitution, which were then referred to the Committee on Style. On September 13, the Committee on Style sent to all members the proposed Constitution for the new government that was eventually accepted by the states. The copyright passage read: "The Congress shall have power: To promote the progress of science and useful arts, by securing, for limited times, to authors and inventors, the exclusive right to their respective writings and discoveries."

The Congress's declaration of intent in the Constitution to protect authors' rights established the general principle of copyright in the United States, but it did not address the matter of administrative procedures for registration or enforcement. Given the wording of the constitutional passage, it was not surprising that writers assumed that they were required to apply directly to Congress for a private copyright bill. Almost immediately after the initial session of the first Congress, David Ramsay of South Carolina and John Churchman of Pennsylvania appealed to the legislators for bills to protect their works. Ramsay, a prominent physician and political leader in his state, had written *The History of the Revolution of South Carolina* and was planning to publish a general history of the American Revolution. His book, he argued, had taken much of his time and had cost him significant amounts of money since he had funded publication. Churchman had invented a new method of navigation that he planned to use to publish globes, maps, and tables. He reasoned that he should receive all payments for publications that used his system. Also included among the copyright applications during the first session was one by Jedidiah Morse for *The American Geography*. An even greater number of patent requests added to the pressure to devise some procedure for handling the individual requests efficiently. A general bill for copyright was offered during the session, but it was tabled with the many petitions for private copyright bills.

On January 8, 1790, at the start of the second session, President George Washington, the most influential person in the country, addressed Congress, reviewing the accomplishments of the first session and outlining his sense of direction for the coming months. Washington's speech gave great impetus to a national copyright law. Washington announced: "Nor am I less persuaded that you will agree with me in opinion, that there is nothing which can better deserve your patronage than the promotion of science and literature." While Congress considered Washington's proposals, requests for protection of books under Article 1, Section 8, continued to arrive. Some members of Congress were aware that the Constitution was not adequately helping authors. Aedanus Burke of South Carolina pointed out (January 25) that while Congress was considering copyright for Jedidiah Morse's *American Geography,* the maps published in the volume had already been reproduced without consent.

Congress quickly responded to Washington's request for action on copyright during the second session of the first Congress, and on May 21, 1790, the President signed into law An Act for the Encouragement of Learning, by Securing the Copies of Maps, Charts, and Books, to the Authors and Proprietors of Such Copies, during the Times Therein Mentioned. For the national copyright law, Congress adopted some of the common elements of the state laws. A claimant had to be a resident of the United States. The term was set for fourteen years and was renewable. Any book, map, or chart printed without the copyright owner's consent was forfeited, and the guilty party fined fifty cents for each sheet printed. A claim accompanied by a proposed title page was filed at the local federal district court. Congress decided to adopt the Massachusetts precedent by making a claimant deposit a copy of his work, though decreeing that the secretary of state should receive the deposited book rather than a university librarian, which had been the case in Massachusetts. Also, unlike all other early American copyright acts, the 1790 statute required the owner of a copyright to publish a public record of his claim in a newspaper.

Authors like David Ramsay, who had already petitioned Congress for his histories of the American revolution, swiftly took advantage of the new law and immediately registered their books. However, many writers and publishers ignored it. Fewer than eight hundred of the more than fifteen thousand imprints published between 1790 and 1800 were copyrighted. Even if the lost Connecticut copyright records were added to these figures and the number of reprinted English works ineligible for copyright were subtracted, it is unlikely that the percentage of American books that were copyrighted would be significantly larger. One of the most remarkable things about the Act to Encourage Learning was how selectively it was used. Whole categories like almanacs, juvenile stories, broadsides, sermons, speeches, newspapers, government documents, and club and society rules and charters are almost entirely absent. Yet these were the staples of early American printers. Most writing during the early years of the Republic was considered ephemeral by its creators and publishers. These books and pamphlets were thought to have a market that would be quickly saturated and a usefulness that would be short-lived.

Plays and poetry are also underrepresented. Though works of original literature and criticism did not constitute a large part of the publishing output of American printers, such works have a particularly low representation in the list of books copyrighted between 1790 and 1800. Most American novels of the period, representing a large monetary commitment by either the printer or author, were registered; but, in total, there were only a handful of serious imaginative works copyrighted in all states, including Hugh Henry Brackenridge's *Modern Chivalry,* Francis Hopkinson's *The Miscellaneous Essays,* Royall Tyler's *The Contrast,* Thomas Ordiorne's *The Progress of Refinement,* and Charles Brockden Brown's *Wieland, Arthur Mervyn,* and *Ormond.* Practical or commercially useful books, on the other hand, were present in much greater numbers, accounting for a majority of the entries. Judging by a sampling of the subject index to Charles Evans' *American Bibliography,* works of instruction, business, and scientific and geographical description did not make up a high proportion of the complete product of the American publishing industry at this time. Of the first 100 copyright entries in Pennsylvania, almost one-half were textbooks, manuals, geographical atlases, and commercial directories. These figures are duplicated in other states. Practical books rather than literary works were thought to have enough long-lasting commercial value to copyright. This trend continued. There are approximately twice as many instructional works in the last 100 Pennsylvania entries as in the first 100. Unlike the federal law, state copyright laws were passed because of constant pressure from composers and writers of belles lettres, and a larger proportion of state copyright registrations than federal registrations were for imaginative works.

The imbalance in the types of books registered under the federal act would have pleased early political leaders who had championed the national copyright law. The Constitution's encouragement of useful knowledge must be seen against the background of the prejudice of an influential segment of society against novels. Works of fiction aroused passions that were better left dormant, according to the novel's critics, and also robbed valuable time from more productive endeavors. An impassioned statement against novels came from Thomas Jefferson: "A great obstacle to good education is the inordinate passion prevalent for novels, and the time lost in that reading which should be instructively employed. When this poison infects the mind, it destroys its tone and revolts it against wholesome reading. Reason and fact, plain and unadorned, are rejected."[21] Similar criticisms were voiced by many of the generation's cultural leaders. One commentator, reviewing the attitude of late eighteenth-century authorities against novel reading, remarked in 1824: "In those days, it was almost as disreputable to be detected reading a novel, as to be found betting at a cock-fight, or a gaming table. Those who had sons would have supposed them forever incapacitated for any useful pursuit in life . . . and those who had daughters who exhibited such an inclination, would have considered them as totally unfitted for ever becoming good wives or mothers."[22] Those who had enjoyed imaginative literature in their youth decided in their maturity that they could not afford such a waste of time. Writing to William Bradford, James Madison remarked, "I was afraid you would not easily have loosened your Affections from the Belles Lettres . . . . I myself use [sic] to have too great a hankering after those amusing Studies. Poetry wit and Criticism Romances Plays &c captivated me much: but I begin [to] discover that they deserve but a moderate portion of a *mortal's* Time. and that something more substantial more durable more profitable befits a riper Age."[23] Even apologists for fiction were reduced to proving its worth by attesting to its usefulness to society. In the preface to *The Gamesters*, Mrs. Caroline Warren defended her profession. She wrote that she "cordially agreed with the objector, that *some* novels have exhibited too highly coloured portraits of life; and have like an *ignis fatuus*, too frequently led the young mind astray; yet the writer believes that were novels devoted to the cause of moral virtue, they might become as *useful*, as they are thought to be pernicious."[24] There was a voracious reading public in America for English novels that gave rise to the strenuous vocal opposition by those who tried to shape public opinion. The constitutional copyright provisions' emphasis on the useful arts sought not to bolster a professional literary establishment of novelists, poets, and critics such as the one that existed in England but rather to ensure that books with demonstrably practical benefits to American society would be available to the readers of the new Republic.

The 1790 statute allowed claimants the option to register as either the author or proprietor of the work, the latter being in most cases the printer or publisher. There is no evidence that the rights of author and proprietor claimants differed. Some individuals decided to claim a work as both proprietor and author. Those who filed works in both categories usually had written and financed the publication of a book, as did Absalom Jones and Richard Allen for *A Narrative of the Proceedings of the Black People, during the Late Awful Calamity in Philadelphia.* The ratio of author to proprietor claims changed noticeably from 1790 to 1800. In Massachusetts between 1790 and 1794, 45 books were claimed by authors and only 25 by proprietors. Between 1795 and 1800, however, the proportion of claims by authors and proprietors reversed, with 62 registered by the first group and 63 by the second. The turnabout was more dramatic in Pennsylvania. Of the 78 registrations in that state between 1790 and 1794, 43 were claimed by authors. During the last six years of the decade, 63 claims were filed by authors and 113 by proprietors. In other states the general trend held true, though the point when proprietors outnumber authors differed. In New York, for example, there were 34 author claimants and 24 proprietor registrants in the 1791–97 period. During the final three years of the decade, the balance shifted to 28 proprietors and 18 authors. The figures underestimate the movement from author to proprietor claims during this period, because many publishers and printers who issued anthologies or textbooks claimed to be the author in registering the book.

Most scholars have assumed that the Copyright Act of 1790 was an immediate and major advance for American literature, because it gave authors a legal stake in their works. Benjamin Spencer in *The Quest for Nationality; An American Literary Campaign* viewed the 1790 law as an eagerly sought step in establishing the professions of novelist, poet, and playwright in America and in encouraging a national literature. Spencer wrote that the copyright law was meant "to protect and nurture the literary efforts of the nation." The national copyright law gave authors a legally defined commodity to sell to publishers, and this property was potentially more valuable than that which writers could offer during the state copyright period or before. Contracts between authors and publishers show that copyright was a point of negotiation. The profession of authorship in America during the nineteenth century would have been crippled without the Copyright Act.

A law like the Copyright Act of 1790 that so completely altered the ground rules of the community that it regulated must be seen, however, in its entirety. Its effects were multidimensional and sometimes even contradictory. One section of the law undercut other sections that supported American authors. The grant of copyright protection only to American citizens pushed the publishing industry in a direction that injured those who sought to make a living by creative writing in America. Since the law allowed printers to reprint British authors without negotiating for copyright, these books offered great monetary rewards. During the prerevolutionary period, colonial booksellers had imported the work of popular writers from England. After the Revolution, American printers were free from any constraints either at home or abroad in issuing these books. When an American publisher looked for a profitable novel or poem to publish, he did not need to pay an American writer, because he could print free anything in English literature. In 1793 alone, the works of the following British authors were issued in American editions: Joseph Addison, Jonathan Swift, James Thomson, Robert Blair, William Cowper, Robert Dodsley, Oliver Goldsmith, William Guthrie, John Love, Alexander Pope, and Laurence Sterne. An added effect of the 1790 law was that it gave to copyright owners a national monopoly on their product and therefore set the stage for the concentration of the publishing business in dominant urban areas with access to wide distribution systems. If the Constitution and the 1790 act had continued the method of state registration in force under the Articles of Confederation, the printing and publishing industries in each state would have been strengthened. Successful publishers would have been forced to maintain active contact with state affiliates in order to ensure that registration requirements were met in every instance.

The United States Constitution played a major role in changing the American economic system's domination by craftsmen with restricted spheres of communication and distribution. As the old society disintegrated, the framework of a modern capitalistic state arose in which political leaders thought progress was driven by the economic self-interest of the middle class. The American legislators intended to harness personal initiative to the public good. The copyright law was introduced in the spirit of economic individualism that characterized the Constitution. Free and easy access to information was necessary for the political self-determination and equal economic opportunity that American political theorists of the time thought were crucial for the success of the democratic experiment in the United States. The framers of the Constitution saw books and ideas as tools to control experience and the environment. The copyright records between 1790 and 1800 show that the practical literature of self-improvement was the deepest native literary tradition. The domination of today's publishing scene by reference works, textbooks, and how-to-do-it manuals indicates that this preference is still part of the American character.

In "The Genius and the Copyright: Economic and Legal Conditions of the Emergence of the 'Author,'" Martha Woodmansee linked the formation of copyright law with the development of the image of the creative writer as an independent professional and of a book as "an imprint or record of a unique individual," an idea that first appeared in the eighteenth century.[25] It is necessary not to view the copyright law as primarily centered on the needs of the author but to place it within the scope of the publishing industry and society as a whole. The 1790 act only incidentally served as an author's law. Its purpose was to protect those authors' and publishers' practices that were thought to serve the best interest of the entire community. Early supporters of the American copyright law such as Joel Barlow and John Trumbull could not have foreseen the immediate results of the copyright statute. The profession of authorship was strengthened by the act, but the law also helped lay the foundation for the powerful nineteenth-century publishers who held all except the most popular literary authors in their control.

---

[1] Perry Miller, *The New England Mind: From Colony to Province* (Cambridge: Harvard University Press, 1953), p. vii.

[2] James Willard Hurst, "Legal Elements in United States History," in *Law in American History,* ed. Donald Fleming and Bernard Bailyn (Boston: Little, Brown and Company, 1971).

[3] An overview of the involvement of the Stationers' Company with copyright can be found in Lyman Ray Patterson's *Copyright in Historical Perspective* (Nashville: Vanderbilt University Press, 1968). Marjorie Plant puts the Stationers' Company in an industry-wide historical perspective in *The English Book Trade* (London: George Allen and Unwin, Ltd., 1965).

[4] For the early development of the Patent Law see Bruce W. Bugbee's *Genesis of American Patent and Copyright Law* (Washington: Public Affairs Press, 1967). The American colonists' interest in science is the subject of numerous articles and books. One example among many that could be cited on this topic is Raymond Phineas Stearns' *Science in the British Colonies of America* (Urbana: University of Illinois Press, 1970), which is notable for its comprehensive treatment.

[5] Larzer Ziff, "The Literary Consequences of Puritanism," in *The American Puritan Imagination: Essays in Revaluation*, ed. Sacvan Bercovitch (London: Cambridge University Press, 1974), p. 41.

[6] For a description of the music publishing trade during this period, see Richard Crawford and D. W. Krummel, "Early American Music Printing and Publishing," in *Printing and Society in Early America*, ed. William Joyce *et al.* (Worcester: American Antiquarian Society, 1983), pp. 186–227.

[7] David McKay and Richard Crawford, *William Billings of Boston: Eighteenth-Century Composer* (Princeton: Princeton University Press, 1975).

[8] Irving Lowens, "Andrew Law and the Pirates," in *Music and Musicians in Early America* (New York: W. W. Norton Company, Inc., 1964), pp. 58–88. See also Richard A. Crawford, *Andrew Law, American Psalmodist* (Evanston: Northwestern University Press, 1968), p. 71.

[9] Hellmut Lehmann-Haupt, *The Book in America* (New York: Bowker, 1951), pp. 103–4.

[10] Alexander Cowie proposes John Trumbull as the author of this editorial in his *John Trumbull, Connecticut Wit* (Chapel Hill: University of North Carolina Press, 1936).

[11] Harry R. Warfel, *Noah Webster, Schoolmaster to America* (New York: Octagon Books, 1966), p. 54.

[12] Warfel, *Noah Webster,* pp. 57–58.

[13] Barlow to [Boudinot], 10 Jan. 1783, Papers of the Continental Congress, item 78, 4:369, National Archives and Records Administration.

[14] Alexis Charles Henri Maurice Clerel de Tocqueville, *Democracy in America,* ed. Phillips Bradley, 2 vols. (New York: Alfred A. Knopf, 1948), 2:61.

[15] The full text of all American copyright laws and the relevant section of the Articles of the Confederation and the United States Constitution are given in *Copyright Enactments* (Washington: Copyright Office, Library of Congress, 1973).

[16] Earle Coleman, "Copyright Deposits at Harvard," *Harvard Library Bulletin* 10 (1956), pp. 135–41.

[17] A listing of the available state deposit records can be found in G. Thomas Tanselle's "Copyright Records and the Bibliographer," *Studies in Bibliography* 22 (1969), p. 83.

[18] See Emily Ellsworth Ford's *Notes on the Life of Noah Webster* (New York: Privately printed, 1912), and Harry R. Warfel, ed., *Letters of Noah Webster* (New York: Library Publishers, 1953).

[19] Rollo Silver, *The American Printer, 1787-1825* (Charlottesville: University of Virginia Press, 1967), pp. 107-8.

[20] Jesse Root, *Reports of Cases Adjudged in the Superior Court and Supreme Court of Errors,* 2 vols. (Hartford: Printed by Hudson and Goodwin, 1798), 1:133-34.

[21] *The Writings of Thomas Jefferson*, ed. A. A. Lipscomb and A. E. Berg (Washington: The Thomas Jefferson Memorial Association of the United States, 1903), 15:166.

[22] Herbert Ross Brown, *The Sentimental Novel in America, 1789-1860* (Durham: Duke University Press, 1940), p. 4.

[23] *The Papers of James Madison*, ed. William J. Hutchinson and William M. E. Rachal (Chicago: University of Chicago Press, 1962), 1:104-6. I owe thanks to Thomas Mason, associate editor of *The Papers of James Madison*, for calling this letter to my attention.

[24] G. Harrison Orians, "Censure of Fiction in American Romances and Magazines, 1789-1810," *Publications of the Modern Language Association* 52 (1937), p. 207. A survey of anti-novel literature in America is in Robert Winans' "The Reading of English Novels in Eighteenth-Century America, 1750-1800" (Ph.D. diss., New York University, 1972).

[25] Martha Woodmansee, "The Genius and the Copyright: Economic and Legal Conditions of the Emergence of the 'Author,'" *Eighteenth-Century Studies* 17 (1984), pp. 405-24.

Pennsylvania

1790

1.

District Court Ledger, 262 PA 1

date of deposit: June 9, fourteenth year of Independence

claimant: A: John Barry

author: . . ., Master of the Free School of the Protestant Episcopal Church.

title: The Philadelphia Spelling Book, arranged upon a plan entirely new, adapted to the capacities of children, and designed as an immediate improvement, in spelling and reading the English Language. The whole being recommended by several eminent teachers, as the most useful performance to expedite the institution of youth.—<author statement>

Title Page Deposit

author: JOHN BARRY, *Master of the Free/ School of the Protestant Episcopal Church.*

title: THE/ PHILADLEPHIA/ SPELLING BOOK/ ARRANGED UPON A PLAN ENTIRELY NEW,/ ADAPTED TO THE CAPACITIES OF CHILDREN,/ AND DESIGNED/ AS AN IM MEDIATE IMPROVEMENT IN/ SPELLING AND READING/ THE/ ENGLISH LAN GUAGE./ The whole being recommended by several emi-/ nent Teachers, as the most useful performance/ to expedite the instruction of youth./ <rule>/ <author statement>/ <double rule>

imprint: <below double rule> PHILADELPHIA:/ PRINTED BY *JOSEPH JAMES*/ M,DCC,XC.

note: Two pages of preface are also deposited.

2.

District Court Ledger, 262 PA 1

date of deposit: June 15, fourteenth year of Independence

claimant: P: Thomas Wignell

author: a citizen of the United States; <Royall Tyler>

title: The Contrast, a Comedy; in five acts: <author statement> performed with applause at the Theatres in New York, Philadelphia, and Maryland; and published (under an assignment of the copyright) by Thomas Wignell <quotation in Latin>

note: According to the *National Index of American Imprints,* the author is Royall Tyler.

Title Page Deposit

author: CITIZEN OF THE *UNITED STATES;*

title: THE/ CONTRAST,/ A/ COMEDY;/ IN FIVE ACTS:/ <author statement>/ Performed with Applause at the Theatres in NEW-YORK,/ PHILADELPHIA, and MARYLAND;/ AND PUBLISHED (*under an Assignment of the Copy-Right)* BY/ THOMAS WIGNELL./ <thick rule>/ <Latin quotation with English translation>/ <thick rule>

imprint: <below thick rule> PHILADELPHIA:/ FROM THE PRESS OF *PRICHARD & HALL,* IN MARKET STREET,/ BETWEEN SECOND AND FRONT STREETS./ M.DCC.XC.

note: One and a half pages of an advertisement, a dedication, and a half title also deposited.

3.

District Court Ledger, 262 PA 2

date of deposit: June 17, fourteenth year of Independence

claimant: A: John Churchman

author: . . ., late land surveyor for the district of the counties of Delaware and Chester, and for part of Lancaster and Berks, Pennsylvania.

title: An Explanation of the Magnetic Atlas, or Variation Chart, hereunto annexed; projected on a plan entirely new, by which the Magnetic Variation on any part of the Globe may be precisely determined, for any time, past, present, or future: and the variation and latitude being accurately known, the Longitude is of consequence truly determined. <author statement>

note: In the ledger the entry for this date records the deposit of a book and a chart, represented in this list by entry numbers 3 and 4.

Title Page Deposit

author: JOHN CHURCHMAN,/ *Late land surveyor for the district of the counties of* DELAWARE *and* CHESTER,/ *and for part of* LANCASTER *and* BERKS, PENNSYLVANIA.

title: AN/ EXPLANATION/ OF THE/ MAG NETIC ATLAS,/ OR/ VARIATION CHART,/ HEREUNTO ANNEXED;/ PROJECTED ON A PLAN/ ENTIRELY NEW,/ BY WHICH THE MAGNETIC VARIATION ON ANY PART OF/ THE GLOBE MAY BE PRE CISELY DETERMINED, FOR ANY TIME,/ PAST, PRESENT, OR FUTURE: AND THE VARIATION AND LATI-/ TUDE BEING ACCURATELY KNOWN, THE LONGITUDE IS/ OF CONSEQUENCE TRULY DETER MINED./ <thick rule>/ <author statement>/ <thick rule>

imprint: <below thick rule> PHILADELPHIA:/ PRINTED BY *JAMES & JOHNSON.*/ M.DCC.XC.

4.

District Court Ledger, 262 PA 2

date of deposit: June 17, fourteenth year of Independence

claimant: A: John Churchman

author: . . . late land surveyor for the district of the counties of Delaware and Chester, and for part of Lancaster and Berks, Pennsylvania.

title: To George Washington, President of the United States of America, this Magnetic Atlas or Variation Chart, is humbly inscribed <author statement>

format: chart

Title Page Deposit

author: JOHN CHURCHMAN.

title: <on lower right hand side of page> <script> To/ <script> George Washington/ <first and seventh words in script> President of the United States of America/ THIS/ MAG NETIC ATLAS/ or/ *VARIATION CHART/ Is humbly inscribed by/* <author statement>

note: This engraved title page is located in the Geography and Map Division.

5.

District Court Ledger, 262 PA 3

date of deposit: June 22, fourteenth year of Independence

claimant: A: A. J. Dallas

author: . . ., Esquire.

title: Reports of Cases ruled and adjudged in the Courts of Pennsylvania, before and since the Revolution: <author statement> <quotation in Latin>

Title Page Deposit

author: A. J. DALLAS, ESQUIRE.

title: REPORTS/ OF/ CASES/ RULED AND ADJUDGED IN THE/ COURTS OF PENN SYLVANIA,/ BEFORE AND SINCE THE/ *REVOLUTION:/* <author statement>/ <thick rule>/ <quotation in Latin>/ <rule>

imprint: <below rule> *PHILADELPHIA:/* <thick rule>/ PRINTED, FOR THE REPORTER, BY T. BRADFORD./ M,DCC,XC.

note: A recommendation, two pages of dedication, two pages of preface, and a table of the names of the cases are also deposited.

6.

District Court Ledger 262 PA 4

date of deposit: July 30, fifteenth year of Independence

claimant: P: Thomas Dobson

author: Benjamin Rush, M. D. Professor of the Theory and Practice of Medicine, in the College of Philadelphia.

title: An Eulogium in honor of the late Dr. William Cullen, Professor of the practice of Physic, in the University of Edinburgh; delivered before the College of Physicians of Philadelphia, on the 9th of July; agreeably to their vote of the 4th of May, 1790. <author statement> Published by order of the College of Physicians.

Title Page Deposit

author: BENJAMIN RUSH, M. D./ Professor of the Theory and Practice of Medicine, in the/ College of Philadelphia.

title: AN/ EULOGIUM/ IN HONOR OF THE LATE/ DR. WILLIAM CULLEN,/ PROFES SOR OF THE PRACTICE OF PHYSIC/ IN THE UNIVERSITY OF EDINBURGH;/ DE LIVERED BEFORE THE/ COLLEGE OF PHYSICIANS OF PHILADELPHIA,/ On the 9th of July, agreeably to their Vote of the 4th of May, 1790./ <rule>/ <author statement>/ <rule>/ PUBLISHED BY ORDER OF THE COLLEGE OF/ PHYSICIANS./ <thick rule>

imprint: <below thick rule> *PHILADELPHIA:/* PRINTED BY THOMAS DOBSON, BOOK SELLER AT THE/ STONE HOUSE IN SEC OND STREET./ M,DCC,XC.

note: The recommendation by the College of Physicians and a note of thanks are also deposited.

7.

District Court Ledger, 262 PA5

date of deposit: August 7, fifteenth year of Independence.

claimant: P: William Hall

title: The Book of Common Prayer, and Administration of the Sacraments, and other Rites and Ceremonies of the Church, according to the use of the Protestant Episcopal Church in the United States of America: together with the Psalter, or Psalms of David.

Title Page Deposit

title: The BOOK of/ COMMON PRAYER,/ And ADMINISTRATION of the/ SACRAMENTS,/ AND OTHER/ Rites and Ceremonies of the Church,/ ACCORDING TO THE USE OF/ *The Protestant Episcopal Church/* IN THE/ UNITED STATES/ OF/ *AMERICA:/* TOGETHER WITH THE/ PSALTER,/ OR/ PSALMS OF DAVID./ <thick rule>

imprint: <below thick rule> *PHILADELPHIA:/* Printed by HALL & SELLERS, in MARKET-STREET./ <short broken rule>/ MDCCXC.

8.

District Court Ledger, 262 PA 5

date of deposit: August 16, fifteenth year of Independence

claimant: A: Samuel Hampton

title: Longitude: or, the art of measuring at Sea or Land made easy; shewing by plain and practical Rules, to measure the distance of one place to that of another; with new Tables for the ease of the measurer. Also, a standard for invariable Measures and Weights. <author statement>

Title Page Deposit

author: SAMUEL HAMPTON.

title: LONGITUDE:/ OR, THE/ Art of Measuring at Sea or Land made easy;/ SHEWING,/ By plain and practical Rules,/ TO/ Measure the Dis tance of one Place to that of another;/ WITH/ NEW TABLES/ FOR THE EASE OF THE MEASURER./ ALSO,/ A Standard for invariable Measures and Weights./ <thick rule>/ <author statement>/ <thick rule>

imprint: <below thick rule> PHILADELPHIA, 19th. of Seventh Month, 1785.

9.

District Court Ledger, 262 PA 6

date of deposit: September 16, fifteenth year of Independence

claimant: P: Samuel Sower

title: Das Kleine Davidische Psalter Spiel der Kinder Zion, Von Alten und Neuen auserlesenen Geistes Gesängen, Allen wahren Heilsbegierig Säuglingen der Weisheit, Insonderheit aber jenen Gemeinden des Herrn, zum Dienst und gebrauch mit Fleiss Zusammen getragen in gegenwärtig beliebiger Form und Ordnung, Nebst einem dreÿfachen darzu nützlichen und der Materien halben nöthigen Register.

Title Page Deposit

title: <entire title page in Gothic script> Das Kleine/ Davidische/ Psalterspiel/ Der/ Kinder Zions,/ von Alten und Neuen auserlesenen/ Geistes Gesängen,/ Allen wahren Heils = begieri = / gen Säuglingen der Weisheit,/ Insonderheit aber/ Denen Gemeinden des HERRN,/ zum Dienst und Gebrauch mit Fleiss zu = / sammen getragen/ in gegenwärtig = beliebiger Form und Ordnung,/ Nebst einem dreyfachen, darzu nützlichen und der/ Materien halben nöthigen/ Register./ <rule>/ Zum vierten mal ans Licht gegeben./ <double rule>

imprint: <below double rule> Germantown, gedruckt bey Christoph Saur, 1777.

10.

District Court Ledger, 262 PA 7

date of deposit: October 15, fifteenth year of Independence

claimant: A: Charles Christopher Reiche

author: . . ., M.A.

title: Fifteen Discourses on the Marvellous Works in Nature delivered by a Father to his Children: calculated to make mankind feel, in every thing, the very presence of a Supreme Being, and to influence their minds with a Permanent delight in, and firm reliance upon, the directions of an Almighty, All-good, and All-wise Creator, and Governor. <author statement>

Title Page Deposit

author: CHARLES CHRISTOPHER REICHE, M.A.

title: FIFTEEN/ DISCOURSES/ ON THE/ MAR VELLOUS WORKS/ IN/ NATURE,/ DE LIVERED BY A/ FATHER TO HIS CHILDREN:/ CALCULATED TO MAKE MANKIND FEEL, IN EVERY/ THING, THE VERY PRESENCE OF A SUPREME BE-/ ING, AND TO INFLUENCE THEIR MINDS WITH/ A PERMANENT DELIGHT IN, AND FIRM/ RELIANCE UPON, THE DIREC TIONS/ OF AN ALMIGHTY, ALL-GOOD,/ AND ALL-WISE CREATOR,/ AND GOVER NOR./ <thick rule>/ <author statement>/ <thick rule>

imprint: <below thick rule> PHILADELPHIA:/ PRINTED for the AUTHOR, by JAMES & JOHNSON,/ and to be sold by them, the Author, and all the/ Booksellers in the city./ MDCCXCI./ <rule>

note: <below rule> Price, neatly bound, to the subscribers, 3s. 9d./ Ditto, — — to non subscribers. 4s. 6d./ Ditto unbound to ditto, — — 3s. 9d.

11.

District Court Ledger, 262 PA 7

date of deposit: November 18, fifteenth year of Independence

claimant: A: Andrew Adgate

author: . . ., P. U. A.

title: Rudiments of Music. <author statement>

Title Page Deposit

author: *ANDREW ADGATE,* P. U. A.

title: <ornamental border encloses the title page> RUDIMENTS/ OF/ MUSIC./ <rule>/ <author statement>/ <rule>

imprint: <below rule> PHILADELPHIA, Printed and sold by JOHN M'CULLOCH, in *Third-street,* near *Market-street.*/ <short double rule>/ M.DCC.LXXX.IX.

note: On the verso of the title page is a printed note by J. B. Smith, Prothonotary of the Court of Common Pleas of Philadelphia County, certifying Andrew Adgate's deposit. The title page is located in the Music Division.

1791

12.

District Court Ledger, 262 PA 8

date of deposit: January 3, fifteenth year of Independence

claimant: A: James Wilson

author: . . . L.L.D.

title: An Introductory Lecture to a Course of Law Lectures. <author statement> To which is added, a Plan of the Lectures.

Title Page Deposit

author: *JAMES WILSON,* L.L.D.

title: AN/ INTRODUCTORY/ LECTURE/ TO A/ COURSE OF LAW LECTURES./ <author statement>/ <thick rule>/ TO WHICH IS ADDED,/ A PLAN OF THE LECTURES./ <thick rule>

imprint: <below thick rule> *PHILADELPHIA:*/ FROM THE PRESS OF T. DOBSON./ M,DCC,XCI.

note: Although the title page indicates this work was published in 1791, the clerk has written on the verso that the title page was deposited on January 30, 1790.

13.

District Court Ledger, 262 PA 8

date of deposit: January 11, fifteenth year of Independence

claimant: A: Reading Howell

title: A map of the state of Pennsylvania, (one of the United States of America.) Including the triangle lately purchased of Congress—and containing the boundary lines of the state, as run by the respective Commissioners, with part of Lake Erie, and Presqu' isle. Also, by actual survey, the rivers Susquehanna, it's north-east and west branches, Tioga Sinnamahoning, Juniata, Lehigh, Lechawaxen, Schuylkill, and the western rivers—Ohio, Alleghany, Connowango, part of the Chataughque Lake, and French Creek, agreeably to the late discoveries—Monungahalia, Youghagania, and Kiskamenetus, and the larger creeks, and most of the lesser streams; mountains; the old principal roads, with the many new ones in the northern and western parts of the state, and the portages and communications from the late surveys by order of government—The division lines of the respective counties, and townships—Delineation of the districts of depreciation and donation lands, with all the other districts in the new purchase—The seats of justice in the respective counties—Iron works, manufactories, minorals, and other noted places—<author statement>

format: map

Title Page Deposit

author: READING HOWELL.

title: <on right hand side of page> <decorative rule>/ A MAP/ OF THE/ State of Pennsyl vania,/ (One of the United States of America.)/ INCLUDING the triangle lately purchased of Congress—and/ <. . .>/ <author statement>/ <decorative rule>

note: The title page is located in the Geography and Map Division.

14.

District Court Ledger, 262 PA 9

date of deposit: January 12, fifteenth year of Independence

*claimant:*P: Michael Billmeyer

title: Ein wohl eingerichtetes deutsches A B C, Buchstabir und Lesebuch zum Gebrauch deutscher Schulen./ Enthaltend/ 1. Das A B C nebst einer grossen Menge Buchstabir und Leseübungen./ 2. Das Gebät des Herrn, die Gebote, den Glauben nebst dem 5, 6, und 7ten Capitel aus Mattheo. 3. Einen hinreichenden, gründlichen und fasslichen Unterricht das Deutsche richtig zu lernen. 4. Ein Anweisung den Kindern das Schreiben und Rechnen leichter und begreiflicher zu machen. 5. Einige angenehme und moralische Geschichten und Erzählungen für Kinder. 6. Einige moralische Fabeln für Kinder mit Kupfern. 7. Eine Erdbeschreibung und allgemeine Nachricht von der Erde und den vier Welttheilen Europa, Asia Africa und Columbia, oder America, zum Nutzen der Erwachsenen so wohl, als der Kinder.

note: See also entry number 26.

Title Page Deposit

title: <entire title page in Gothic script> Ein/ wohl eingerichtetes deutsches/ A B C,/ Buchstabir und Lesebuch/ zum Gebrauch/ deutscher Schulen./ Enthalted/ I. Das A B C, nebst einer grossen Menge Buchstabir = und Leseübungen./ 2. Das Gebät des HErrn, die Gebote, den Glauben, nebst dem 5, 6, und 7ten/ Capitel aus Matthäo. 3. Einen hinreichenden, gründlichen und fasslichen Un = / terricht das Deutsche richtig zu lernen. 4. Eine Anweisung den Kindern das/ Schreiben und Rechnen leichter und begreiflicher zu machen. 5. Einige ange = / nehme und moralische Geschichten und Erzählungen für Kinder. 6. Einige/ moralische Fabeln für Kinder, mit Kupfern. 7. Eine Erdbeschreibung/ und allge meine Nachricht von der Erde und den vier Welt theilen/ Europa, Asia, Africa und Columbia, oder America, zum Nu = / tzen der Erwachsenen sowohl, als der Kinder./ <relief cut of two cherubs>/ <rule>

imprint: <below rule> Germantaun:/ Gedruckt bey Michael Billmeyer, 1790.

note: The clerk's note on the verso of the title page, in addition to giving the date of deposit as January 12, 1791, also states: "Recorded and deposited on the same Deposited Title 17th Oct 1791—SC <Samuel Caldwell>." See entry number 26.

15.

District Court Ledger, 262 PA 10

date of deposit: February 22, fifteenth year of Independence

claimant: A: William Waring

title: A Journal for Lunar Observations, by which the Calculation of Longitude is much expedited, the Mariner being led through the operation by a regular printed Form in each Page, having only to fill the Blanks from the Nautical Almanac and proper Tables, as indicated by the leading lines to the respective Numbers: containing also, in the same page, Blanks for calculating the Latitude from the Moon's meridional Altitude. With directions exemplified, <author statement>

Title Page Deposit

author: WILLIAM WARING.

title: A/ JOURNAL/ FOR/ LUNAR OBSERVA TIONS,/ BY WHICH THE/ CALCULATION/ OF/ LONGITUDE/ IS MUCH EXPEDITED;/ The MARINER being led through the Opera tion/ BY/ A regular printed Form in each Page,/ HAVING ONLY/ To fill the Blanks from the Nautical Almanac and proper Tables, as indicated by the/ leading Lines to the respective Numbers:/ CONTAINING ALSO, IN THE SAME PAGE,/ *Blanks for calculating the* LATITUDE *from the* MOON'S *meridional Altitude.*/ With Directions ex emplified, &c./ <short thick rule>/ <author statement>/ <short thick rule>

imprint: <below short thick rule> *PHILADEL PHIA:*/ PRINTED BY ZACHARIAH POULSON, JUNIOR, No. 30, FOURTH-STREET, NEAR THE COLLEGE./ M D C C X C I.

16.

District Court Ledger, 262 PA 11

date of deposit: February 23, fifteenth year of Independence

claimant: A: Nathan Dorsey

author: Doctor . . ., Fellow of the College of Physicians of Philadelphia.

title: A new and complete System of Instructions, for the safe and successful Administration of Medicines, in those Diseases incident to Mariners. <author statement>

Title Page Deposit

author: DOCTOR *NATHAN DORSEY,*/ FELLOW OF THE COLLEGE OF PHYSICIANS OF/ PHILADELPHIA.

title: A/ NEW AND COMPLETE/ SYSTEM/ OF/ INSTRUCTIONS,/ FOR THE SAFE AND SUCCESSFUL/ ADMINISTRATION OF/ MEDICINES,/ IN THOSE/ DISEASES/ INCI DENT TO/ MARINERS./ <author statement>/ <thick rule>

imprint: <below thick rule> PHILADELPHIA:/ PRINTED BY P. STEWART, No. 34, SOUTH SECOND-STREET./ M,DCC,XCI.

17.

District Court Ledger, 262 PA 11

date of deposit: February 23, fifteenth year of Independence

claimant: A: John Adlum

author: . . . & John Wallis.

title: A Geographical and Hydrographical Map, exhibiting a general View of the Roads and inland Navigation of Pennsylvania, and Part of the adjacent States, which are now the Object of Improvement, with a View to bring to Market, by the most easy Land & Water Carriage, the Trade of the Susquehanna and Ohio Waters, and of that extensive Territory, bounding on, and connected with the great Lakes. Compiled from actual Surveys, at the particular Request of the Society lately formed in Pennsylvania, for promoting the "Improvement of Roads and inland Navigation," humbly inscribed to his Excellency Thomas Mifflin, Governor, and the General Assembly of the Commonwealth of Pennsylvania, <author statement>

Title Page Deposit
author: JOHN ADLUM, &/ JOHN WALLIS.
title: A/ GEOGRAPHICAL AND HYDROGRA PHICAL/ <black letter> Map,/ EXHIBITING/ A GENERAL VIEW/ OF/ THE ROADS AND INLAND NAVIGATION/ OF/ *Pennsylvania,*/ AND/ PART OF THE ADJACENT STATES,/ <. . .>/ COMPILED from actual Surveys, at the particular Request of the *Society* late-/ ly formed in Pennsylvania, for promoting the "Improvement of Roads and In-/ land Navigation," Humbly inscribed/ TO/ HIS EXCELLENCY/ Thomas Mifflin, *Governor,*/ AND THE/ *General Assembly of the Commonwealth*/ OF/ Pennsylvania,/ <author statement>
note: The title page is located in the Geography and Map Division.

18.

District Court Ledger, 262 PA 12
date of deposit: February 26, fifteenth year of Independence
claimant: A: John Churchman
author: . . ., Author of the Magnetic Atlas.
title: A Dissertation on Gravitation. <author statement>

Title Page Deposit
author: JOHN CHURCHMAN,/ AUTHOR OF THE MAGNETIC ATLAS.
title: A/ DISSERTATION/ ON/ GRAVITATION./ <thick rule>/ <author statement>/ <short thick rule>

19.

District Court Ledger, 262 PA 13
date of deposit: March 18, fifteenth year of Independence
claimant: A: Clement Biddle
title: The Philadelphia Directory. <author statement>

Title Page Deposit
author: CLEMENT BIDDLE.
title: THE/ PHILADELPHIA/ DIRECTORY./ <thick rule>/ <author statement>/ <short thick rule>
imprint: <below short thick rule> PHILADEL PHIA:/ PRINTED BY *JAMES & JOHNSON,* No. 147, HIGH-STREET,/ <two rules, one above and one below the following three words, have been inserted in ink> FOR THE *EDITOR.*/ M,DCC,XCI.

20.

District Court Ledger, 262 PA 13
date of deposit: May 18, fifteenth year of Independence
claimant: A: Vincent M. Pelosi
title: Pelosi's Marine List and Price Current, containing the inward and outward bound Vessels in every Port of the Union, with other interesting Occurrences. A compendious Price Current, chiefly intended to accomodate the Merchants, Traders and their foreign Connections: published every Monday Morning at the Merchants and Exchange Coffee-House.

Title Page Deposit
title: PELOSI's/ <black letter> Marine List and Price Current,/ *Containing the Inward and Outward bound vessels in every Port of the Union,/ with other interesting Occurrences./ A COMPENDIOUS PRICE CURRENT,*/ Chiefly intended to accommodate the Merchants, Traders and their/ foreign connec tions; published every Monday morning at the Mer-/ chants and Exchange Coffee-House.
note: Price One Guinea per Annum./ <thick rule>/ ***Commercial Intelligence and Subscriptions will be thankfully receiv-/ ed at the Merchants and Exchange Coffee-House, 1791.

21.

District Court Ledger, 262 PA 14
date of deposit: June 13, fifteenth year of Independence
claimant: A: Reading Howell
title: A Map of Pennsylvania, and the Parts connected therewith, relating to the Roads and inland Navigation, especially as proposed to be improved by the late Proceedings of Assembly. (Copied from his larger Map) <author statement>
format: map

Title Page Deposit
author: READING HOWELL.
title: A MAP/ OF/ PENNSYLVANIA,/ AND the parts connected therewith, relating to/ the Roads and inland Navigation, especially as pro-/ posed to be improved by the late proceedings of/ Assembly. (Copied from his larger Map) by/ <author statement>
note: The title page is located in the Geography and Map Division.

22.

District Court Ledger, 262 PA 15
date of deposit: August 19, sixteenth year of Independence

claimant: P: Thomas Dobson
author: Nicholas B. Waters, M. D. Fellow of the College of Physicians of Philadelphia, and one of the Physicians and surgeons to the Philadelphia Dispensary.
title: A System of Surgery, extracted from the works of Benjamin Bell Edinburgh: <author statement> Illustrated with notes and Copper plates.

Title Page Deposit
author: NICHOLAS B. WATERS, M. D./ FEL LOW OF THE COLLEGE OF PHYSICIANS OF PHILADELPHIA,/ AND ONE OF THE PHYSICIANS AND SURGEONS/ TO THE PHILADELPHIA DISPENSARY.
title: A/ SYSTEM/ OF/ SURGERY./ EX TRACTED FROM THE WORKS OF/ BENJAMIN BELL, OF *EDINBURGH:/* <author statement>/ <thick rule>/ ILLUSTRATED WITH NOTES AND COPPERPLATES./ <thick rule>
imprint: <below thick rule> *PHILADELPHIA:/* PRINTED BY *T. DOBSON,* AT THE *STONE-HOUSE,/* No. 41, SOUTH SECOND-STREET./ M,DCC,XCI.

23.
District Court Ledger, 262 PA 15
date of deposit: August 20, sixteenth year of Independence
claimant: A: Lewis Nicolas
title: The Divinity of Jesus Christ considered, from Scripture Evidences. In three parts. 1. Texts of Scripture favorable or adverse thereto. 2. Conjecture on his true nature, as countenanced by sacred Writ. 3. His agency in Creation. To which is added, an Attempt to account for the general Deluge. <author statement> <quotation in Latin>

Title Page Deposit
author: LEWIS NICOLAS.
title: THE/ DIVINITY/ OF/ JESUS CHRIST/ CONSIDERED, FROM/ SCRIPTURE EVI DENCES./ *IN THREE PARTS.*/ I. Texts of Scripture favorable or adverse thereto./ II. Con jecture on his true Nature, as contenanced by Sacred Writ./ III. His Agency in Creation./ TO WHICH IS ADDED,/ An Attempt to account for the general Deluge./ <short thick rule>/ <author statement>/ <short thick rule>/ <quotation in Latin>/ <thick rule>
imprint: <below thick rule> *PHILADELPHIA:/* Printed by ELEAZER OSWALD, No. 156, Market-street./ between Fourth & Fifth-streets./ <short rule>/ M,DCC,XCI.
note: Three pages of a preface and two pages of an intended address are also deposited.

24.
District Court Ledger, 262 PA 16
date of deposit: August 22, sixteenth year of Independence
claimant: P: Zachariah Poulson
author: sundry Teachers in and near Philadelphia.
title: The American Tutor's Assistant; or, a compendious System of practical Arithmetic; containing, the several Rules of that useful Science, concisely defined, methodically arranged, and fully exemplified.—The whole particularly adapted to the easy and Regular Instruction of Youth in our American Schools: <author statement>

Title Page Deposit
author: By sundry TEACHERS *in and near* Philadelphia.
title: THE/ American Tutor's Assistant;/ OR,/ A COMPENDIOUS SYSTEM/ OF/ PRACTICAL ARITHMETIC;/ CONTAINING,/ The several Rules of that useful Science,/ *Concisely defined, methodically arranged, and fully exemplified./* THE WHOLE/ PARTICULARILY ADAPTED TO THE EASY AND REGULAR/ Instruction *of* Youth *in our* American Schools:/ <thick rule>/ <author statement>/ <thick rule>
imprint: <below thick rule> *PHILADELPHIA:/* PRINTED AND SOLD BY ZACHARIAH POULSON, JUNIOR,/ No. 30, FOURTH-STREET, NEAR THE COLLEGE./ M D C C X C I.

25.
District Court Ledger, 262 PA 17
date of deposit: August 26, sixteenth year of Independence
claimant: A: William Bartram
title: Travels through North & South Carolina, Georgia, East & West Florida, the Cherokee Country, the Extensive Teritories of the Muscogulges, or Creek Confederacy, and the Country of the Chactaws; Containing an Account of the Soil and Natural productions of those Regions, together with observations on the Manners of the Indians. Embellished with Copper-plates <author statement>

Title Page Deposit
author: WILLIAM BARTRAM.

title: TRAVELS/ THROUGH/ NORTH & SOUTH CAROLINA,/ GEORGIA,/ EAST & WEST FLORIDA,/ THE CHEROKEE COUN TRY, THE EXTENSIVE/ TERRITORIES OF THE MUSCOGULGES,/ OR CREEK CON FEDERACY, AND THE/ COUNTRY OF THE CHACTAWS;/ CONTAINING/ AN AC COUNT OF THE SOIL AND NATURAL/ PRODUCTIONS OF THOSE REGIONS, TOGE-/ THER WITH OBSERVATIONS ON THE/ MANNERS OF THE INDIANS./ *EMBELLISHED WITH COPPER-PLATES.*/ <thick rule>/ <author statement>/ <thick rule>
imprint: <below thick rule> PHILADELPHIA:/ PRINTED BY *JAMES & JOHNSON.*/ M,DCC,XCI.
note: Six pages describing the contents are also deposited.

26.
District Court Ledger, 262 PA 17
date of deposit: October 17, sixteenth year of Independence
claimant: P: Michael Billmeyer
title: Ein wohl eingerichtetes deutsches A B C, Buchstabir und Lese = buch zum Gebrauch deutscher Schulen./ Enthaltend/ 1. Das A.B.C. nebst einer grosen Menge Buchstabir = und Lese = übungen./ 2. Das Gebät des HErrn, die Gebote, den Glauben, nebst den 5, 6, und 7ten Capitel aus Matheo. 3. Einen hinreichenden, gründlichen und fasslichen Unterricht das Deutsche richtig zu lernen. 4. Eine Anweisung den Kindern das Schreiben und Rechnen leichter und begreiflicher zu machen. 5. Einige angenehme und moralische Geschichten und Erzählungen für Kinder. 6. Einige moralische Fabeln für Kinder, mit Kupfern. 7. Eine Erdbeschreibung und allgemeine Nachricht von der Erde, und den vier Welttheilen, Europa, Asia, Africa, und Columbia, oder America, zum Nutzen der Erwachsenen, sowohl, als der Kinder.
note: See entry number 14.

27.
District Court Ledger, 262 PA 18
date of deposit: November 14, sixteenth year of Independence
claimant: P: Matthew Carey
title: A brief Examination of Lord Sheffield's Observations of the Commerce of the United States. In seven Numbers. With two supplementary Notes on American Manufactures.

Title Page Deposit
title: A BRIEF/ <second letter "A" crossed out in ms. and an "A" inserted between "X" and "M"> E<A>XAMINATION/ OF LORD SHEFFIELD'S/ OBSERVATIONS/ OF THE/ COMMERCE/ OF THE/ UNITED STATES./ <rule>/ <tear> IN SEVEN NUMBERS./ WITH TWO SUPPLEMENTARY NOTES ON/ AMERICAN MANUFACTURES./ <rule>
imprint: <below rule> *PHILADELPHIA:*/ FROM THE PRESS OF M. CAREY./ <last three numerals inserted in ms.> M.DCC.XCI.

28.
District Court Ledger, 262 PA 19
date of deposit: November 25, sixteenth year of Independence
claimant: A: John Aitkin
title: A Compilation of the Litanies Vespers Hymns & Anthems as they are sung in the Catholic Church

Title Page Deposit
title: <script> A/ COMPILATION/ <script> of the/ <script> Litanies/ VESPERS HYMNS & ANTHEMS/ <script> As they are sung in the/ CATHOLIC CHURCH/ <thick rule>
imprint: <below thick rule> PHILADELPHIA/ PRINTED AND SOLD BY JOHN AITKEN 1791
note: The title page is engraved.

29.
District Court Ledger, 262 PA 20
date of deposit: December 9, sixteenth year of Independence
claimant: P: John Mc.Culloch
author: Benjamin Workman A M
title: Elements of Geography designed for young Students in that Science In seven Sections Sect 1 Of the solar System Sect 2 Of the Earth in particular Sect 3 Of Maps and Globes The three foregoing Sections contain the Scientific or Astronomical Part of Geography digested in a clear and comprehensive Manner Sect 4 Of the different Religions Governments and Languages of Nations Sect 5 Of the Political Divisions of the Earth into Empires Kingdoms &c or the Historical Part of Geography Sect 6 Of Natural Philosophy or the Properties of Matter &c Sect. 7 Of Chronology <author statement> The third Edition Illustrated with 1 A Map of the World 2 A Plate of the Solar System 3 A Map of North America 4 A Map of the United States 5 A Map

of South America 6 A Map of Europe 7 A Map of Asia 8 A Map of Africa—

Title Page Deposit
author: BENJAMIN WORKMAN, *A.M.*
title: ELEMENTS/ OF/ GEOGRAPHY,/ DE SIGNED FOR/ Young Students in that Science./ IN SEVEN SECTIONS./ <. . .>/ <rule>/ <author statement>/ <rule>/ THE THIRD EDITION./ <rule>/ *Illustrated with,* I. *A Map of the World.* 2. *A Plate/ of the Solar System.* 3. *A Map of North America./* 4. *A Map of the United States.* 5. *A Map of South/ America.* 6. *A Map of Europe.* 7. *A Map of Asia./* 8. *A Map of Africa./* <double rule>
imprint: <below double rule> PHILADELPHIA:/ Printed and sold by JOHN McCULLOCH, in *Third-/ street,* NO. 1, above *Market-street./* M,DCC,XC.
note: The title page is located in the Geography and Map Division.

1792

30.

District Court Ledger, 262 PA 21
date of deposit: January 18, sixteenth year of Independence
claimant: A: John Rouelle
author: . . . M D
title: A complete Treatise on the mineral Waters of Virginia containing a Description of their Situation their natural History their Analysis Contents and their Use in Medicine <author statement> <two lines of poetry in English>

Title Page Deposit
author: JOHN ROUELLE, M. D.
title: A COMPLETE/ TREATISE/ ON THE/ MINERAL WATERS/ OF/ *VIRGINIA:/* CON TAINING/ A DESCRIPTION OF THEIR SIT UATION,/ THEIR NATURAL HISTORY, THEIR/ ANALYSIS, CONTENTS, AND THEIR/ USE IN MEDICINE./ <rule>/ <author statement>/ <rule>/ <two lines of poetry in English>/ <double rule>
imprint: <below double rule> PHILADELPHIA:/ PRINTED FOR THE AUTHOR, BY CHARLES CIST,/ AND TO BE SOLD BY THOMAS DOBSON./ M,DCC,XCII.

31.

District Court Ledger, 262 PA 22
date of deposit: February 14, sixteenth year of Independence
claimant: A: H H Brackenridge
title: Modern Chivalry; containing the Adventures of Captain John Ferrago, and Teague ORegan, his servant, Volume 1. <author statement> <quotation in Latin>

Title Page Deposit
author: H. H. BRACKENRIDGE.
title: <black letter> Modern Chivalry:/ CON TAINING THE/ ADVENTURES/ OF/ Captain John Farrago,/ AND/ TEAGUE OREGAN,/ HIS SERVANT./ VOLUME I./ <author statement>/ <thick rule>/ <quotation in Latin>/ <thick rule>
imprint: <below thick rule> *PHILADELPHIA:/* Printed and sold by JOHN M'CULLOCH, No. 1./ North *Third-street./* MDCCXCII.

32.

District Court Ledger, 262 PA 22
date of deposit: March 8, sixteenth year of Independence
claimant: A: Ebenezer Hazard
author: . . . A. M. Member of the American Philosophical Society, held at Philadelphia for Promoting useful Knowledge; and fellow of the American Academy of Arts and Sciences.
title: Historical Collections; Consisting of State Papers and other authentic Documents; intended as materials for an History of the United States of America <author statement> Volume 1. <quotation in Latin>

Title Page Deposit
author: EBENEZER HAZARD, A. M./ MEMBER OF THE AMERICAN PHILOSOPHICAL SOCIETY, HELD AT/ PHILADELPHIA, FOR PROMOTING USEFUL KNOWLEDGE;/ AND FELLOW OF THE AMERICAN ACADEMY/ OF ARTS AND SCIENCES.
title: HISTORICAL COLLECTIONS;/ CON SISTING OF/ STATE PAPERS,/ AND OTHER AUTHENTIC DOCUMENTS; INTENDED AS MATERIALS FOR/ AN HISTORY OF THE/ UNI TED STATES OF AMERICA./ <thick rule>/ <author statement>/ <short thick rule>/ VOLUME I./ <short thick rule>/ <quotation in Latin>/ <double rule>
imprint: <below double rule> PHILADELPHIA:/ PRINTED BY T. DOBSON, FOR THE AUTHOR./ M DCC XCII.
note: Two pages of preface are also deposited.

33.

District Court Ledger, 262 PA 23
date of deposit: March 13, sixteenth year of Independence

claimant: P: Benjamin Franklin Bache
author: William Smith D. D. one of the Vice-Presidents of the said Society and Provost of the College and Academy of Philadelphia
title: Eulogium on Benjamin Franklin L.L.D. President of the American Philosophical Society held at Philadelphia for promoting useful Knowledge Fellow of the Royal Society of London Member of the Royal Academy of Sciences at Paris of the Royal Society at Gottingen the Batavian Society in Holland and of many other literary Societies in Europe and America late Minister Plenipotentiary for the United States of America at the Court of Paris sometime President and for more than half a Century a revered Citizen of the Commonwealth of Pennsylvania Delivered March 1. 1791. in the German Lutheran Church of the City of Philadelphia before the American Philosophical Society and agreeably to their Appointment <author statement> The Memory of the deceased was honored also at the Delivery of this Eulogium with the Presence of the President Senate and House of Representatives of the Commonwealth of Pennsylvania the Corporation and most of the public Bodies as well as respectable private Citizens of Philadelphia.

Title Page Deposit
author: WILLIAM SMITH, D.D./ ONE OF THE VICE-PRESIDENTS OF THE SAID SOCIETY, AND PROVOST OF THE/ COLLEGE, AND ACADEMY OF PHILADELPHIA.
title: EULOGIUM/ ON/ <script> BENJAMIN FRANKLIN,/ L.L.D./ *PRESIDENT* OF THE *AMERICAN PHILOSOPHICAL SOCIETY,/* HELD AT PHILADELPHIA, FOR PRO MOTING USEFUL KNOWLEDGE,/ FELLOW OF THE ROYAL SOCIETY OF LONDON,/ MEMBER OF THE ROYAL ACADEMY OF SCIENCES AT PARIS,/ OF THE ROYAL SOCIETY AT GOTTINGEN,/ THE BATA VIAN SOCIETY IN HOLLAND,/ AND OF MANY OTHER LITERARY SOCIETIES IN EUROPE AND/ AMERICA;/ LATE MINIS TER PLENIPOTENTIARY FOR THE UNITED STATES/ OF AMERICA AT THE COURT OF PARIS,/ SOMETIME *PRESI DENT,* AND FOR MORE THAN HALF A CENTURY/ A REVERED *CITIZEN,* OF THE COMMONWEALTH OF/ *PENNSYLVANIA./* DELIVERED MARCH 1, 1791, IN THE GER MAN LUTHERAN CHURCH OF THE/ CITY OF PHILADELPHIA,/ BEFORE THE AMERI CAN PHILOSOPHICAL SOCIETY, AND AGREEABLY TO/ THEIR APPOINTMENT,/ <author statement>/ THE MEMORY OF THE DECEASED WAS HONORED ALSO, AT THE DELIVERY/ OF THIS EULOGIUM, WITH THE PRESENCE OF/ THE PRESI DENT, SENATE AND HOUSE OF REPRE SENTATIVES OF THE/ UNITED STATES OF AMERICA,/ THE SENATE AND HOUSE OF REPRESENTATIVES OF THE COMMON WEALTH/ OF PENNSYLVANIA,/ THE COR PORATION, AND MOST OF THE PUBLIC BODIES, AS WELL AS RES-/ PECTABLE PRIVATE CITIZENS, OF PHILADELPHIA./ <double rule>
imprint: <below double rule> PRINTED BY/ *BENJAMIN FRANKLIN BACHE,/* PHILA DELPHIA, 1792.
note: A note of thanks, a note of acknowledgment, and a list of corrections and alterations are also deposited.

34.
District Court Ledger, 262 PA 24
date of deposit: March 30, sixteenth year of Independence
claimant: A: Joseph Lippincott
title: A Collection of Tables 1. A Table shewing the Value of any Number of Pounds Shillings and Pence in Dollars and Cents from one Cent to ten thousand Dollars. 2. A Table of the Weight and Value of Coins as they now pass in the respective States of the Union with their sterling and federal Value. 3. A Table of the Money of the United States. 4. Tables of Interest at six and seven per cent. per Annum—With several other useful Tables—Calculated by <author statement>

Title Page Deposit
title: A/ COLLECTION OF/ TABLES./ . . ./ WITH SEVERAL OTHER USEFUL TABLES./ <thick rule>/ *CALCULATED BY/* JOSEPH LIPPINCOTT./ <double rule>/ *PHILADELPHIA:/* PRINTED BY *BENJAMIN JOHNSON,/ M,DCC,XCII.*

35.
District Court Ledger, 262 PA 25
date of deposit: May 1, sixteenth year of Independence
claimant: P: Michael Billmeyer
title: Ein wohl eingerichtetes deutsches A, B, C.= Buchstabir=und Lesebuch zum Gebrauch deutscher Schulen. Enthal=tend: das A B, C, nebst vielen Arten Buchstabir=und

Leseübungen. Eine Anweisung das Deutsche recht zu lernen, mit einem kurzen Unterricht vom Schreiben und Rechnen. Etliche angenehme und lehrreiche Erzählungen, Fabeln mit Kupfern, und poetische Stücke. Eine Kurze Erdbeschreibung, und ein sinnreiches Bild vor dem Buche/ Germantown/ Gedruckt beÿ Michael Billmeÿer, 1792.

Title Page Deposit

title: <entire title page in Gothic script> Ein/ wohl eingerichtetes deutsches/ A B C= / Buchstabir= und Lesebuch/ zum Gebrauch/ deutscher Schulen./ Enthaltend:/ Das A B C, nebst vielen Arten Buchstabir=und Lese= / übungen. Eine Anweisung das Deutsche recht zu ler= / nen, mit einem kurzen Unterricht vom Schreiben/ und Rechnen./ Etliche angenehme und lehrreiche Erzählungen, Fabeln mit Ku= / pfern, und poetische Stücke./ Eine kurze Erdbeschreibung, und ein sinnreiches Bild vor dem/ Buche./ <relief cut of two cherubs>/ <thick rule>

imprint: <below thick rule> Germantaun:/ Gedruckt bey Michael Billmeyer, 1792.

36.

District Court Ledger, 262 PA 26

date of deposit: September 24, seventeenth year of Independence

claimant: A: John Ely

author: . . . a teacher of little Children in Philadelphia

title: The Child's Instructor consisting of easy Lessons for Children on Subjects which are familiar to them in Language adapted to their Capacities <author statement> <biblical quotation> Volume 1—

Title Page Deposit

author: A TEACHER OF LITTLE CHILDREN/ IN PHILADELPHIA.

title: THE/ Child's Instructor:/ CONSISTING OF/ EASY LESSONS/ FOR/ CHILDREN;/ ON/ SUBJECTS which are FAMILIAR to them,/ IN/ LANGUAGE ADAPTED TO THEIR CAPACI TIES./ <thick rule>/ <author statement>/ <thick rule> <biblical quotation>/ <decorative rule>/ VOLUME I./ <decorative rule>

imprint: <below decorative rule> Printed by JOHN M'CULLOCH, No. 1, North *Third-street.*/ <short broken rule>/ M.DCC.XCII.

37.

District Court Ledger, 262 PA 27

date of deposit: October 2, seventeenth year of Independence

claimant: P: Joseph Hopkinson

author: Francis Hopkinson Esq.—

title: The miscellaneous Essays and occasional Writings <author statement>

note: The deposit includes title pages for vols. 2 and 3.

Title Page Deposit

author: FRANCIS HOPKINSON, ESQ.

title: THE/ MISCELLANEOUS ESSAYS/ AND/ OCCASIONAL WRITINGS/ <author statement>/ <thick rule>/ VOLUME I./ <thick rule>

imprint: <below thick rule> *PHILADELPHIA:*/ PRINTED BY *T. DOBSON,* AT THE STONE-HOUSE, No 41,/ SECOND STREET./ M,DCC,XCII.

note: Title pages for volumes 2 and 3, identical to title page for volume 1 except for the volume numbers, are also deposited.

38.

District Court Ledger, 262 PA 27

date of deposit: November 19, seventeenth year of Independence

claimant: A: Tobias Hirte

title: Ein Neues, auserlesenes, gemein nütziges Hand = Buchlein. Heraus gegeben von Tobias Hirte: Philadelphia

Title Page Deposit

note: A decorative paper cover and three leaves of blank paper deposited. On the cover is inscribed: "Tobias Hirte's Book Deposited 19th Nov. 1792."

39.

District Court Ledger, 262 PA 28

date of deposit: December 1, seventeenth year of Independence

claimant: P: Joseph C. Sykes

author: a literary Society—

title: The Lady's Magazine and Repository of entertaining Knowledge—Vol. 1 for 1792—<author statement> <quotation in English>

Title Page Deposit

author: a Literary Society.

title: THE/ <script> Lady's Magazine;/ <script> AND/ REPOSITORY/ <script> of/ *ENTER TAINING KNOWLEDGE.*/ <thick rule>/ VOL: I. for 1792./ <thick rule>/ <author statement>/ <rule>/ <quotation in English>/ <double rule>

imprint: <below double rule> PHILADELPHIA:/ <first five words in script> Printed for the Pro prietors, by W: GIBBONS/ <script> North Third Street/ <script> No,, 144.
note: The title page is engraved.

1793

40.

District Court Ledger, 262 PA 29
date of deposit: January 17, seventeenth year of Independence
claimant: P: John Carey
title: The System of Short-hand practised by W. Thomas Lloyd in taking down the Debates of Congress and now (with his Permission) published for general Use—by J. C.

Title Page Deposit
title: THE SYSTEM OF/ SHORT-HAND,/ PRAC TISED <torn page, word supplied> <BY>/ Mr. THOMAS LLOYD,/ IN TAKING DOWN THE/ DEBATES OF CONGRESS;/ AND NOW/ (with his permission)/ *PUBLISHED for GENERAL USE,*/ BY J. C./ <thick rule>
imprint: <below thick rule> SOLD BY H. AND P. RICE, No. 50. MARKET-STREET,/ *PHILA DELPHIA:*/ <short rule>/ 1793.

41.

District Court Ledger, 262 PA 29
date of deposit: March 13, seventeenth year of Independence
claimant: P: Thomas Dobson
author: William Bradford Esquire—
title: An Enquiry how far the Punishment of Death is necessary in Pennsylvania with Notes and Illustrations <author statement> To which is added an Account of the Gaol and Penitentiary House of Philadelphia and of the interior Management thereof—By Caleb Lownes of Philadelphia— <quotation in English>

Title Page Deposit
author: WILLIAM BRADFORD, ESQ.
Title: AN/ ENQUIRY/ HOW FAR/ THE PUNISH MENT OF DEATH IS NECESSARY/ IN PENN SYLVANIA./ WITH/ NOTES AND ILLUSTRA TIONS./ <author statement>/ <thick rule>/ To which is added,/ AN ACCOUNT OF THE GAOL AND PENITENTIARY HOUSE OF/ PHILADELPHIA, AND OF THE INTERIOR MANAGE-/ MENT THEREOF./ BY CALEB LOWNES, OF PHILADELPHIA./ <thick rule>/ <quotation in English>/ <thick rule>
imprint: <below thick rule> PHILADELPHIA:/ PRINTED BY T. DOBSON AT THE STONE-HOUSE, NO. 41,/ SOUTH SECOND-STREET./ M,DCC,XCIII.

42.

District Court Ledger, 262 PA 31
date of deposit: March 16, seventeenth year of Independence
claimant: P: Samuel Sower
title: Der/ Geschwinde Rechner, oder des Händlers nützlicher Gehülfe/ in/ Kauffung und Verkauffung allerley Sachen/ sowohl im Grossen als Kleinen,/ nach dem Föderal Geld/ berechnet;/ da auf einmal gezeigt wird/ Den Werth von allerley Waaren und Sachen von einem/ halben Cent bis auf einen Föderal Thaler/ und darüber, es seÿ auch von was für/ Benennung es wolle, bis auf/ 5,000./ Nebst Interessen Tabellen cc/ Und solches auf eine so leichte Weise, dass sich eine Person, die/ sonst nichts von der Rechenkunst versteht dennoch darnach richten/ kan, und dem der rechnen kan, ist es eine geschwinde Anzeige,/ wodurch er Mühe und Zeit erspahrt.—/ Erste Auflage—

Title Page Deposit
title: <entire title page in Gothic script> Der/ Geschwinde Rechner,/ Oder: des/ Händlers nüz licher Gehülfe/ in/ Kauffung und Verkauffung allerley Sachen/ sowohl im Grossen als Kleinen,/ nach dem Föderal Geld/ berechnet;/ da auf einmal gezeigt wird/ Den Werth von allerley Waaren und Sachen, von ei =/ nem halben Cent bis auf einen Föderal Thaler/ und drüber, es sey auch von was für/ Benennung es wolle, bis auf/ 5,000./ Nebst Interessen Tabellen, &c. &c./ Und solches auf eine so leichte Weise, dass sich eine Person,/ die sonst nichts von der Rechenkunst verstehet den =/ noch darnach richten kan, und dem der/ rechnen kan, ist es eine geschwinde/ Anzeige, wodurch er Mühe/ und Zeit erspahrt./ <rule>/ Erste Auflage./ <rule>
imprint: <below rule> Chesnuthill, gedruckt bey Samuel Saur, 1793.

43.

District Court Ledger, 262 PA 32
date of deposit: March 18, seventeenth year of Independence
claimant: P: Samuel Sower
title: The federal or new ready Reckoner and Trader's useful Assistant in Buying and Selling all Sorts of Commodities either wholesale or Retail

adapted to the federal Money shewing at one View the Amount or Value of any Number or Quantity of Goods or Merchandise from half a Cent to one Dollar and upwards either by Weight or Measure together with Interest. Tables &c — In so plain and easy a Manner that Persons quite unacquainted with Arithmetic may hereby asertain the Value in federal Money of any Quantity of Goods in Weight or Measure at any Price whatever. The first Edition—

Title Page Deposit

title: THE/ Federal/ OR NEW/ Ready Reckoner;/ AND/ Trader's useful ASSISTANT,/ IN/ Buying and Selling all Sorts of Com-/ modities either Wholesale or Retail./ Adapted to the FEDERAL MONEY,/ Shewing at one View/ The Amount or Value of any Num-/ ber or Quantity of Goods or Merch-/ andise from half a Cent to one Dol-/ lar and upwards, either by Weight/ or Measure, together with Interest-/ Tables, &c./ In so plain and easy a Manner, that/ Persons quite unacquainted with A-/ rithmetic may hereby asertain the/ Value in Federal Money of any/ quantity of Goods, in Weight or/ Measure at any Price whatever./ <rule>/ THE FIRST EDITION./ <rule>

imprint: <below rule> SAMUEL SOWER. 1793.

44.

District Court Ledger, 262 PA 33

date of deposit: June 27, seventeenth year of Independence

claimant: A: Tobias Hirte

title: Der Freund in der Noth, oder Zweiter Theil, des Neuen Auserlesenen Gemein nützigen Hand=Büchleins, darinnen allerhand Arten Solcher nützliche Kentnisse und Wissenschaften zu finden, die alle Gattungen von Menschen, wes Standes, Geschlechts und Alter er ist, nahe angehet, und beÿdes Nutzen und Vergnügen schaffen wird. Von welchen der Inhalt auf folgender Seite, und mehrere Nachricht in dem Vorbericht befindlich ist. Für die Deutsche Nation in America heraus gegeben von Tobias Hirte. Philadelphia.

Title Page Deposit

title: <entire title page in Gothic script> Der Freund in der Noth,/ Oder/ Zweyter Theil,/ des Neuen Auserlesenen Gemeinnützigen/ Hand= Büchleins,/ Darinnen allerhand Arten solcher nützliche Kenntnisse/ und Wissenschaften zu finden, die alle Gattungen von/ Menschen, wes Standes, Geschlechts und Alter er ist,/ nahe angehet, und beydes Nuzen und Vergnügen/ schaffen wird./ <the following three lines have been put in parentheses inserted in ms.> Von welchen der Inhalt/ auf folgender Seite, und mehrere Nachricht in dem/ Vorbericht befindlich ist./ Für die Deutsche Nation in America,/ heraus gegeben von/ Tobias Hirte. Philadelphia./ <double rule>

imprint: <below double rule> Germantaun: Gedruckt bey Peter Leibert, 1793.

45.

District Court Ledger, 262 PA 34

date of deposit: August 13, eighteenth year of Independence

claimant: P: Thomas Dobson

title: Transactions of the College of Physicians of Philadelphia—Volume 1.—Part 1. <quotation in Latin>

Title Page Deposit

title: TRANSACTIONS/ OF THE/ COLLEGE OF PHYSICIANS,/ OF PHILADELPHIA./ <short thick rule>/ VOLUME I.—PART I./ <short thick rule>/ <quotation in Latin>/ <thick rule>

imprint: <beneath thick rule> *PHILADELPHIA:*/ PRINTED BY T. DOBSON, No. 41, SO. SECOND-STREET./ <short rule>/ M DCC XCIII.

46.

District Court Ledger, 262 PA 34

date of deposit: August 13, eighteenth year of Independence

claimant: P: Thomas Dobson

author: Benjamin Rush M. D.—Professor of the Institutes of Medicine and of Clinical Practice in the University of Pennsylvania—

title: Medical Inquiries and Observations <author statement> Volume II.

Title Page Deposit

author: BENJAMIN RUSH, M. D./ PROFESSOR OF THE INSTITUTES OF MEDICINE, AND OF/ CLINICAL PRACTICE IN THE UNI VERSITY/ OF PENNSYLVANIA:

title: MEDICAL/ INQUIRIES/ AND/ OBSERVA TIONS./ <author statement>/ <thick rule>/ VOLUME II./ <thick rule>

imprint: <below thick rule> PHILADELPHIA:/ PRINTED BY T. DOBSON, AT THE STONE-HOUSE, NO. 41,/ SOUTH SECOND-STREET./ <short rule>/ M,DCC,XCIII.

47.

District Court Ledger, 262 PA 35

date of deposit: September 12, eighteenth year of Independence

claimant: P: Philip Derrick

author: <Richard Snowden>

title: The American Revolution written in the Style of ancient History—In two Volumes—<quotation in French> Vol:1—

note: According to the *National Index of American Imprints* the author is Richard Snowden.

Title Page Deposit

title: THE/ AMERICAN/ REVOLUTION;/ WRITTEN IN THE STYLE OF ANCIENT HISTORY./ *IN TWO VOLUMES./* <double rule>/ <quotation in French>/ <double rule>/ VOL. I./ <thick rule>

imprint: <below thick rule> PHILADELPHIA:/ PRINTED BY *JONES, HOFF & DERRICK.*/ M,DCC,XCIII./ <following line inserted in manuscript> Philip Derrick

48.

District Court Ledger, 262 PA 36

date of deposit: November 14, eighteenth year of Independence

claimant: A: Mathew Carey

title: A Short Account of the malignant Fever lately prevalent in Philadelphia with a Statement of the Proceedings that took Place on the Subject in different Parts of the United States—<author statement>

Title Page Deposit

author: MATHEW CAREY.

title: A SHORT/ ACCOUNT/ OF THE/ MALIG NANT FEVER,/ LATELY PREVALENT IN/ PHILADELPHIA:/ WITH A STATEMENT OF THE/ PROCEEDINGS/ THAT TOOK PLACE ON THE SUBJECT IN DIFFERENT/ PARTS OF THE/ UNITED STATES./ <short rule>/ <author statement>/ <short double rule>

imprint: <below short double rule> PHILA DELPHIA:/ PRINTED BY THE AUTHOR./ *November* 14, 1793.

49.

District Court Ledger, 262 PA 37

date of deposit: November 22, eighteenth year of Independence

claimant: P: Mathew Carey and Richard Folwell

author: D. Nassy M. D. Member of the American Philosophical Society &c.

title: Observations on the Cause Nature and Treatment of the epidemic Disorder prevalent in Philadelphia <author statement>

note: According to the *National Index of American Imprints,* the author is David de Isaac Cohen Nassy.

Title Page Deposit

author: D. NASSY, *M. D. Member of the American/ Philosophical Society, &c.*

title: OBSERVATIONS/ ON THE/ CAUSE, NATURE, and TREATMENT/ OF THE/ EPI DEMIC DISORDER,/ PREVALENT IN PHILADELPHIA./ <author statement>/ <thick rule>

imprint: <below thick rule> *PHILADELPHIA:/* Printed by Parker & Co. for M. Carey./ Nov. 26,—1793./ <deleted in ms.> <(Registered agreeable to law.)>

note: A printed text in French is on the verso of the title page.

50.

District Court Ledger, 262 PA 38

date of deposit: December 13, eighteenth year of Independence

claimant: A: Mathew Carey

title: Observations on Dr. Rush's Enquiry into the Origin of the late epidemic Fever in Philadelphia—<author statement>

Title Page Deposit

author: MATHEW CAREY.

title: OBSERVATIONS/ ON/ DR. RUSH's ENQUIRY/ INTO THE ORIGIN OF THE LATE/ EPIDEMIC FEVER/ IN PHILADEL PHIA:/ <short thick rule>/ <"smaller" is written in ms. next to thick rule and a ms. line drawn through rule>/ <author statement>

note: The bottom part of title page is torn off, therefore no imprint information is available.

51.

District Court Ledger, 262 PA 38

date of deposit: December 13, eighteenth year of Independence

claimant: A: Justus Henry Christian Helmuth

author: J. Heinrich C. Helmuth, Evangelisch Luther. Prediger.

title: Kurze Nachricht von dem sogenanten gelben Fieber in Philadelphia; für den nachdenkenden Christen, <author statement>

Title Page Deposit

author: J. Heinrich C. Helmuth,/ Evangelisch Luther. Prediger.

title: <entire title page in Gothic script> Kurze/ Nachricht/ von dem sogenannten/ gelben Fieber/ in Philadelphia;/ für den nachdenkenden Christen;/ <author statement>/ <double rule>
imprint: <There is a curved ms. line on the left side of the imprint.> <below double rule> Philadelphia:/ Gedruckt bey Steiner und Kämmerer./ 1793.

1794

52.

District Court Ledger, 262 PA 39
date of deposit: January 6, eighteenth year of Independence
claimant: P: Benjamin Carr
author: a Lady of Philadelphia
composer: R Taylor
title: The Kentucky Volunteer a new Song <author statement> <composer statement>
note: According to the *National Index of American Imprints* the composer is Raynor Taylor.

53.

District Court Ledger, 262 PA 39
date of deposit: January 8, eighteenth year of Independence
claimant: P: Mathew Carey
title: A Short Account of Algiers containing a Description of the Climate of that Country of the Manners & Customs of the Inhabitants and of their several Wars against Spain, France, England, Holland Venice and other Powers of Europe from the Usurpation of Barbarossa and the Invasion of the Emporer Charles V to the present time with a concise View of the Rupture between Algiers and the United States <quotation in Latin>

(53a)

Title Page Deposit
title: A/ SHORT ACCOUNT/ OF/ ALGIERS,/ CONTAINING/ <The last two letters of the second word have been underlined; "of the" has been inserted in ms.> A DESCRIPTION of the/ CLIMATE OF THAT COUNTRY,/ OF THE/ MANNERS AND CUSTOMS/ OF THE/ INHABITANTS,/ AND OF THEIR SEVERAL WARS AGAINST SPAIN,/ FRANCE, ENGLAND, HOLLAND, VENICE AND/ OTHER POWERS OF EUROPE, FROM/ THE USURPATION OF *BARBAROSSA*/ AND THE INVASION OF THE/ EMPEROR *CHARLES V.* TO/ THE PRESENT TIME,/ WITH A CONCISE/ VIEW OF THE RUPTURE/ BETWEEN/ ALGIERS AND THE UNITED STATES./ <rule>/ <quotation in Latin>/ <rule>
imprint: <below rule> *PHILADELPHIA:*/ Printed by J. Parker for M. Carey, No. 118, Market-street./ *January* 8, 1794.

(53b)

Title Page Deposit
title: A/ SHORT ACCOUNT/ OF/ ALGIERS,/ CONTAINING/ A DESCRIPTION/ OF THE/ CLIMATE OF THAT COUNTRY,/ OF THE/ MANNERS AND CUSTOMS/ OF THE/ INHABITANTS,/ AND OF THEIR SEVERAL WARS AGAINST SPAIN,/ FRANCE, ENGLAND, HOLLAND, VENICE, AND/ OTHER POWERS OF EUROPE, FROM/ THE USURPATION OF *BARBAROSSA*/ AND THE INVASION OF THE/ EMPEROR *CHARLES V.* TO/ THE PRESENT TIME;/ WITH A CONCISE/ VIEW OF THE ORIGIN/ OF THE RUPTURE/ BETWEEN/ ALGIERS AND THE UNITED STATES./ <rule>/ <quotation in Latin>/ <rule>
imprint: <below rule> *PHILADELPHIA:*/ Printed by J. Parker for M. Carey, No. 118, Market-street/ *January* 8, 1794.
note: The registration as it is written in the ledger is printed on the verso of this title page. On the verso of 53b the clerk has written that it was deposited on January 8, but there is no note on title page 53a.

54.

District Court Ledger, 262 PA 40
date of deposit: January 15, eighteenth year of Independence
claimant: A, P: David Hale and John Phillips Ripley
title: The United States Register for the year 1794 being the 18–9th of National Sovereignty

Title Page Deposit
title: THE/ <black letter> United States/ REGISTER,/ FOR THE YEAR 1794;/ Being the 18—9th of/ NATIONAL SOVEREIGNTY./ <thick rule>/ <relief cut of an American eagle>/ <thick rule>
imprint: <below thick rule> *PHILADELPHIA:*/ PRINTED, FOR THE EDITORS,/ By *Stewart & Cochran,* No. 34, South Second-street,/ and *John M'Culloch,* No. 1, North Third-street./ M,DCC,XCIV.

55.

District Court Ledger, 262 PA 41

date of deposit: January 23, eighteenth year of Independence

claimant: A, P:Absolam Jones and Richard Allen

author: A. J. and R A.

title: A Narrative of the Proceedings of the Black People during the late Awful Calamity in Philadelphia in the year 1793 and a Refutation of some Censures thrown upon them in some late Publications <author statement>

note: The *National Union Catalog* lists Absalom Jones as author.

Title Page Deposit

author: A. J. AND R. A.

title: A/ NARRATIVE/ OF THE/ PRO CEEDINGS/ OF THE/ BLACK PEOPLE,/ DURING THE LATE/ Awful Calamity in Phila delphia,/ IN THE YEAR 1793:/ AND/ A REFU TATION/ OF SOME/ CENSURES,/ *Thrown upon them in some late Publications.*/ <short double rule>/ <author statement>/ <double rule>

imprint: <below double rule> PHILADELPHIA: PRINTED FOR THE AUTHORS,/ *BY WILLIAM W. WOODWARD, AT FRANKLIN's HEAD,*/ NO. 41, CHESTNUT-STREET./ <short rule>/ 1794.

56.

District Court Ledger, 262 PA 41

date of deposit: February 24, eighteenth year of Independence

claimant: A: Robert Davidson

author: an American

title: Geography Epitomized or a Tour round the World being a short but Comprehensive Description of the Terraqueous Globe Attempted in Verse (for the sake of Memory) and principally designed for the use of Schools <author statement>

Title Page Deposit

author: AN AMERICAN.

title: GEOGRAPHY/ EPITOMIZED;/ OR, A/ TOUR *round the* WORLD:/ BEING/ A SHORT BUT COMPREHENSIVE/ DESCRIPTION/ OF THE/ *TERRAQUEOUS GLOBE:*/ ATTEMPTED IN VERSE,/ (FOR THE SAKE OF MEM ORY;)/ And principally designed for the Use of SCHOOLS./ <rule>/ <author statement>/ <broken double rule>

imprint: <below broken double rule> *PHILADEL PHIA:*/ PRINTED AND SOLD BY JOSEPH CRUKSHANK, IN MARKET-/ STREET, BE TWEEN SECOND AND THIRD-/ STREETS. MDCCLXXXIV.

57.

District Court Ledger, 262 PA 42

date of deposit: February 26, eighteenth year of Independence

claimant: A: Reading Howell

title: A Map of the United States of America shewing or containing the Boundaries or Division Lines of the different and respective States (with their respective divisions into Counties &c)—Lakes Rivers & principal Creeks Mountains Canals Roads Portages and Communications Forts Cities Towns and all other Matter and Things worthy of insertion Compiled from the best Authorities <author statement> Philadelphia Feb. 26th 1794

format: map

Title Page Deposit

author: READING HOWELL.

title: A MAP of the UNITED STATES of AMERICA,/ shewing or containing the Boun daries or Division Lines/ of the different and respective States (with their respec-/ tive Divisions into Counties, &c.)—Lakes, Rivers, and/ prin cipal Creeks, Mountains, Canals, Roads, Por tages/ and Communications, Forts, Cities, Towns, and all o-/ ther Matter and Things worthy of insertion. Compil-/ ed from the best Authorities, by/ <author statement>

imprint: <below author statement on the lower left hand side, set off by a decorative bracket> PHILADELPHIA,/ *Feb. 26th,* 1794.

note: The title page is located in the Geography and Map Division.

58.

District Court Ledger, 262 PA 42

date of deposit: March 5, eighteenth year of Independence

claimant: A: Reading Howell

title: A Map of the County of Philadelphia in Pennsylvania shewing the Rivers Delaware and Schuylkill and the other Waters Hills Townships Lines Canals Roads Water-works Public Houses Gentlemens' Seats &c—Exhibiting also the Ground Plan of the City of Philadelphia Southwark and the Liberties &c—Houses of Worship &c <author statement> Philadelphia March 5th 1794

format: map

Title Page Deposit

author: READING HOWELL.

title: <top of page> A MAP of the COUNTY of PHILADELPHIA,/ in *Pennsylvania,* shewing the

Rivers *Delaware* and/ *Schuylkill,* and the other Waters;—Hills, Townships,/ Lines, Canals, Roads, Water-works, Public Houses,/ Gentlemens' Seats, &c.—Exhibiting also the Ground/ Plan of the City of *Philadelphia, Southwark,* and the/ *Liberties,* &c. Houses of Worship, &c. by/ <author statement>

imprint: <below author statement, on the lower left hand side> PHILADELPHIA, *March* 5*th,* 1794.

note: The title page is located in the Geography and Map Division.

59.

District Court Ledger, 262 PA 43

date of deposit: March 7, eighteenth year of Independence

claimant: P: Matthew Clarkson<,> Caleb Lownes<,> and John Connelly

title: Minutes of the Proceedings of the Committee, appointed on the 14th September, 1793, by the Citizens of Philadelphia, the Northern Liberties and the District of Southwark, to attend to and alleviate the Sufferings of the Afflicted with the Malignant Fever, prevalent, in the City and its vicinity, with An Appendix.

Title Page Deposit

title: MINUTES/ OF THE/ *PROCEEDINGS*/ OF/ THE COMMITTEE,/ *APPOINTED ON THE* 14*th SEPTEMBER,* 1793,/ *BY THE CITIZENS OF*/ PHILADELPHIA,/ THE NORTHERN LIBERTIES/ AND THE/ DISTRICT OF SOUTHWARK,/ TO ATTEND TO AND ALLEVIATE THE SUFFERINGS OF THE/ AFFLICTED WITH/ *THE MALIGNANT FEVER,*/ PREVALENT,/ *IN THE CITY AND ITS VICINITY,*/ WITH AN APPENDIX./ <thick rule>

imprint: <below thick rule> *PHILADELPHIA:*/ PRINTED BY *R. AITKEN & SON,* AND SOLD BY J. CRUK-/ SHANK, W. YOUNG, T. DOB SON AND THE OTHER BOOKSELLERS./ <short broken rule>/ M.DCC.XCIV.

note: There is also a ms. note on a separate sheet with the names of the proprietors Matthew Clarkson, Caleb Lownes, and John Connelly.

60.

District Court Ledger, 262 PA 44

date of deposit: March 24, eighteenth year of Independence

claimant: A: Ebenezer Hazard

author: . . . , A. M. Member of the American Philosophical Society, held at Philadelphia for promoting useful knowledge; Fellow of the American Academy of Arts and Sciences; and correspondent member of the Massachusetts Historical Society.

title: Historical Collections; consisting of State Papers, and other authentic documents; intended as materials for an History of the United States of America. <author statement> Volume II. <quotation in Latin>

Title Page Deposit

author: EBENEZER HAZARD, A. M./ MEMBER OF THE AMERICAN PHILOSOPHICAL SO CIETY, HELD AT PHI-/ LADELPHIA, FOR PROMOTING USEFUL KNOWLEDGE; FELLOW/ OF THE AMERICAN ACADEMY OF ARTS AND SCIENCES;/ AND CORRE SPONDENT MEMBER OF THE MASSA-/ CHUSETTS HISTORICAL SOCIETY.

title: HISTORICAL COLLECTIONS;/ CON SISTING OF/ STATE PAPERS,/ AND OTHER AUTHENTIC DOCUMENTS; INTENDED AS MATERIALS FOR/ AN HISTORY OF THE/ UNITED STATES OF AMERICA./ <thick rule>/ <author statement>/ <short thick rule>/ VOLUME II./ <short thick rule>/ <quotation in Latin>/ <double rule>

imprint: <below double rule> PHILADELPHIA:/ PRINTED BY T. DOBSON, FOR THE AUTHOR./ M DCC XCIV.

note: Two pages of preface are also deposited.

61.

District Court Ledger, 262 PA 45

date of deposit: April 12, eighteenth year of Independence

claimant: P: Benjamin Davies

author: A P Folie;

title: A Ground Plan of the City and Suburbs of Philadelphia, taken from actual Survey; Containing an exact description of all the Squares, Streets and Alleys in the City and Liberties; of the Situation of all the principal public Buildings, of the Rivulets and as much of the Canal as lies within the Compass of the Draft <author statement> and published by the Proprietor Benjamin Davies.

format: map

Title Page Deposit

author: A. P. Folie;

title: A/ GROUND PLAN/ OF THE/ *CITY AND SUBURBS*/ OF/ *Philadelphia,*/ Taken from actual Survey;/ CONTAINING an exact description of all squares, streets,/ and alleys in the CITY and LIBERTIES; of the situation of all the/ principal Public Buildings; of the Rivuletts, and as much of

the Canal/ as lies within the compass of the Draft by/ <author statement>
imprint: <below author statement> and published by the Proprietor,/ Benjamin Davies.

62.

District Court Ledger, 262 PA 45
date of deposit: April 19, eighteenth year of Independence
claimant: A: James Carson
title: A Practical Grammar of the English Tongue containing all that is necessary to be committed to memory for rightly understanding the Englis Language composed chiefly for the benefit of his own School <author statement> <quotation in Latin>

Title Page Deposit
author: JAMES CARSON.
title: A/ PRACTICAL GRAMMAR/ OF THE/ ENGLISH TONGUE./ CONTAINING/ ALL THAT IS NECESSARY TO BE COM MITTED/ TO MEMORY FOR RIGHTLY UNDER-/ STANDING THE ENGLISH/ LANGUAGE./ <double rule>/ Composed chiefly for the benefit of his own School./ <author statement>/ <double rule>/ <quotation in Latin>/ <thick rule>
imprint: <below thick rule> *PHILADELPHIA:/* PRINTED BY FRANCIS BAILEY, AT YORICK'S-/ HEAD, NO. 116, HIGH-STREET./ M,DCC,XCIV.

63.

District Court Ledger, 262 PA 46
date of deposit: April 23, eighteenth year of Independence
claimant: P: John Poor
title: The Rise & Progress of the Young-Ladies' Academy of Philadelphia: containing an Account of a Number of Public Examinations & Commencements; the Charter & Bye-Laws; Likewise, a Number of Orations delivered by the young ladies And several by the Trustees of said Institution

Title Page Deposit
title: THE/ RISE AND PROGRESS/ OF THE/ <black letter> Young = Ladies' Academy/ OF PHILADELPHIA:/ Containing an Account of a Number of/ PUBLIC EXAMINATIONS & COMMENCEMENTS;/ *The Charter and Bye-Laws;/ Likewise,* A Number of ORATIONS delivered/ By the YOUNG LADIES,/ And several by the *Trustees* of said Institution./ <double rule>
imprint: <below double rule> *PHILADELPHIA:/* Printed by STEWART & COCHRAN, No. 34, South Second-street./ M,DCC,XCIV.

64.

District Court Ledger, 262 PA 46
date of deposit: April 30, eighteenth year of Independence
claimant: A, P: Thomas Timmings Christopher Appleton & John Gregory
title: The Philadelphia Cabinet and Chair Makers Book of Prices Instituted April 14th 1794

Title Page Deposit
title: THE/ *PHILADELPHIA/* CABINET/ AND/ CHAIR MAKERS/ <black letter> Book of Prices./ <rule>/ *INSTITUTED APRIL 14th,* 1794./ <rule>
imprint: <below rule> *PHILADELPHIA:/* PRINTED BY *R. AITKEN & SON* No. 22, MARKET STREET./ <short rule>/ M.DCC.XCIV.

65.

District Court Ledger, 262 PA 47
date of deposit: May 17, eighteenth year of Independence
claimant: A: Tobias Hirte
title: Phrophetische Muthmassungen über die französische Staatsveränderung und andere neuere in kurzem zu erwartende Begebenheiten. Nebst lehrreichen Erzählungen von Handlungen Joseph's des zweÿten, des besten Kaisers, den Deutschland jemals verehrte, dann ist unser Waschington mit diesem Joseph, der seine Laufbahn 1790 vollendet, verglichen. Und einer Beschreibung dreÿer Gedächtniss = Medaillen mit der von den Amerikanisch Englischen Colonien verfochtenen Freiheit.

Title Page Deposit
title: <entire title page in Gothic script> Pro phetische Muthmassungen/ über die/ Fran zösische/ Staatsveränderung/ und andere neuere/ in kurzem zu erwartende Begebenheiten./ Nebst/ lehrreichen Erzählungen von Handlungen/ Josephs des Zweyten,/ des besteu Kaisers,/ den Deutschland jemals verehrte./ Dann ist unser/ Waschington/ mit diesem Joseph, der seine Lauf bahn 1790 vollen= / det, verglichen./ Und einer Beschreibung/ dreyer Gedächtniss=Medaillen/ mit der von den Amerikanisch Englischen

Colonien/ erfochtenen Freyheit./ <insertion of a rule in ms.>/ <thick rule>
imprint: <below thick rule> Philadelphia:/ Gedruckt bey Samuel Saur, 1794.
note: A handwritten note at the bottom of the title page states: "Herausgegeben von Tobias Hirte."

66.

District Court Ledger, 262 PA 47
date of deposit: June 6, eighteenth year of Independence
claimant: A: John Deveze
author: . . . Maître en Chirurgie du Cap-Francis Mêdecin de l'Hôpital Bush-Hill Chirurgien-major et Médecin en chef de l'Hôpital militaire établi à Philadelphie au compte de la République Française—
title: Recherches et Observations sur les Causes et les Effets de la Maladie Epidémique qui a régné à Philadelphie depuis le Mois d'Août jusque vers le milieu du Mois de Décembre de l'Ann'ee 1793— <author statement> <quotation in French>

Title Page Deposit
author: Par JEAN DEVEZE, Maître en Chirurgie,/ du Cap-Français, Médecin de l'Hôpital/ Bush-hill, Chirurgien-major et Médecin/ en chef de l'Hôpital militaire établi à/ Philadelphie au compte de la République/ Française.
title: RECHERCHES/ ET/ OBSERVATIONS,/ Sur les Causes et les Effets de la Maladie/ Épidémique qui a régné à Philadelphie,/ depuis de mois d'Août jusques vers le milieu/ du mois de Décembre de l'année 1793;/ <author statement>/ <rule>/ <quotation in French>/ <rule>/ <short thick rule>
imprint: <below short thick rule> A PHILADEL PHIE,/ De l'Imprimerie de PARENT.
note: One page of the text translated in English is printed on the verso of the title page.

67.

District Court Ledger, 262 PA 48
date of deposit: July 14, nineteenth year of Independence
claimant: A: John Simmons
title: A new Pennsylvania Primer <author statement>

Title Page Deposit
author: JOHN SIMMONS.
title: A/ *NEW/* Pennsylvania/ PRIMER./ <author statement>
imprint: PHILADELPHIA:/ Printed by Mordecai Jones./ MDCCXCVI.

68.

District Court Ledger, 262 PA 49
date of deposit: July 15, nineteenth year of Independence
claimant: A: Collinson Read
author: . . . Esquire
title: Precedents in the Office of a Justice of Peace to which is added a short System of Conveyancing in a method entirely new with an Appendix containing a variety of the most useful forms <author statement>

Title Page Deposit
author: COLLINSON READ, ESQUIRE.
title: PRECEDENTS/ IN THE/ OFFICE/ OF A/ *JUSTICE OF PEACE./* TO WHICH IS ADDED/ A Short SYSTEM of CONVEYANCING,/ IN A METHOD ENTIRELY NEW./ WITH AN/ APPENDIX,/ CONTAINING A VARIETY OF THE MOST USEFUL FORMS./ <thick rule>/ <author statement>/ <thick rule>
imprint: <below thick rule> M.DCC.XCIV.

69.

District Court Ledger, 262 PA 49
date of deposit: July 23, nineteenth year of Independence
claimant: A: Joseph Boggs
title: The Philadelphia Directory for the Year 1795. <author statement>

Title Page Deposit
author: JOSEPH BOGGS.
title: THE/ PHILADELPHIA/ <black letter> Directory,/ FOR THE YEAR/ 1795./ <short thick double rule>/ <author statement>/ <thick double rule>
imprint: <below thick double rule> *PHILA DELPHIA:/ Printed for the* AUTHOR *by/ WILLIAM W. WOODWARD,/ No.* 41, *Chesnut-street.*

70.

District Court Ledger, 262 PA 50
date of deposit: August 4, nineteenth year of Independence
claimant: P: Thomas Dobson
author: Benjamin Rush M. D. Professor of the Institutes and of Clinical Medicine in the University of Pennsylvania—

title: An Account of the Bilious remitting Yellow Fever as it appears in the City of Philadelphia in the Year 1793. <author statement>

Title Page Deposit

author: Benjamin Rush, M. D./ PROFESSOR OF THE INSTITUTES, AND OF CLINICAL MEDICINE,/ IN THE UNIVERSITY OF PENNSYLVANIA.

title: AN/ *ACCOUNT/* OF THE/ Bilious remitting Yellow Fever,/ AS/ *IT APPEARED/* IN THE/ CITY OF PHILADELPHIA,/ IN THE YEAR 1793./ <double rule>/ <author statement>/ <double rule>/ <short thick rule>

imprint: <below short thick rule> PHILA DELPHIA,/ PRINTED BY THOMAS DOB SON,/ AT THE STONE-HOUSE, No 41, SOUTH SECOND-STREET./ <rule>/ MDCCXCIV.

note: A handwritten note signed by T. Dobson which was found in the title page collection with this title page states: "Dr. Rush's Work on the Yellow Fever to be Entered in the name of Tho. Dobson as Proprietor<.> Dr. Priestley's three <see entries 71-73> to be entered in his name as author<.>"

71.

District Court Ledger, 262 PA 51

date of deposit: August 4, nineteenth year of Independence

claimant: A: Joseph Priestley

author: . . . L.L.D. F.R.S. &c

title: An Appeal to the serious and candid Professors of Christianity on the following Subjects viz—1. The Use of Reason in Matters of Religion—2. The Power of Man to do the Will of God—3. Original Sin—4. Election and Reprobation—5. The Divinity of Christ—and—6. Atonement for Sin by the Death of Christ—<author statement> to which are added a concise History of the Rise of those Doctrines and an Account of the Trial of Mr. Elwall for Heresy and Blasphemy at Stafford Assizes—<biblical quotation>

Title Page Deposit

author: JOSEPH PRIESTLEY, LL.D. F.R.S. &c.

title: AN/ APPEAL/ TO THE/ *SERIOUS AND CANDID/* PROFESSORS OF CHRISTIANITY,/ ON THE FOLLOWING SUBJECTS, VIZ./ I. The Use of Reason in Matters of Religion./ II. The Power of Man to do the Will of GOD./ III. Original Sin./ IV. Election and Reprobation./ V. The Divinity of Christ. And,/ VI. Atonement for Sin by the Death of Christ./ <author statement>/ TO WHICH ARE ADDED,/ A concise History of the Rise of those Doctrines;/ AND AN ACCOUNT OF/ THE TRIAL OF MR. ELWALL,/ *FOR HERESY AND BLASPHEMY,/* AT STAFFORD ASSIZES./ <short double rule>/ <biblical quotation>/ <short thick rule>

imprint: <below thick rule> PHILADELPHIA,/ PRINTED BY THOMAS DOBSON,/ AT THE STONE HOUSE, No 41, SOUTH SECOND-STREET./ M,DCC,XCIV.

note: See note for title page deposit for entry number 70.

72.

District Court Ledger, 262 PA 52

date of deposit: August 4, nineteenth year of Independence

claimant: A: Joseph Priestley

author: . . . L.L.D—F.R.S. &c. &c.

title: Letters addressed to the <the following word has been crossed out in ms.> <Lawyers> Philosophers and Politicians of France on the Subject of Religion—To which are prefixed Observations relating to the Causes of the general Prevalence of Infidelity—<author statement> <quotation in Latin>

Title Page Deposit

author: Jospeh Priestley, L.L.D. F.R.S. &c.&c.

title: LETTERS/ ADDRESSED TO THE/ *Philosophers and Politicians of France,/* ON THE/ SUBJECT OF RELIGION./ TO WHICH ARE PREFIXED,/ *OBSERVATIONS/* RELATING TO THE/ CAUSES OF THE GENERAL PREVA LENCE OF/ INFIDELITY./ <author statement>/ <short double rule>/ <quotation in Latin>/ <short double rule>

imprint: <below short double rule> PHILA DELPHIA:/ PRINTED BY THOMAS DOBSON,/ AT THE STONE-HOUSE, No 41, SOUTH SECOND-STREET./ M.DCC.XCIV.

note: See note for title page deposit for entry 70.

73.

District Court Ledger, 262 PA 53

date of deposit: August 4, nineteenth year of Independence

claimant: A: Joseph Priestley

author: . . . L.L.D., F.R.S. &c—

title: Two Sermons—viz—I. The present State of Europe compared with antient Prophecies preached on the Fast-Day in 1794—with a Preface containing the Reasons for the Author's leaving

England—II. The Use of Christianity especially in difficult Times being the Author's Farewell Discourse to his Congregation at Hackney—<author statement>

Title Page Deposit
author: JOSEPH PRIESTLEY, L.L.D. F.R.S.&c.
title: TWO SERMONS/ VIZ./ I. *The present State of Europe compared with/ Antient Prophecies;/* PREACHED ON/ *THE FAST-DAY IN* 1794;/ WITH/ A PREFACE,/ CONTAINING THE/ REASONS FOR THE AUTHOR's LEAVING/ ENGLAND./ <short thick rule>/ II. *The Use of Christianity, especially in difficult/ Times;/* BEING THE *AUTHOR's/* FAREWELL DISCOURSE/ TO HIS CONGREGATION AT HACKNEY./ <author statement>
imprint: PHILADELPHIA:/ PRINTED BY THOMAS DOBSON, AT THE STONE-HOUSE,/ No 41, SOUTH SECOND-STREET./ MDCCXCIV.
note: See note for title page deposit for entry number 70.

74.

District Court Ledger, 262 PA 54
date of deposit: September 18, nineteenth year of Independence
claimant: P: J. E. G. M. de la Grange
author: J. E. G. M. de la Grange Habitant de Saint Domingue et Avocat au Conseil supérieur du Cap-Français
translator: John Moore
title: Journal durant un Séjour en France depuis le Commencement d'Août jusqu' à la mi-Décembre 1792 auquel est ajouté un Récit des Événements les plus remarquables qui ont eu lieu à Paris depuis cette Époque jusqu' à la Mort du feu Roi de France Traduit de l'Anglais de <translator statement> <author statement> En deux Volumes—

Title Page Deposit
author: J. E. G. M. DE LA GRANGE, Habitant de/ Saint-Domingue, et Avocat au Conseil supérieur/ du Cap Français.
translator: JOHN MOORE, Dr. M.
title: JOURNAL/ DURANT UN SÉJOUR/ EN FRANCE,/ DEPUIS le commencement d'Août jusqu' à la/ mi-Décembre 1792; auquel est ajouté un Récit/ des événemens les plus remarquables qui ont eu/ lieu à Paris, depuis cette époque, jusqu à la/ mort du feu roi de France./ *Traduit de l'Anglais de* <translator statement>/ <author statement>/ EN DEUX VOLUMES./ <rule>/ <quotation in Latin>/ <rule>/ <thick rule>
imprint: <below thick rule> PHILADELPHIE:/ Chez MATHEW CAREY, rue du Marché./ <thick rule>/ 1794./ *Enregistré suivant la loi.*

75.

District Court Ledger, 262 PA 55
date of deposit: October 14, nineteenth year of Independence
claimant: P: Hoff and Derrick
title: A New and Concise History of the Revolution in France; from its commencement to the execution of the Gironde Party and the death of the Duke of Orleans.

Title Page Deposit
title: A/ NEW AND CONCISE HISTORY/ OF THE/ REVOLUTION IN FRANCE;/ FROM/ ITS COMMENCEMENT/ TO THE/ EXECU TION/ OF THE/ *GIRONDE PARTY/* AND/ THE DEATH OF/ THE/ *DUKE OF ORLEANS./* <thick rule>
imprint: <below thick rule> *PHILADELPHIA:/* PRINTED BY *HOFF* AND *DERRICK,/* M,DCC,XCIV./ <next three words inserted in ms.> Hoff & Derrick Proprietors

76.

District Court Ledger, 262 PA 56
date of deposit: October 24, nineteenth year of Independence
claimant: P: William Hall, Wrigley, & Berriman
author: Tench Coxe, of Philadelphia;
title: A View of the United States of America, in a series of papers, written at various times between the years 1787 and 1794 <author statement> interspersed with Authentic Documents the whole tending to exhibit the progress and present State of Civil and Religious Liberty, population, Agriculture, Exports, Imports, Fisheries, Navigation, Ship-Building, Manufactures, and General Improvement.

Title Page Deposit
author: Tench Coxe, of Philadelphia;
title: A/ VIEW/ OF THE/ UNITED STATES/ OF/ AMERICA,/ *IN A SERIES OF PAPERS,/* WRIT TEN AT VARIOUS TIMES, BETWEEN THE YEARS/ 1787 AND 1794,/ <author statement>/ INTERSPERSED WITH/ AUTHENTIC DOC UMENTS:/ THE WHOLE TENDING TO EX HIBIT THE PROGRESS AND PRE-/ SENT STATE OF CIVIL AND RELIGIOUS LIB - ERTY, POPU-/ LATION, AGRICULTURE,

EXPORTS, IMPORTS, FISHE-/ RIES, NAVI GATION, SHIP-BUILDING, MANUFAC-/ TURES, AND GENERAL IMPROVEMENT./ <short thick rule>
imprint: <below short thick rule> *PHILADEL PHIA:/* PRINTED FOR WILLIAM HALL, No. 51, Market Street, and/ WRIGLEY & BERRIMAN, No. 149, Chesnut Street./ <short double rule>/ 1794.

77.
District Court Ledger, 262 PA 56
date of deposit: November 1, nineteenth year of Independence
claimant: P: David Sower
title: Ein ganz Neu eingerichtetes Lutherisches A B C Buchstabier und Namenbuch zu nützlichem Gebrauch Deutscher Schulen.

78.
District Court Ledger, 262 PA 57
date of deposit: November 13, nineteenth year of Independence
claimant: P: James Thomson Callender
author: <James Thomson Callender>
title: The political Progress of Britain or an impartial History of Abuses in the Government of the British Empire in Europe Asia and America from the Revolution in 1688 to the present Time the whole tending to prove the ruinous Consequences of the popular System of Taxation War and Conquest—<quotation in English> Part first—Second Edition—
note: According to the *National Index of American Imprints,* the author is James Thomson Callender.

Title Page Deposit
title: THE/ POLITICAL PROGRESS/ OF/ *BRI TAIN:/* OR, AN/ IMPARTIAL HISTORY/ OF/ ABUSES IN THE GOVERNMENT/ OF THE/ BRITISH EMPIRE,/ IN/ EUROPE, ASIA, AND AMERICA:/ *FROM THE REVOLUTION IN* 1688, *TO THE PRESENT TIME:/* THE WHOLE TENDING TO PROVE THE RUINOUS CON SEQUENCES OF/ THE POPULAR SYSTEM OF TAXATION, WAR, AND CONQUEST./ <double rule>/ <quotation in English>/ <double rule>/ PART FIRST./ <black letter> Second Edition./ <short thick rule>
imprint: <below short thick rule> *PHILADEL PHIA:/* PRINTED BY WRIGLEY & BER RIMAN, for W. YOUNG, Chesnut-Street,/ T. ALLEN, New-York, and A. KEDDIE, Balti more./ <short double rule>/ M,DCC,XCIV.
note: [PRICE HALF A DOLLAR.] A two-page advertisement is also deposited.

79.
District Court Ledger, 262 PA 58
date of deposit: December 4, nineteenth year of Independence
claimant: A: Sebastian Kunckler
author: von Einem das Landleben Liebenden.
title: Poesien und Anecdoten zum Zeitvertreib, für die Lieben Landleute, am Sonn = und Wercktage, ohne Nachtheil zu gebrauchen, <author statement> Erstes Bandgen <quotation in German>

Title Page Deposit
author: Geschrieben von einem das Land = Leben = Liebenden.
title: <entire title page in Gothic script> Poesien/ und/ Anecdoten,/ Zum/ Zeitvertreib,/ Für die lieben Landleute,/ Am Sonn und Wercktage/ ohne Nachtheil zu gebrauchen./ <author statement>/ <rule>/ Erstes Bändgen./ <thick rule>/ <quotation in German>/ <rule>/ <decorative rule>/ <rule>
imprint: <below rule> Germantaun:/ Gedruckt bey Peter Leibert, 1795.
note: The German quotation on the title page is phrased differently from that recorded in the ledger: "Prüfet alles, behaltet das Gute" as opposed to the ledger transcription, "Prüfet alles das gute behaltet."

80.
District Court Ledger, 262 PA 59
date of deposit: December 5, nineteenth year of Independence
claimant: P: Mathew Carey
title: The United States Register for the Year 1795—being the 19–20th of national Sovereignty

Title Page Deposit
title: THE/ UNITED STATES/ REGISTER,/ FOR/ *THE YEAR* 1795;/ BEING THE 19–20th/ OF/ NATIONAL SOVEREIGNTY./ <double rule>
imprint: <below double rule> *PHILADELPHIA:/* PRINTED FOR MATHEW CAREY,/ NO. 118, MARKET-STREET./ <short rule>/ DEC. 4, 1794.

81.
District Court Ledger, 262 PA 59
date of deposit: December 23, nineteenth year of Independence
claimant: A: Susannah Rowson
author: Mrs . . .

title: Slaves in Algiers or a Struggle for Freedom a Play interspersed with Songs in three Acts <author statement> as performed at the New-Theatres in Philadelphia and Baltimore

Title Page Deposit
author: MRS. ROWSON.
title: SLAVES IN ALGIERS;/ OR, A/ STRUG GLE FOR FREEDOM:/ A PLAY,/ INTER SPERSED WITH SONGS,/ IN THREE ACTS./ <author statement>/ AS PERFORMED/ AT THE/ <black letter> NEW THEATRES,/ IN/ PHILADELPHIA AND BALTIMORE./ <short thick rule>
imprint: <below short thick rule> *PHILADEL PHIA:*/ PRINTED FOR THE AUTHOR, BY WRIGLEY AND/ BERRIMAN, No. 149, CHESNUT-STREET./ <short double rule>/ M,DCC,XCIV.

1795

82.
District Court Ledger, 262 PA 60
date of deposit: January 19, nineteenth year of Independence
claimant: A,P: Oliver Evans
author: . . . of Philadelphia—
title: The Young Mill-Wright and Miller's Guide—in five Parts—embellished with twenty five Plates. containing Part 1. Mechanics & Hydraulics shewing Errors in the old and establishing a new System of Theories of Water-Mills by which the Power of Mill-Seats and the Effects they will produce may be as-certained by Calculation—Part 2. Rules for applying the Theories to Practice Tables for proportioning Mills to the Power and Fall of the Water and Rules for finding Pitch Circles with Tables from 6 to 130 Cogs—Part 3. Directions for constructing and using all the Authors patented Improvements in Mills—Part 4. The Art of manufacturing Meal and Flour in all its Parts as practised by the most skilful Millers in America—Part 5. The practical Mill-Wright containing Instructions for building Mills with Tables of their Proportions suitable for all Falls from three to Thirty six Feet. Appendix containing Rules for discovering new Improvements—exemplified in improving the Art of cleaning and threshing Grain hulling Rice warming Rooms and venting Smoke by Chimneys &c <author statement>

Title Page Deposit
author: OLIVER EVANS, OF PHILADELPHIA.
title: THE/ *YOUNG*/ MILL-WRIGHT & MILLER'S/ GUIDE./ <rule>/ IN FIVE PARTS—EMBELLISHED WITH TWENTY FIVE PLATES./ <rule>/ CONTAINING,/ <. . .>/ <short decorative rule>/ <author statement>/ <thick rule>
imprint: <below thick rule> PHILADELPHIA:/ PRINTED FOR, AND SOLD BY THE AUTHOR, No. 215,/ NORTH SECOND STREET./ <short rule>/ 1795.

83.
District Court Ledger, 262 PA 61
date of deposit: January 20, nineteenth year of Independence
claimant: P: Edmund Hogan
title: The Pennsylvania State Trials containing the Impeachment Trial and Acquittal of Francis Hopkinson and John Nicholson Esquires the former being Judge of the Court of Admiralty and the latter the Comptroller-General of the Commonwealth of Pennsylvania—Vol: 1.—<quotation in Latin>

Title Page Deposit
date of deposit: January 21, 1795
title: THE/ <Gothic script> Pennsylvania State Trials:/ CONTAINING THE/ IMPEACH MENT, TRIAL, AND ACQUITTAL/ OF/ FRANCIS HOPKINSON,/ AND/ JOHN NICHOLSON, ESQUIRES./ THE FORMER BEING/ JUDGE OF THE COURT OF ADMIRALTY,/ AND THE LATTER,/ THE COMPTROLLER-GENERAL/ OF THE/ COMMONWEALTH OF PENNSYLVANIA./ <double rule>/ VOL. I./ <thick rule>/ <quotation in Latin>/ <double rule>
imprint: <below double rule> *PHILADELPHIA:*/ PRINTED BY FRANCIS BAILEY,/ AT YORICK'S HEAD, No. 116, HIGH-STREET, FOR/ EDMUND HOGAN./ M,DCC,XCIV.

84.
District Court Ledger, 262 PA 62
date of deposit: January 24, nineteenth year of Independence
claimant: P: Benjamin Franklin Bache
author: Peter Pindar Esq.
title: Pindariana—or—Peter's Port-Folio—containing—Tale Fable Translation—Ode Elegy Epigram—Song Pastoral Letters—with Extracts from Tragedy Comedy Opera &c. <author statement> <quotation in Latin> <six lines of poetry in English>

Title Page Deposit
author: *PETER PINDAR,* ESQ.
title: PINDARIANA;/ OR/ PETER'S PORT FOLIO./ CONTAINING/ <each of the following three line divisions represents a separate column divided from the other columns by perpendicular double rules> TALE, FABLE, TRANSLA TION,/ <perpendicular double rule>/ ODE, ELEGY, EPIGRAM,/ <perpendicular double rule>/ SONG, PASTORAL, LETTERS./ WITH EXTRACTS FROM/ TRAGEDY, COMEDY, OPERA, &c./ <author statement>/ <short double rule>/ <quotation in Latin>/ <six lines of poetry in English>/ <double rule>
imprint: <below double rule> PHILADELPHIA:/ PRINTED FOR BENJAMIN FRANKLIN <"E" crossed out in ms.> B<E>ACHE./ <short rule>/ M.DCC.XCIV.

85.
District Court Ledger, 262 PA 63
date of deposit: January 30, nineteenth year of Independence
claimant: P: Thomas Bradford
title: Observations—on the—Emigration—of—Dr. Joseph Priestley—and on the several Addresses delivered to him on his Arrival at New=York—with Additions—containing many curious and interesting Facts on—the Subject not Known here when the—first Edition was published—together with—a comprehensive Story—of a—Farmer's Bull—the third Edition—<four lines of poetry in French>

Title Page Deposit
title: OBSERVATIONS/ ON THE/ EMIGRA TION/ OF/ DR. JOSEPH PRIESTLEY,/ AND ON THE SEVERAL ADDRESSES DE LIVERED TO HIM, ON/ HIS ARRIVAL AT NEW-YORK,/ WITH ADDITIONS;/ CON TAINING MANY CURIOUS AND INTER ESTING FACTS ON/ THE SUBJECT, NOT KNOWN HERE, WHEN THE/ FIRST EDI TION WAS PUBLISHED:/ TOGETHER WITH/ A COMPREHENSIVE STORY/ OF A/ FARMER'S BULL/ <short thick rule>/ THE *THIRD EDITION.*/ <double rule>/ <four lines of poetry in French>/ <double rule>
imprint: <below double rule> PHILADELPHIA:/ PUBLISHED BY THOMAS BRADFORD, NO. 8, South-/Front-Street./ <short double rule>/ 1795.
note: Four pages of introduction and two pages of text are also deposited.

86.
District Court Ledger, 262 PA 64
date of deposit: January 30, nineteenth year of Independence
claimant: P: Thomas Bradford
title: A—Bone to gnaw—for the—Democrats—or—Observations—on—a Pamplet—entited—"The political Progress of Britain"—

Title Page Deposit
title: A/ BONE TO GNAW,/ FOR THE/ DEMO CRATS;/ OR,/ OBSERVATIONS/ ON/ A PAMPHLET,/ ENTITLED,/ *"The Political Progress of Britain."*/ <double rule>
imprint: <below double rule> *PHILADELPHIA:*/ PRINTED for the PURCHASERS./ <short double rule>/ 1795.
note: Three pages of preface and two pages of text are also deposited.

87.
District Court Ledger, 262 PA 65
date of deposit: February 12, nineteenth year of Independence
claimant: P: Elizabeth Hall
author: William Cullen M.D. &c &c—
translator: Henry Wilkins M.D.
title: A Synopsis—of—methodical Nosology—in which the—Genera of Disorders—are—particularly defined—and the—Species added—with the—Synonimous of those from Sauvages <author statement> From the fourth Edition corrected & much enlarged <translator statement>

Title Page Deposit
author: W1ILLIAM CULLEN, M.D. &c. &c.
translator: HENRY WILKINS, M.D.
title: A/ SYNOPSIS/ OF/ METHODICAL NOSOLOGY,/ IN WHICH THE/ *GENERA* OF DISORDERS/ ARE/ PARTICULARLY DE FINED,/ AND THE/ *SPECIES* ADDED/ WITH THE/ SYNONIMOUS OF THOSE FROM *SAUVAGES.*/ <author statement>/ FROM THE FOURTH EDITION CORRECTED AND MUCH ENLARGED./ <translator statement>/ <thick rule>
imprint: <below thick rule> PHILADELPHIA:/ PRINTED AND SOLD BY *PARRY HALL,* NO. 149. CHESNUT STREET,/ NEAR FOURTH STREET./ <short rule>/ M.DCC.XCIII.

88.
District Court Ledger, 262 PA 66
date of deposit: March 2, nineteenth year of Independence
claimant: A: Benjamin Davies

title: The American Repository—of useful Information—containing—a Calendar—of the present Years—an—Account of the United States—their Territory and Population—of the Federal Government—and—Courts of Justice —with other various interesting Matter—Ornamented in the 12 Vignettes & a Frontispiece—to be continued annually

Title Page Deposit

title: *THE*/ AMERICAN REPOSITORY/ OF/ <script> Useful Information:/ <script> con taining/ *A CALENDAR*/ of the present Year:/ AN/ <script> Account of the United States,/ Their Territory and Population;/ <script> *of the Federal Government*/ &/ <script> Courts of Justice/ <script> with other various interesting matter./ Ornamented with 12 Vignettes, & a Frontispiece,/ <next four words deleted in ms.> <script> <Engraved by J. Smither and E. Trenchard.>/ <rule>/ To be continued Annually./ <rule>

imprint: <below rule> <script> Philadelphia./ <script> *Printed for B: Davies, No: 68, High Street.*/ <short rule> 1795 <short rule>

note: The title page is engraved. "J. Smther Sculpt." is printed at the bottom right-hand side of the title page.

89.

District Court Ledger, 262 PA 66

date of deposit: March 7, nineteenth year of Independence

claimant: P: Thomas Stephens

title: Proceedings—of the—Society—of—United Irishmen—of—Dublin.

Title Page Deposit

title: PROCEEDINGS/ OF THE/ SOCIETY/ OF/ UNITED IRISHMEN,/ OF/ DUBLIN./ <short double rule>/ <engraving of a woman and a harp with a quotation in English>/ <short double rule>

imprint: <below short double rule> *PHILADEL PHIA:*/ PRINTED FOR THOMAS STEPHENS NO. 57, SOUTH SECOND-STREET/ BY JACOB JOHNSON, & Co./ <short rule>/ 1795

90.

District Court Ledger, 262 PA 67

date of deposit: March 17, nineteenth year of Independence

claimant: P: Thomas Bradford

author: William Cobbet

title: Le—Tuteur Anglais au—Grammaire regulière de la Langue Anglaise en deux Parties—Premiere Partie contenant une Analyse des Parties de l'oraison— Seconde Partie contenant la Syntaxe complète—de la Langue Anglaise avec des Thèmes—analogues aux differens Sujets—qu'on y a traités—<author statement>

Title Page Deposit

author: WILLIAM COBBETT.

title: LE/ TUTEUR ANGLAIS,/ OU/ GRAM MAIRE REGULIÈRE/ DE LA/ LANGUE ANGLAISE/ EN/ DEUX PARTIES./ *PRE MIERE PARTIE,* CONTENTANT UNE ANALYSE/ DES PARTIES DE L'ORAISON./ *SECONDE PARTIE,* CONTENANT LA SYN TAXE COMPLETE/ DE LA LANGUE ANGLAISE, AVEC DES thèmes,/ ANALOGUES AUX différens SUJETS/ QU' ON Y A traités./ <rule>/ <author statement>/ <rule>

imprint: <below rule> A PHILADELPHIE:/ CHEZ *THOMAS BRADFORD,* LIBRAIRE,/ Première Rue Sud, No. 8./ <short rule>/ 1795.

note: Two pages of table of contents, two pages of preface, and a title page for "Premier Partie" are also deposited.

91.

District Court Ledger, 262 PA 68

date of deposit: March 17, nineteenth year of Independence

claimant: P: Thomas Bradford

author: Peter Porcupine—Author of the Bone to gnaw for the Democrats—

title: A—Kick for a Bite—or—Review upon Review—with a—critical Essay—on the Works of—Mrs. S. Rowson—in—a Letter—to the Editor or Editors—of the American monthly Review—<author statement> <quotation in French>

Title Page Deposit

author: PETER PORCUPINE,/ Author of the Bone to Gnaw, for the Democrats.

title: A/ KICK FOR A BITE;/ OR,/ REVIEW UPON REVIEW;/ WITH A/ CRITICAL ESSAY,/ ON THE WORKS OF/ MRS. S. ROWSON;/ IN/ *A LETTER*/ TO THE EDI TOR, OR EDITORS,/ OF THE/ AMERICAN MONTHLY REVIEW./ <rule>/ <author statement>/ <rule>/ <quotation in French>/ <double rule>

imprint: <below double rule> PHILADELPHIA:/ PRINTED BY THOMAS BRADFORD, NO. 8, SOUTH/ FRONT STREET./ <short rule>/ 1795.

note: Four pages of a note to the editor and an advertisement are also deposited.

92.

District Court Ledger, 262 PA 69

date of deposit: March 18, nineteenth year of Independence

claimant: P: Michael Billmeyer

title: Erbauliche Lieder = Sammlung zum Gottesdienstlichen Gebrauch in den Vereinigten Evangelisch = Lutherischen Gemeinen in Pennsÿlvanien und den benachbarten Staaten. Gesammlet, eingerichtet und zum Druck befördert durch das hiesige Deutsche Evangelisch = Lutherische Ministerium. Zweite Auflage. Germantaun: Gedruckt beÿ Michael Billmeÿer 1795.

Title Page Deposit

title: <entire title page in Gothic script> Erbau liche/ Lieder = Sammlung/ zum/ Gottes dienstlichen Gebrauch/ in den/ Vereinigten Evangelisch = Lutherischen/ Gemeinen/ in/ Penn sylvanien/ und den benachbarten Staaten./ Gesamlet, eingerichtet und zum Druck befördert/ durch das hiesige/ Deutsche Evangelisch = Lutherische Ministerium./ <relief cut of two angels>/ <thick rule>/ Zweyte Auflage./ <decorative rule>

imprint: <below decorative rule> Germantaun:/ Gedruckt bey Michael Billmeyer, 1795.

93.

District Court Ledger, 262 PA 70

date of deposit: March 26, nineteenth year of Independence

claimant: P: Thomas Dobson

author: Jo. Fred. Blumenbach M.D.—Professor of Medicine in Ordinary at Goettingen—Member of the Royal Society of Sciences at—Goettingen and of several other Societies in—different Parts of Europe—

translator: Charles Caldwell—

title: Elements of Physiology—<author statement> translated from the original Latin—and—interspersed with occasional Notes—<translator statement> To which is subjoined by the Translator—an Appendix—exhibiting a brief and compendious View—of the existing Discoveries—relative to the Subject of—Animal Electricty—Volume 1.

Title Page Deposit

author: JO. FRED. BLUMENBACH, M.D./ PRO FESSOR OF MEDICINE IN ORDINARY AT GOETTINGEN,/ MEMBER OF THE ROYAL SOCIETY OF SCIENCES AT/ GOETTINGEN, AND OF SEVERAL OTHER SOCIETIES IN/ DIFFERENT PARTS OF EUROPE.

translator: CHARLES CALDWELL.

title: Elements of Physiology;/ <author statement>/ *Translated from the Original Latin,/* AND/ INTER SPERSED WITH OCCASIONAL NOTES./ <translator statement>/ <double rule>/ TO WHICH IS SUBJOINED, BY THE TRANS LATOR,/ *An* APPENDIX,/ EXHIBITING A BRIEF AND COMPENDIOUS VIEW/ OF THE EXISTING DISCOVERIES/ Relative to the Subject of/ *ANIMAL ELECTRICITY./* <short double rule>/ VOLUME I./ <double rule>

imprint: <below double rule> PHILADELPHIA,/ *PRINTED BY THOMAS DOBSON,/* AT THE STONE-HOUSE, No 41, SOUTH SECOND-STREET./ <short rule>/ M.DCC.XCV.

94.

District Court Ledger, 262 PA 71

date of deposit: March 26, nineteenth year of Independence

claimant: P: Thomas Dobson

author: Thomas Truxtun—

title: Remarks Instructions and Examples relating to the—Latitude & Longitude—also—the Variation of the Compass—&c &c &c—to which is annexed—a general Chart of the Globe—where the Route made by the Author in different—Ships under his Command—to the—Cape of Good Hope Batavia Canton in China the different Parts of India Europe and—the Cape de Verde Islands are marked for the Purpose of shewing the best Tract of Sea—to meet the most favorable Winds and avoid those perplexing Calms which too often attend—Asiatic Voyages—together—with a short but general Account—of—variable Winds Trade Winds Monsoons Hurricanes—Tornadoes Tuffoons Calms Currents—and —particular Weather met with in those Voyages—&c &c &c—<author statement>

Title Page Deposit

author: Thomas Truxtun.

title: Remarks, Instructions, and Examples/ RELATING TO THE/ LATITUDE & LONGITUDE;/ *ALSO,/* The Variation of the Compass,/ &c. &c. &c./ <black letter> To which is Annexed,/ A GENERAL CHART OF THE GLOBE,/ WHERE THE ROUTE MADE BY THE AUTHOR, IN DIFFERENT/ SHIPS UNDER HIS COMMAND,/ TO THE/ CAPE of GOOD HOPE, BATAVIA, CANTON in CHINA, the different parts of INDIA, EUROPE, and/ the CAPE DE VERDE ISLANDS *are marked,* . . . / TOGETHER/ *With a Short,*

but General Account/ OF/ VARIABLE WINDS, TRADE-WINDS, MONSOONS, HURRI CANES,/ <. . .>/ <short thick rule>/ <author statement>/ <short thick rule>
imprint: <below short thick rule> PHILADEL PHIA,/ PRINTED BY T. DOBSON, AT THE STONE-HOUSE, SOUTH SECOND-STREET./ M,DCC,XCIV.
note: The title page is located in the Geography and Map Division.

95.
District Court Ledger, 262 PA 72
date of deposit: March 26, nineteenth year of Independence
claimant: A: Joseph Priestley
author: . . . L.L.D. F.R.S. &c &c—
title: A—Continuation—of the—Letters—to the—Philosophers and Politicians of France—on the Subject of—Religion—and of the—Letters to a Philosophical Unbeliever—in Answer to—Mr. Paine's Age of Reason—<author statement>

Title Page Deposit
author: JOSEPH PRIESTLEY, L.L.D. F.R.S. &c. &c.
title: A/ CONTINUATION/ OF THE/ LETTERS/ TO THE/ *Philosophers and Politicians of France,/* ON THE SUBJECT OF/ RELIGION;/ AND OF THE/ *Letters to a Philosophical Unbeliever;/* IN ANSWER TO/ MR. PAINE's AGE OF REA SON./ <thick rule>/ <author statement>/ <thick rule>
imprint: <below thick rule> NORTHUMBER LAND-TOWN:/ PRINTED BY *ANDREW KENNEDY./* <short rule>/ M,DCC,XCIV.

96.
District Court Ledger, 262 PA 73
date of deposit: April 14, nineteenth year of Independence
claimant: A: Susanna Rowson
author: . . . of the new Theatre Philadelphia Author of Charlotte Fille de Chambre Inquisitor &c &c
title: Trials of the Human Heart a Novel in four Volumes <author statement> <two quotations in English> VOL II

Title Page Deposit
author: MRS. ROWSON,/ *OF THE NEW THEATRE, PHILADELPHIA,/* AUTHOR OF CHARLOTTE, FILLE DE CHAMBRE,/ INQUISITOR, &c. &c.
title: TRIALS/ OF THE/ HUMAN HEART,/ A NOVEL./ IN FOUR VOLUMES./ <double rule>/ <author statement>/ <double rule>/ <two quotations in English>/ <short thick rule>/ VOL. II./ <thick rule>
imprint: <below thick rule> *PHILADELPHIA:/* PRINTED FOR THE AUTHOR,/ BY WRIGLEY & BERRIMAN, NO. 149, CHESNUT-STREET./ SOLD BY MESSRS. CAREY, RICE, CAMPBELL, ORMROD,/ YOUNG; AND THE AUTHOR, CORNER OF SEVENTH/ AND CHESNUT STREETS./ <short rule>/ M.DCC.XCV.

97.
District Court Ledger, 262 PA 73
date of deposit: May 1, nineteenth year of Independence
claimant: A: James Ph. Puglia
author: . . . teacher of the Spanish & Italian Languages and Author of the Spanish work entitled El Desengaño del Hombre or the Man undeceived &c &c
title: The Federal Politician <author statement> <quotation in Latin>

Title Page Deposit
author: JAMES PH. PUGLIA,/ TEACHER OF THE SPANISH AND ITALIAN LAN GUAGES,/ AND AUTHOR OF THE SPAN ISH WORK,/ ENTITLED/ El Desengaño del Hombre,/ OR, THE/ MAN UNDECEIVED. &c. &c.
title: THE/ FEDERAL POLITICIAN:/ <author statement>/ <thick rule>/ <quotation in Latin>/ <thick rule>
imprint: <below thick rule> *PHILADELPHIA:/* PRINTED BY FRANCIS & ROBERT BAILEY, AT YORICK'S/ HEAD, No. 116, HIGH-STREET./ <double rule>/ M DCC XCV.

98.
District Court Ledger, 262 PA 74
date of deposit: May 5, nineteenth year of Independence
claimant: A: John Cox
author: . . . , a native of Philadelphia.
title: Rewards & Punishments, or, Satan's Kingdom Aristocratical. to which is subjoined a voyage to London, and an Acrostic. <author statement>

Title Page Deposit
author: JOHN COX, A NATIVE OF PHILADELPHIA.
title: REWARDS/ AND/ PUNISHMENTS,/ OR,/ *Satan's Kingdom Aristocratical./* TO WHICH IS SUBJOINED/ *A VOYAGE TO LONDON,/* AND/

AN ACROSTIC./ <short thick rule>/ <author statement>/ <short thick rule>/ <double rule>

imprint: <below double rule> *PHILADELPHIA,/* PRINTED FOR THE AUTHOR, AT NO. 41, CHESNUT-STREET./ <thick rule>/ MAY, 1795.

99.

District Court Ledger, 262 PA 74

date of deposit: May 6, nineteenth year of Independence

claimant: A: James Leach

author: an American Citizen.

title: A new & easy plan to redeem the American Captives in Algiers: comprising A benevolent subscription for their immediate relief <author statement>

Title Page Deposit

author: AN AMERICAN CITIZEN. <James Leach>

title: A/ *NEW & EASY*/ PLAN/ TO REDEEM THE/ American Captives in Algiers:/ COM PRISING/ A BENEVOLENT SUBSCRIPTION/ FOR THEIR/ IMMEDIATE RELIEF./ <author statement>/ <thick rule>

note: At the bottom of the title page the clerk's note states that the author is James Leach.

100.

District Court Ledger, 262 PA 75

date of deposit: May 28, nineteenth year of Independence

claimant: P: Thomas Dobson

author: William Buchan M.D. fellow of the Royal College of Physicians, Edinburgh:

adaptor: Samuel Powel Griffitts, M.D. Professor of Materia Medica in the University of Pennsylvania

title: Domestic Medicine: or a Treatise on the prevention and cure of Diseases, by Regimen & simple Medicines. with an Appendix, containing a dispensatory for the use of private practitioners. <author statement> Revised and adapted to the Diseases and Climate of the United States of America, <adaptor statement>

Title Page Deposit

author: WILLIAM BUCHAN, M.D./ FELLOW OF THE ROYAL COLLEGE OF PHYSICIANS,/ EDINBURGH:

adaptor: SAMUEL POWEL GRIFFITTS, M.D./ PROFESSOR OF MATERIA MEDICA IN THE UNIVERSITY/ OF PENNSYLVANIA.

title: Domestic Medicine:/ OR, A/ TREATISE/ ON/ THE PREVENTION AND CURE/ OF/ *DISEASES,/* BY REGIMEN AND SIMPLE MEDICINES./ WITH/ AN APPENDIX,/ *CON TAINING A DISPENSATORY FOR THE USE/ OF PRIVATE PRACTITIONERS./* <author statement>/ <double rule>/ REVISED AND ADAPTED TO THE/ *Diseases and Climate of the United States of America,/* <adaptor statement>/ <thick rule>

imprint: <below thick rule> PHILADELPHIA,/ PRINTED BY THOMAS DOBSON,/ AT THE STONE HOUSE No 41, SOUTH SECOND-STREET./ <short rule>/ 1795.

101.

District Court Ledger, 262 PA 76

date of deposit: May 29, nineteenth year of Independence

claimant: P: Thomas Bradford

author: Peter Porcupine.

title: Part II. A Bone to Gnaw for the Democrats containing 1st Observations on a Patriotic pamphlet. entitled proceedings of the United Irishmen. 2dly Democratic principles Exemplified by Example. 3dly Democratic Memoires or an account of some recent feats performed by the Frenchified Citizens of the United States of America <author statement> <four lines of poetry in English>

Title Page Deposit

author: PETER PORCUPINE.

title: Part II./ <short double rule>/ A/ BONE TO GNAW,/ FOR THE/ DEMOCRATS;/ CON TAINING,/ Ist. OBSERVATIONS ON A PATRIOTIC PAMPHLET./ ENTITLED,/ "PROCEEDINGS OF THE UNITED IRISH MEN."/ 2dly. DEMOCRATIC PRINCIPLES EXEMPLIFIED BY EXAMPLE./ 3dly. DEMOCRATIC MEMOIRES; OR AN ACCOUNT OF SOME RE-/ CENT FEATS PERFORMED BY THE FRENCHIFIED CI-/ TIZENS OF THE UNITED STATES/ OF AMERICA./ <double rule>/ <author statement>/ <double rule>/ <four lines of poetry in English>/ <thick rule>

imprint: <below thick rule> PHILADELPHIA:/ Printed & sold by THOMAS BRADFORD, No. 8, South/ Front Street./ <short double rule>/ 1795.

note: Six pages of preface are also deposited.

102.

District Court Ledger, 262 PA 76

date of deposit: June 1, nineteenth year of Independence

claimant: A: James Thomson Callender

title: The Political Register, or, proceedings in the Session of Congress, commencing November 3d, 1794, and ending March 3d, 1795, with an Appendix, containing a selection of papers laid before Congress during that period. <author statement> Vol. I.

Title Page Deposit

author: JAMES THOMSON CALLENDER.

title: THE/ *Political Register;*/ OR,/ PRO CEEDINGS/ IN THE/ *SESSION OF CON GRESS,*/ COMMENCING NOVEMBER 3d, 1794, AND/ ENDING MARCH 3d, 1795./ <double rule>/ WITH/ *An APPENDIX,*/ CON TAINING/ A SELECTION *OF* PAPERS/ LAID BEFORE CONGRESS DURING THAT PERIOD./ <thick rule>/ <author statement>/ <double rule>/ VOL. I./ <short thick rule>

imprint: <below short thick rule> PHILADEL PHIA,/ *PRINTED BY THOMAS DOBSON,*/ AT THE STONE-HOUSE, No 41, SOUTH SECOND-STREET./ <short rule>/ M.DCC.XCV

note: Four pages of preface and a half title are also deposited.

103.

District Court Ledger, 262 PA 77

date of deposit: June 15, nineteenth year of Independence

claimant: P: Thomas Stephens

author: James Hardie.

title: The Philadelphia Directory and Register containing the Names Occupations and Places of abode of the Citizens, arranged in Alphabetical Order: A Register of the Executive, Legislative, and Judicial Magistrates of the United States and the State of Pennsylvania, with their Salaries; the Governors of the different States, and the Magistrates of the City: to which is added, a short account of the City; and of the Charitable & Literary institutions therein. the second edition <author statement>

Title Page Deposit

author: JAMES HARDIE, A.M.

title: THE/ PHILADELPHIA/ DIRECTORY/ AND/ REGISTER:/ CONTAINING/ THE NAMES, OCCUPATIONS, AND PLACES OF ABODE OF/ THE CITIZENS; ARRANGED IN ALPHABET-/ ICAL ORDER:/ A REGISTER/ OF THE EXECUTIVE, LEGISLATIVE, AND JUDICIAL/ MAGISTRATES OF THE UNITED STATES AND THE/ STATE OF PENNSYLVANIA, WITH THEIR SA-/ LARIES; THE GOVERNORS OF THE DIF-/ FERENT STATES, AND THE MAGIS-/ TRATES OF THE CITY:/ TO WHICH IS ADDED,/ A SHORT ACCOUNT OF THE CITY; AND OF THE CHA-/ RITABLE AND LITERARY INSTITUTIONS/ THEREIN./ <thick rule>/ THE SECOND EDITION./ <thick rule>/ <author statement>/ <double rule>

imprint: <below double rule> *PHILADELPHIA:*/ *Printed for the Author, by* JACOB JOHNSON & CO. No./ 147, *Market-Street.*/ M DCC XCIV.

note: [Price 62 1-2 Cents.]

104.

District Court Ledger, 262 PA 78

date of deposit: July 1, nineteenth year of Independence

claimant: A: James Hardie

author: . . . A.M.

title: The American Remembrancer and universal Tablet of Memory containing a List of the most eminent Men whether in ancient or modern Times with the Atchievements for which they have been particularly distinguished as also the most memorable Events in History from the earliest Period till the Year 1795. classed under distinct Heads with their respective Dates—To which is added a Table comprehending the Periods at which the most remarkable Cities and Towns were founded their present Population Latitude and Longitude—The whole being intended to form a comprehensive Abridgement of History and Chronology particularly of that Part which relates to America—<author statement> <quotation in Latin>

Title Page Deposit

author: JAMES HARDIE, A.M.

title: THE/ AMERICAN REMEMBRANCER,/ AND/ *Universal Tablet of Memory:*/ CONTAIN ING/ A LIST OF THE MOST EMINENT MEN, WHE-/ THER IN ANCIENT OR MODERN TIMES,/ *With the Atchievements for which they have been par-/ ticularly distinguished:*/ AS ALSO/ *THE MOST MEMORABLE EVENTS IN HISTORY,*/ From the earliest period till the year 1795, classed un-/ der distinct Heads, with their respective dates./ *To which is added,*/ A TABLE,/ COMPREHENDING THE PERIODS AT WHICH THE MOST/ REMARKABLE CITIES AND TOWNS WERE FOUNDED,/ THEIR PRESENT POPULATION, LATITUDE, AND/ LONGITUDE./ *The whole being intended to form a comprehensive/ abridgement of History and Chronology, particu-/ larly of that part which relates to America.*/ <double rule>/ <author statement>/ <rule>/ <quotation in Latin>/ <rule>

imprint: <below rule> PHILADELPHIA,/ PRINTED FOR THE AUTHOR BY THOMAS DOBSON,/ AT THE STONE-HOUSE, No 41, SOUTH/SECOND-STREET./ <short rule>/ M.DCC.XCV.

note: A half title is also deposited.

105.

District Court Ledger, 262 PA 79

date of deposit: July 15, twentieth year of Independence

claimant: P: Charles Cist

title: Lesebuch für Deutsche Schulkinder herausgegeben von Georg Gottfried Otterbein, Diener des Gottlichen Worts zu Duisburg am Rhein mit Veränderungen und Zusätzen zum Gebrauch Americanischer Schulen.

Title Page Deposit

title: <entire title page in Gothic script> Lesebuch/ für/ Deutsche Schulkinder./ Herausgegeben/ von/ Georg Gottfried Otterbein,/ Diener des göttlichen Worts zu Duisburg am Rhein./ <decorative rule>/ Mit Veränderungen und Zusätzen,/ zum Gebrauch Americanischer Schulen./ <decorative rule>

imprint: <below decorative rule> Philadelphia, 1795./ Gedruckt und verlegt bey Carl Cist.

106.

District Court Ledger, 262 PA 80

date of deposit: August 4, twentieth year of Independence

claimant: P: John McCulloch

title: A concise History of the United States from the Discovery of America till 1795. With a correct Map of the United States

Title Page Deposit

title: A CONCISE/ HISTORY/ OF THE/ UNITED STATES,/ FROM THE/ DISCOVERY OF AMERICA TILL 1795:/ *With a correct Map of the United States.*/ <rule>/ <relief cut of an American eagle>/ <rule>

imprint: <below rule> *PHILADELPHIA:*/ Printed and sold by JOHN M'CULLOCH, No. 1,/ North *Third-street.*—1795.

107.

District Court Ledger, 262 PA 80

date of deposit: August 8, twentieth year of Independence

claimant: A: Joseph Scott

title: The United States Gazetteer containing an Authentic description of the Several States their Situation Extent Boundaries Soil Produce Climate Population Trade and Manufactures together with the Extent Boundaries and Population of their respective Counties Also an exact account of the Cities Towns Harbours Bays Rivers Lakes Mountains &c Illustrated with nineteen Maps. <author statement>

Title Page Deposit

author: JOSEPH SCOTT.

title: <entire title page in script> The United States/ GAZETTEER:/ Containing/ An Authentic Description of the/ SEVERAL STATES:/ Their Situation, Extent, Boundaries, Soil, Produce,/ Climate, Population, Trade and Manufactures./ Together with the/ Extent, Boundaries and Popu lation of their/ Respective Counties/ Also, an/ Exact Account of the Cities, Towns, Harbours, Bays,/ Rivers, Lakes, Mountains, &c./ Illustrated with Nineteen Maps./ <thick rule>/ <author statement>/ <thick rule>

note: The bottom of the title page is missing, making imprint information unavailable. The title page is engraved.

108.

District Court Ledger, 262 PA 81

date of deposit: August 11, twentieth year of Independence

claimant: P: Joseph Crukshank

compiler: John Peirce

title: The new American Spelling-Book improved in three parts containing I Tables of common words from one to five syllables classed together agreeably to their proper Sounds and also Tables of proper Names with natural & easy Lessons dispersed through the whole which are adapted to the capacities of Children.—II A Collection of words of two three & four syllables divided into three Tables being accented and explained for the instruction of youth in the Knowledge of words as well as spelling together with a Table of words alike in sound but different in spelling and signification Also Tables of words the same in spelling but different in sound & signification with reading Lessons &c III A plain and easy introduction to English Grammar particularily adapted to the Capacities of Youth <compiler statement> the first Revised Edition—

Title Page Deposit

compiler: JOHN PEIRCE.

title: THE/ *NEW AMERICAN*/ SPELLING-BOOK,/ IMPROVED./ IN THREE PARTS./ CONTAINING,/ . . . / <thick rule>/ <compiler statement>/ <thick rule>/ THE FIRST REVISED EDITION./ <decorative rule>

imprint: <below decorative rule> *PHILADELPHIA:*/ PRINTED FOR AND SOLD BY JOSEPH CRUKSHANK, NO. 87,/ HIGH-STREET, BETWEEN SECOND AND/ THIRD-STREETS./ <short rule>/ 1795.

note: Two pages of preface are also deposited.

109.

District Court Ledger, 262 PA 82

date of deposit: August 15, twentieth year of Independence

claimant: P: Thomas Bradford

author: Peter Porcupine—

title: A little plain English addressed to the People of the United States on the Treaty negociated with his Britannic Majesty and on the Conduct of the President relative thereto in Answer to "The Letters of Franklin"—with a Supplement containing an Account of the Turbulent and factious Proceedings of the Opposers of the Treaty—<author statement> <eight lines of poetry in English>

Title Page Deposit

author: PETER PORCUPINE.

title: A LITTLE/ PLAIN ENGLISH,/ ADDRESSED TO/ THE PEOPLE OF THE UNITED STATES,/ ON/ THE TREATY/ NEGOCIATED WITH/ HIS BRITANNIC MAJESTY,/ AND ON THE CONDUCT OF/ THE PRESIDENT/ RELATIVE THERETO./ IN ANSWER TO/ "THE LETTERS OF FRANKLIN."/ WITH A/ SUPPLEMENT/ CONTAINING AN ACCOUNT OF THE TUR BULENT AND FAC-/ TIOUS PROCEEDINGS OF THE OPPOSERS OF/ THE TREATY./ <short thick rule>/ <author statement>/ <short thick rule>/ <eight lines of poetry in English>/ <thick rule>

imprint: <below thick rule> PHILADELPHIA:/ PRINTED BY THOMAS BRADFORD, NO. 8, SOUTHF RONT ST./ <short rule>/ 1795.

110.

District Court Ledger, 262 PA 83

date of deposit: September 7, twentieth year of Independence

claimant: P: Thomas Stephens, Denoon & Condie

title: Sentiments upon the Religion of Reason and Nature, carefully translated from the Original French Manuscript, communicated by the Author.

Title Page Deposit

title: SENTIMENTS/ UPON/ THE RELIGION OF REASON/ AND NATURE,/ CAREFULLY TRANSLATED FROM THE/ ORIGINAL FRENCH MANUSCRIPT,/ COMMUNI CATED BY THE AUTHOR./ <double rule>/ *ENTERED AS THE ACT DIRECTS.*/ <double rule>/ <thick rule>

imprint: <below thick rule> <first word in black letter> Philadelphia—Printed/ FOR T. STEPHENS, AND DENOON & CONDIE./ BY BIOREN & MADAN./ <short rule>/ M DCCXCV.

note: Five pages of preface and four pages of text are also deposited.

111.

District Court Ledger, 262 PA 84

date of deposit: September 15, twentieth year of Independence

claimant: James Thompson Callender

title: The Political Progress of Britain: or an Impartial History of abuses in the Government of the British Empire, in Europe, Asia, and America, from the revolution, in 1688, to the present time: the whole tending to prove the ruinous consequences of the popular System of Taxation, War, & Conquest. <biblical quotation> Part second.—

note: The ledger does not name the claimant as either proprietor or author. The *National Index of American Imprints* lists him as author.

Title Page Deposit

title: THE/ POLITICAL PROGRESS/ OF/ BRIT AIN:/ OR, AN/ IMPARTIAL HISTORY/ OF/ ABUSES IN THE GOVERNMENT/ OF THE/ BRITISH EMPIRE,/ IN/ Europe, Asia, and America./ *FROM THE REVOLUTION, IN* 1688, *TO THE PRESENT TIME:*/ THE WHOLE TENDING TO PROVE THE RUINOUS CON SEQUENCES OF/ THE POPULAR SYSTEM OF/ TAXATION, WAR, AND CONQUEST./ <double rule>/ <biblical quotation>/ <double rule>/ PART SECOND./ <thick rule>

imprint: <below thick rule> PHILADELPHIA:/ Printed for *RICHARD FOLWELL*, No. 33, MULBERRY-STREET./ AND SOLD IN NEW-YORK BY *JAMES RIVINGTON.*/ 1795.
note: [PRICE THREE SHILLINGS.]

112.

District Court Ledger, 262 PA 85
date of deposit: September 19, twentieth year of Independence
claimant: A: John Murdock
author: an American and a Citizen of Philadelphia—
title: The Triumphs of Love or Happy Reconciliation. A Comedy in four Acts—<author statement> Acted at the New-Theatre—Philadelphia—First Edition—

Title Page Deposit
author: Written by an American, and a Citizen of Philadelphia.
title: THE/ TRIUMPHS OF LOVE;/ OR,/ Happy Reconciliation./ A COMEDY./ IN FOUR ACTS./ <rule>/ <author statement>/ <rule>/ Acted at the New Theatre,/ PHILADELPHIA./ <thick rule>/ *FIRST EDI TION.*/ <thick rule>
imprint: <below thick rule> PHILADELPHIA:/ PRINTED BY R. FOLWELL, NO. 33, ARCH-STREET./ <short rule>/ SEPTEMBER 10, 1795.
note: A list of Dramatis Personae on the verso of the title page is also deposited.

113.

District Court Ledger, 262 PA 85
date of deposit: October 5, twentieth year of Independence
claimant: A: Edmund Hogan
title: The Prospect of Philadelphia and Check on the next Directory—Part 1. Giving at a single View the Numbers of the Houses Names of the Streets Lanes Couts and Alleys with the Names of the present Inhabitants and their Occupations—together with other interesting Occurrences and useful Observations. <author statement>

Title Page Deposit
claimant: A,P: Edmund Hogan
author: EDMUND HOGAN.
title: THE/ PROSPECT/ OF/ PHILADELPHIA,/ AND/ CHECK/ ON THE NEXT/ *DIREC TORY.*/ <double rule>/ PART I./ <double rule>/ *GIVING, AT A SINGLE VIEW,*/ THE NUMBERS OF THE HOUSES, NAMES OF THE STREETS, LANES,/ COUTS, AND ALLEYS; WITH THE NAMES OF THE PRE SENT/ INHABITANTS, AND THEIR OCCU PATIONS: TOGETHER/ WITH OTHER INTERESTING OCCURRENCES, AND/ USEFUL OBSERVATIONS./ <double rule>/ <author statement>/ <double rule>
imprint: <below double rule> *PHILADELPHIA:*/ PRINTED BY FRANCIS & ROBERT BAILEY, AT YORICK'S/ HEAD, No. 116, HIGH-STREET./ <short double rule>/ M.DCC.XCV.
note: The clerk's note on the verso of the title page states that Edmund Hogan is both author and proprietor.

114.

District Court Ledger, 262 PA 86
date of deposit: November 7, twentieth year of Independence
claimant: A: Constantin François Volney
author: . . . .One of the Deputies of the Constituent Assemby of M, DCC, LXXX IX Author of Travels in Syria and Egypt &c. &c. &c.
title: The Ruins or Meditations on the Revolutions of Empires—<author statement> The American Edition from the English translation of the French corrected by the Author himself upon the Spot with considerable Additions—

Title Page Deposit
author: C. F. VOLNEY,/ ONE OF THE DEPUTIES OF THE CONSTITUENT ASSEMBLY OF/ *M,DCC,LXXXIX*; AUTHOR OF *TRAVELS IN SYRIA AND EGYPT,*/ &c. &c. &c.
title: THE/ RUINS:/ OR,/ MEDITATIONS/ ON THE/ REVOLUTIONS OF EMPIRES./ <thick rule>/ <author statement>/ <double rule>/ THE AMERICAN EDITION,/ FROM THE ENGLISH TRANSLATION OF THE FRENCH, CORRECTED BY/ THE AUTHOR, HIMSELF, UPON THE SPOT, WITH CON-/SIDERABLE ADDITIONS./ <double rule>
imprint: <below double rule> *PHILADELPHIA:*/ PRINTED FOR THOMAS STEPHENS, BY/ *FRANCIS & ROBERT BAILEY.*/ <short double rule>/ M.DCC.XCV.

115.

District Court Ledger, 262 PA 87
date of deposit: November 7, twentieth year of Independence
claimant: A: Constantin François Volney

author: C. F. Volney. Author of "The Ruins or Meditations on the Revolutions of Empires" and "Elements of the Study of History read at Paris "in the Ecole Normale" &c.&c.
title: Travels through Syria and Egypt in the Years 1783. 1784. and 1785. containing the present natural and political State of those Countries their Productions Arts Manufactures and Commerce with Observations on the Manners Customs and Government of the Turks and Arabs—<author statement> In two Volumes

Title Page Deposit
author: C. F. VOLNEY,/ AUTHOR OF "THE RUINS, OR MEDITATIONS ON THE REVOLUTIONS OF/ "EMPIRES;" AND "ELEMENTS OF THE STUDY OF HIS TORY,/ "READ AT PARIS IN THE ECOLE NORMALE," &c. &c.
title: TRAVELS/ THROUGH/ SYRIA AND EGYPT,/ IN THE YEARS/ 1783, 1784, AND 1785./ *CONTAINING,*/ THE PRESENT NATURAL AND POLITICAL STATE OF THOSE/ COUNTRIES, THEIR PRODUC TIONS, ARTS, MANUFACTURES,/ AND COMMERCE; WITH OBSERVATIONS ON THE MAN-/ NERS, CUSTOMS, AND GOVERNMENT, OF THE/ TURKS AND ARABS./ <double rule>/ <author statement>/ <thick rule>/ IN TWO VOLUMES./ <thick rule>
imprint: <below thick rule> *PHILADELPHIA:*/ PRINTED FOR THOMAS STEPHENS, BY/ *FRANCIS & ROBERT BAILEY.*/ <short double rule>/ M.DCC.XCV.

116.
District Court Ledger, 262 PA 88
date of deposit: November 7, twentieth year of Independence
claimant: A: Constantin François Volney
author: C. F. Volney—Author of Travels through Syria and Egypt the Ruins &c.
title: Elements of the Study of History read at Paris in the Ecole Normale instituted by the Convention to superintend the Plan of national Education in the French Republic. <author statement>

Title Page Deposit
author: C. F. VOLNEY,/ AUTHOR OF *TRAVELS THROUGH SYRIA AND EGYPT*, THE *RUINS*, &c.
title: ELEMENTS/ OF THE/ *STUDY*/ OF/ HISTORY./ READ AT PARIS,/ IN THE/ *ECOLE NORMALE,*/ INSTITUTED BY THE *CONVENTION*, TO SUPERINTEND THE *PLAN*/ OF *NATIONAL EDUCATION*, IN THE *FRENCH REPUBLIC.*/ <thick rule>/ <author statement>/ <thick rule>
imprint: <below thick rule> *PHILADELPHIA:*/ PRINTED FOR THOMAS STEPHENS, BY/ *FRANCIS & ROBERT BAILEY.*/ <short rule>/ M.DCC.XCV.

117.
District Court Ledger, 262 PA 89
date of deposit: November 9, twentieth year of Independence
claimant: P: Samuel Harrison Smith
author: <Edmund Randolph>
title: A Vindication of Mr. Randolph's Resignation—
note: According to the *National Index of American Imprints* the author is Edmund Randolph.

Title Page Deposit
title: A/ VINDICATION/ OF/ MR. RANDOLPH'S/ RESIGNATION./ <double rule>
imprint: <below double rule> PHILADELPHIA:/ PRINTED BY SAMUEL H. SMITH,/ NO. 118, CHESNUT STREET./ M.DCC.XCV.

118.
District Court Ledger, 262 PA 90
date of deposit: November 30, twentieth year of Independence
claimant: P: John Lindsey, and the Federal Society
title: The Journeymen Cabinet and Chair-Makers Philadelphia Book of Prices—Second Edition corrected & enlarged—

Title Page Deposit
title: THE/ *JOURNEYMEN*/ CABINET/ AND/ CHAIR-MAKERS/ PHILADELPHIA/ *BOOK OF PRICES.*/ <double rule>/ *SECOND EDITION CORRECTED AND ENLARGED.*/ <double rule>
imprint: <below double rule> PHILADELPHIA:/ PRINTED BY ORMROD AND CONRAD/ AT FRANKLIN's HEAD, No. 41,/ CHESNUT-STREET./ M.DCCXCV.

119.
District Court Ledger, 262 PA 91
date of deposit: December 4, twentieth year of Independence
claimant: P: Thomas Bradford
author: Mr. Martens—Professor of Law in the University of Gottingen—<Georg Friedrich von Martens>

translator: William Cobbett—
title: Summary of the Law of Nations founded on the Treaties and Customs of the Modern Nations of Europe with a List of the principal Treaties concluded since the Year 1748 down to the present Time indicating the Works in which they are to be found—<author statement> Translated from the French <translator statement>
note: According to the *National Index of American Imprints* the author is Georg Friedrich von Martens.

Title Page Deposit
author: *MR. MARTENS,*/ PROFESSOR OF LAW IN THE UNIVERSITY OF GOTTINGEN.
translator: WILLIAM COBBETT.
title: SUMMARY/ OF THE/ LAW OF NATIONS,/ FOUNDED ON/ THE TREATIES AND CUSTOMS/ OF THE/ MODERN NATIONS/ OF/ EUROPE;/ WITH/ *A LIST OF THE PRINCIPAL TREATIES,*/ CONCLUDED SINCE THE YEAR 1748 DOWN TO THE PRESENT TIME,/ INDICATING THE WORKS IN WHICH THEY ARE/ TO BE FOUND./ <thick rule>/ <author statement>/ <double rule>/ *Translated from the French*/ <translator statement>/ <double rule>
imprint: <below double rule> PHILADELPHIA:/ *PUBLISHED BY THOMAS BRADFORD, PRINTER,*/ BOOKSELLER & STATIONER,/ No. 8, South Front Street./ <short double rule>/ 1795.

120.
District Court Ledger, 262 PA 92
date of deposit: December 24, twentieth year of Independence
claimant: A: Elhanan Winchester
title: A plain political Catechism intended for the Use of Schools in the United States of America where in the great Principles of Liberty and of the Federal Government are laid down and explained in the Way of Question and Answer Made level to the lowest Capacities <author statement>

Title Page Deposit
author: ELHANAN WINCHESTER.
title: A Plain Political Catechism,/ INTENDED/ FOR THE USE OF SCHOOLS,/ IN/ *The United States of America:*/ WHEREIN/ THE GREAT PRINCIPLES OF LIBERTY,/ AND/ OF THE FEDERAL GOVERNMENT,/ Are laid down and explained, in the way of/ *Question and Answer.*/ MADE LEVEL TO THE LOWEST CAPACITIES./ <triple rule>/ <author statement>/ <thick rule>
imprint: <below thick rule> PHILADELPHIA:/ PRINTED BY R. FOLWELL, No. 33, MULBERRY-STREET./ 1795.

1796
121.
District Court Ledger, 262 PA 93
date of deposit: January 2, twentieth year of Independence
claimant: P: M. L. E. Moreau de Saint-Mery
author: un Européen—<François Alexandre Frédéric, duc de La Rochefoucauld Liancourt>
title: Des Prisons de Philadelphie—<author statement>
note: The *National Index of American Imprints* states that the author is François Alexandre Frédéric, duc de La Rochefoucauld Liancourt.

Title Page Deposit
author: UN EUROPÉEN.
title: DES/ PRISONS/ DE/ PHILADELPHIE./ <double rule>/ <author statement>/ <double rule>/ <relief cut of wreath surrounding initials "S" and "M">
imprint: <below relief cut> *PHILADELPHIE.*/ Imprimê & se trouve chez MOREAU DE ST-MÉRY, Imprimeur-/ Libraire, au coin de Front & de Walnut streets, No. 84./ <thick rule>/ JANVIER 1796.

122.
District Court Ledger, 262 PA 93
date of deposit: January 2, twentieth year of Independence
claimant: P: M. L. E. Moreau de Saint-Mery
author: an European—<François Alexandre Frédéric, duc de La Rouchefoucauld Liancourt>
title: On the Prisons of Philadelphia—<author statement>
note: The *National Index of American Imprints* states that the author is François Alexandre Frédéric, duc de La Rochefoucauld Liancourt.

Title Page Deposit
author: *AN EUROPEAN.*
title: ON THE/ PRISONS/ OF/ PHILADELPHIA./ <double rule>/ <author statement>/ <double rule>
imprint: <below double rule> *PHILADELPHIA:*/ PRINTED AND SOLD BY MOREAU DE SAINT-MERY,/ PRINTER & BOOKSELLER, No. 84, SOUTH FRONT-STREET./ <short thick rule>/ JANUARY 1796.

123.

District Court Ledger, 262 PA 94

date of deposit: January 2, twentieth year of Independence

claimant: A: M. L. E. Moreau de Saint-Mery

author: . . . Membre de la Société Philosophique de Philadelphie

title: Description topographique et politique de la Partie Espagnole de l'Isle Saint-Domingue avec des Observations générales sur le Climat la Population les Productions le Caractère & les Moeurs de Habitans de cette Colonie & un Tableau raisonné des différentes Parties de son Administration—Accompagnée d'une nouvelle Carte de la Totalité de l'Isle—<author statement> Tome premier—

Title Page Deposit

author: M. L. E. MOREAU DE SAINT-MÉRY,/ Membre de la Société Philosophique de Philadelphie.

title: DESCRIPTION/ TOPOGRAPHIQUE ET POLITIQUE/ DE LA/ PARTIE ESPAGNOLE/ DE L'ISLE/ SAINT-DOMINGUE;/ AVEC des Observations générales sur le Climat, la Population,/ les Productions, le Caractère & les Moeurs des Habitans de/ cette Colonie, & un Tableau raisonné des différentes parties de/ son Administration;/ *Accompagnée d'une nouvelle Carte de la totalité de l'Isle.*/ <double rule>/ <author statement>/ <double rule>/ TOME PREMIER./ <relief cut of palm leaves and a sun>

imprint: <below relief cut> PHILADELPHIE,/ Imprimé & se trouve chez MOREAU DE ST-MÉRY, Imprimeur—/ Libraire, au coin de Front & de Walnut streets, No 84./ <short double rule>/ 1796.

124.

District Court Ledger, 262 PA 95

date of deposit: January 2, twentieth year of Independence

claimant: P: M. L. E. Moreau de Saint-Mery

author: M. L. E. Moreau de Saint Mery Member of the Philosophical Society of Philadelphia &c—

translator: William Cobbet—

title: A topographical and political Description of the Spanish Part of Saint Domingo containing general Observations on the Climate Population and Productions on the Character and Manners of the Inhabitants with an Account of the several Branches of the Government—to which is prefixed a new correct and elegant Map of the whole Island—<author statement> Translated from the French <translator statement> Vol. 1.—

Title Page Deposit

author: M. L. E. MOREAU DE SAINT-MERY./ MEMBER OF THE PHILOSOPHICAL SOCIETY OF PHILADELPHIA, &c.

translator: WILLIAM COBBETT.

title: A/ TOPOGRAPHICAL AND POLITICAL/ DESCRIPTION/ OF THE/ *SPANISH PART/* OF/ SAINT-DOMINGO,/ CONTAINING,/ . . . / TO WHICH IS PREFIXED,/ A NEW, CORRECT, AND ELEGANT MAP OF THE/ WHOLE ISLAND./ <rule>/ <author statement>/ <rule>/ TRANSLATED FROM THE FRENCH/ <translator statement>/ <double rule>/ *VOL. I./* <short thick rule>

imprint: <below short thick rule> PHILADELPHIA:/ PRINTED AND SOLD BY MOREAU DE SAINT-MERY, PRINTER/ AND BOOKSELLER, No. 84, SOUTH FRONT-STREET./ <short thick rule>/ 1796.

125.

District Court Ledger, 262 PA 96

date of deposit: January 6, twentieth year of Independence

claimant: P: Thomas Bradford

author: Peter Porcupine

title: A New-Year's Gift to the Democrats or Observations on a Pamphlet entitled "A Vindication of Mr. Randolph's Resignation"—<author statement> <six lines of poetry in English>

Title Page Deposit

author: PETER PORCUPINE.

title: A/ NEW-YEAR'S GIFT/ TO/ *THE DEMOCRATS;/* OR/ OBSERVATIONS/ ON/ *A PAMPHLET,/* ENTITLED,/ *"A VINDICATION/ OF/ Mr. RANDOLPH's RESIGNATION."/* <thick rule>/ <author statement>/ <thick rule>/ <six lines of poetry in English>/ <double rule>

imprint: <below double rule> PHILADELPHIA:/ *PUBLISHED BY THOMAS BRADFORD, PRINTER,/* BOOK-SELLER & STATIONER,/ No. 8,/ South Front-Street./ <short double rule>/ 1796.

note: Two pages of preface and four pages of text are also deposited. The "h" in the word South and the first "t" in the word Street in the imprint are dropped.

126.

District Court Ledger, 262 PA 96

date of deposit: January 7, twentieth year of Independence

claimant: P: Thomas Stephens
title: Stephens's Philadelphia Directory for 1796. or Alphabetical Arrangement containing the Names Occupations and Places of Abode of the Citizens with a Register of the Executive Legislative and Judicial Magistrates of the United States and the State of Pennsylvania with their Salaries—the Governors of the different States and the Magistrates of the City—also an Account of the different Societies charitable and literary Institutions with the Names of their present Officers—and an accurate Table of the Duties on Goods Wares and Merchandize together with a general Abstract from the Revenue Laws—relative to the Duty of Masters of Vessels—of the owners Consignees of Goods. of Officers of the Customs—of the Payment of Duties &c. and of the Manner in which Goods must be imported—To all which are added—A complete Account of the Post-Office Establishment—The Banks and different Monies &c with an Alphabetical List of the Streets Lanes and Alleys—

Title Page Deposit
title: <black letter> Stephens's/ Philadelphia Directory,/ For 1796;/ OR,/ *ALPHABETICAL ARRANGEMENT:*/ CONTAINING/ THE NAMES, OCCUPATIONS, AND PLACES/ OF ABODE OF THE CITIZENS:/ WITH/ <. . .>/ TO ALL WHICH ARE ADDED,/ A complete Account of the Post Office Establishment/—The Banks, and different Monies, &c./ *With an Alphabetical List of the Streets, Lanes, and Alleys.*
imprint: *PHILADELPHIA:*/ PRINTED FOR *THOMAS STEPHENS,* No 60,/ SOUTH SECOND STREET; BY W. WOODWARD.

127.
District Court Ledger, 262 PA 98
date of deposit: February 5, twentieth year of Independence
claimant: P: Benjamin Davies
title: Revolutionary Justice displayed or an inside View of the various Prisons of Paris under the Government of Robespierre and the Jacobins—Taken principally from the Journals of the Prisoners themselves—<two lines of poetry in English> Translated from the French with an Appendix containing an Account of the Promulgation of the new Religion of France the impious Attack on the ancient and the Violation and Plunder of the sacred Receptacles of the Dead—

Title Page Deposit
title: Revolutionary Justice,/ *DISPLAYED;*/ OR,/ AN INSIDE VIEW/ OF THE/ *Various Prisons of Paris,*/ UNDER THE GOVERNMENT OF/ Robespierre and the Jacobins./ <short thick rule>/ Taken principally from the Journals of the Prisoners themselves./ <thick rule>/ <quotation in English>/ <thick rule>/ Translated from the French./ <thick rule>/ WITH AN APPENDIX—containing—an Account of/ the Promulgation of the new Religion of France,/ the impious Attack on the ancient, and the/ Violation and Plunder of the sacred/ Receptacles of the Dead./ <thick rule>
imprint: <below thick rule> *PHILADELPHIA: Printed for* BENJAMIN DAVIES,/ *No.* 68, *High street, by* RICHARD FOLWELL, *No.* 33, *Mulberry-street.*

128.
District Court Ledger, 262 PA 99
date of deposit: February 24, twentieth year of Independence
claimant: P: Thomas Bradford
author: Peter Porcupine.
title: A Prospect from the Congress-Gallery during the Session begun December 7. 1795. containing the President's Speech the Addresses of both Houses some of the Debates in the Senate and all the principal Debates in the House of Representatives each Debate being brought under one Head and so digested and simplified as to give the Reader the completest View of the Proceedings with the least possible Fatigue—With occasional Remarks—<author statement>

Title Page Deposit
author: PETER PORCUPINE.
title: A/ PROSPECT/ FROM THE/ *CONGRESS-GALLERY,*/ DURING THE/ SESSION,/ BEGUN DECEMBER 7, 1795./ CONTAIN ING,/ The President's Speech, the addresses of both Houses, some of the/ debates in the Senate, and all the principal debates in the House of/ Representatives; each debate being brought under one head, and/ so digested and simplified as to give the reader the completest view/ of the pro ceedings with the least possible fatigue./ WITH/ OCCASIONAL REMARKS,/ <double rule>/ <author statement>/ <double rule>
imprint: <below double rule> PHILADELPHIA:/ PUBLISHED BY THOMAS BRADFORD, PRINTER/ *BOOK-SELLER & STATIONER,*/ No. 8,/ *South Front-Street,*/ 1796.
note: Two pages of preface and four pages of text are also deposited.

129.
District Court Ledger, 262 PA 100
author: C.. F.. Volney
title: Law of Nature/ or/ Principles of Morality/ deduced/ from the Physical constitution/ of/ Mankind and the Universe/ <author statement>/ <short rule>/ T Suphem/ Philadelphia/ 1796—
note: This registration is on a separate sheet of paper inserted into the District Court Ledger representing ledger entry number 128. The printer's name does not appear in Roger Bristol's *Index of Printers, Publisher's, and Booksellers Indicated by Charles Evans in His American Bibliography.*

130.
District Court Ledger, 262 PA 101
date of deposit: March 8, twentieth year of Independence
claimant: P: Benjamin Davies
author: Peter Porcupine—
title: The Bloody Buoy thrown out as a Warning to the political Pilots of America or a faithful Relation of a Multitude of Acts of horrid Barbarity such as the Eye never witnessed the Tongue never expressed or the Imagination conceived until the Commencement of the French Revolution—To which is added an instructive Essay tracing these dreadful Effects to their real Causes—Illustrated with four striking Copper-Plates—<author statement> <quotation in English>

Title Page Deposit
author: PETER PORCUPINE.
title: THE/ BLOODY BUOY/ THROWN OUT AS/ A warning to the Political Pilots of America;/ OR A/ FAITHFUL RELATION/ OF/ A MULTITUDE OF ACTS OF HORRID BARBARITY,/ Such as the eye never witnessed, the tongue never/ Expressed, or the imagination conceived,/ Until the commencement of/ THE FRENCH REVOLUTION./ TO WHICH IS ADDED/ AN INSTRUCTIVE ESSAY,/ Tracing these dreadful effects to their real/ Causes./ <decorative rule>/ *Illustrated with four striking Copper-plates.*/ <short decorative rule>/ <author statement>/ <short decorative rule>/ <quotation in English>/ <double rule>
imprint: <below double rule> *PHILADELPHIA:/ PRINTED FOR* BENJAMIN DAVIES *NO.* 68. HIGH-STEET./ MDCCXCVI.

131.
District Court Ledger, 262 PA 102
date of deposit: April 4, twentieth year of Independence
claimant: P: Benjamin Davies
author: Peter Porcupine
title: The Political Censor or monthly review of the most interesting political Occurrences relative to the United States of America <author statement>

Title Page Deposit
author: PETER PORCUPINE.
title: THE/ *POLITICAL*/ CENSOR,/ OR/ MONTHLY REVIEW/ OF THE/ *Most interesting Political Occurences,*/ RELATIVE TO/ *THE UNITED STATES*/ OF/ *AMERICA.*/ <double rule>/ <author statement>/ <double rule>
imprint: <below double rule> *PHILADELPHIA:/ PRINTED FOR* BENJAMIN DAVIES, NO. 68, HIGH-STREET./ MDCCXCVI.
note: Page 8 of the text is printed on the verso of the title page.

132.
District Court Ledger, 262 PA 102
date of deposit: April 6, twentieth year of Independence
claimant: P: Benjamin Franklin Bache
author: Thomas Paine Author of the works entitled Common Sense Rights of man part first & second the first part of the Age of Reason and Dissertations on first principles of Government.
title: The Age of Reason part the second being an investigation of true and of Fabulous Theology <author statement>

Title Page Deposit
author: THOMAS PAINE,/ AUTHOR OF THE WORKS ENTITLED COMMON SENSE,—/ RIGHTS OF MAN, PART FIRST AND SECOND,—THE/ FIRST PART OF THE AGE OF REASON,—AND DIS-/ SERTATIONS ON FIRST PRINCIPLES OF GOVERNMENT.
title: THE/ AGE OF REASON./ PART THE SECOND./ <short double rule>/ BEING AN/ INVESTIGATION/ OF/ TRUE AND OF FABULOUS/ THEOLOGY./ <thick rule>/ <author statement>/ <double rule>
imprint: <below double rule> PRINTED FOR THE AUTHOR./ MDCCXCV.

133.
District Court Ledger, 262 PA 103
date of deposit: April 25, twentieth year of Independence
claimant: A: Abraham Bradley junior
title: A Map of the United States exhibiting Post-Roads and Distances <author statement> the

first Sheet comprehending the nine Northern States with Parts of Virginia and the Territory North of Ohio
format: map

Title Page Deposit
author: <script> Abraham Bradley Junr,,
title: *A MAP/* OF THE/ <script> United States/ Exhibiting Post Roads & Distances/ <author statement>/ <script> The first Sheet compre hending the/ <script> Nine Northern States, with parts of Virginia/ <script> and the Terri tory North of Ohio.
note: This deposit page is a copy of the entire map and is located in the Geography and Map Division (call number: G3710 1796.B7). The title page is engraved.

134.
District Court Ledger, 262 PA 104
date of deposit: April 29, twentieth year of Independence
claimant: P: Gouin Dufief Junr.
title: A Plan of the City of New York and its Environs taken from Actual Survey—
format: map

Title Page Deposit
title: A/ PLAN/ OF THE/ CITY/ OF/ NEW-YORK,/ AND ITS/ ENVIRONS:/ *Taken from actual survey.*
note: This title, printed on 6.6 cm x 7.2 cm paper, is located in the Geography and Map Division.

135.
District Court Ledger, 262 PA 104
date of deposit: April 29, twentieth year of Independence
claimant: P: Gouin Dufief Junr.
title: A Plan of the City of Philadelphia and its environs taken from Actual Survey—
format: map

Title Page Deposit
title: A/ PLAN/ OF THE/ CITY/ OF/ PHILADELPHIA,/ AND ITS/ ENVIRONS:/ *Taken from actual survey.*
note: This title, printed on 6.6 cm x 7 cm paper, is located in the Geography and Map Division.

136.
District Court Ledger, 262 PA 105
date of deposit: May 13, twentieth year of Independence
claimant: A, P: Charles Wilson Peale
author: C. W. Peale, Member of the American Philosophical Society and AMFJ Beauvois Member of the Society of Arts & Sciences of St. Domingo of the American Philosophical Society and correspondent to the Museum of Natural History at Paris
title: A Scientific & Descriptive Catalogue of Peale's Museum, <author statement> <relief cut of an open book> <five lines of poetry in English>

Title Page Deposit
author: C. W. PEALE, Member of the American Philosophical Society, and A. M. F./ J. BEAUVOIS, Member of the Society of Arts and Sciences of St. Domingo; of/ the American Philosophical Society; and correspondent to the Museum of Natural/ History at Paris.
title: A/ SCIENTIFIC AND DESCRIPTIVE/ CATALOGUE/ OF/ PEALE'S MUSEUM,/ <author statement>/ <rule>/ <relief cut of an open book>/ <rule>/ <five lines of poetry in English>/ <thick rule>
imprint: <below thick rule> *PHILADELPHIA:/* PRINTED BY SAMUEL H. SMITH, No. 118 CHESNUT-STREET./ <short double rule>/ M.DCC.XCVI.
note: Six pages of an Advertisement are also deposited.

137.
District Court Ledger, 262 PA 105
date of deposit: May 16, twentieth year of Independence
claimant: P: Samuel Harrison Smith
author: William Findley Member of the House of Representatives of the United States
title: History of the Insurrection in the four Western Counties of Pennsylvania in the Year M,DCC,XCIV—with a Recital of the Circumstances specially connected therewith—and an historical Review of the previous Situation of the Country—<author statement>

Title Page Deposit
author: *WILLIAM FINDLEY,/* MEMBER OF THE HOUSE OF REPRESENTATIVES OF THE UNITED STATES.
title: HISTORY/ OF THE/ INSURRECTION,/ IN THE/ FOUR WESTERN COUNTIES/ OF/ PENNSYLVANIA:/ IN THE YEAR M.DCC.XCIV./ WITH A RECITAL OF THE CIRCUMSTANCES SPECI-/ ALLY CON NECTED THEREWITH:/ AND AN/ HISTORICAL REVIEW OF THE PREVIOUS

SITUATION OF THE COUNTRY./ <short double rule>/ <author statement>/ <double rule>

imprint: <below double rule> *PHILADELPHIA:/* PRINTED BY SAMUEL HARRISON SMITH,/ No. 118, CHESNUT-STREET./ <short rule>/ M.DCC.XCVI.

note: Four pages of preface are also deposited.

138.

District Court Ledger, 262 PA 106

date of deposit: May 23, twentieth year of Independence

claimant: P: Francis Shallus

author: Andrew Barton, Esqr.

title: The Disappointment; or the force of Credulity. a new Comic-Opera of three Acts. <author statement> second edition, revised and corrected with large additions by the Author. <four lines of poetry in English>

Title Page Deposit

author: ANDREW BARTON, *Esq.*

title: THE/ DISAPPOINTMENT;/ OR, THE/ *FORCE OF CREDULITY./* A NEW COMIC-OPERA,/ *OF THREE ACTS./* <author state ment>/ <short thick rule>/ *Second Edition, revised and corrected with large/ additions by the Author./* <double rule>/ <four lines of poetry in English>/ <double rule>

imprint: <below double rule> PHILADELPHIA:/ *PRINTED FOR, AND SOLD BY/* FRANCIS SHALLUS No. 40, VINE-STREET./ <short double rule>/ M.DCC.XCVI.

139.

District Court Ledger, 262 PA 107

date of deposit: June 24, twentieth year of Independence

claimant: P: John Ormrod

author: Charles H. Wharton. D.D. and Member of the Philosophical Society of Philadelphia—

title: A short and candid Enquiry into the Proofs of Christ's Divinity in which Doctor Priestley's Opinion concerning Christ is occasionally considered—In a Letter to a Friend—<author statement> <biblical quotation>

Title Page Deposit

author: CHARLES H. WHARTON, D. D./ *And Member of the Philosophical Society of Philadelphia.*

title: A/ *SHORT AND CANDID/* ENQUIRY/ INTO THE/ *PROOFS OF CHRIST's DIVINITY;/* IN WHICH/ Doctor PRIESTLEY'S Opinion/ *CON CERNING CHRIST,/* IS OCCASIONALLY CONSIDERED./ IN A LETTER TO A FRIEND./ <short thick rule>/ <author statement>/ <double rule>/ <biblical quotation>/ <double rule>

imprint: <below double rule> *PHILADELPHIA:/* PRINTED BY ORMROD & CONRAD, No. 41, CHESNUT-STREET./ <short thick rule>/ 1796.

note: Six pages of preface are also deposited.

140.

District Court Ledger, 262 PA 108

date of deposit: July 19, twenty-first year of Independence

claimant: P: Thomas Dobson

author: James Hardie A.M. Teacher of the Greek and Latin Languages.

title: Selectae e veteri Testamento, Historiae or select Passages from the old Testament—To which is added an alphabetical Vocabulary or Dictionary of the Words contained in this Book wherein the <the following word has been crossed out in ms.> <Principles> Primitives of compound and derivative Words are minutely traced and the Irregularities of anomalous Nouns and Verbs are particularly mentioned—For the Use of those who are entering on the Study of the Latin Language <quotation in Latin> <author statement>

Title Page Deposit

author: JAMES HARDIE, A.M./ TEACHER OF THE GREEK AND LATIN LANGUAGES.

title: SELECTAE/ E Veteri Testamento, Historiae;/ OR,/ SELECT PASSAGES/ From the Old Testa ment./ TO WHICH IS ADDED,/ *AN ALPHA BETICAL VOCABULARY,/* OR/ *Dictionary of the Words/* CONTAINED IN THIS BOOK;/ *WHEREIN/* THE PRIMITIVES OF COMPOUND AND DERIVATIVE/ WORDS ARE MINUTELY TRACED,/ *AND/* THE IRREGULARITIES OF ANOMALOUS NOUNS AND/ VERBS ARE PARTICULARLY MENTIONED./ <short double rule>/ *For the use of those who are entering on the study of the/ Latin Language./* <rule>/ <quotation in Latin>/ <rule>/ <author statement>/ <thick rule>

imprint: <below thick rule> PHILADELPHIA,/ *PRINTED BY THOMAS DOBSON,/* AT THE STONE-HOUSE, No 41, SOUTH SECOND-STREET./ <short rule>/ M.DCC.XCV.

141.

District Court Ledger, 262 PA 109

date of deposit: July 19, twenty-first year of Independence
claimant: P: Thomas Dobson
author: Joseph Priestley L.L.D. F.R.S. &c. &c.
title: Unitarianism explained and defended in a Discourse delivered in the Church of the Universalist, at Philadelphia 1796. <author statement> <three biblical quotations>

Title Page Deposit

author: JOSEPH PRIESTLEY, LL.D F.R.S./ *&c. &c.*
title: Unitarianism explained and defended,/ IN A/ DISCOURSE/ DELIVERED IN THE/ CHURCH OF THE UNIVERSALISTS,/ AT PHILADELPHIA, 1796./ <author statement>/ <double rule>/ <three biblical quotations>/ <thick decorative rule>
imprint: <below thick decorative rule> PHILADLEPHIA,/ PRINTED BY JOHN THOMPSON./ 1796./ <short rule>

142.

District Court Ledger, 262 PA 110

date of deposit: July 19, twenty-first year of Independence
claimant: P: Thomas Dobson
author: Joseph Priestley L.L.D. F.R.S. &c. &c.
title: Discourses relating to the Evidences of revealed Religion delivered in the Church of the Universalists at Philadelphia 1796. and published at the Request of many of the Hearers—<author statement> <biblical quotation>

Title Page Deposit

author: JOSEPH PRIESTLEY, LL.D. F.R.S./ &c. &c.
title: DISCOURSES/ RELATING TO/ *The Evidences of Revealed Religion,*/ DELIVERED IN THE/ CHURCH OF THE UNIVERSALISTS,/ AT PHILADELPHIA, 1796./ AND/ PUB LISHED AT THE REQUEST OF MANY OF THE/ HEARERS./ <author statement>/ <double rule>/ <biblical quotation>/ <thick decorative rule>
imprint: <below thick decorative rule> PHILADELPHIA,/ PRINTED FOR T. DOBSON, BY JOHN THOMPSON./ 1796./ <short rule>

143.

District Court Ledger, 262 PA 111

date of deposit: July 19, twenty-first year of Independence
claimant: P: Thomas Dobson
author: Joseph Priestley L.L.D. F.R.S. &c. &c.
title: Considerations on the Doctrine of Phlogiston and the Decomposition of Water—<author statement> <quotation in Latin>

Title Page Deposit

author: JOSEPH PRIESTLEY, *LL.D.F.R.S.&c. &c.*
title: CONSIDERATIONS/ ON THE/ *DOCTRINE*/ OF/ PHLOGISTON,/ AND/ *The Decomposition of Water.*/ <thick rule>/ <author statement>/ <short double rule>/ <quotation in Latin>/ <short thick rule>
imprint: <below short thick rule> PHILADELPHIA;/ PRINTED BY THOMAS DOBSON, AT THE STONE-HOUSE,/ No 41, SOUTH SECOND-STREET./ 1796.

144.

District Court Ledger, 262 PA 112

date of deposit: August 2, twenty-first year of Independence
claimant: P: Tobias Hirte
title: Gemeinnützige Sammlung/ zum Gebrauch/ der/ Deutschen in America/ Vornemlich/ der/ Landleute in Pennsylvanien

Title Page Deposit

title: <entire title page in Gothic script> Gemeinnützige Sammlung/ Zum Gebrauch/ der/ Deutschen in America,/ Vornehmlich/ der/ Landleute in Pennsylvanien./ <thick rule>/ <rule>/ ENTERED ACCORDING TO LAW./ <rule>/ <thick decorative rule>
imprint: <below thick decorative rule> Ephrata: gedruckt für den Herausgeber, bey/ Benjamin Mayer, 1796./ Und zu haben, beym Dutzend und Einzelu, bey folgenden/ Herrn: In Philadelphia bey Gottfried Beder, Buchhänd=/ ler in der Rees=strasse, No. 59. In Germanton bey Peter/ Leibert. In Lancaster bey Carl Heinitz,
note: 2c. Preis 4 s. 2./ Beym Dutzend wird ein billiges nachgelassen.

145.

District Court Ledger, 262 PA 113

date of deposit: August 5, twenty-first year of Independence
claimant: P: William Cobbett
author: Peter Porcupine himself.
title: The Life and Adventures of Peter Porcupine with a full and fair Account of all his authoring Transactions being a sure and infallible Guide for all enterprising young Men who wish to make a Fortune by writing Pamphlets—<author statement> <quotation in English>

Title Page Deposit
author: PETER PORCUPINE Himself.
title: THE/ LIFE AND ADVENTURES/ OF/ PETER PORCUPINE,/ WITH/ A FULL AND FAIR ACCOUNT/ OF/ All his Authoring Trans actions;/ BEING A SURE AND INFALLIBLE GUIDE FOR ALL ENTERPRISING YOUNG/ MEN WHO WISH TO MAKE A FORTUNE BY WRITING/ PAMPHLETS./ <thick rule>/ <author statement>/ <thick rule>/ <quotation in English>/ <decorative rule>
imprint: <below decorative rule> PHILADELPHIA:/ Printed for, and sold by, WILLIAM COBBETT, at No./ 25, North Second Street, opposite Christ Church./ M.DCC.XCVI.

146.

District Court Ledger, 262 PA 114
date of deposit: August 22, twenty-first year of Independence
claimant: P: Moreau de St. Mery
author: James QuickSilver
title: The blue Shop or impartial and humorous Observations on the Life and Adventures of Peter Porcupine with the real Motives which gave Rise to his Abuse of our distinguished Patriotic Characters together with a full and fair Review of his late Scare-Crow. <author statement>

Title Page Deposit
author: JAMES QUICKSILVER.
title: THE/ BLUE SHOP/ OR/ IMPARTIAL AND HUMOROUS OBSERVATIONS/ ON THE/ LIFE AND ADVENTURES/ OF/ PETER PORCUPINE,/ WITH THE/ *REAL MOTIVES WHICH GAVE RISE TO HIS/ ABUSE OF OUR DISTINGUISHED/ PATRIOTIC CHARACTERS;/* TOGETHER WITH/ A FULL AND FAIR REVIEW OF HIS LATE/ SCARE-CROW./ <thick rule>/ <author statement>/ <thick rule>
imprint: <below thick rule> PHILADELPHIA:/ Printed by MOREAU DE ST-MÉRY, No 84. Corner of/ Front and Walnut Streets./ <thick rule>/ August 1796.

147.

District Court Ledger, 262 PA 115
date of deposit: August 23, twenty-first year of Independence
claimant: P: M. L. E. Moreau de St. Méry
title: Carte de l'Isle St. Domingue dressé pour l'Ouvrage de M.L.E. Moreau de St. Méry dessinée par I. Sonis. 1790. gravée par Vallance

Title Page Deposit
title: CARTE/ DE/ L'ISLE ST. DOMINGUE/ <script> dressée pour l'Ouvrage de/ M.L.E. MOREAU DE ST. MÉRY/ Dessinée par J. SONIS 1796/ <script> Gravée par Vallance.
note: This deposit is a copy of the entire map and is located in the Geography and Map Division (call number: G4930 1796.M). The title page is engraved.

148.

District Court Ledger, 262 PA 116
date of deposit: August 31, twenty-first year of Independence
claimant: A: Robert J. Turnbull
title: A Visit to the Phialdelphia Prison being an accurate and particular Account of the wise and humane Administration adopted in every Part of that Building containing also an Account of the gradual Reformation and present improved State of the penal Laws of Pennsylvania with Observations on the Impolicy and Injustice of capital Punishments—In a Letter to a Friend—<author statement> <quotation in Latin> <quotation in English>

Title Page Deposit
author: ROBERT J. TURNBULL.
title: A/ VISIT/ TO THE/ PHILADELPHIA PRISON;/ BEING AN/ ACCURATE AND PARTICULAR ACCOUNT OF THE WISE AND HUMANE ADMINI-/ STRATION ADOPTED IN EVERY PART OF THAT BUILDING;/ CONTAINING ALSO/ An Account of the Gradual Reformation, and Present Improved State,/ OF THE/ PENAL LAWS OF PENNSYLVANIA:/ WITH/ OBSERVATIONS/ ON THE/ IMPOLICY AND INJUSTICE/ OF/ CAPITAL PUNISHMENTS./ *In a Letter to a Friend.*/ <thick rule>/ <author statement>/ <thick rule>/ <quotation in Latin>/ <short rule>/ <quotation in English>/ <decorative rule>
imprint: <below decorative rule> PHILADELPHIA:/ PRINTED BY BUDD AND BARTRAM, No. 58, NORTH SECOND STREET./ <short rule>/ M.DCC.XCVI.

149.

District Court Ledger, 262 PA 117
date of deposit: September 1, twenty-first year of Independence
claimant: P: Benjamin Franklin Bache
author: Jonathan Pindar Esq. a Cousin of Peter's

and Candidate for the Post of Poet-Laureat to the C. U. S.—
title: The Probationary Odes <author statement> In two Parts—<quotation in Latin>

Title Page Deposit
author: JONATHAN PINDAR, Esq./ A/ COUSIN OF *PETER's,*/ AND/ CANDIDATE FOR THE POST OF POET LAUREAT/ TO THE *C. U. S.*
title: THE/ *Probationary Odes*/ <author statement>/ <short double rule>/ IN TWO PARTS./ <short double rule>/ <quotation in Latin>/ <double rule>
imprint: <below double rule> *PHILADELPHIA:*/ PRINTED FOR BENJ. FRANKLIN BACHE,/ M.DCC.XCVI./ <short double rule>

150.

District Court Ledger, 262 PA 118
date of deposit: September 3, twenty-first year of Independence
author: Timothy Ticketoby—
title: The Impostor detected or a Review of some of the Writings of "Peter Porcupine"—<author statement> <two lines of poetry in English> To which is annexed a Refreshment for the Memory of William Cobbet by Samuel F. Bradford—
note: The *National Union Catalog* gives the author of this book as Samuel Fisher Bradford, 1776–1837.

Title Page Deposit
author: *TIMOTHY TICKLETOBY.*
title: THE/ *IMPOSTOR DETECTED,*/ OR/ A REVIEW/ OF/ *SOME OF THE WRITINGS*/ OF/ "PETER PORCUPINE."/ <short thick rule>/ <author statement>/ <short thick rule>/ <two lines of poetry in English>/ <thick rule>/ TO WHICH IS ANNEXED/ *A REFRESHMENT FOR THE MEMORY OF*/ William Cobbet,/ BY/ SAMUEL F. BRADFORD./ <double rule>
imprint: <below double rule> PHILADELPHIA:/ FROM THE FREE AND INDEPENDENT/ *POLITICAL & LITERARY*/ *PRESS* OF/ THOMAS BRADFORD,/ *PRINTER, BOOKSELLER & STATIONER,*/ No. 8, South Front Street./ <short thick rule>/ 1796.
note: Six pages of an Address to the Reader are also deposited.

151.

District Court Ledger, 262 PA 119.
date of deposit: September 14, twenty-first year of Independence
claimant: A: Frederic Molineux
title: Plan of the Town of Erie on Lake Erie—
format: map

Title Page Deposit
title: *PLAN*/ of the Town of/ <script> Erie/ on LAKE *Erie.*
note: This deposit is a copy of the entire map and is located in the Geography and Map Division (call number: G3824.E8 1796 .M). The title page is engraved.

152

District Court Ledger, 262 PA 120
date of deposit: September 17, twenty-first year of Independence
claimant: P: M.L.E. Moreau de Saint Méry
author: James Quicksilver. Author of the Blue Shop.
title: The political Massacre or unexpected Observations on the Writings of our present Scribblers—<author statement>

Title Page Deposit
author: JAMES QUICKSILVER,/ AUTHOR OF THE BLUE SHOP.
title: THE/ POLITICAL MASSACRE,/ OR/ UNEXPECTED OBSERVATIONS/ ON THE/ WRITINGS OF OUR PRESENT/ SCRIBBLERS./ <thick rule>/ <author statement>/ <thick rule>/ <relief cut of a horn, harp, and book>
imprint: <below relief cut> PHILADELPHIA:/ Printed by MOREAU DE ST-MÉRY, No. 84, Corner of/ Front and Walnut Streets./ <thick rule>/ September 1796.

153.

District Court Ledger, 262 PA 121
date of deposit: September 17, twenty-first year of Independence
claimant: A: William Mitchell
title: A new and complete System of Book-Keeping by an improved Method of Double Entry adapted to Retail domestic and foreign Trade exhibiting a Variety of Trans-actions which usually occur in Business—The whole comprised in three Sets of Books the last Set being a Copy of the second according to those Systems most generally in Use is given in Order to exhibit by a comparative View the Advantages of the System now laid down To which is added a Table of the Duties payable on Goods Wares and Merchandise imported into the United States of America The whole in Dollars and Cents—<author statement>

Title Page Deposit
author: WILLIAM MITCHELL.
title: A/ NEW AND COMPLETE SYSTEM/ OF/ BOOK-KEEPING,/ BY AN IMPROVED METHOD/ OF/ DOUBLE ENTRY;/ ADAPTED TO/ RETAIL, DOMESTIC AND FOREIGN TRADE:/ EXHIBITING A VARIETY OF TRANSACTIONS/ WHICH USUALLY OCCUR IN BUSINESS./ THE WHOLE COMPRISED IN THREE SETS OF BOOKS;/ The last Set, being a copy of the Second according to those systems/ most generally in use, is given in order to exhibit, by a com-/ parative view, the advantages of the system now laid down./ TO WHICH IS ADDED,/ A TABLE OF THE DUTIES PAYABLE ON GOODS, WARES/ AND MERCHANDISE, IMPORTED INTO THE/ UNITED STATES OF AMERICA./ THE WHOLE IN DOLLARS AND CENTS./ <author statement>/ <double rule>
imprint: <below double rule> <black letter> Philadelphia,/ PRINTED BY BIOREN & MADAN./ 1796.

154.
District Court Ledger, 262 PA 122
date of deposit: September 24, twenty-first year of Independence
claimant: P: William Cobbett
author: Peter Porcupine—
title: The Political Censor or Review of the most interesting political Occurrences relative to the United States of America—<author statement>

Title Page Deposit
author: *PETER PORCUPINE.*
title: THE/ *POLITICAL*/ CENSOR;/ OR/ REVIEW/ OF THE/ *Most interesting Political Occurrences,*/ RELATIVE TO/ *THE UNITED STATES*/ OF/ *AMERICA.*/ <double rule>/ <author statement>/ <double rule>
imprint: <below double rule> *PHILADELPHIA:*/ PRINTED FOR, AND SOLD BY, WILLIAM COBBETT, NORTH/ SECOND STREET, OPPOSITE CHRIST CHURCH./ M.DCC.XCVI.

155.
District Court Ledger, 262 PA 123
date of deposit: September 26, twenty-first year of Independence
claimant: A: Abraham Bradley
author: . . . jun
title: Map of the United States exhibiting the Post-Roads the Situations Connections and Distances of the Post-Offices Stage Roads Counties Ports of Entry and Delivery for foreign Vessels and the Principal Rivers—<author statement>
format: map

Title Page Deposit
author: <script> Abraham Bradley junr
title: <bottom of page> <script> Map/ of the/ <script> United States,/ *Exhibiting the*/ POST-ROADS, the situations, connections & distances of the POST-OFFICES/ *Stage Roads, Counties, Ports of Entry and*/ Delivery for Foreign Vessels, and the Principal Rivers./ <author statement>
note: This deposit is a copy of part of the map and is located in the Geography and Map Division (call number: G3700 1796.B).

156.
District Court Ledger, 262 PA 123
date of deposit: September 29, twenty-first year of Independence
claimant: P: M.L.E. Moreau de Saint Méry
title: Idée Générale au Abrigé des Sciences et des Arts à l'Usage de la Jeunesse—Publié par M.L.E. Moreau De Saint-Mery.

Title Page Deposit
title: IDÉE GÉNÉRALE/ OU/ ABRÉGE/ DES/ SCIENCES ET DES ARTS/ A L'USAGE DE LA JEUNESSE./ Publié par M.L.É. MOREAU/ DE SAINT-MÉRY./ <relief cut of horn, harp, and book>
imprint: <below relief cut> A PHILADELPHIE:/ Imprimé par l'EDITEUR, Libraire-Impri-/ meur au coin de Front & de Walnut/ Streets, No. 84./ <thick rule>/ Octobre 1796.

157.
District Court Ledger, 262 PA 124
date of deposit: September 30, twenty-first year of Independence
claimant: P: Matthew Carey
author: St. George Tucker Professor of Law in the University of William and Mary and one of the Judges of the general Court in Virginia
title: A Dissertation on Slavery with a Proposal for the gradual Abolition of it in the State of Virginia—<author statement> <quotation in English>

Title Page Deposit
author: ST. GEORGE TUCKER,/ *PROFESSOR OF LAW IN THE UNIVERSITY OF WILLIAM*/

AND MARY, AND ONE OF THE JUDGES OF THE/ GENERAL COURT, IN VIRGINIA.
title: <torn, first letter supplied> A/ DISSERTATION/ ON/ *SLAVERY:*/ WITH/ A PROPOSAL/ FOR THE/ GRADUAL ABOLITION OF IT,/ IN THE/ *STATE OF VIRGINIA.*/ <thick rule>/ <author statement>/ <thick rule>/ <quotation in English>/ <thick rule>
imprint: <below thick rule> PHILADELPHIA:/ PRINTED FOR MATHEW CAREY,/ NO. 118, MARKET-STREET./ <short rule>/ 1796.

158.
District Court Ledger, 262 PA 125
date of deposit: September 30, twenty-first year of Independence
claimant: P: Matthew Carey
title: Plat of the seven Ranges of Townships being Part of the Territory of the United States N. W. of the River Ohio which by a late Act of Congress are directed to be sold—
format: map

Title Page Deposit
title: *PLAT*/ <script> of/ THE SEVEN RANGES OF TOWNSHIPS/ <script> being Part of the/ <first through third, sixth, and seventh words in script> Territory of the *UNITED STATES N. W.* of the/ River Ohio/ <script> Which by a late act of Congress are directed to be sold.
imprint: <at the bottom of the page below border> <script> Published by Matthew Carey No. 118 Market Street Philada.
note: This deposit is a copy of the entire map and is located in the Geography and Map Division (call number: G4082.S4B3 1796.H). The title page is engraved.

159.
District Court Ledger, 262 PA 126
date of deposit: October 3, twenty-first year of Independence
claimant: P: Thomas Bradford
author: Peter Grievous junr.—
title: A Congratulatory Epistle to the redoubtable "Peter Porcupine" on his "complete Triumph over the once towering but fallen and despicable Faction in the United States"—A poem <author statement> <two lines of poetry in English> To which is annexed the Vision a Dialogue between Marat and Peter Porcupine in the infernal Regions—

Title Page Deposit
author: *PETER GRIEVOUS,* JUNr.
title: A/ *Congratulatory Epistle*/ TO THE/ *REDOUBTABLE* "PETER PORCUPINE."/ ON HIS/ "COMPLETE TRIUMPH/ OVER THE/ Once towering but fallen and despicable faction,/ in the UNITED STATES:"/ A POEM,/ <thick rule>/ <author statement>/ <short thick rule>/ <two lines of poetry in English>/ <thick rule>/ TO WHICH IS ANNEXED/ THE VISION,/ *A DIALOGUE*/ Between MARAT and PETER PORCUPINE,/ in the Infernal Regions./ <double rule>
imprint: <below double rule> PHILADELPHIA:/ FROM THE FREE AND INDEPENDENT/ *POLITICAL & LITERARY*/ *PRESS* OF/ THOMAS BRADFORD,/ PRINTER, BOOKSELLER & STATIONER,/ No. 8, South Front Street./ <short thick rule>/ 1796.

160.
District Court Ledger, 262 PA 127
date of deposit: November 17, twenty-first year of Independence
claimant: P: Stacy Budd & Archibald Bartram
author: Thomas Say
compiler: his Son—<Benjamin Say>
title: A short Compilation of the extraordinary Life and Writings of Thomas Say in which is faithfully copied from the original Manuscript the uncommon Vision which he had when a young Man—<compiler statement>

Title Page Deposit
compiler: HIS SON. <Benjamin Say>
title: A SHORT/ COMPILATION/ OF THE EXTRAORDINARY/ LIFE AND WRITINGS/ OF/ THOMAS SAY;/ IN WHICH IS FAITHFULLY COPIED, FROM THE ORIGINAL/ MANUSCRIPT,/ THE/ UNCOMMON VISION,/ Which he had when a young Man./ <thick rule>/ <compiler statement>/ <thick rule>/
imprint: <below thick rule> PHILADELPHIA:/ PRINTED AND SOLD BY BUDD AND BARTRAM,/ NO. 58, NORTH SECOND STREET./ <short rule>/ 1796.
note: Ten pages of text are also deposited.

161.
District Court Ledger, 262 PA 128
date of deposit: November 18, twenty-first year of Independence
claimant: P: Benjamin Franklin Bache
author: Thomas Paine Author of the Works entitled Common Sense—Rights of Man—Age of Reason &c—

title: Letter to George Washington President of the United States of America on Affairs Public and Private—<author statement>

Title Page Deposit

author: THOMAS PAINE,/ AUTHOR OF THE WORKS ENTITLED, COMMON SENSE,/ RIGHTS OF MAN, AGE OF REASON, &c.

title: LETTER/ TO/ GEORGE WASHINGTON,/ *PRESIDENT OF THE UNITED STATES OF/ AMERICA.*/ ON/ *AFFAIRS PUBLIC AND PRIVATE.*/ <double rule>/ <author statement>/ <double rule>

imprint: <below double rule> *PHILADELPHIA:/* PRINTED BY BENJ. FRANKLIN BACHE, NO. 112 MAR-/ KET STREET./ 1796.

162.

District Court Ledger, 262 PA 129

date of deposit: November 24, twenty-first year of Independence

claimant: P: William Cobbett

author: Peter Porcupine—

title: History of the American Jacobins commonly denominated Democrats—<author statement> <quotation in English>

Title Page Deposit

author: PETER PORCUPINE.

title: HISTORY/ OF THE/ *AMERICAN JACOBINS,*/ COMMONLY DENOMINATED/ DEMOCRATS./ <thick rule>/ <author statement>/ <thick rule>/ <quotation in English>/ <decorative rule>

imprint: <below decorative rule> PHILADELPHIA:/ PRINTED FOR WILLIAM COBBETT, NORTH SECOND/ STREET, OPPOSITE CHRIST CHURCH./ <short rule>/ NOV. 1796.

163.

District Court Ledger, 262 PA 129

date of deposit: December 30, twenty-first year of Independence

claimant: P: Robert Campbell and Company

title: A new Method of keeping Bill-Books adapted for the Ease and Convenience of Merchants in general but particularily for those who are extensively concerned in Trade exhibiting at one View all the Bills which a Merchant may have to receive or pay in the Course of the whole Year for each Month seperately and thereby preventing the Trouble and Inconvenience attendant on the Mode now in Use of selecting the Bills due in each Month from the promiscuous Entries of several Months—To which is prefixed a Table shewing the Number of Days from any Day of any Month to the same Day in any other Month—

Title Page Deposit

title: <double rule>/ <entire title page in script> A New Method of Keeping Bill Books/ Adapted for the Ease and Convenience of Merchants in general./ <rule> But Particularly <rule>/ For those who are Extensively concerned in Trade/ Exhibiting at One View, all the Bills which a Merchant may have to receive, or pay, in the course of the whole year,/ for Each Month Seperately; And thereby preventing the trouble & inconvenience, attendant on the mode now in/ use of Selecting the Bills due in Each Month from the promiscuous Entries of Several Months./ <rule> <rule>/ To which is prefixed A Table, Shewing the number of days from any day of any Month,/ to the same day in any other month/ <table>

imprint: <below table> PHILADELPHIA/ *Printed For & Sold by/ Robert Campbell & Co./* 1797

note: The deposited title page is in ms.

1797

164.

District Court Ledger, 262 PA 131

date of deposit: January 3, twenty-first year of Independence

claimant: P: Joseph Hawkins

author: Joseph Hawkins of New-York who has since become blind and for whose Benefit it is now published by his Friends—

title: A History of a Voyage to the Coast of Africa and Travels into the Interior of that Country containing particular Descriptions of the Climate and Inhabitants and interesting Particulars concerning the Slave-Trade—<author statement>

Title Page Deposit

author: JOSEPH HAWKINS,/ OF NEW YORK,/ Who has since become Blind; and for whose benefit it is/ now published by his Friends.

title: A/ HISTORY/ OF A/ VOYAGE TO THE COAST OF/ *AFRICA,/* AND/ *Travels into the Interior of that/ Country;/* CONTAINING/ Particular descriptions of the Climate and Inhabitants,/ and interesting particulars concerning the/ SLAVE TRADE./ <short thick rule>/ <author statement>/ <double rule>

imprint: <below double rule> *PHILADELPHIA:/* PRINTED FOR THE AUTHOR,/ BY S. C USTICK, & CO./ 1797.

165.
District Court Ledger, 262 PA 132
date of deposit: January 11, twenty-first year of Independence
claimant: P: Francis Bailey
author: George Logan M. D.—
title: Fourteen Agricultural Experiments to ascertain the best Rotation of Crops addressed to the "Philadelphia Agricultural Society" <author statement>

Title Page Deposit
author: GEORGE LOGAN, *M.D.*
title: FOURTEEN/ Agricultural Experiements,/ TO/ ASCERTAIN/ THE/ BEST ROTATION/ OF/ CROPS:/ ADDRESSED/ TO THE/ *"Philadelphia Agricultural Society."*/ <author statement>/ <thick rule>
imprint: <below thick rule> *PHILADELPHIA:*/ PRINTED BY FRANCIS AND ROBERT BAILEY, AT YOR-/ ICK'S-HEAD, No. 116, HIGH-STREET./ <short double rule>/ M,DCC,XCVII.

166.
District Court Ledger, 262 PA 133
date of deposit: January 17, twenty-first year of Independence
claimant: P: Gotlob Jungman
title: Eine schöne Samlung der Neuesten Lieder zum Gesellschaftlichen Vergnugen

Title Page Deposit
title: <entire title page in Gothic script> Eine/ schöne/ Sammlung/ der/ Neuesten Lieder/ zum/ gesellschaftlichen Vergnügen./ <relief cut of a cherub>/ <decorative rule>
imprint: <below decorative rule> Reading,/ Gedruckt, bey Gottlob Jungmann und Comp.

167.
District Court Ledger, 262 PA 134
date of deposit: January 17, twenty-first year of Independence
claimant: P: Mathew Carey
author: Samuel Lewis
title: A Map of Part of the N. W. Territory of the United States compiled from actual Surveys and the best Information <author statement> 1796
format: map

Title Page Deposit
author: <script> Samuel Lewis
title: A MAP/ <script> of part of the/ N: W: TERRITORY/ of the/ *UNITED STATES:*/ <script> compiled/ from Actual Surveys, and the best Information,/ <author statement> 1796
note: This deposit is a copy of the entire map and is located in the Geography and Map Division (call number: G4070 1796 .L). The title page is engraved.

168.
District Court Ledger, 262 PA 135
date of deposit: January 19, twenty-first year of Independence
claimant: P: Bioren and Madan
title: The American Annual Register or historical Memoirs of the United States for the Year 1796

Title Page Deposit
title: THE/ *American Annual Register,*/ OR,/ HISTORICAL MEMOIRS/ OF THE/ *UNITED STATES,*/ FOR THE YEAR 1796./ <double rule>
imprint: <below double rule> *PHILADELPHIA:*/ PRINTED AND SOLD BY BIOREN & MADAN, NO. 77, DOCK-STREET./ <short double rule>/ January 19th, 1797.

169.
District Court Ledger, 262 PA 136
date of deposit: January 20, twenty-first year of Independence
claimant: P: Charles Cist
title: Sketches on Rotations of Crops and other rural Matters—To which are annexed Intimations on Manufactures—on the Fruits of Agriculture and on new Sources of Trade interfering with Products of the United States of America in foreign Markets—

Title Page Deposit
title: SKETCHES/ ON/ ROTATIONS/ OF/ *CROPS,*/ AND OTHER/ RURAL MATTERS./ TO WHICH ARE ANNEXED/ INTIMATIONS ON MANUFACTURES; ON THE/ FRUITS OF AGRICULTURE; AND ON NEW/ SOURCES OF TRADE, INTERFERING WITH/ PRODUCTS OF THE UNITED STATES OF/ AMERICA IN FOREIGN MARKETS./ <double rule>
imprint: <below double rule> *PHILADELPHIA:*/ PRINTED BY CHARLES CIST, NO. 104. NORTH/ SECOND-STREET, M,DCC,XCVI.

170.
District Court Ledger, 262 PA 136
date of deposit: January 20, twenty-first year of Independence

claimant: P: Charles Cist and John Markland
author: Richard Peters
title: Agricultural Enquiries on Plaister of Paris—Also Facts Observations and Conjectures on that Substance when applied as Manure—Collected chiefly from the Practice of Farmers in Pennsylvania and published as much with a View to invite as to give Information—<author statement>

Title Page Deposit
author: RICHARD PETERS.
title: *AGRICULTURAL ENQUIRIES/* ON/ PLAISTER OF PARIS./ ALSO,/ FACTS, OBSERVATIONS/ AND/ CONJECTURES ON THAT SUBTANCE,/ WHEN APPLIED AS MANURE./ Collected, chiefly from the practice of farmers in Pennsylvania, and/ published as much with a view to invite, as to give informa tion./ <decorative rule>/ <author statement>/ <decorative rule>/ <thick rule>
imprint: <below thick rule> *PHILADELPHIA:/* PRINTED BY CHARLES CIST, No. 104, NORTH SECOND STREET,/ AND/ JOHN MARKLAND, No. 91, SOUTH FRONT STREET./ <short rule>/ 1797.

171.
District Court Ledger, 262 PA 137
date of deposit: January 24, twenty-first year of Independence
claimant: P: John Thompson
author: William Smith of South Carolina L.L.D. and Member of the Congress of the United States—
title: A comparative View of the Constitutions of the several States with each other and with that of the United States exhibiting in Tables the prominent Features of each Constitution and classing together their most important Provisions under the several Heads of Administration with Notes and Observations—<author statement>

Title Page Deposit
author: *William Smith,* OF SOUTH CAROLINA, L.L.D./ AND MEMBER OF THE CONGRESS OF THE UNITED STATES.
title: A/ COMPARATIVE VIEW/ OF THE/ CON STITUTIONS/ OF THE/ SEVERAL *STATES* WITH EACH OTHER, AND WITH THAT/ OF THE *UNITED STATES:/* EXHIBITING IN/ TABLES/ *The prominent Features of each Constitu tion,/* AND CLASSING TOGETHER THEIR MOST IMPORTANT PROVISIONS UNDER THE/ SEVERAL HEADS OF ADMINISTRA TION;/ WITH/ Notes and Observations./ <double rule>/ <author statement>/ <double rule>/ <following words crossed out in ms.> *<Dedicated to the People of the United States.>/* <double rule>
imprint: <imprint crossed out in ms.> <below double rule> *Philadelphia,/* PRINTED BY JOHN THOMPSON, AND SOLD BY ALL THE BOOKSELLERS/ IN THE UNITED STATES./ <short rule>/ 1796.
note: A dedication is also deposited.

172.
District Court Ledger, 262 PA 138
date of deposit: February 17, twenty-first year of Independence
claimant: A: Robert Proud
title: The History of Pennsylvania in North America from the original Institution and Settlement of that Province under the first Proprietor and Governor William Penn in 1681. 'till after the Year 1742—with an Introduction respecting the Life of W. Penn prior to the Grant of that Provence and the religious Society of the People called Quakers with the first Rise of the neighbouring Colonies more particularly of West-New-Jersey and the Settlement of the Dutch and Swedes on Delaware—To which is added a Brief Description of the said Province and of the general State in which it flourished principally between the Years 1760 and 1770. the whole including a Variety of Things useful and interesting to be known respecting that Country in early Time &c—With an Appendix—Written principally between the Years 1776 and 1780. <author statement> <two quotations in Latin>

Title Page Deposit
author: *ROBERT PROUD.*
title: THE/ History of Pennsylvania,/ IN/ *NORTH AMERICA,/* FROM/ The original Institution and Settlement of that Province,/ UNDER THE/ *First Proprietor and Governor* WILLIAM PENN,/ In 1681, till after the Year 1742;/ WITH AN/ INTRODUCTION,/ RESPECTING,/ The Life of W. PENN, prior to the grant of that Province, and/ the religious Society of the People called QUAKERS;/ WITH THE/ First Rise of the neighbouring Colonies,/ MORE PARTICU LARLY OF/ *West-New-Jersey,* and the Settlement of the *Dutch/* and *Swedes* on *Delaware./* TO WHICH IS ADDED,/ A brief Description of the said Province,/ AND OF THE/ General State, in which it flourished, principally between the Years 1760 and 1770./ The whole including a Variety of

Things,/ Useful and interesting to be known, respecting that Country in early Time, &c./ With an APPENDIX./ <rule>/ Written principally between the Years 1776 and 1780,/ <author statement>/ <rule>/ <two quotations in Latin>

173.

District Court Ledger, 262 PA 140

date of deposit: February 21, twenty-first year of Independence

claimant: A: Samuel Relf

title: Infidelity or the Victims of Sentiment—A Novel in a Series of Letters—<quotation in English>

Title Page Deposit

title: INFIDELITY,/ OR THE/ VICTIMS OF SENTIMENT./ A NOVEL,/ IN A SERIES OF LETTERS./ <thick rule>/ <quotation in English>/ <short thick rule>

imprint: <below short thick rule> PHILADELPHIA:/ PRINTED BY W. W. WOODWARD, No. 17,/ CHESNUT-STREET./ <short rule>/ 1797.

note: The ledger entry states that Samuel Relf is the author, and the clerk's note on the verso of the title page indicates that he is both author and proprietor.

174.

District Court Ledger, 262 PA 141

date of deposit: March 1, twenty-first year of Independence

claimant: A: C. C. Tanguy de la Boissiere

translator: Samuel Chandler—

title: Observations on the Dispatch written the 16th January 1797 by Mr. Pickering Secretary of State of the United States of America to Mr. Pinkney Minister Plenipotentiary of the United States near the French Republic—<author statement> Translated from the French <translator statement>

Title Page Deposit

author: C. C. TANGUY DE LA BOISSIÈRE.

translator: SAMUEL CHANDLER.

title: OBSERVATIONS/ ON THE DISPATCH/ WRITTEN THE 16th. JANUARY 1797,/ *By Mr. PICKERING, Secratary of State of the/ United States of America,/* To Mr. PINKNEY, Minister Plenipotentiary of/ the United Sates near the French Republic./ <double rule>/ <author statement>/ <double rule>/ TRANSLATED FROM THE FRENCH/ <translator statement>/ <relief cut of horn, harp, and book>

imprint: <below relief cut> PHILADELPHIA:/ Printed and sold by MOREAU DE SAINT-MERY, Book-seller/ and Printer, corner of Front and Walnut Streets/ <short double rule>/ 1797.

175.

District Court Ledger, 262 PA 142

date of deposit: March 6, twenty-first year of Independence

claimant: A: Thomas Dobson

title: First Lessons for Children—

Title Page Deposit

title: First/ *LESSONS/* FOR/ Children./ <short thick rule>

imprint: <below short thick rule> PHILADELPHIA;/ Printed by T. Dobson, No. 41. So./ Second Street./ 1797.

176.

District Court Ledger, 262 PA 143

date of deposit: March 6, twenty-first year of Independence

claimant: A: Thomas Dobson

title: First Lessons for Children—Volume second—

Title Page Deposit

title: First/ *LESSONS/* FOR/ Children./ <short broken double rule>/ *Volume Second./* <thick rule>

imprint: <below thick rule> PHILADELPHIA;/ Printed by T. Dobson, No. 41. So./ Second Street./ 1797.

177.

District Court Ledger, 262 PA 144

date of deposit: March 16, twenty-first year of Independence

claimant: A: Charles Wilson Peale

author: . . . .Proprietor of the Museums in Philadelphia—

title: An Essay on building wooden Bridges—<author statement>

Title Page Deposit

author: CHARLES W. PEALE,/ *Proprietor of the Museum in Philadelphia.*

title: AN/ ESSAY/ ON BUILDING/ *WOODEN BRIDGES./* <author statement>/ <thick rule>

imprint: <below thick rule> *PHILADLEPHIA:/* PRINTED BY FRANCIS BAILEY, No. 116, HIGH-STREET,/ FOR THE AUTHOR—1797.

178.

District Court Ledger, 262 PA 145
date of deposit: March 23, twenty-first year of Independence
claimant: A: Thomas Dobson
title: The Holiday or Children's social Amusement

Title Page Deposit
title: THE/ HOLIDAY,/ OR/ *CHILDREN'S/ Social Amusement.* / <thick rule>
imprint: <below thick rule> PHILADELPHIA;/ Printed by T. Dobson, No. 41. So./ Second Street./ 1797./ <short rule>

179.

District Court Ledger, 262 PA 145
date of deposit: April 1, twenty-first year of Independence
claimant: A: Samuel Stanton
author: . . . Esq. an Officer (of twenty Years standing) in the British Army—Author of miscellaneous Letters on every Subject from the Prince to the Peasant—The Principles of Duelling—A Treatise on the Slave Trade—Sentiments and Information respecting the Slave Trade delivered in Writing to the British House of Commons and afterwards printed by Bell—Duelling explained from Philanthropic Motives—Two Elegiac Poems &c—
title: Answer to Thomas Paine's Letter to General Washington President of the United States on Affairs public and private—<author statement> The Character of the illustrious Washington is here justly defended from Motives of the strictest Honour viz. The Veneration and Respect the Author has ever had for George Washington—

Title Page Deposit
author: SAMUEL STANTON, Esq. / An Officer of (twenty years standing) in the British Army./ AUTHOR OF/ Miscellaneous Letters, on every Subject, from the Prince to the Peasant./ The Principles of Duelling - - - A Treatise on the Slave Trade./ Sentiments and information respec ting the Slave Trade, delivered in/ writing to the British House of Commous, and afterwards/ Printed by Bell./ Duelling explained from Philan thropic Motives./ Two Elegiac Poems, &c.
title: ANSWER/ TO/ THOMAS PAINE's LET TER/ TO/ *General Washington,* / PRESIDENT OF THE UNITED STATES, ON AFFAIRS PUBLIC/ AND PRIVATE./ <double rule>/ <author statement>/ <double rule>/ *The character of the illustrious Washington is here/ justly defended from motives of the strictest/ honour;* viz *The veneration and respect the/ Author has ever had for George Washingtou.* / <short double rule>
imprint: <below short double rule> Philadelphia,/ PRINTED FOR THE AUTHOR,/ 1797.

180.

District Court Ledger, 262 PA 147
date of deposit: May 19, twenty-first year of Independence
claimant: P: Solomon Myer
title: Die Wahre Brantwein Brennerey oder Brantwein Gin und Cordialmacher Kunst wie auch die ächte färbe Kunst wie man alle Couleuren auf Seide Leinen und Wolle färben kan

Title Page Deposit
title: <entire title page in Gothic script> Die/ Wahre/ Brantewein = Brennerey;/ oder,/ Brantwein = Gin = und Cordialmacher = / Kunst;/ wie auch/ die ächte Färbe = Kunst,/ Wie man alle Couleuren auf Seide,/ Leinen und Wolle, färben kan./ <thick rule>
imprint: <below thick rule> York:/ Gedruckt bey Salomon Mäyer,/ 1797.
note: The clerk's note on the back of the title page states that Col. T. Hartley deposited the title page for Solomon Myer.

181.

District Court Ledger, 262 PA 148
date of deposit: May 20, twenty-first year of Independence
claimant: A: Thomas Dobson
title: Pleasing Instructions for young Minds—

Title Page Deposit
title: Pleasing/ INSTRUCTIONS/ FOR/ *YOUNG MINDS.* / <thick rule>
imprint: <below thick rule> PHILADELPHIA;/ Printed by T. Dobson, No. 41. So./ Second Street./ 1797./ <short rule>
note: [Copy Right Secured.]

182.

District Court Ledger, 262 PA 148
date of deposit: June 1, twenty-first year of Independence
claimant: P: Benjamin Davies
author: Peter Porcupine
title: Die Blut Fahne, ausgestecket zur Warnung der politischen Wegweiser in America, oder Eine getreue Erzählung einer grossen Anzahl Handlungen der abscheulichsten Grausamkeit solche als nie ein Auge gesehen, nie eine Zunge ausgesprochen, oder die Einbildungskraft gedacht

hat vor dem Anfang der Französischen Revolution, welchem beÿgefügt ist, Ein unterrichtender Versuch, welcher diesen schrecklichen Thatsachen bis auf ihren wahren Ursprung nachforschet, Ausgeziert mit vier treffenden Kupferstichen <author statement>

183.

District Court Ledger, 262 PA 149

date of deposit: June 13, twenty-first year of Independence

claimant: P: André Everard Van Braam Houckgeest

author: Le tout tiré du Journal d'André Everard Van Braam Houckgeest Chef de la Direction de la Compagnie des Indes Orientales Hollandaises à la Chine & Second dans cette Ambassade ancien Directeur de la Société des Sciences & Arts de Harlem en Hollande de la Société Philosophique de Philadelphie etc. etc.—Et orné de Cartes & de Gravures Publié en Francais par M. L. E. Moreau de St. Méry—

title: Voyage de l'Ambassade de la Compagnie des Indes Orientales Hollandaises vers l'Empereur de la Chine dans les Années 1794 & 1795. où se trouve la Description des plusieurs Parties de la Chine inconnues aux Européens & que cette Ambassade à donné l'Occasion de traverser— <author statement> Tome premier—

Title Page Deposit

author: LE tout tiré du Journal d'ANDRÉ EVERARD VAN BRAAM HOUCKGEEST,/ Chef de la Direction de la Compagnie des Indes Orientales Hollandaises à/ la Chine, & Second dans cette Ambassade; ancien Directeur de la Société/ des Sciences & Arts de Harlem en Hollande; de la Société Philosophique/ de Philadelphie, &c.&c.

title: VOYAGE/ DE L'AMBASSADE/ DE LA/ COMPAGNIE DES INDES/ ORIENTALES HOLLANDAISES,/ VERS L'EMPEREUR DE LA CHINE,/ DANS LES ANNÉES 1794 & 1795:/ Où se trouve la description de plusieurs parties de la Chine/ inconnues aux Européens, & que cette Ambassade à/ donné l'occasion de traverser:/ <author statement>/ Et orné de Cartes & de Gravures./ <double rule>/ *Publié en Français par M.L.E. MOREAU DE SAINT-MÉRY.*/ <double rule>/ TOME PREMIER./ <decorative thick rule>

imprint: <below decorative thick rule> A PHILADELPHIE; <printed to the left of the following three lines> Et se trouve chez . . . / <decorative bracket>/ L'ÉDITEUR, Imprimeur-Libraire au coin de la première rue Sud & de Walnut, No. 84./ Les Principaux Libraires des États-Unis d'Amérique./ Les Libraires des principales Villes d'Europe./ <thick rule>/ 1797.

184.

District Court Ledger, 262 PA 150

date of deposit: June 15, twenty-first year of Independence

claimant: A: James Woodhouse

author: . . . M. D. Professor of Chemistry in the University of Pennsylvania, President of the Chemical Society of Philadelphia &c—

title: The Young Chemist's Pocket Companion being a Description of a portable Laboratory in which are contained a philosophic Apparatus and a great Variety of chemical Agents by which any Person may perform on endless Variety of amusing and instructing Experiments designed for the Use of Ladies and Gentlemen and intended to promote the Cultivations of the Science of Chemistry in the United States of America—<author statement> <quotation in English>

Title Page Deposit

author: JAMES WOODHOUSE, M.D./ *Professor of Chemistry in the University of Pennsylvania, Pre-/ sident of the Chemical Society of Philadelphia, &c.*

title: THE/ *Young Chemist's Pocket Companion;*/ BEING/ A DESCRIPTION/ OF/ <black letter> A Portable Laboratory;/ IN WHICH ARE CON TAINED/ A PHILOSOPHIC APPARATUS,/ AND A GREAT VARIETY OF/ CHEMICAL AGENTS;/ BY WHICH ANY PERSON MAY PERFORM AN ENDLESS/ VARIETY OF AMUSING AND INSTRUCTING/ EXPERIMENTS;/ <sixth word has been crossed out in ms.> DESIGNED FOR THE USE OF <PHILOSOPHIC> LADIES/ AND GENTLEMEN,/ AND INTENDED TO PROMOTE THE CULTIVATION OF/ THE SCIENCE OF CHEMISTRY IN THE/ UNITED STATES OF AMERICA./ <short double rule>/ <author statement>/ <short double rule>/ <quotation in English>

note: There is no imprint on the title page.

185.

District Court Ledger, 262 PA 152

date of deposit: June 16, twenty-first year of Independence

claimant: A: Benjamin Smith Barton

author: . . . M. D. Correspondent-Member of the Society of the Antiquaries of Scotland Member of the American Philosophical Society Fellow of the American Academy of Arts and Sciences of Boston corresponding Member of the Massachusetts historical Society and Professor of Materia Medica Natural History and Botany in the University of Pennsylvania—
title: New Views of the Origin of the Tribes & Nations of America—<author statement>

Title Page Deposit
author: BENJAMIN SMITH BARTON, M. D./ CORRESPONDENT-MEMBER OF THE SOCIETY OF THE ANTIQUARIES/ OF SCOTLAND; MEMBER OF THE AMERICAN PHILOSOPHICAL/ <The punctuation after "SOCIETY" has been crossed out in ms.; a semicolon has been inserted in ms. as a replacement for the deleted mark.> SOCIETY; FELLOW OF THE AMERICAN ACADEMY OF/ ARTS AND SCIENCES OF BOSTON; CORRESPONDING/ MEMBER OF THE MASSACHUSETTS HIS-/ TORICAL SOCIETY,/ AND PROFESSOR OF MATERIA MEDICA, NATURAL HISTORY/ AND BOTANY/ IN THE/ *UNIVERSITY OF PENNSYLVANIA.*
title: <"VIEWS" has been divided between "E" and "W" by a pen line, and "nearer" is written in ms. above the "w."> NEW VIEWS/ OF THE/ *ORIGIN*/ OF THE/ TRIBES AND NATIONS/ OF/ AMERICA./ <short double rule>/ <author statement>/ <double rule>
imprint: <below double rule> *PHILADELPHIA:*/ PRINTED, FOR THE AUTHOR,/ BY JOHN BIOREN./ 1797.

186.

District Court Ledger, 262 PA 153
date of deposit: June 23, twenty-first year of Independence
claimant: P: Benjamin Franklin Bache
title: Remarks occasioned by the late Conduct of Mr. Washington as President of the United States—M,DCC,XCVI.

Title Page Deposit
title: REMARKS/ OCCASIONED BY THE LATE CONDUCT/ OF/ MR. WASHINGTON,/ AS/ *PRESIDENT OF THE UNITED STATES.*/ <short double rule>/ M.DCC.XCVI./ <double rule>
imprint: <below double rule> PHILADELPHIA:/ *PRINTED FOR BENJAMIN FRANKLIN BACHE,*/ No. 112, MARKET-STREET./ 1797./ <short broken rule>
note: <below short broken rule> [COPY-RIGHT SECURED ACCORDING TO LAW.]

187.

District Court Ledger, 262 PA 154
date of deposit: June 24, twenty-first year of Independence
claimant: P: Snowdon and Mc.Corkle
title: The History of the United States for 1796—including a Variety of interesting Particulars relative to the federal Government previous to that Period—

Title Page Deposit
title: THE/ HISTORY/ OF THE/ UNITED STATES/ FOR 1796,/ INCLUDING A VARIETY OF/ INTERESTING PARTICULARS/ RELATIVE TO THE/ FEDERAL GOVERNMENT/ PREVIOUS TO THAT PERIOD./ <thick rule>
imprint: <below thick rule> PHILADELPHIA:/ FROM THE PRESS OF *SNOWDEN & M'CORKLE,*/ NO. 47, NORTH FOURTH-STREET./ <short rule>/ 1797.

188.

District Court Ledger, 262 PA 154
date of deposit: June 24, twenty-first year of Independence
claimant: P: Thomas Bradford
author: Addressed by Robert Goodloe Harper of South Carolina to his Constituents in May 1797—
title: Observations on the Dispute between the United States and France—<author statement>

Title Page Deposit
author: ROBERT GOODLOE HARPER, OF SOUTH CAROLINA,
title: OBSERVATIONS/ ON THE/ DISPUTE/ BETWEEN THE/ <black letter> United States and France,/ *ADDRESSED*/ <double rule>/ <author statement>/ <double rule>/ TO HIS/ *CONSTITUENTS,*/ IN MAY, 1797.
imprint: <below double rule> PHILADELPHIA:/ PRINTED & SOLD BY THOMAS BRAD FORD,/ *BOOK-SELLER & STATIONER,*/ No. 8,/ *South Front-Street.*/ <short double rule>/ 1797.

189.

District Court Ledger, 262 PA 155
date of deposit: July 26, twenty-second year of Independence

claimant: P: John Fenno
author: Written by himself—<Alexander Hamilton>
title: Observations on certain Documents contained in No. V & VI of "The History of the United States for the Year 1796" in which the Charge of Speculation against Alexander Hamilton late Secretary of the Treasury is fully refuted—<author statement>

Title Page Deposit
author: WRITTEN BY HIMSELF. <Alexander Hamilton>
title: OBSERVATIONS/ ON/ CERTAIN DOCUMENTS/ CONTAINED IN NO. V & VI OF/ "THE HISTORY OF THE UNITED STATES/ FOR THE YEAR 1796,"/ IN WHICH THE/ *CHARGE OF SPECULATION*/ AGAINST/ ALEXANDER HAMILTON,/ LATE SECRETARY OF THE TREASURY,/ IS FULLY REFUTED./ <author statement>/ <thick rule>
imprint: <below thick rule> PHILADELPHIA:/ PRINTED FOR JOHN FENNO, BY JOHN BIOREN./ 1797.

190.
District Court Ledger, 262 PA 156
date of deposit: August 7, twenty-second year of Independence
claimant: P: William Hendel
title: Das neue und Verbesserte Gesang Buch worinnen die Psalmen Davids Samt einer Sammlung alter und neuer Geistreicher Lieder sowohl für Privat und Haussandachten, als auch für den offentlichen Gottesdienst enthalten sind nebst einem anhang des Heÿdelbergischen Catechismus Wie auch Erbaulicher Gebäten nach einem Sÿnodal Schluss zusammen getragen und eingerichtet vor die Evangelisch Reformirten Gemeinen in den Vereinigten Staaten von America—

Title Page Deposit
title: <entire title page in Gothic script> Das/ Neue und Verbesserte/ Gesang=Buch,/ worinnen die/ Psalmen Davids/ Samt einer Sammlung/ alter und neuer/ Geistreicher Lieder/ sowohl für privat und Haussandachten, als auch für/ den öffent lichen Gottesdienst enthalten sind./ Nebst einem Anhang des/ Heydelbergischen Catechismus,/ wie auch/ Erbaulicher Gebäter./ <short thick rule>/ Nach einem Synodal Schluss zusammen=/ getragen und eingerichtet/ vor die/ Evange lisch=Reformirten Gemeinen/ in den Vereinigten Staaten von America./ <double rule>
imprint: <below double rule> Philadelphia:/ Gedruckt bey Steiner und Kämmerer,/ und H. Kämmerer, jun./ 1797.
note: In a note at the bottom of the title page, written in a hand different from that of the clerk, William Hendel's title is given as "President of the Synod of the German Reformed Congregations in the U. S. of America." On the verso of the title page, the clerk's note states that Hendel has deposited the title page as proprietor "for the Use and on the Behalf of the Synod of the German Reformed Congregations."

191.
District Court Ledger, 262 PA 157
date of deposit: August 7, twenty-second year of Independence
claimant: P: Hogan and Mc.Elroy
author: James Wilson Stevens—
title: An historical and geographical Account of Algiers comprehending a novel and interesting Detail of Events relative to the American Captives—<author statement>

Title Page Deposit
author: *JAMES WILSON STEVENS.*
title: AN/ HISTORICAL AND GEOGRAPHICAL/ ACCOUNT/ OF/ ALGIERS;/ COMPREHEND ING/ A NOVEL AND INTERESTING/ *DETAIL OF EVENTS*/ RELATIVE TO/ THE AMERICAN CAPTIVES./ <thick rule>/ <author statement>/ <thick rule>
imprint: <below thick rule> PHILADELPHIA:/ PRINTED BY *HOGAN & M'ELROY,* GEORGE-STREET/ THIRD DOOR BELOW SOUTH-STREET./ August, 1797.

192.
District Court Ledger, 262 PA 158
date of deposit: August 30, twenty-second year of Independence
claimant: P: Richard Folwell
author: William Buchan M. D. Fellow of the Royal College of Physicians Edinburgh—
adaptor: Isaac Cathrall—
title: Domestic Medicine or a Treatise on the Prevention and Cure of Diseases by Regimen and simple Medicines With an Appendix containing a Dispensatory for the Use of private Practitioners—<author statement> Adapted to the Climate and Diseases of America <adaptor statement>

Title Page Deposit
author: WILLIAM BUCHAN, M.D./ FELLOW OF THE ROYAL COLLEGE OF PHYSICIANS,/ EDINBURGH.
adaptor: ISAAC CATHRALL.
title: DOMESTIC MEDICINE:/ OR, A/ TREATISE/ ON THE/ PREVENTION AND CURE/ OF/ *DISEASES,*/ BY REGIMEN AND SIMPLE MEDICINES:/ WITH/ AN APPEN DIX,/ *CONTAINING A DISPENSATORY FOR THE USE OF/ PRIVATE PRACTITIONERS.*/ <thick rule>/ <author statement>/ <short thick rule>/ *ADAPTED TO THE/* Climate and Diseases of America,/ <adaptor statement>/ <thick rule>
imprint: <below thick rule> PHILADELPHIA:/ *PRINTED BY RICHARD FOLWELL.*/ <short rule>/ 1797.
note: A preface and five pages of a Table of Contents are also deposited.

193.

District Court Ledger, 262 PA 159
date of deposit: November 9, twenty-second year of Independence
claimant: A: P. R. Wouves
title: A Syllabical and Steganographical Table—

Title Page Deposit
title: A/ SYLLABICAL/ AND/ *STEGANOGRAPHICAL/* TABLE./ <double rule>/ *ENTERED ACCORDING TO LAW.*/ <double rule>
second title: TABLEAU/ SYLLABIQUE/ ET/ *STÉGANOGRAPHIQUE.*/ <double rule>/ *Enregistré conformément à la loi.*/ <double rule>
imprint: <below double rule> *PHILADELPHIA:/ PRINTED* by BENJAMIN FRANKLIN BACHE, No. 112, Market-street.
second imprint: <below double rule> *PHILADELPHIE:*/ De l'imprimerie de BENJAMIN FRANKLIN BACHE, No. 112, rue de Marché <A period is inserted in ms.>
note: Parallel title pages and sections of text of this bilingual edition are deposited on a full printer's sheet. The sections of text are heavily annotated with proofreader's marks.

194.

District Court Ledger, 262 PA 160(a)
date of deposit: November 13, twenty-second year of Independence
claimant: P: Matthew Carey
author: by a Philadelphian
title: The Age of Error or a Poetical Essay on the course of Human Action <author statement> <quotation in Latin>

Title Page Deposit
author: BY A PHILADELPHIAN.
title: THE/ AGE OF ERROR,/ OR A/ POETICAL ESSAY/ ON THE/ *COURSE/* OF/ HUMAN ACTION./ <author statement>/ <quotation in Latin>
imprint: <below quotation> <first word in black letter> Philadelphia: PRINTED FOR THE AUTHOR./ <short dotted rule>/ 1797.

195.

District Court Ledger, 262 PA 160(a)
date of deposit: November 30, twenty-second year of Independence
claimant: P: M. L. E. Moreau de Saint-Mery
translator: Michael Fortune—
title: General View or Abstract of the Arts and Sciences adapted to the Capacity of Youth—Published by M. L. E. Moreau de Saint-Mery and translated from the French <translator statement> <quotation in Latin>

Title Page Deposit
translator: MICHAEL FORTUNE.
title: GENERAL VIEW/ OR/ ABSTRACT/ OF/ THE ARTS AND SCIENCES,/ ADAPTED TO THE CAPACITY OF/ YOUTH./ Published by M. L. E. MOREAU DE SAINT-/MERY;/ *And translated from the French by/* <translator statement>/ <rule>/ <quotation in Latin>/ <two ornaments>
imprint: <below two ornaments> *PHILADELPHIA:*/ Printed by the Editor, Printer, at the Corner of/ Front and Callow-Hill street./ <double rule>/ October 1797.
note: Two pages of an advertisement are also deposited.

196.

District Court Ledger, 262 PA 160(a)
date of deposit: December 21, twenty-second year of Independence
claimant: P: Benjamin Franklin Bache
author: James Monroe late Minister Plenipotentiary to the said Republic.
title: A View of the Conduct of the Executive in the foreign Affairs of the United States connected with the Mission to the French Republic during the Years 1794, 5, &6. <author statement> Illustrated by his Instructions and Correspondence and other authentic Documents—

Title Page Deposit

author: *James Monroe,/ Late Minister Plenipotentiary to the said Republic:*

title: A/ VIEW/ OF THE/ Conduct of the Executive,/ IN THE/ FOREIGN AFFAIRS/ OF THE/ *United States,*/ CONNECTED WITH THE MISSION TO THE/ *FRENCH REPUBLIC,*/ DURING THE YEARS 1794, 5, & 6./ <short thick rule>/ <author statement>/ <short thick rule>/ ILLUSTRATED BY HIS/ Instructions and Correspondence/ AND OTHER/ AUTHEN TIC DOCUMENTS./ <double rule>/ COPY RIGHT SECURED ACCORDING TO LAW./ <double rule>

imprint: <below double rule> *PHILADELPHIA:*/ Printed by and for BENJ. FRANKLIN BACHE, and to be had at the/ Office of the AURORA, No. 112, Market-street,/ M,DCCXCVII.

note: An advertisement, a list of errors, and two pages of text are also deposited.

1798

197.

District Court Ledger, 262 PA 160(b)

date of deposit: January 4, twenty-second year of Independence

claimant: P: Thomas Dobson

title: Encyclopaedia or a Dictionary of Arts Sciences and miscellaneous Literature constructed on a Plan by which the different Sciences and Arts are digested into the Form of distinct Treatises or Systems comprehending the History Theory and Practice of each according to the latest Discoveries and Improvements and full Explanations given of the various detached Parts of knowledge whether relating to natural and artificial Objects or to Matters ecclesiastical civil military commercial &c—including Elucidation, of the most important Topics relative to Religion Morals Manners and the Oeconomy of Life—together with a Description of all the Countries Cities principal Mountains Seas Rivers &c throughout the World—a general History ancient and modern of the different Empires Kingdoms and States and an Account of the Lives of the most eminent Persons in every Nation from the earliest Ages down to the present Times—Compiled from the Writings of the best Authors in several Languages—the most approved Dictionaries as well of general Science as of its particular Branches—the Transactions Journals and Memoirs of various learned Societies—the MS. Lectures of eminent Professors on different Sciences—and a Variety of original Materials furnished by an extensive Correspondence—The first American Edition in eighteen Volumes greatly improved—Illustrated with five hundred and forty two Copper-Plates. <quotation in Latin>

Title Page Deposit

title: *ENCYCLOPAEDIA;* / OR, A/ DICTIONARY/ OF/ ARTS, SCIENCES,/ AND/ MISCELLA NEOUS LITERATURE;/ Constructed on a PLAN,/ BY WHICH/ THE DIFFERENT SCIENCES AND ARTS/ Are digested into the FORM of Distinct/ TREATISES OR SYSTEMS,/ COMPREHENDING/ THE HISTORY, THEORY, and PRACTICE, of each,/ According to the Latest Discoveries and Improvements;/ <. . .>/ <rule>/ Compiled from the writings of the best Authors, in several languages; the most approved Dictionaries, as well of general science as of its/ particular branches; the Transactions, Journals, and Memoirs, of various Learned Societies, the MS. Lectures of Eminent/ Professors on different sciences; and a variety of Original Materials, furnished by an Extensive Correspondence./ <rule>/ *THE FIRST AMERICAN EDITION, IN EIGHTEEN VOLUMES, GREATLY IMPROVED.*/ <thick rule>/ ILLUSTRATED WITH FIVE HUNDRED AND FORTY-TWO COPPERPLATES./ <rule>/ <double rule>/ <quotation in Latin>/ <double rule>

imprint: <below double rule> *PHILADELPHIA:*/ PRINTED BY THOMAS DOBSON, AT THE STONE HOUSE, No 41, SOUTH SECOND STREET./ M.DCC.XCVIII.

note: [*Copy-Right secured according to law.*]

198.

District Court Ledger, 262 PA 162

date of deposit: January 4, twenty-second year of Independence

claimant: A: Richard Folwell

title: Short History of the Yellow Fever that broke out in the City of Philadelphia in July 1797—with a List of the Dead—of the Donations for the Relief of the Poor and a Variety of other interesting Particulars—

Title Page Deposit

title: SHORT HISTORY/ OF THE/ YELLOW FEVER,/ THAT BROKE OUT/ IN THE/ *CITY OF PHILADELPHIA,*/ IN JULY, 1797:/ WITH/ A LIST OF THE DEAD;/ OF THE/ *DONATIONS FOR THE RELIEF OF THE POOR,*/ AND A/ VARIETY OF OTHER INTERESTING PARTICULARS./ <thick rule>

imprint: <below thick rule> *PHILADELPHIA:/* PRINTED BY RICHARD FOLWELL,/ No. 33, Carter's-Alley./ <short thick rule>/ M.DCCXCVII.
note: Six pages of text are also deposited.

199.
District Court Ledger, 262 PA 163
date of deposit: January 12, twenty-second year of Independence
claimant: P: Thomas and Samuel F. Bradford
author: Benjamin Rush—M.D. and Professor of the Institutes of Medicine and Clinical Practice in the University of Pennsylvania—
title: Essays literary moral and Philosophical <author statement>

Title Page Deposit
author: *BENJAMIN RUSH,* M.D./ <double rule>/ *AND PROFESSOR OF THE INSTITUTES OF MEDICINE/ AND CLINICAL PRACTICE/* IN THE/ University of Pennsylvania.
title: ESSAYS,/ <black letter> Literary, Moral & Philosophical/ <double rule>/ <author statement>/ <decorative thick rule>
imprint: <below decorative thick rule> <black letter> Philadelphia:/ *PRINTED BY THOMAS & SAMUEL F. BRADFORD,/* No. 8, *SOUTH FRONT STREET./* <dotted rule>/ 1798.

200.
District Court Ledger, 262 PA 164
date of deposit: January 16, twenty-second year of Independence
claimant: A: William Currie
author: . . . Fellow of the College of Physicians of Philadelphia &c.
title: Observations on the Causes and Cure of remitting or bilious Fevers. To which is annexed an Abstract of the Opinions and Practice of different Authors—and an Appendix exhibiting Facts and Reflections relative to the Synochus Icteroides or Yellow Fever—<author statement> <quotation in English>

Title Page Deposit
author: WILLIAM CURRIE,/ *Fellow of the College of Physicians of Philadelphia, &c.*
title: OBSERVATIONS/ ON THE/ CAUSES AND CURE/ OF/ *REMITTING/* OR/ BILIOUS FEVERS./ TO WHICH IS ANNEXED, AN/ ABSTRACT OF THE OPINIONS AND PRACTICE/ OF DIFFERENT AUTHORS;/ AND AN APPENDIX,/ EXHIBITING FACTS AND REFLECTIONS RELATIVE TO THE/ Synochus Icteroides, or Yellow Fever./ <double rule>/ <author statement>/<double rule>/ <quotation in English>/ <short double rule>
imprint: <below short double rule> PHILA DELPHIA:/ PRINTED FOR THE AUTHOR, BY WILLIAM T. PALMER,/ NO. 18, NORTH THIRD-STREET./ 1798
note: A two-page advertisement is also deposited.

201.
District Court Ledger, 262 PA 165
date of deposit: January 22, twenty-second year of Independence
claimant: A, P: Benjamin Carr
author: J. E. Harwood—
composer: Benjamin Carr—
title: Ellen arise a Ballad <author statement> <composer statement> as sung at the Philadelphia and New-York Theatres by Mrs. Oldmixon and Mrs. Hodgkinson—

Copy Deposit
author: <script> J. E. Harwood,
composer: <script> B. Carr
title: <script> Ellen Arise/ A BALLAD/ <author statement> <composer statement>/ As Sung at the PHILADELPHIA and NEW YORK THEATRES by/ <script> Mrs,, Oldmixon & Mrs,, Hodgkinson/ <short thick rule> Price 25 Cents <short thick rule>/ <imprint>
imprint: Printed and Sold at B: Carr's Musical Repository Philadelphia, J: Hewitt's New York and at J: Carr's Baltimore
note: The deposit copy is located in the Music Division.

202.
District Court Ledger, 262 PA 165
date of deposit: January 22, twenty-second year of Independence
claimant: A,P: Benjamin Carr
author: Mrs. Rowson—<Susanna Haswell Rowson>
composer: B. Carr—
title: The little Sailor Boy—a Ballad—sung at the Theatres and other public Places in Philadelphia Baltimore New-York &c by Messrs. J. Darley-Williamson Miss Broadhurst Mrs. Hodgkinson & Mrs. Oldmixon—<author statement> <composer statement>
note: According to the *National Index of American Imprints* the author is Susanna (Haswell) Rowson.

Copy Deposit
author: Mrs. ROWSON

composer: <script> B. Carr
title: <script> The little Sailor Boy/ A BALLAD/ Sung at the Theatres & other Public Places in Philadelphia, Baltimore, New York &c by/ <script> Messrs. J. Darley Williamson, Miss Broadhurst,/ <script> Mrs. Hodgkinson & Mrs. Oldmixon./ <author statement>/ <composer statement>/ <short thick rule> Price 25 Cents <short thick rule>
imprint: Printed and Sold at the Authors Musical Repository Philadelphia, J: Carrs Baltimore & J: Hewitts New York
note: This is the deposit copy and is located in the Music Division.

203.

District Court Ledger, 262 PA 166
date of deposit: February 8, twenty-second year of Independence
claimant: A: James Thomson Callender
title: Sketches of the History of America <author statement>

Title Page Deposit
author: JAMES THOMSON CALLENDER.
title: SKETCHES/ OF THE/ HISTORY/ OF/ AMERICA./ <double rule>/ <author statement>/ <double rule>/ [ENTERED ACCORD ING TO LAW.]/ <thick rule>
imprint: <below thick rule> PHILADELPHIA:/ FROM THE PRESS OF SNOWDEN & M'CORKLE, NO. 47,/ NORTH FOURTH-STREET./ 1798./ <short rule>
note: [Price ONE DOLLAR.]

204.

District Court Ledger, 262 PA 167
date of deposit: February 8, twenty-second year of Independence
claimant: A: Felix Pascalis Ouviere
author: . . . M.D. corresponding Member of the Medical Society of Connecticut and resident Member of the Philadelphia Academy of Medicine—
title: An Account of the contagious epidemic Yellow Fever which prevailed in Philadelphia in the Summer and Autumn of 1797. comprising the Questions of its Causes and domestic Origin—Characters—medical Treatment and Preventives—<author statement> <quotation in Latin>

Title Page Deposit
author: FELIX PASCALIS OUVIERE, M.D./ CORRESPONDING MEMBER OF THE MEDICAL SOCIETY OF/ CONNECTICUT, AND RESIDENT MEMBER OF THE/ PHILADEDPHIA ACADEMY OF/ MEDICINE.
title: AN/ ACCOUNT/ OF THE/ Contagious Epidemic Yellow Fever,/ WHICH PREVAILED IN/ PHILADELPHIA/ IN THE/ *SUMMER and AUTUMN of* 1797;/ COMPRISING/ *The questions of its causes and domestic origin, characters,/ medical treatment, and preventives./* <double rule>/ <author statement>/ <thick rule>/ <quotation in Latin>/ <thick rule>
imprint: <below thick rule> PHILADELPHIA:/ FROM THE PRESS OF SNOWDEN & M'CORKLE, NO. 47,/ NORTH FOURTH-STREET./ <short rule>/ 1798.

205.

District Court Ledger, 262 PA 168
date of deposit: March 12, twenty-second year of Independence
author: . . . M.D. one of the Honorary Members of the Society and Professor of Materia Medica natural History and Botany in the University of Pennsylvania—
title: Collections for an Essay towards a Materia Medica of the United States—Read before the Philadelphia Medical Society on the twenty first of February 1798.—<author statement> <two quotations in Latin>

Title Page Deposit
author: BENJAMIN SMITH BARTON, M.D./ ONE OF THE HONORARY MEMBERS OF THE SOCIETY,/ AND/ <three ms. lines surround first word; the meaning of the notation is unclear> PROFESSOR OF MATERIA MEDICA, NATURAL HISTORY, AND BOTANY,/ IN THE UNIVERSITY OF PENN SYLVANIA.
title: COLLECTIONS/ FOR/ AN ESSAY/ TOWARDS A/ MATERIA MEDICA/ OF THE/ UNITED-STATES./ *READ BEFORE THE PHILADELPHIA MEDICAL SOCIETY, ON THE/ TWENTY-FIRST OF FEBRUARY,* 1798./ <thick rule>/ <author statement>/ <double rule>/ <quotation in Latin>/ <double rule>/ <quotation in Latin>/ <short double rule>
imprint: <below short double rule> *PHILADEL PHIA:/* PRINTED, FOR THE AUTHOR,/ BY WAY & GROFF, No. 27, ARCH-STREET./ 1798.

206.

District Court Ledger, 262 PA 169
date of deposit: April 5, twenty-second year of Independence

claimant: P: T B Freeman
title: Thespian Oracle or Monthly Mirror consisting of Original Pieces and Selections from performances of merit relating chiefly to the most admired Dramatic Compositions and Interspersed with Theatrical Anecdotes Volume first No. 1—

Title Page Deposit
title: THESPIAN ORACLE,/ OR/ <black letter> Monthly Mirror,/ CONSISTING OF/ *ORIGINAL PIECES/ And Selections from performances of merit, relating chiefly to/ the most admired/* DRAMATIC COMPOSITIONS,/ AND INTERSPERSED WITH THEATRICAL ANECDOTES./ <double rule>/ VOLUME FIRST. No. I./ <double rule>
imprint: <below double rule> <black letter> Philadelphia:/ PRINTED FOR *T. B. FREEMAN,* No. 39, SOUTH FRONT/ STREET, OPPOSITE THE POST-OFFICE./ <dotted rule>/ 1798.

207.
District Court Ledger, 262 PA 170
date of deposit: April 24, twenty-second year of Independence
claimant: A: Samuel Jones
author: . . . D.D.
title: A Treatise of Church Discipline and a Directory—Done by Appointment of the Philadelphia Baptist Association—<author statement> <two biblical quotations>

Title Page Deposit
author: SAMUEL JONES, D.D.
title: A/ *Treatise of Church Discipline,/* AND A/ DIRECTORY./ Done by Appointment of the PHILADELPHIA BAPTIST/ ASSOCIATION./ <decorative thick rule>/ <author statement>/ <decorative thick rule>/ <two biblical quotations>/ <double rule>
imprint: <below double rule> *Philadelphia:/* Printed by S. C. USTICK, No. 79, North Third-Street./ 1798.

208.
District Court Ledger, 262 PA 170
date of deposit: May 29, twenty-second year of Independence
claimant: P: Mathew Carey
title: The Columbian Spelling and Reading Book or an easy and alluring Guide to spelling and reading—Containing—I. Lessons in spelling from one Syllable to seven—II. A large Collection of Proverbs and Maxims of one and two Syllables—III Eighty one of Dodsley's Fables being more than half of the Number in that entertaining Book—each ornamented with a handsome metal Cut—IV—A Collection of Words nearly alike in Sound but different in Sense—V. A Table of Contractions—VI—An Explanation of the Use of Points Stops and certain Marks used in writing and printing—VII. Essay on the Sounds of the Letters in the English Language—

Title Page Deposit
title: THE/ COLUMBIAN/ Spelling and Reading Book:/ OR,/ AN EASY AND ALLURING GUIDE TO/ SPELLING AND READING./ CONTAINING:/ <. . .>/ <thick rule>
imprint: <below thick rule> PRINTED FOR/ MATHEW CAREY,/ No. 118, Market-street, Philadelphia,/ By W. & R. DICKSON, Lan caster./ <short rule>/ [*Copy Right secured according to Act of Congress.*]
note: A preface printed on the verso of the title page is also deposited.

209.
District Court Ledger, 262 PA 171
date of deposit: May 30, twenty-second year of Independence
claimant: P: Ephraim Conrad
author: a Teacher of Philadelphia <Ralph Harrison>
title: A New Edition with corrections and additions <author statement> of Harrison's Rudiments of English Grammar containing I the different Kinds Relations & Changes of Words II Syntax or the right construction of Sentences with an Appendix comprehending a Table of Verbs irregularly inflected Remarks on some Grammatical Figures Rules of <the following word has been crossed out in ms.> <Pronunciation> Punctuation a praxis on the Grammar and Examples of true & false construction <quotation in Latin>
note: According to the *National Index of American Imprints* the author is Ralph Harrison.

Title Page Deposit
author: A TEACHER OF PHILADELPHIA;
title: A NEW EDITION/ *WITH CORRECTIONS AND ADDITIONS,/* <author statement>/ OF HARRISON'S/ RUDIMENTS/ OF/ English Grammar;/ CONTAINING/ I. The different Kinds, Relations, and/ Changes of Words;/ II. Syntax, or the Right Construction/ of Sentences./ WITH AN/ APPENDIX,/ COMPREHENDING A TABLE OF VERBS IRRE-/ GULARLY INFLECTED;/ Remarks on some Grammatical

Figures, Rules of/ Punctuation; a Praxis on the Grammar, and/ examples of true and false construction./ <quotation in Latin>/ <short rule>/ *Entered according to Law./* <short rule>
imprint: <below short rule> *PHILADELPHIA:/* Printed by JOHN BIOREN,/ 1798.

210.

District Court Ledger, 262 PA 172
date of deposit: June 1, twenty-second year of Independence
claimant: A: James Davidson
author: . . . Professor of Humanity in the University of Pennsylvania—
title: An Easy and practical Introduction to the Knowledge of the Latin Tongue or An Exemplification of the Rules of Construction corresponding to those of the Philadelphia Grammar with two Indexes & afew necessary Cautions to assist youth in Translating with more Accuracy To these there is added an Epitome of General History and some Account of the affairs of Greece from the days of Epaminondas until they coincide with the History of Rome Some Examples of Themes are Annexed with a few Select Discourses on Various Subjects <quotation in Latin> <author statement>

Title Page Deposit
author: JAMES DAVIDSON,/ *Professor of Humanity in the University of Pennsylvania.*
title: AN EASY AND PRACTICAL/ INTRODUC TION/ TO THE KNOWLEDGE OF THE/ LATIN TONGUE:/ OR AN/ *EXEMPLIFICA TION/* OF THE/ RULES OF CONSTRUC TION,/ CORRESPONDING TO THOSE OF THE/ PHILADELPHIA GRAMMAR;/ *With two* INDEXES *and a few necessary* CAUTIONS,/ To assist YOUTH in Translating with more Accuracy./ TO THESE THERE IS ADDED AN/ EPITOME OF GENERAL HISTORY,/ AND SOME ACCOUNT OF THE AFFAIRS OF GREECE,/ From the days of *Epaminondas,* until they coincide with the/ History of *Rome./* SOME EXAMPLES OF THEMES ARE ANNEXED, WITH A/ FEW SELECT DISCOURSES ON VARIOUS SUBJECTS./ <rule>/ <quotation in Latin>/ <rule>/ <author statement>/ <rule>

211.

District Court Ledger, 262 PA 173
date of deposit: June 1, twenty-second year of Independence
claimant: A,P: Samuel Jones
author: . . . D. D. and Burgis Allison A. M.
title: A Selection of Psalms and Hymns done under the Appointment of the Philadelphian Association—<author statement>

Title Page Deposit
author: SAMUEL JONES, D.D./ AND/ *BURGIS ALLISON,* A.M.
title: A/ SELECTION/ OF/ *PSALMS* AND *HYMNS,/* DONE UNDER THE APPOINT MENT/ OF THE/ *PHILADELPHIAN ASSOCIA TION./* <rule>/ <author statement>/ <rule>
imprint: <below rule> *PHILADELPHIA:/* PRINTED BY *R. AITKEN & SON,* AT/ No. 22. MARKET STREET,/ <short rule>/ M.DCC.XC.
note: The clerk's note on the verso of the title page states only that Samuel Jones is proprietor.

212.

District Court Ledger, 262 PA 174
date of deposit: June 15, twenty-second year of Independence
claimant: P: Edward Stammers and William Little
author: Edward Stammers William Little—
title: The Easy Instructor or a New Method of teaching Sacred Harmony containing the Rudiments of Music on an improved Plan wherein the Naming & Timing of the Notes are familiarized to the weakest capacity—Likewise an Essay on Composition with directions to enable any person with a tolerable voice to take the Air of any piece of Music at sight and perform it by word without singing it by note—Also the Transposition of Mi rendering all the keys in Music as easy as the Natural key whereby the errors in Composition & the press may be known Together with a choice collection of Psalm Tunes & Anthems from the most celebrated Authors in Europe with a number composed in Europe & America entirely new suited to all metres sung in the different Churches in the United States Published for the use of singing societies in general but more particularly for those who have not the advantage of an instructor <author statement>

Title Page Deposit
author: EDWARD STAMMERS,/ WILLIAM LITTLE.
title: THE *Easy Instructor,* or a New Method of teaching *Sacred Harmony,* containing/ . . . / Published for the use of Singing Societies in general, but more particularly for those/ who have not the advantage of an Instructor./ <author statement>/ <short double rule>

note: This title page deposit, printed on 11.1 cm x 7.7 cm paper, is located in the Music Division.

213.

District Court Ledger, 262 PA 175

date of deposit: June 16, twenty-second year of Independence

claimant: P: Thomas Dobson

author: John Campbell late adjutant in the British 73.d Regiment of Foot—

title: The Complete Soldier's Pocket companion; or a plain and easy method of Military discipline. containing: the new System of manual and Platoon exercise, now practised in the army of Great Britain; together with filing, grounding, advancing, handling, easing and reversing of arms with field manoeuvres, camp and garrison duty. To which are added, forms of—morning reports, monthly returns, recruiting returns, muster rolls, returns of arms, accoutrements, cloathing &c with a roll of country age size and servitude. Also the field piece and great-gun exercise, with some extracts and observations from Baron Steuben's publication. <author statement>

Title Page Deposit

author: JOHN CAMPBELL,/ Late Adjutant in the British 73d Regiment of Foot.

title: THE COMPLETE/ Soldier's Pocket Compan ion;/ OR,/ A PLAIN AND EASY METHOD OF/ *MILITARY DISCIPLINE./* CONTAINING:/ <. . .>/ <short double rule>/ <author statement>/ <double rule>

imprint: <below double rule> *PHILADELPHIA:/* PRINTED BY THOMAS DOBSON, AT THE STONE-/ HOUSE, No. 41, SOUTH SECOND-STREET./ <short rule>/ M,DCC,XCVIII.

214.

District Court Ledger, 262 PA 176

date of deposit: June 19, twenty-second year of Independence

claimant: A: James Ross

author: . . . A.M. Teacher of the Latin and greek Languages and rector of the Franklin Academy in Chambersburg—

title: A plain, short, comprehensive, practical Latin Grammar comprising all the rules and Observations necessary to an accurate knowledge of the Latin classics, with the signs of quantity—affixed to certain syllables to shew their right pronunciation. <author statement> <two quotations in Latin> <four lines of poetry in English>

Title Page Deposit

author: JAMES ROSS, A.M./ TEACHER OF THE LATIN AND GREEK LANGUAGES/ AND RECTOR OF THE FRANKLIN ACADEMY/ IN CHAMBERSBURG.

title: A/ PLAIN, SHORT, COMPREHENSIVE, PRACTICAL/ LATIN GRAMMAR,/ COM PRISING ALL THE RULES AND OBSERVA TIONS/ NECESSARY TO AN ACCURATE KNOWLEDGE/ OF THE/ LATIN CLASSICS,/ WITH THE SIGNS OF QUANTITY AFFIXED TO/ CERTAIN SYLLABLES TO SHEW THEIR RIGHT/ PRONUNCIATION./ <double rule>/ <author statement>/ <double rule>/ <two quotations in Latin>/ <four lines of poetry in English>/ <short thick rule>

imprint: <below short thick rule> *CHAMBERSBURG:/* PRINTED FOR THE AUTHOR,/ BY ROBERT HARPER./ MDCCXCVIII.

215.

District Court Ledger, 262 PA 177

date of deposit: June 25, twenty-second year of Independence

claimant: P: William Cobbett

author: G. W. Snyder, A. M.—

title: The Age of Reason unreasonable; or the folly of rejecting revealed religion. In a series of letters to a friend—<author statement>

Title Page Deposit

author: G. W. SNYDER, A.M.

title: THE/ *AGE OF REASON/* UNREASONABLE;/ OR, THE/ FOLLY OF REJECTING/ REVEALED RELIGION./ *In a Series of Letters to a Friend./* <double rule>/ <author statement>/ <double rule>

imprint: <below double rule> *PHILADELPHIA:/* PUBLISHED BY WILLIAM COBBETT,/ OPPOSITE CHRIST CHURCH./ <short rule>/ MAY, 1798.

216.

District Court Ledger, 262 PA 177

date of deposit: July 23, twenty-third year of Independence

claimant: P: Jeremiah Paul

title: A Collection of Copies for Writing—alphabetically arranged—<quotation in English>

Title Page Deposit

title: A/ Collection/ OF/ COPIES FOR WRITING,/ Alphabetically Arranged./ <double rule>/ <quotation in English>/ <double rule>

imprint: <below double rule> PHILADELPHIA:/ PRINTED BY BUDD & BARTRAM,/ No. 58, NORTH SECOND STREET./ <short double rule>/ 1798.

217.

District Court Ledger, 262 PA 178

date of deposit: August 12, twenty-third year of Independence

claimant: A: Benjamin Smith Barton

author: . . . M.D. Correspondent-Member of the Society of the Antiquaries of Scotland—Member of the American Philosophical Society—Fellow of the American Academey of Arts and Sciences of Boston—corresponding Member of the Massachusetts Historical Society and Professor of Materia Medica Natural History and Botany in the University of Pennsylvania—

title: New Views of the Origin of the Tribes and Nations of America—<author statement> Philadelphia—Printed for the Author by John Bioren 1798.—

Title Page Deposit

author: BENJAMIN SMITH BARTON, M.D./ <an "i" has been inserted in ms. between the "T" and "Q" in the eighth word> CORRE SPONDENT-MEMBER OF THE SOCIETY OF THE ANTiQUARIES/ OF SCOTLAND; MEMBER OF THE AMERICAN PHILOSOPH ICAL/ SOCIETY; FELLOW OF THE AMERICAN ACADEMY OF/ ARTS AND SCIENCES OF BOSTON; CORRESPOND ING/ MEMBER OF THE MASSACHUSETTS HIS-/ TORICAL SOCIETY,/ AND PRO FESSOR OF MATERIA MEDICA, NATURAL HISTORY/ AND BOTANY,/ IN THE/ *UNIVERSITY OF PENNSYLVANIA.*

title: NEW VIEWS/ OF THE/ *ORIGIN*/ OF THE/ TRIBES AND NATIONS/ OF/ AMERICA./ <double rule>/ <author statement>/ <double rule>

imprint: <below double rule> *PHILADELPHIA:*/ PRINTED, FOR THE AUTHOR,/ BY JOHN BIOREN./ 1798.

218.

District Court Ledger, 262 PA 179

date of deposit: December 10, twenty-third year of Independence

claimant: A: John Lambert

title: A short and practical Essay on Farming being the Experience of a Farmer of about sixty Years of Age near forty Years of which were spent in England Essex County on Land where Farming is done in the greatest Perfection and near seven Years on three hundred and twenty Acres of worn out Land in Patty grove and Alloway Creek in Salem County West Jersey—Shewing the Means whereby these worn out Lands may be improved and that the Means are in the Power of almost every Farmer—

1799

219.

District Court Ledger, 262 PA 180

date of deposit: January 12, twenty-third year of Independence

claimant: A: Alexander James Dallas

author: . . . Esquire

title: Reports of Cases ruled and adjudged in the several Courts of the United States and of Pennsylvania held at the Seat of the Federal Government—<author statement> Vol. II. <quotation in Latin>

Title Page Deposit

author: A. J. DALLAS.

title: REPORTS/ OF/ CASES/ *RULED AND ADJUDGED IN THE*/ SEVERAL COURTS/ OF THE/ UNITEDSTATES, AND OF PENN SYLVANIA,/ HELD AT THE SEAT OF THE/ FEDERAL GOVERNMENT./ <author statement>/ <short rule>/ VOL. II./ <short thick rule>/ <quotation in Latin>/ <double rule>

imprint: <below double rule> PHILADELPHIA:/ PRINTED FOR THE REPORTER, AT THE AURORA OFFICE,/ M,DCC,XCVIII.

note: Four pages of the table containing the names of the cases are also deposited.

220.

District Court Ledger, 262 PA 181

date of deposit: January 19, twenty-third year of Independence

claimant: A: Mathew Carey

author: his obliged Friend . . .

title: A Plumb Pudding for the humane chaste valiant enlightened Peter Porcupine—<author statement> <biblical quotation> <quotation in English> <two lines of poetry in English>

Title Page Deposit

author: HIS OBLIGED FRIEND,/ MATHEW CAREY.

title: A/ PLUMB PUDDING/ FOR THE/ HUMANE, CHASTE, VALIANT, ENLIGHT ENED/ *PETER PORCUPINE.*/ <short thick

rule>/ <author statement>/ <rule>/ <biblical quotation>/ <quotation in English>/ <two lines of poetry in English>/ <rule>/ <relief cut of a porcupine being hanged>
imprint: <below relief cut> PHILADELPHIA:/ PRINTED FOR THE AUTHOR.

221.

District Court Ledger, 262 PA 182
date of deposit: January 21, twenty-third year of Independence
claimant: A: Andrew Law
title: The musical Magazine containing a Number of favorite Pieces European and American— <author statement> Number fifth

Title Page Deposit
author: ANDREW LAW.
title: THE/ MUSICAL MAGAZINE:/ CONTAIN ING A NUMBER OF/ FAVORITE PIECES,/ European and American./ <decorative rule>/ <author statement>/ <decorative rule>/ NUMBER FIFTH./ <thick rule>/ *Published as the Act directs.*/ <double rule>/ January. 1799.
note: There is no imprint on the title page.

222.

District Court Ledger, 262 PA 183
date of deposit: January 31, twenty-third year of Independence
claimant: P: Asbury Dickins
author: the reverend Ezekiel Cooper—
title: A Funeral Discourse on the Death of that eminent Man the late reverend John Dickins <author statement> <two biblical quotations>

Title Page Deposit
author: REVEREND EZEKIEL COOPER.
title: A FUNERAL DISCOURSE,/ ON THE DEATH/ OF THAT EMINENT MAN/ THE LATE/ REVEREND JOHN DICKINS./ <double rule>/ <author statement>/ <double rule>/ <two biblical quotations>/ <double rule>
imprint: <below double rule> PHILADELPHIA:/ PRINTED BY H. MAXWELL, FOR ASBURY DICKINS,/ BOOKSELLER, NO 41, MARKET STREET./ <short dotted rule>/ 1799.

223.

District Court Ledger, 262 PA 184
date of deposit: February 20, twenty-third year of Independence
claimant: A: Richard Parkinson
author: . . . , late of Doncaster in the county of York, England,
title: The Experienced Farmer, an entire new work, in which the whole system of Agriculture, husbandry and breeding of cattle, will be explained and copiously enlarged upon—and the best methods with the most recent improvements pointed out; with considerable alterations and additions. <author statement> likewise, the Author's opinion upon the cultivation of the different Soils, and crops proper for each soil, and the various kinds of manure and composts in the United States—importation of Horses, cattle &c—

Title Page Deposit
author: *RICHARD PARKINSON,*/ LATE OF DONCASTER, IN THE COUNTY OF YORK, ENGLAND.
title: THE EXPERIENCED FARMER,/ *AN ENTIRE NEW WORK,*/ IN WHICH THE WHOLE SYSTEM OF/ AGRICULTURE, HUSBANDRY, AND BREEDING OF CATTLE,/ WILL BE EXPLAINED AND COPIOUSLY ENLARGED UPON,/ AND/ THE BEST METHODS, WITH THE MOST RECENT IMPROVEMENTS, POINTED OUT:/ WITH CONSIDERABLE ALTERA TIONS AND ADDITIONS./ <author statement>/ *LIKEWISE,*/ THE AUTHOR'S OPINION UPON THE CULTIVATION OF THE DIFFERENT SOILS,/ AND CROPS PROPER FOR EACH SOIL, AND THE VARIOUS KINDS OF MANURE AND COMPOSTS/ IN THE UNITED STATES, IMPORTATION OF HORSES, CATTLE, &c./ <thick rule>
note: There is no imprint on the title page.

224.

District Court Ledger, 262 PA 185
date of deposit: February 22, twenty-third year of Independence
claimant: A: Alexander Reinagle
title: The Music in the Historical play of Columbus, composed and adapted, for the Piano Forte—Flute or violin—<author statement>

Title Page Deposit
author: ALEXANDER REINAGLE.
title: THE/ MUSIC/ IN THE/ *HISTORICAL PLAY,*/ OF/ COLUMBUS,/ COMPOSED AND ADAPTED,/ FOR THE/ *PIANO FORTE, FLUTE OR VIOLIN,*/ <author statement>
imprint: <below author statement> *Philadelphia, Feb. 9th,* 1799.

225.

District Court Ledger, 262 PA 186

date of deposit: February 25, twenty-third year of Independence

claimant: P: Charles B. Brown

author: The Author of Wieland and Ormond or the secret Witness—

title: Arthur Mervyn or Memoirs of the Year 1793—<author statement>

226.

District Court Ledger, 262 PA 187

date of deposit: March 1, twenty-third year of Independence

claimant: A: Mathew Carey

title: The Porcupiniad A Hudibrastic Poem—addressed to William Cobbett <author statement> <four quotations in English>

Title Page Deposit

author: MATHEW CAREY.

title: THE/ PORCUPINIAD:/ A/ *HUDIBRASTIC POEM.*/ ADDRESSED TO/ WILLIAM COBBETT,/ <author statement>/ <short thick rule>/ <four quotations in English with ms. corrections>/ <double rule>

imprint: <below double rule> *PHILADELPHIA:*/ Printed for and sold by the AUTHOR./ *March* 2, 1799.

227.

District Court Ledger, 262 PA 188

date of deposit: March 8, twenty-third year of Independence

claimant: P: Cornelius William Stafford

author: Cornelius William Stafford—

title: The Philadelphia Directory for 1799—containing the Names Occupations and Places of Abode of the Citizens arranged in alphabetical Order also a Register of the Executive Legislative and Judicial Magistrates of the United States—The Constitution of the United States—Officers of the Commonwealth of Pennsylvania—and the Magistrates of the City—with an accurate Table of the Duties on Goods Wares and Merchandize—together with a general Abstract from the Revinue Laws relative to the Duty of Masters of Vessels—of the Owners or Consignees of Goods—of Officers of the Customs—of Payment of Duties &c—and the Form of Entry at the Custom-House on the Importation of Goods—to all which are added An Account of the Post-Office Establishment—the Banks—Stamp Duties—Tables of Monies &c—with an alphabetical List of the Streets Lanes and Alleys—<author statement>

Title Page Deposit

author: CORNELIUS WILLIAM STAFFORD.

title: THE/ PHILADELPHIA DIRECTORY,/ FOR 1799:/ CONTAINING/ *THE NAMES, OCCUPATIONS, AND PLACES OF ABODE OF THE/ CITIZENS,*/ ARRANGED IN ALPHA BETICAL ORDER:/ ALSO/ A REGISTER/ *OF THE/* Executive, Legislative and Judicial Magistrates of the/ United States—The Constitution of the United/ States—Officers of the Commonwealth of Penn-/ sylvania—And the Magistrates of the City:/ . . . / TO ALL WHICH ARE ADDED,/ An Account of the Post-Office Establishment—The Banks—Stamp Du-/ ties—Tables of Monies &c.—With an Alphabetical List of the Streets,/ Lanes and Alleys./ <short thick rule>/ <author statement>/ <short thick rule>

imprint: <below short thick rule> Printed for the Editor, by/ WILLIAM W. WOODWARD, No. 17, Chesnut Street./ 1799.

228.

District Court Ledger, 262 PA 189

date of deposit: March 19, twenty-third year of Independence

claimant: P: George Douglas

author: Daniel Fenning—late School Master at Buries in Suffolk—Author of the Royal English Dictionary—Practical Arithmetick—The young Man's Book of Knowledge &c—

title: The universal Spelling Book improved being a new and easy Guide to the English Language—containing—I. Tables of useful Words from one to eight Syllables diversified with a great Variety of religious and moral Precepts and accompanied by a Number of instructive Fables and Stories—a large Collection of Words nearly alike in Sound but different in Spelling and Signification—Remarks on the various Pronunciations of the Vowels and Consonants—and a new Catalogue of the most useful Contractions—II. An easy and comprehensive Guide to English Grammar adapted to young Capacities in a familiar Dialogue between Master and Scholar whereby the Learner may very soon become acquainted with the first Principles of his native Language—III. Tables of the principal Parts of Speech—viz. Substantives—Adjectives—and Verbs of two three and four Syllables ranged alphabetically under their respective Heads and explained from the best Authority in the easiest and most comprehensive Terms—IV. A Variety of select alphabetical Sentences calculated for writing Pieces—moral

Poems and Precepts—concise Forms of Graces and Prayers—with other useful and instructing Articles very necessary for the Information of the young Scholar—and a copious chronological Table of the most remarkable Events from the Creation of the World to the present Period &c. &c. &c—<author statement> <two lines of poetry in English> The first American Edition With considerable Additions and Improvements—

Title Page Deposit

author: DANIEL FENNING,/ *Late School-Master at Buries in Suffolk, Author of the/ Royal English Dictionary, Practical Arithmetick,/ the Young Man's Book of Knowledge, &c.*

title: THE/ *Universal* SPELLING-BOOK/ <black letter> Improved,/ BEING/ A NEW AND EASY GUIDE/ TO THE/ *ENGLISH LANGUAGE./* CONTAINING,/ <. . .>/ <rule>/ <author statement>/ <rule>/ <two lines of poetry in English>/ <rule>/ <black letter> The First American Edition./ *With considerable Additions and Improvements./* <double rule>

imprint: <below double rule> *PHILADELPHIA:/* PRINTED BY JOHN BIOREN FOR/ *G. DOUGLAS, BOOKSELLER—M.DCC.XCIX.*

229.

District Court Ledger, 262 PA 191

date of deposit: March 30, twenty-third year of Independence

claimant: A: James Ross

author: . . . A. M.—Teacher of the latin and Greek languages and rector of the Franklin Academy in Chambersburg—.

title: A Practical, new vocabulary latin and English; consisting of more than Two thousand nouns substantive, appellative and proper; serving to exemplify and illustrate the rules for the Declensions and genders of nouns in the latin Grammar; with an appendix of Adjectives, every one of which may be adapted to one or other of the foregoing substantives—<author statement> <two quotations in Latin>

Title Page Deposit

author: JAMES ROSS, A.M./ *TEACHER OF THE LATIN AND GREEK LANGUAGES; AND/ RECTOR OF THE FRANKLIN ACADEMY IN/ CHAMBERSBURG.*

title: A PRACTICAL, NEW/ VOCABULARY/ LATIN AND ENGLISH;/ CONSISTING OF MORE THAN TWO THOUSAND/ Nouns Substantive,/ APPELLATIVE AND PROPER;/ SERVING TO EXEMPLIFY AND ILLUSTRATE THE RULES/ FOR THE/ DECLENSIONS AND GENDERS OF NOUNS IN THE/ LATIN GRAMMAR:/ WITH AN/ APPENDIX OF ADJECTIVES,/ Every one of which may be adapted to one or other of/ the foregoing substantives./ <double rule>/ <author statement>/ <double rule>/ <two quotations in Latin>/ <thick rule>

imprint: <below thick rule> CHAMBERSBURG:/ FROM THE PRESS OF SNOWDEN AND M'CORKLE./ <short thick rule>/ *Nov.* 10, 1798.

note: Two pages of preface have also been deposited.

230.

District Court Ledger, 262 PA 193

date of deposit: April 23, twenty-third year of Independence

claimant: A: Thomas Dobson

title: Letters on the existence and character of the Deity—and on the moral State of Man.

Title Page Deposit

title: *LETTERS/ ON THE/ EXISTENCE AND CHARACTER/* OF THE/ DEITY,/ AND ON THE/ MORAL STATE/ OF/ MAN./ <double rule>

imprint: <below double rule> *PHILADELPHIA:/* PRINTED FOR THOMAS DOBSON, AT THE STONE/ HOUSE, No 41, SOUTH SECOND STREET./ <short rule>/ 1799.

231.

District Court Ledger, 262 PA 193

date of deposit: April 23, twenty-third year of Independence

claimant: P: Thomas Dobson

title: Plat of that tract of country in the Territory Northwest—of the Ohio appropriated for military Services and described in the act of Congress, instituted an Act regulating the grants of land appropriated for military Services and for the society of United Brethren for propagating the Gospell among the Heathen—Survey'd under the direction of Rufus Putnam—Surveyor General to the United States—

format: map

Title Page Deposit

title: <"title page" is in fact the top portion of a map> <script> Plat of that Tract of Country in the Territory Northwest of the Ohio apporiated/ <script> for Military Services; and described in the Act of Congress, instituted An Act regulating/ <script> the Grants of Land appropriated for

Military Services and for the Society of United/ < script > Brethren for propagating the Gospell among the Heathen Survey'd under the direction/ < script > of Rufus Putnam Surveyor General to the United States

note: The clerk's note on the top left-hand side of the title page states that Thomas Dobson is the proprietor. The title page is located in the Geography and Map Division.

232.

District Court Ledger, 262 PA 194

date of deposit: May 7, twenty-third year of Independence

claimant: P: Thomas Carpenter

title: The Trials of John Fries and others on indictments for Treason: Together with a brief report of the trials of several other persons for insurrection, In the Counties of Bucks, Northampton and Montgomery, in the Circuit Court of the United States before the Hon: James Iredell and Richard Peters Esquires—begun at the city of Philadelphia, April 30. 1799—Taken in short hand by Thomas Carpenter—

Title Page Deposit

title: THE/ TRIALS/ OF/ JOHN FRIES, and OTHERS,/ on Indictments for/ TREASON:/ *TOGETHER WITH A BRIEF REPORT OF THE TRIALS OF SEVERAL OTHER/ PERSONS FOR/* INSURRECTION,/ In the Counties of BUCKS, NORTHAMPTON & MONTGOMERY,/ *In the Circuit Court of the United States,/* Before the/ Hon. JAMES IREDELL, and RICHARD PETERS, Esquires,/ *Begun at the City of Philadelphia, April* 30, 1799./ < short double rule > / TAKEN IN SHORT HAND BY THOMAS CARPENTER./ < short double rule > / [*COPY RIGHT SECURED.*]/ < thick rule >

imprint: < below thick rule > Printed at Philadel phia, for the EDITOR./ < short rule > / 1799.

233.

District Court Ledger, 262 PA 195

date of deposit: May 17, twenty-third year of Independence

claimant: A: Benjamin Carr

composer: B. Carr—

title: Three Ballads—viz—The New Somebody—Mary will Smile—and Poor Richard— < composer statement >

Title Page Deposit

composer: < script > B Carr.

title: THREE/ < script > Ballads/ VIZ/ The New Somebody < short thick rule > Mary will smile/ < ornament > and Poor Richard < ornament > / < composer statement > / < short thick rule > Price 62 Cents < short thick rule > / < the word cents is printed above the colon that precedes it > or in seperate Sheets at 25:cents each/ Copyright Seccur'd according to law/ < double rule >

imprint: < below double rule > Printed and sold at B. Carrs Musical Repository Philadelphia J: Carrs Baltimore & J: Hewitts New York

note: < below imprint is printed > Just Published/ Three Canzonetts by Haydn/ and shortly will be Published/ Musical Bagatelles or Six little Ballads selected from some late English Publications. < The first page of "The New Somebody" is printed on the verso of the title page. This title page is located in the Music Division. >

234.

District Court Ledger, 262 PA 196

date of deposit: May 20, twenty-third year of Independence

claimant: P: William W. Woodward

title: The Trial of John Fries on an indictment for Treason; together with a brief report of the trials of several other persons for—insurrection, in the counties of Bucks,—Northampton and Montgomery—In the Circuit Court of the United States, Before the Hon: James Iredell and Richard Peters, Esquires—Begun at the city of Philadelphia, April 30, 1799—Taken in short hand by Thomas Carpenter.—

Title Page Deposit

title: THE/ TRIAL/ OF/ JOHN FRIES,/ on an Indictment for/ < brackets around the following word have been inserted in ms. > [TREASON;]/ *TOGETHER WITH A BRIEF REPORT OF THE TRIALS OF SEVERAL OTHER/ PERSONS FOR/* INSURRECTION,/ In the Counties of BUCKS, NORTHAMPTON and MONTGOMERY;/ *In the Circuit Court of the United States,/* Before the/ < two pen lines surround first word > Hon. JAMES IREDELL and RICHARD PETERS, Esquires:/ *Begun at the City of Philadelphia, April* 30, 1799./ < short double rule > / TAKEN IN SHORT HAND BY THOMAS CARPENTER./ < short double rule > / [*COPY RIGHT SECURED.*]/ < thick rule >

imprint: < below thick rule > Philadelphia: Printed and sold by W. W. Woodward, Ches-/ nut street, No. 17, near Front street./ < short rule > / 1799.

235.

District Court Ledger, 262 PA 197

date of deposit: May 27, twenty-third year of Independence

claimant: A: Benjamin Smith Barton

author: . . . M. D. Correspondent—Member of the Society of the Antiquaries of Scotland—Member of the American Philosophical Society—Fellow of the American Academy of Arts and Sciences of Boston—Corresponding Member of the Massachusetts Historical Society—Member of the Physical Society of Jena—one of the foreign Members of the Linnaean Society of London—and Professor of Materia Medica natural History and Botony in the University of Pennsylvania—

title: Fragments of the Natural History of Pennsylvania—<author statement> Part first—<two quotations in Latin>

Title Page Deposit

author: BENJAMIN SMITH BARTON, M.D./ CORRESPONDENT-MEMBER OF THE SOCIETY OF THE ANTIQUARIES OF SCOTLAND; MEMBER/ OF THE AMERI CAN PHILOSOPHICAL SOCIETY; FELLOW OF THE AMERICAN ACADEMY/ OF ARTS AND SCIENCES OF BOSTON; CORRE SPONDING MEMBER OF THE/ MASSACHU SETTS HISTORICAL SOCIETY; MEMBER OF THE PHY-/ SICAL SOCIETY OF JENA; ONE OF THE FOREIGN MEMBERS/ OF THE LINNAEAN SOCIETY OF LONDON;/ AND/ *PROFESSOR OF MATERIA MEDICA, NATURAL HISTORY AND BOTANY,*/ IN THE/ UNIVERSITY OF PENNSYLVANIA.

title: FRAGMENTS/ OF THE/ NATURAL HISTORY/ OF/ PENNSYLVANIA./ <thick rule>/ <author statement>/ <short double rule>/ *PART FIRST.*/ <short double rule>/ <two quotations in Latin>/ <double rule>

imprint: <below double rule> *PHILADELPHIA:*/ PRINTED, FOR THE AUTHOR, BY WAY & GROFF,/ No. 48, NORTH THIRD-STREET./ 1799.

236.

District Court Ledger, 262 PA 198

date of deposit: June 3, twenty-third year of Independence

claimant: A: Jeremiah Paul

title: The Child's Assistant: containing a plain and easy introduction to arithmetic.—<quotation in English>

Title Page Deposit

title: THE/ Child's Assistant:/ CONTAINING, A/ PLAIN AND EASY/ INTRODUCTION/ TO/ ARITHMETIC./ <short thick rule>/ <quotation in English>/ <thick rule>

imprint: <below thick rule> *PHILADELPHIA:*/ PRINTED FOR *JEREMIAH PAUL,* No. 35,/ SOUTH FOURTH STREET./ 1799.

237.

District Court Ledger, 262 PA 199

date of deposit: June 12, twenty-third year of Independence

claimant: A: Joseph Scott

title: The new and universal Gazetteer; or Modern Geographical Dictionary containing a full and authentic description of the different empires, Kingdoms republics, states, Provinces, Islands, cities towns, Forts, mountains caves, capes, canals, Rivers, lakes, Oceans, Seas, Bays, Harbours &c in the Known World—; the Government, customs, manners and religion of the inhabitants; the situation, extent, boundaries subdivisions, climate, soil, natural productions and curiosities of each country; the manufactures and trade of the cities and towns; their longitudes from the Meridian of Philadelphia—their latitudes; the sieges they have undergone and the battles fought near them—including the New Political Divisions of Europe—and several hundred places in the United States of America never before published. The whole containing many thousand places not found in any similar Geographical work; and wherein upwards of Five hundred Errours are corrected in the Encyclopedia Britannica, and in Millar, Payne, Guthrie Watson, Brooks, Walker, Morse, &c—to which is added a new and easy introduction to Geography and astronomy, with a nomenclature, explaining the essential terms in each science. Illustrated with Twenty five Maps an Armillary Sphere, and several Diagrams—<author statement>/ in four volumes—/ VOL I./ <short rule>

Title Page Deposit

author: JOSEPH SCOTT.

title: THE/ New and Universal Gazetteer;/ *OR,*/ <black letter> Modern Geographical Dictionary./ CONTAINING/ *A FULL AND AUTHENTIC DESCRIPTION OF THE DIFFERENT EMPIRES, KINGDOMS, RE-/ PUBLICS, STATES, PROVINCES, ISLANDS, CITIES, TOWNS, FORTS, MOUNTAINS,/ CAVES, CAPES, CANALS, RIVERS, LAKES,*

OCEANS, SEAS, BAYS, HARBOURS, &c./ IN THE/ KNOWN WORLD;/ <. . .>/ *Illustrated with twenty-five Maps, an Armillary Sphere, and several Diagrams.*/ <rule>/ <author statement>/ <rule>/ IN FOUR VOLUMES./ <short rule>/ VOL I./ <short thick rule>
imprint: <below short thick rule> *PHILADEL PHIA:*/ PRINTED BY FRANCIS & ROBERT BAILEY, AT YORICK'S-/ HEAD, No. 116, HIGH-STREET./ 1799.

238.
District Court Ledger, 262 PA 200
date of deposit: August 1, twenty-fourth year of Independence
claimant: A: Alexander James Dallas
author: . . . Esquire
title: Reports of Cases ruled and adjudged in the several Courts of the United States and of Pennsylvania held at the Seat of the Federal Government—<author statement>/ Volume III./ <quotation in Latin>

Title Page Deposit
author: A. J. DALLAS.
title: REPORTS/ OF/ CASES/ RULED AND ADJUDGED IN THE/ *SEVERAL COURTS*/ OF THE/ <black letter> United States,/ AND OF/ *PENNSYLVANIA,*/ HELD AT THE SEAT OF THE/ <black letter> Federal Government./ <double rule>/ <author statement>/ <double rule>/ VOLUME III./ <quotation in Latin>/ <thick rule>
imprint: <below thick rule> <black letter> Phila delphia:/ PRINTED FOR THE *REPORTER,* BY *J. ORMROD.*/ <short rule>/ 1799.
note: One page of the index to titles of the cases is also deposited.

239.
District Court Ledger, 262 PA 201
date of deposit: August 9, twenty-fourth year of Independence
claimant: A: Jonathan Williams
title: Thermometrical Navigation. being a series of experiments and observations tending to prove, that by ascertaining the relative heat of the seawater from time to time, The Passage of a Ship through the Gulph Stream, and from Deep Water into soundings may be discovered in time to avoid danger. although (owing to tempestuous weather) it may be impossible to heave the lead or observe the Heavenly Bodies.—Extracted from the American Philosophical Transactions. Vol. 2 & 3. with Additions and improvements. <quotation in English>

Title Page Deposit
title: THERMOMETRICAL/ NAVIGATION./ BEING/ A Series of Experiments and Observa tions,/ TENDING TO PROVE,/ THAT BY/ *ASCERTAINING*/ *The* RELATIVE HEAT *of the* SEA-WATER/ FROM TIME TO TIME,/ <black letter> The Passage of a Ship/ THROUGH/ THE GULPH STREAM,/ AND/ FROM DEEP WATER INTO SOUNDINGS,/ *May be discovered in Time to avoid Danger,*/ ALTHOUGH (OWING TO TEMPESTUOUS WEATHER,)/ IT MAY BE IMPOSSIBLE/ To heave the Lead or observe the Heavenly Bodies./ <short thick rule>/ *Extracted from the American Philosophical Transactions. Vol.* 2 & 3./ WITH/ ADDITIONS AND IMPROVEMENTS./ <double rule>/ <quotation in English>/ <double rule>
imprint: <below double rule> *PHILADELPHIA:*/ PRINTED AND SOLD BY R. AITKEN, No. 22, MARKET STREET./ <short thick decorative rule>/ 1799.
note: The clerk's note on the verso of the title page states that Jonathan Williams is the author.

240.
District Court Ledger, 262 PA 202
date of deposit: November 1, twenty-fourth year of Independence
claimant: P: James Carey
title: A View of the New England Illuminati: Who are indefatigably engaged in destroying the religion and Government of the United States; under a feigned regard for their Safety—And under an impious abuse of true religion.

Title Page Deposit
title: A/ VIEW,/ OF THE/ *New-England Illuminati:*/ WHO ARE INDEFATIGABLY ENGAGED IN/ DESTROYING THE *RELIGION* AND *GO-/ VERNMENT* OF THE *UNITED STATES;*/ UNDER A FEIGNED REGARD FOR THEIR SAFETY—AND/ UNDER AN IMPIOUS ABUSE OF TRUE RELIGION./ <double rule>
imprint: <below double rule> *PHILADELPHIA:*/ PRINTED BY JAMES CAREY, No. 16, CHESNUT-STREET./ <short thick rule>/ 1799./ <short thick decorative rule>

241.

District Court Ledger, 262 PA 203

date of deposit: December 11, twenty-fourth year of Independence

claimant: A: Mathew Carey

title: The Columbian Reading Book or historical Preceptor a Collection of authentic Histories Anecdotes Characters &c. &c. calculated to incite in young Minds a Love of Virtue from its intrinsic Beauty and a Hatred of Vice from its disgusting Deformity—

Title Page Deposit

title: THE/ Columbian Reading Book,/ OR/ HISTORICAL PRECEPTOR:/ A COL LECTION OF AUTHENTIC/ HISTORIES, ANECDOTES,/ CHARACTERS, &c. &c./ CAL CULATED TO INCITE IN YOUNG MINDS/ A LOVE OF VIRTUE,/ FROM ITS INTRIN SIC BEAUTY,/ AND/ A HATRED OF VICE,/ FROM ITS DISGUSTING DEFORMITY./ <decorative rule>

imprint: <below decorative rule> *PHILADEL PHIA:/* PRINTED FOR MATHEW CAREY./ November 30th, 1799./ <short rule>

note: [*Copy secured according to Law.*] <The clerk's manuscript note at the bottom of the title page states, "To be secured as compiler." On the verso of the title page a note indicates that Mathew Carey is the author.>

242.

District Court Ledger, 262 PA 204

date of deposit: December 24, twenty-fourth year of Independence

claimant: P: Robert Campbell

author: Joseph Priestley—LLD. F.RS. &c—

title: Letters to the inhabitants of Northumberland and its neighborhood on subjects interesting to the author and to them.—Part. I. <author statement> <quotation in Latin>

Title Page Deposit

author: JOSEPH PRIESTLEY, L.L.D.F.R.S.&c.

title: LETTERS/ TO THE/ INHABITANTS/ OF/ NORTHUMBERLAND/ AND ITS/ *NEIGHBOURHOOD,/ On Subjects interesting to the* AUTHOR,/ *and to* THEM./ PART I./ <thick rule>/ <author statement>/ <thick rule>/ <quotation in Latin>/ <thick rule>

imprint: <below thick rule> *NORTHUMBER LAND:/ Printed for the* AUTHOR *by ANDREW KENNEDY./* <rule>/ MDCCXCIX.

243.

District Court Ledger, 262 PA 205

date of deposit: December 24, twenty-fourth year of Independence

claimant: P: Robert Campbell

author: Joseph Priestley—L.L.D. F.R.S. &c.

title: A Comparison of the institutions of Moses with those of the Hindoos and other ancient nations; with remarks on Mr. Dupuis's origin of all religions, The laws and institutions of Moses methodized, And an address to the Jews on the present State of the world and the propecies relating to it <author statement> <quotation in Latin>

Title Page Deposit

author: JOSEPH PRIESTLEY, L.L.D.F.R.S.&c.

title: A/ COMPARISON/ OF THE/ INSTITU TIONS OF MOSES/ WITH THOSE OF/ THE HINDOOS/ AND/ OTHER ANCIENT NATIONS;/ WITH/ REMARKS on MR. DUPUIS'S ORIGIN of all/ RELIGIONS,/ The LAWS and INSTITUTIONS of MOSES/ METHODIZED,/ AND/ An ADDRESS to the JEWS on the present state of the/ WORLD and the PROPHECIES relating to it./ <thick rule>/ <author statement>/ <thick rule>/ <quotation in Latin>/ <thick rule>

imprint: <below thick rule> NORTHUMBER LAND:/ *PRINTED* FOR THE *AUTHOR* BY *A. KENNEDY./* <rule>/ MDCCXCIX.

244.

District Court Ledger, 262 PA 206

date of deposit: December 28, twenty-fourth year of Independence

claimant: P: David Hogan

author: Robert Slender—O.S.M.

title: Letters on various interesting and important Subjects; many of which have appeared in the Aurora.—corrected and much enlarged. <author statement> <two lines of poetry in English>

Title Page Deposit

author: ROBERT SLENDER, *O.S.M.*

title: LETTERS/ ON/ *Various interesting and important Subjects;/* MANY OF WHICH HAVE APPEARED/ in the/ *AURORA./* CORRECTED AND MUCH ENLARGED./ <short thick decorative rule>/ <author statement>/ <short thick decorative rule>/ <two lines of poetry in English>/ <double rule>

imprint: <below double rule> PHILADELPHIA:/ *PRINTED FOR THE AUTHOR./* FROM THE PRESS OF *D. HOGAN—/* And sold at his Store,

No. 222, South *Third-street,* and at/ the Office of the *Aurora.*/ <short thick rule>/ December 30, 1799.

1800

245.

District Court Ledger, 262 PA 207
date of deposit: January 9, twenty-fourth year of Independence
claimant: P: John Rowlett
title: Table of Discount of Interests (accurately calculated) From 50 Cents to 5,000 Dollars from 1 day to 123 days inclusive; at 6 perCent—

Title Page Deposit
title: TABLE OF DISCOUNT,/ OR/ INTEREST,/ *(ACCURATELY CALCULATED)*/ From 50 Cents to 5,000 Dollars, from 1 Day to 123 Days inclusive; at 6 per Cent.
note: Only the top portion of the title page is deposited.

246

District Court Ledger, 262 PA 208
date of deposit: January 9, twenty-fourth year of Independence
claimant: P: John Rowlett
title: Table of Discount or Interest (accurately calculated) from 50 Cents to 5,000 Dollars, from 1 day to 123 days inclusive; at 7 per Cent—

Title Page Deposit
title: TABLE OF DISCOUNT,/ OR/ INTEREST,/ *(ACCURATELY CALCULATED)*/ From 50 Cents to 5,000 Dollars, from 1 Day to 123 Days inclusive; at 7 per Cent.
note: Only the top portion of the title page is deposited.

247.

District Court Ledger, 262 PA 209
date of deposit: January 11, twenty-fourth year of Independence
claimant: P: Collinson Read and George Davis
author: Drawn by Collinson Read—
title: Ten Blank Declarations, Elegantly engraven on Copper Plate—viz: <no.s 1-5 on left hand column; no.s 6-10 on right hand column> 1. Debt on Bond, 2.—by Assignee, 3.—on single Bill, 4.—on penal Bill, 5. Indebitatus Assumsit, 6. Quantum meruit, 7. Quantum valebant, 8. On Promissory Note, 9. Same by Indorsee, 10. Tresspass and Ejectment, For the use of the Professors of the Law. <author statement>

Title Page Deposit
author: DRAWN BY/ COLLINSON READ.
title: TEN/ <black letter> Blank Declarations,/ ELEGANTLY ENGRAVEN/ ON/ *COPPER-PLATE,*/ VIZ./ . . . / <thick decorative rule>/ *FOR THE USE OF THE PROFESSORS OF THE LAW.*/ <short thick decorative rule>/ <author statement>/ <double rule>
imprint: <below double rule> *PHILADELPHIA:*/ PRINTED FOR THE PROPRIETORS, AND SOLD BY/ <black letter> George Davis,/ NO. 319, HIGH-STREET./ <short rule>/ *MDCCC.*

248.

District Court Ledger, 262 PA 210
date of deposit: January 17, twenty-fourth year of Independence
claimant: P: Collinson Read
author: . . . Esq.
title: An Abridgement of the Laws of Pennyslvania containing a complete digest of all such acts of Assembly as concern the commonwealth at large. To which is added An Appendix containing a great variety of Precedents, adapted to the several Acts, for the use of Justices of the Peace, Sherriffs, Attornies and conveyancers. With a complete index to the whole.—<author statement>

Title Page Deposit
author: COLLINSON READ, ESQ.
title: AN/ <two small squares of paper are sealed onto the title page on either side of the following word> <black letter> Abridgment/ OF THE/ *LAWS OF PENNSYLVANIA,*/ CONTAIN ING/ . . . / *WITH A COMPLETE INDEX TO THE WHOLE.*/ <thick decorative rule>/ <author statement>/ <double rule>
note: There is no imprint on the title page.

249.

District Court Ledger, 262 PA 248
date of deposit: January 30, twenty-fourth year of Independence
claimant: P: John Rowlett
author: . . . , Accomptant, Bank of North America.
title: Rowlett's Tables of Discount, or Interest, on every Dollar from one to two thousand, and by tens, from two thousand to two thousand five hundred; by fiftys, from two thousand five hundred to three thousand, and by five hundreds, from three thousand to five thousand, on each sum from one day to sixty-four days inclusive, At Six per Cent, comprizing, in the whole, upwards

of One hundred and thirty-two thousand one hundred and fifty calculations of Discount, all performed according to the equitable principles of the Banks, and as practised between individuals throughout the United States. With Notes preceding the work, shewing how by means of the Tables, to ascertain the Discount, At Seven and at Eight per Cent. Reckoning either 360 or 365 days to the year: explained by examples. Also, another Note under the first Page of the Work, shewing the mode of calculation on cents, Likewise, the ready way to use the tables for any number of days exceeding sixty-four, To all which is added, the principles of computation of the various exchanges between each state respectively, and between all these and London and Paris, at different rates of Exchange.—<author statement>

Title Page Deposit
author: JOHN ROWLETT, Accomptant, Bank of North America.
title: ROWLETT's/ Tables of Discount, or Interest,/ *On every Dollar/* . . . / TO ALL WHICH IS ADDED,/ The principles of com putation of the various exchanges between *each state respectively,* and between all/ these and LON DON and PARIS, at *different rates of Exchange./* <double rule>/ <author statement>/ <double rule>
imprint: <below double rule> *PHILADELPHIA:/* PRINTED FOR THE PROPRIETOR,/ *Anno Domini* 1800,/ And the twenty-fifth Year of the Independence of the United States of America./ <thick rule>
note: COPY-RIGHT SECURED ACCORDING TO ACT OF CONGRESS. <The preface has also been deposited.>

250.

District Court Ledger, 262 PA 212
date of deposit: January 31, twenty-fourth year of Independence
claimant: P: John Rowlett
author: . . . Accomptant, Bank of North America
title: Rowlett's Tables of Discount, or Interest, On every Dollar from one to two thousand; on every ten dollars from two thousand to two thousand five hundred; on every fifty, from two thousand five hundred to three thousand, and on every five hundred, from three thousand to five thousand, From One day to sixty-four days inclusive, At six per Cent—comprizing, in the whole, upwards of one hundred and thirty-two thousand one hundred and fifty Calculations of Discount, All performed according to the equitable principles of the Banks, and as practised between Individuals throughout the United States—With Notes preceding the work, shewing how, by means of the Tables, to ascertain the Discount, At Seven and at Eight per Cent. Reckoning either 360 or 365 days to the Year:—explained by examples. Also, Another note under the first page of the Work, shewing the mode of calculation on Cents, Likewise, the ready way to use the Tables for any number of days exceeding sixty-four. To all which is added, The principles of computation of the various exchanges between each state respectively, and between all these and London and Paris at different rates of Exchange. <author statement>

Title Page Deposit
author: JOHN ROWLETT, Accomptant, Bank of North America.
title: ROWLETT's/ Tables of Discount, or Interest,/ *On every Dollar/* . . . / TO ALL WHICH IS ADDED,/ The principles of computation of the various exchanges between *each state respectively,* and between all/ these and LONDON and PARIS, at *different rates of Exchange./* <double rule>/ <author statement>/ <double rule>
imprint: <below double rule> *PHILADELPHIA:/* PRINTED FOR THE PROPRIETOR,/ *Anno Domini* 1800,/ And the twenty-fourth Year of the Independence of the United States of America./ <thick rule>
note: COPY-RIGHT SECURED ACCORDING TO ACT OF CONGRESS.

251.

District Court Ledger, 262 PA 214
date of deposit: February 25, twenty-fourth year of Independence
claimant: P: William W. Woodward
author: Rev. John Witherspoon D.D. L.L.D. Late President of the College at Princeton New-Jersey.
title: The Works of <author statement> To which is Prefixed An Account of the Author's life, in a sermon occasioned by his death. By the Rev. Dr. John Rodgers—of New York—. In Three volumes—Vol. 1.

Title Page Deposit
author: <black letter> Rev. John Witherspoon,/ D.D. L.L.D./ LATE PRESIDENT OF THE COLLEGE, AT PRINCETON NEW-JERSEY.
title: THE/ WORKS/ OF THE/ <author statement>/ TO WHICH IS PREFIXED/ An

Account of the Author's Life, in a Sermon occasioned/ by his Death, by the/ REV. DR. JOHN RODGERS,/ OF NEW YORK./ <double rule>/ IN THREE VOLUMES./ <double rule>/ VOL. I./ <double rule>
imprint: <below double rule> <black letter> Philadelphia:/ Printed and published by WIL LIAM W. WOODWARD, No. 17,/ Chesnut near Front Street./ <short double rule>/ 1800.
note: [*COPY RIGHT SECURED.*]

252.
District Court Ledger, 262 PA 215
date of deposit: February twenty-eighth, twenty-fourth year of Independence
claimant: P: John Ormrod
author: Major William Jackson—Aid-de-camp to the late President of the United States and Secretary-general of the Cincinnati—
title: Eulogium on the character of General Washington late President of the United States; Pronounced before the Pennsylvania Society of the Cincinnati—On the twenty second day of February Eighteen hundred—At the German Reformed Church in the City of Philadelphia. <author statement>

Title Page Deposit
author: MAJOR WILLIAM JACKSON,/ Aid-de-camp to the late President of the United/ States, and Secretary-general of the Cincinnati.
title: EULOGIUM,/ On the Character of/ GENERAL WASHINGTON,/ LATE/ PRESIDENT OF THE UNITED STATES;/ *Pronounced before the/* PENNSYLVANIA SOCIETY/ OF THE/ <black letter> Cincinnati,/ ON THE TWENTY-SECOND DAY OF FEBRUARY, EIGHTEEN HUNDRED./ AT THE GERMAN REFORMED CHURCH,/ IN THE/ CITY OF PHILADELPHIA./ <thick decorative rule>/ <author statement>/ <double rule>
imprint: <below double rule> *Philadelphia:/* PRINTED BY JOHN ORMROD, NO. 41, CHESNUT-STREET./ 1800.

253.
District Court Ledger, 262 PA 216
date of deposit: May 7, twenty-fourth year of Independence
claimant: P: Daniel Ebsworth
author: D. E. a Cosmopolite.
title: The Republican Harmonist; being a select collection of Republican, Patriotic and Masonic Songs, Odes, Sonnets—&c—American and European: some of which are Original and most of the others now come for the first time from an American Press. with a collection of Toasts and sentiments. <four lines of poetry in English> <author statement>

Title Page Deposit
author: D. E. *a Cosmopolite.*
title: THE/ REPUBLICAN HARMONIST:/ *BEING/* A SELECT COLLECTION OF/ *Republican, Patriotic, and Masonic/* SONGS, ODES, SONNETS, &c./ AMERICAN AND EUROPEAN:/ *Some of which are Original, and most of the others now come/ for the first time from an American Press./* WITH A COL LECTION OF/ TOASTS AND SENTIMENTS./ <thick rule>/ <four lines of poetry in English>/ <short double rule>/ <author statement>/ <short double rule>
imprint: <below short double rule> <black letter> Philadelphia:/ <ornament>/ 1800.

254.
District Court Ledger, 262 PA 217
date of deposit: June 7, twenty-fourth year of Independence
claimant: A: Benjamin Smith Barton
author: . . . , M.D. Professor of Materia Medica, Natural History and Botany in the University of Pennsylvania, and one of the Physicians to the Pennsylvania Hospital.
title: A Memoir concerning the disease of Goitre as it prevails in different Parts of North America. <author statement> <quotation in English>

Title Page Deposit
author: BENJAMIN SMITH BARTON, M.D./ PROFESSOR OF MATERIA MEDICA, NATURAL HISTORY AND BOTANY,/ IN THE/ *UNIVERSITY OF PENNSYLVANIA,/* AND/ ONE OF THE PHYSICIANS TO THE PENNSYLVANIA HOSPITAL.
title: A/ MEMOIR/ CONCERNING THE/ DISEASE OF GOITRE,/ AS IT PREVAILS/ IN/ DIFFERENT PARTS/ OF/ NORTH-AMERICA./ <short thick rule>/ <author statement>/ <short decorative rule>/ <quotation in English>/ <short decorative rule>
imprint: <below short decorative rule> *PHILADELPHIA:/* PRINTED, FOR THE AUTHOR, BY WAY & GROFF,/ No. 48, North Third-Street./ 1800.

255.
District Court Ledger, 262 PA 218
date of deposit: July 10, twenty-fifty year of Independence

claimant: A: Alexander Addison
author: . . . , President of the Courts of Common Pleas of the Fifth Circuit of the State of Pennsylvania—
title: Reports of Cases in the County Courts of the Fifth Circuit, and in the High Court of Errors & Appeals, of the State of Pennsylvania. And Charges to Grand Juries of those County Courts—<author statement>

Title Page Deposit
author: ALEXANDER ADDISON,/ PRESIDENT OF THE COURTS OF COMMON PLEAS OF/ THE FIFTH CIRCUIT OF THE STATE/ OF PENNSYLVANIA.
title: REPORTS OF CASES/ IN THE/ *County Courts of the Fifth Circuit,*/ AND IN THE/ HIGH COURT of ERRORS & APPEALS,/ OF THE/ STATE OF PENNSYLVANIA./ AND/ Charges to Grand Juries/ OF THOSE/ COUNTY COURTS./ <double rule>/ <author statement>/ <double rule>
imprint: <below double rule> *WASHINGTON:*/ PRINTED BY JOHN COLERICK, AND MAY/ BE HAD OF THE BOOKSELLERS/ IN PHILADELPHIA./ <short thick rule>/ 1800.

256.
District Court Ledger, 262 PA 218
date of deposit: July 15, twenty-fifth year of Independence
claimant: A: Mathew Carey
title: The Child's Guide to Spelling and Reading; or an Attempt, to facilitate the progress of small children when first sent to School.—

Title Page Deposit
title: THE/ CHILD's GUIDE/ TO/ SPELLING AND READING;/ OR/ AN ATTEMPT,/ TO FACILITATE THE PROGRESS/ OF/ SMALL CHILDREN/ WHEN FIRST SENT TO SCHOOL./ <short thick decorative rule>
imprint: <below short thick decorative rule> *PHILADELPHIA:*/ PRINTED FOR MATHEW CAREY,/ No. 118, Market-street./ From the Press of D. HOGAN./ <short thick decorative rule>

257.
District Court Ledger, 262 PA 219
date of deposit: July 15, twenty-fifth year of Independence
claimant: A: Mathew Carey
title: The American Primer; or an easy introduction to Spelling and Reading.

Title Page Deposit
title: THE/ American Primer;/ OR,/ AN EASY INTRODUCTION/ TO/ SPELLING AND READING.
imprint: *PHILADELPHIA:*/ PRINTED FOR MATHEW CAREY,/ No. 118, High-street./ <short thick rule>/ 1800.

258.
District Court Ledger, 262 PA 220
date of deposit: July 31, twenty-fifth year of Independence
claimant: P: John Rowlett
author: . . . , Accomptant, Bank of North America.
title: Rowlett's Tables of Discount, or Interest, On every Dollar (without exception) From one to two thousand, on every ten dollars, from two thousand to two thousand five hundred; on every fifty, from two thousand five hundred to three thousand, and on every five hundred, from three thousand to five thousand, From one day to sixty four days inclusive, At Six Per Cent. Comprizing, in the whole, upwards of one hundred and thirty two thousand one hundred and fifty calculations of Discount. All performed according to the equitable Principles of the Banks, and as practised between individuals throughout the United States. With Notes preceding the work, shewing how, by means of the Tables, to ascertain the Discount, At five, seven, and at eight per Cent. Reckoning either 360 or 365 days to the Year—explained by Examples. Also, Another note, under the first Page of the Work, shewing the mode of calculation on Cents; likewise the ready way to use the tables for any number of days exceeding sixty four. To all which is added, the principles of Computation of the various exchanges between each state respectively, and between these and London and Paris, at different rates of Exchange. <author statement>

Title Page Deposit
author: JOHN ROWLETT, Accomptant, Bank of North America.
title: ROWLETT's/ Tables of Discount, or Interest,/ *On every Dollar (without exception)*/ <. . .>/ TO ALL WHICH IS ADDED,/ The principles of computation of the various exchanges between *each state respectively,* and between all/ these and LONDON and PARIS, at *different rates of Exchange.*/ <double rule>/ <author statement>/ <double rule>
imprint: <below double rule> *PHILADELPHIA:*/ PRINTED FOR THE PROPRIETOR,/ *Anno*

Domini 1800,/ And the twenty-fourth Year of the Independence of the United States of America./ <thick rule>

259.

District Court Ledger, 262 PA 221

date of deposit: August 22, twenty-fifth year of Independence

claimant: P: William Young

title: Essay on Political Society.

Title Page Deposit

title: <double rule>/ ESSAY/ ON/ <script> POLITICAL SOCIETY./ <seven parallel thick rules, four of them decorative, arranged in order of decreasing size>

260.

District Court Ledger, 262 PA 222

date of deposit: November 19, twenty-fifth year of Independence

claimant: A: Charles W. Peale

title: Discourse introductory to a Course of Lectures on the Science of Nature with original Music composed for and sung on the Occasion—Delivered in the Hall of the University of Pennsylvania Nov: 8. 1800. <author statement> <three lines of poetry in English>

note: According to the *National Index of American Imprints,* the author is Charles Willson Peale.

Title Page Deposit

author: CHARLES W. PEALE.

title: DISCOURSE/ INTRODUCTORY/ TO A/ Course of Lectures/ ON THE/ SCIENCE OF NATURE;/ WITH/ ORIGINAL MUSIC,/ *COMPOSED FOR, AND SUNG ON, THE OCCA SION.*/ <short thick rule>/ DELIVERED IN THE HALL OF THE UNIVERSITY/ OF PENNSYLVANIA, NOV. 8, 1800./ <short double rule>/ <author statement>/ <short double rule>/ <three lines of poetry in English>/ <double rule>

imprint: <below double rule> *—Philadelphia:—*/ PRINTED BY ZACHARIAH POULSON, JUNIOR,/ *No.* 106, *Chesnut-street.*/ <short thick rule>/ 1800.

261.

District Court Ledger, 262 PA 222

date of deposit: December 12, twenty-fifth year of Independence

claimant: P: Collinson Read

author: . . . Esquire—

title: An Abridgement of the Laws of Pennsylvania being a complete Digest of all such Acts of Assembly as concern the Commonwealth at Large—To which is added an Appendix containing a Variety of Precedents (adapted to the several Acts) for the Use of Justices of the Peace Sherriffs Attornies and Conveyancers. <author statement>

Title Page Deposit

author: COLLINSON READ, ESQUIRE.

title: AN/ ABRIDGEMENT/ OF THE/ *Laws of Pennsylvania,*/ BEING A COMPLETE/ DIGEST/ OF ALL SUCH/ ACTS OF ASSEMBLY/ AS CONCERN THE COMMONWEALTH AT LARGE./ TO WHICH IS ADDED,/ AN APPENDIX,/ CONTAINING,/ A VARIETY OF PRECEDENTS/ (ADAPTED TO THE SEV ERAL ACTS)/ FOR THE USE OF/ JUSTICES OF THE PEACE, SHERIFFS, ATTOR-/ NIES, AND CONVEYANCERS./ <short thick decorative rule>/ <author statement>/ <short thick decorative rule>

imprint: <below short thick decorative rule> *PHILADELPHIA:* PRINTED FOR THE AUTHOR./ <short rule>/ 1800.

262.

District Court Ledger, 262 PA 223

date of deposit: December 16, twenty-fifth year of Independence

claimant: A: Mathew Carey

title: The School of Wisdom or American Monitor containing a copious Collection of sublime and elegant Extracts from the most eminent Writers on Morals, Religion and Government—<quotation in English>

Title Page Deposit

title: THE/ SCHOOL OF WISDOM:/ OR,/ AMERICAN MONITOR./ CONTAINING/ A COPIOUS COLLECTION OF/ SUBLIME AND ELEGANT EXTRACTS,/ FROM THE/ *MOST EMINENT WRITERS,*/ ON/ *MORALS, RELIGION & GOVERNMENT.*/ <thick decorative rule>/ <quotation in English>/ <thick decorative rule>

imprint: <below thick deocrative rule> *PHILADELPHIA:*/ PRINTED FOR MATHEW CAREY,/ No. 118, MARKET-STREET./ <short thick decorative rule>/ 1800./ <short thick decorative rule>

note: [*Copy-right secured.*] <The clerk's note giving the date of deposit and the claimant appears on a separate piece of paper.>

263.

District Court Ledger, 262 PA 224
date of deposit: December 23, twenty-fifth year of Independence
claimant: P: Asbury Dickens
translator: An American Gentleman—
title: The Origin and Principles of the American Revolution, compared with the Origin and Principles of the French Revolution. Translated from the German of Gentz—<translator statement>

Title Page Deposit
translator: AN AMERICAN GENTLEMAN.
title: THE ORIGIN AND PRINCIPLES/ OF THE/ *AMERICAN REVOLUTION,*/ COM PARED WITH THE/ ORIGIN AND PRIN CIPLES/ OF THE/ FRENCH REVOLUTION./ <short double rule>/ TRANSLATED FROM THE GERMAN OF GENTZ;/ <translator statement>/ <short double rule>/ COPY-RIGHT SECURED./ <double rule>
imprint: <below double rule> PHILADELPHIA:/ PUBLISHED BY ASBURY DICKINS, OPPOSITE CHRIST-CHURCH./ H. MAXWELL, PRINTER, COLUMBIA-HOUSE./ <short dotted rule>/ 1800.

Massachusetts

1790

264.

District Court Ledger, 43 MA 1

date of deposit: July 10, fifteenth year of Independence

claimant: A: Reverend Jedediah Morse

author: . . . A.M. Minister of the Congregation in Charlestown near Boston

title: The American Geography; or a view of the present situation of the United States of America illustrated with two Sheet maps;—One of the southern the other of the Northern States, neatly & elegantly engraved & more correct, than any that have hitherto been publish'd—to which is added a concise abridgement of the Geography of the British, Spanish, French & Dutch Dominions in America & the West = Indies, of Europe, Asia & Africa

note: Numbers 264 and 265 are registered in the same deposit entry in the court ledger.

265.

District Court Ledger, 43 MA 1

date of deposit: July 10, fifteenth year of Independence

claimant: A: Jedediah Morse

author: . . . A.M. Minister of the Congregation in Charlestown near Boston

title: Geography made easy; being an Abridgement of the American Geography;—to which is added a geographical Account of the European settlements in America & of Europe, Asia & Africa; illustrated with eight neat maps & cuts—calculated particularly for the use & improvement of Schools in the United States—<author statement>

note: See the note for entry 264.

266.

District Court Ledger, 43 MA 2

date of deposit: September 13, fifteenth year of Independence

claimant: P: Isaiah Thomas

author: Samuel Deane A.M. Fellow of the American Academy of Arts & Sciences—

title: The New England Farmer; or, Georgical Dictionary containing a compendious account of the ways & methods in which the most important Art of Husbandry, in all it's various branches, is, or may be practised to the greatest advantage in this country. <author statement>

267.

District Court Ledger, 43 MA 2

date of deposit: October 7, fifteenth year of Independence

claimant: P: Isaiah Thomas & Eben. T. Andrews

author: Noah Webster Junior Esquire—

title: "The American spelling book; containing an easy standard of Pronunciation.—being the first part of a grammatical institute of the english language;—And of part the second "a grammatical institute of the english language, comprising an easy, concise & systematic method of education designed for the use of english Schools in America; And of part the third "An American selection of lessons in reading & speaking, calculated to improve the mind and refine the taste of youth &c. <author statement>

note: In the entry in the court ledger the claimants extend their rights as proprietors for this book to Rhode Island, New Hampshire, and Massachusetts. This book is claimed "in three parts."

268.

District Court Ledger, 43 MA 3

date of deposit: October 23, fifteenth year of Independence

claimant: A: Mrs.. M. Warren <Mercy (Otis) Warren>

title: Poems dramatic & miscellaneous <author statement>

note: According to the *National Index of American Imprints* the author is Mercy (Otis) Warren.

269.

District Court Ledger, 43 MA 3

date of deposit: November 15, fifteenth year of Independence

claimant: A: Caleb Bingham

author: . . . AM—.

title: The young Lady's Accidence:—or a short & easy introduction to English Grammar . . . designed principally for the use of young learners, more especially those of the Fair Sex, tho' proper for either. <author statement>

note: The ellipses in the title have been inserted in the deposit entry in the court ledger by the clerk.

270.

District Court Ledger, 43 MA 4

date of deposit: December 13, fifteenth year of Independence

claimant: A: Thomas & John Fleet

title: Fleets Pocket Almanack for the year of our Lord 1791, to which is annexed the Massachusetts Register &c.

note: Numbers 270 and 271 are registered in the same deposit entry in the court ledger.

271.
District Court Ledger, 43 MA 4
date of deposit: December 13, fifteenth year of Independence
claimant: P: Thomas & John Fleet
author: Nathaniel Low
title: An Astronomical Diary or Almanack for the year of the Christian AEra 1791, calculated for the meridian of Boston in America, <author statement>
note: See the note for entry 270.

272.
District Court Ledger, 43 MA 4
date of deposit: December 24, fifteenth year of Independence
claimant: A: John Jenkins
author: . . . writing Master
title: The Art of writing reduced to a plain & easy system on a plan entirely new, in seven books <author statement>

273.
District Court Ledger, 43 MA 4
date of deposit: December 29, fifteenth year of Independence
claimant: A: Montague
title: A systematical compendium of Geography on the face of 52 Cards.
note: The clerk has left a blank space where the claimant's first name should appear in this entry in the ledger.

1791

274.
District Court Ledger, 43 MA 5
date of deposit: January 24, fifteenth year of Independence
claimant: A: Samuel Holyoke
author: . . . A B.
title: Harmonia Americana containing a concise introduction to the Grounds of Music, with a variety of Airs, suitable for divine worship & the use of musical Societies—consisting of three & four parts; <author statement>

275.
District Court Ledger, 43 MA 5
date of deposit: February 24, fifteenth year of Independence
claimant: A: Paul Pinkham
author: surveyed by Capt . . . .
title: A Chart of Nantuckett Shoals, <author statement>
format: chart

276.
District Court Ledger, 43 MA 6
date of deposit: April 20, fifteenth year of Independence
claimant: A: William Croswell
author: . . . Teacher of Navigation.
title: Tables for readily computing the Longitude by the Lunar observations.—partly new & partly taken from the requisite tables of Dr.. Maskelyne. with their application in a variety of Rules & Examples. <author statement>

277.
District Court Ledger, 43 MA 6
date of deposit: July 6, sixteenth year of Independence
claimant: A: Hannah Adams
author: . . . of Medfield.
title: A view of Religion in two parts;—part first containing an Alphabetical compendium of the various religious denominations which have appeared in the world from the beginning of the Christian AEra to the present day;—part second containing a brief Account of the different schemes of Religion now embraced among mankind.—<author statement>

278.
District Court Ledger, 43 MA 7
date of deposit: August 31, sixteenth year of Independence
claimant: A: Jeremy Belknap
author: . . . AM Member of the American Philosophical society held at Philadelphia for promoting useful knowledge—
title: The History of New Hampshire Volume 1. comprehending the events of one complete century from the discovery of the River Piscataqua, <author statement>
note: Numbers 278, 279, 280 and 281 are registered in the same deposit entry in the court ledger.

279.
District Court Ledger, 43 MA 7
date of deposit: August 31, sixteenth year of Independence
claimant: A: Jeremy Belknap

author: . . . AM. Member of the Philosophical Society in Philadelphia, And of the Academy of Arts & Sciences in Massachusetts—
title: the History of New Hampshire Volume II. comprehending the events of seventy five years from MDCCXV to MDCCXC. illustrated by a Map. <author statement>
note: See the note for entry number 278.

280.
District Court Ledger, 43 MA 7
date of deposit: August 31, sixteenth year of Independence
claimant: A: Jeremy Belknap
author: . . . AM Member of the Philosophical Society in Philadelphia & of the Academy of Arts & Sciences in Massachusetts.
title: The History of New Hampshire Volume III. containing a geographical description of the State; with sketches of its natural History, productions, improvements & present state of society & manners, laws & government; <author statement>
note: See the note for entry number 278.

281.
District Court Ledger, 43 MA 7
date of deposit: August 31, sixteenth year of Independence
claimant: A: Jeremy Belknap
title: A New Map of New Hampshire <author statement> 1791.
format: map
note: See the note for entry number 278.

282.
District Court Ledger, 43 MA 8
date of deposit: November 19, sixteenth year of Independence
claimant: A: Thomas & John Fleet
title: Fleets Pocket Almanack for the year of our Lord 1792, being Bissextile or leap year & sixteenth of American Independence. calculated chiefly for the use of the Commonwealth of Massachusetts, to which is annexed the Massachusetts Register &c.
note: Numbers 282 and 283 are registered in the same deposit entry in the court ledger.

283.
District Court Ledger, 43 MA 8
date of deposit: November 19, sixteenth year of Independence
claimant: P: Thomas & John Fleet
title: An Astronomical Diary or Almanack for the year of Christian AEra 1792 for Bissextile or leap year &c—
note: See the note for entry number 282.

284.
District Court Ledger, 43 MA 8
date of deposit: July 29, sixteenth year of Independence
claimant: P: Isaiah Thomas
title: The Worcester Collection of Sacred Harmony. first & second parts. containing first an introduction to the grounds of Musick, or rules for learners—second, a large number of celebrated Psalm and Hymn Tunes from the most approved Authors, suited to all metres usually sung in Churches.—to which is added an Appendix containing a number of excellent Psalm Tunes, several of which are entirely new, and other pieces of sacred vocal musick, many of which were composed by eminent European Authors, and never before published in this Country.—The whole compiled for the use of Schools and singing Societies—

1792

285.
District Court Ledger, 43 MA 9
date of deposit: January 5, sixteenth year of Independence
claimant: P: Belknap & Young
title: The American Apollo Part 1—vol. 1. containing the publications of the Historical Society—

286.
District Court Ledger, 43 MA 10
date of deposit: January 24, sixteenth year of Independence
claimant: A: Caleb Bingham
author: A.M. Author of the young Lady's Accidence—
title: The Child's Companion; being a concise spelling book; containing a selection of words, in modern use properly arranged & divided in such a manner as will most naturally lead the learner to a right pronunciation; together with a variety of lessons for reading &c. designed for the use of schools, <author statement>

287.
District Court Ledger, 43 MA 10
date of deposit: February 11, sixteenth year of Independence

claimant: P: Thomas & Andrews
title: The Foresters, An American Tale:—being a sequel to the History of John Bull the Clothier—in a series of letters to a friend.

288.
District Court Ledger, 43 MA 11
date of deposit: February 21, sixteenth year of Independence
claimant: P: Isaiah Thomas
title: The young Gentlemen & Ladies Accidence; or a compendious American Grammar of the English Tongue plain & easy.—designed for the youth of both sexes—

289.
District Court Ledger, 43 MA 11
date of deposit: February 22, sixteenth year of Independence
claimant: P: Thomas & Andrews
author: William Cooper.
title: An Anthem designed for Thanksgiving day—but proper for any publick occasion. <author statement>

290.
District Court Ledger, 43 MA 12
date of deposit: February 28, sixteenth year of Independence
claimant: A: Caleb Alexander
author: . . . AM.
title: A Grammatical System of the English language;—comprehending a plain & familiar Scheme of teaching young Gentlemen & Ladies the Art of speaking & writing correctly their native tongue. <author statement>

291.
District Court Ledger, 43 MA 12
date of deposit: March 20, sixteenth year of Independence
claimant: A: John Gardiner
title: The speech of John Gardiner Esq. delivered in the House of Representatives, on Thursday the 26.th of January 1792; on the subject of the report of the Committee appointed to consider the expediency of repealing the law against Theatrical exhibitions within this Commonwealth.

292.
District Court Ledger, 43 MA 13
date of deposit: March 13, sixteenth year of Independence
claimant: P: Isaiah Thomas
author: a Farmer of Massachusetts.
title: A complete Guide for the management of Bees, through the year. <author statement> illustrated with a copperplate.

293.
District Court Ledger, 43 MA 13
date of deposit: March 31, sixteenth year of Independence
claimant: A: Elisha Ticknor
author: . . . AM.
title: English exercises in which sentences, falsely constructed, are to be corrected; comprehending all the rules necessary for passing the language;—And arranged in such a manner, as will greatly facilitate the acquisition of Grammatical Knowledge, designed for the use of schools, <author statement>

294.
District Court Ledger, 43 MA 14
date of deposit: April 27, sixteenth year of Independence
claimant: A: P.J.G. De Nancrede
author: . . . , Maitre de langue Françoise, en cette Universite.
title: L'abeille Françoise, ou nouveau recueil, de morceaux brillans, des Auteurs Francois les plus celebres. Ouvrage utile à ceux qui étudient la langue Francoise, et amusant pour ceux qui la connoissent. A l'usage de l'Université de Cambridge. <author statement>

295.
District Court Ledger, 43 MA 14
date of deposit: May 21, sixteenth year of Independence
claimant: A: John Vinal
author: . . . , Teacher of the Mathematicks and Writing in Boston.
title: The Preceptor's Assistant, or Student's Guide. being a systematical treatise of Arithmetick; both vulgar and decimal—calculated for the use of Schools, counting houses and private families. Wherein the most practical branches of that important Art are laid down in so plain and concise a manner, that persons of common capacity may become acquainted, in a short time, with that beneficial Science. <author statement>

296.
District Court Ledger, 43 MA 15
date of deposit: July 16, seventeenth year of Independence

claimant: P: Thomas and Andrews
title: A clear & practical System of Punctuation;—abridged from Robertson's essay on Punctuation, for the use of Schools.

297.
District Court Ledger, 43 MA 15
date of deposit: September 4, seventeenth year of Independence
claimant: A: Joseph Dana
author: . . . AB.
title: A new American selection of lessons in reading & speaking; consisting of sacred, moral and historical extracts; humorous, entertaining, and descriptive pieces; select sentences and maxims; poetry, dialogues &c—to which are added elements of Gesture, illustrated with Copperplate engravings, designed for the use of Schools <author statement>

298.
District Court Ledger, 43 MA 16
date of deposit: September 25, seventeenth year of Independence
claimant: A: Oliver Holden
author: . . . Teacher of Music in Charlestown.
title: American Harmony; containing a variety of Airs, suitable for divine worship on thanksgivings, Ordinations, Christmas fasts, funerals & other occasions.—together with a number of Psalm tunes, in three & four parts—the whole entirely new.—<author statement>

299.
District Court Ledger, 43 MA 17
date of deposit: October 11, seventeenth year of Independence
claimant: A: Thomas & John Fleet
title: Fleets Pocket Almanack for the year of our Lord 1793. to which is annexed the Massachusetts Register &c—
note: Numbers 299 and 300 are registered in the same deposit entry in the court ledger.

300.
District Court Ledger, 43 MA 17
date of deposit: October 11, seventeenth year of Independence
claimant: P: Thomas & John Fleet
author: Nathaniel Low—
title: An Astronomical Diary or Almanack for the year of Christian AEra 1793. calculated for the meridian of Boston in America, latitude 42 deg: 25 min: North <author statement>
note: See the note for entry 299.

301.
District Court Ledger, 43 MA 17
date of deposit: October 15, seventeenth year of Independence
claimant: A: George Richards & Oliver W Lane
title: Psalms, Hymns and Spiritual Songs, selected and Original.—designed for the use of the Church Universal in public & private devotion—

302.
District Court Ledger, 43 MA 18
date of deposit: October 18, seventeenth year of Independence
claimant: A: William Haliburton
author: a Bostonian.
title: Effects of the Stage on the manners of a People;—and the propriety of encouraging and establishing a virtuous Theatre. <author statement>

303.
District Court Ledger, 43 MA 18
date of deposit: October 23, seventeenth year of Independence
claimant: A: Jeremy Belknap
author: . . . D.D.
title: A Discourse intended to commemorate the discovery of America by Christopher Columbus; delivered at the request of the Historical Society in Massachusetts on the twenty third day of October 1792 being the completion of the third Century since that memorable event.—To which are added four dissertations, connected with various parts of the discourse, viz. 1. On the circumnavigation of Africa by the Ancients.—2 An examination of the pretensions of Martin Behaim to a discovery of America, prior to that of Columbus with a Chronological detail of all the discoveries made in the fifteenth Century—3. On the question whether the Honey = Bee is a native of America.?—4. On the colour of the native Americans and the recent population of this Continent. <author statement>

304.
District Court Ledger, 43 MA 19
date of deposit: November 30, seventeenth year of Independence
claimant: A: Benjamin Dearborn
title: The Pupils' Guide or Assistant in Writing, &c <author statement>

305.
District Court Ledger, 43 MA 20
date of deposit: December 7, seventeenth year of Independence
claimant: P: Isaiah Thomas
title: The Constitutions of the ancient and honourable Fraternity of free & accepted Masons: containing their history, Charges, Addresses &c collected and digested from their old records, faithful traditions & Lodge Books, for the use of Masons.—To which are added the History of Masonry in the Commonwealth of Massachusetts, and the Constitution laws & regulations of their Grand Lodge.—together with a large Collection of songs, Epilogues &c—
note: Page 21 in the ledger is blank.

1793

306.
District Court Ledger, 43 MA 22
date of deposit: March 8, seventeenth year of Independence
claimant: P: Isaiah Thomas & Ebenezer T. Andrews
title: The System of Doctrines contained in divine revelation, explained & defended.—showing their consistence & connection with each other.—To which is added, a Treatise on the millenium.—in two volumes. VOL. II.

307.
District Court Ledger, 43 MA 23
date of deposit: March 8, seventeenth year of Independence
claimant: P: Isaiah Thomas
author: Joseph Lathrop, D.D. Pastor of the first Church in West=springfield.
title: Sermons on various subjects, evangelical, devotional and practical, adapted to the promotion of Christian piety, family religion and youthful virtue. <author statement>

308.
District Court Ledger, 43 MA 24
date of deposit: March 22, seventeenth year of Independence
claimant: P: Belknap & Hall
author: an American Lady.
title: The hapless Orphan, or innocent victim of revenge. a novel founded on incidents in real life.—in a series of letters from Caroline Francis to Maria B—in two volumes, <author statement>

309.
District Court Ledger, 43 MA 24
date of deposit: May 9, seventeenth year of Independence
claimant: P: Isaiah Thomas
author: Nicholas Pike Esq. Member of the American Academy of Arts & Sciences.
title: Abridgement of the new & complete System of Arithmetick composed for the use and adapted to the Commerce of the Citizens of the United States. <author statement>

310.
District Court Ledger, 43 MA 25
date of deposit: June 10, seventeenth year of Independence
claimant: A: Jedidiah Morse
author: . . . AM.
title: The American Universal Geography, or a view of the present state of all the Empires, Kingdoms, States & Republics in the known world, & of the United States of America, in particular, in two parts; the first part treats of Astronomical Geography & other useful preliminaries to the Study of Geography, in an enlarged & improved introduction;—of the Western or American Continent;—of its discovery—it's aboriginal inhabitants & whence they came—it's divisions—but more particularly of the United States of America, generally & individually,—of their situation, dimensions, civil divisions, <the following word has been partially blotted out with ink in the ms.> Rivers, Lakes, Climate, Mountains, soil produce, natural history, Commerce, Manufactures, population, Character, Curiosities, Springs, Mines & Minerals, Military Strength, Constitutions, Islands, history of the war & the succeeding events;—with a view of the British, Spanish, French, Portuguese And other dominions on the Continent & in the West=Indies the second part describes at large and from the latest & best Authorities, the present state, in respect to the above mentioned particulars, of the Eastern Continent, and it's Islands, as divided into Europe, Asia & Africa,—and subdivided into Empires Kingdoms & Republics.—To which are added, an improved Catalogue of names of places, and their Geographical situation, alphabetically arranged;—An enlarged chronological table of remarkable events, from the Creation to the present time,—and a list of Ancient & modern learned & eminent men in America, as well as Europe.—The whole comprehending a complete & improved System of modern Geography, calculated for Americans. illustrated with maps of the Countries described. <author statement>

311.
District Court Ledger, 43 MA 26
date of deposit: July 9, eighteenth year of Independence
claimant: A: Thaddeus M. Harris
author: . . . AM. Librarian of Harvard University, Cambridge.
title: The natural history of the Bible:—or a description of all the Beasts, Birds, Fishes, Insects, Reptiles, Trees Plants, metals, precious Stones &c mentioned in the sacred scriptures.—collected from the best Authorities, and alphabetically arranged. <author statement>

312.
District Court Ledger, 43 MA 28
date of deposit: August 1, eighteenth year of Independence
claimant: A: Oliver Holden
author: . . . Author of the American Harmony.
title: The Union Harmony or Universal Collection of sacred Music. —In two volumes; <author statement>

313.
District Court Ledger, 43 MA 28
date of deposit: August 19, eighteenth year of Independence
claimant: P: David West
title: Memoirs of the Lives, Characters, and writings of those two eminent, pious and useful Ministers of Jesus Christ, Dr.. Isaac Watts and Dr.. Philip Doddridge.

314.
District Court Ledger, 43 MA 29
date of deposit: September 13, eighteenth year of Independence
claimant: A: Joseph Stone & Abraham Wood
title: The Columbian Harmony.—containing the Rules of Psalmody;—together with a collection of sacred Music, designed for the use of worshipping Assemblies & singing societies. <author statement>

315.
District Court Ledger, 43 MA 30
date of deposit: October 11, eighteenth year of Independence
claimant: P: Isaiah Thomas & Ebenezer T. Andrews
author: Caleb Alexander, Author of a ''grammatical of the English language.''
title: Grammatical Elements or a comprehensive theory of English Grammar; intended for the use of Children of both sexes. <author statement>

316.
District Court Ledger, 43 MA 30
date of deposit: October 21, eighteenth year of Independence
claimant: A: Thomas & John Fleet
title: A Pocket Almanack for the year of our Lord 1794—to which is annexed the Massachusetts-Register, <author statement>
note: Numbers 316 and 317 are registered in the same deposit entry in the court ledger.

317.
District Court Ledger, 43 MA 30
date of deposit: October 21, eighteenth year of Independence
claimant: P: Thomas & John Fleet
author: Nathaniel Low
title: An Astronomical Diary or Almanack for the year of Christian AEra 1794, calculated for the meridian of Boston in America, lat: 42 deg: 25 min north, <author statement>
note: See the note for entry 316.

318.
District Court Ledger, 43 MA 31
date of deposit: November 15, eighteenth year of Independence
claimant: A: David Townsend
author: . . . , Inspector of Pot & Pearl Ashes for the Commonwealth of Massachusetts.
title: Principles & observations applied to the manufacture & inspection of Pot & Pearl Ashes. <author statement>

319.
District Court Ledger, 43 MA 32
date of deposit: December 3, eighteenth year of Independence
claimant: A: Jacob Kimball
author: . . . Jun. A.B.
title: The rural harmony, being an original composition, in three & four parts. for the use of singing Schools & musical Societies. <author statement>

1794

320.
District Court Ledger, 43 MA 32
date of deposit: January 20, eighteenth year of Independence

claimant: P: Isaiah Thomas
author: Peter Whitney AM Minister of the Gospel in Northborough in said County.
title: The History of the County of Worcester, in the Commonwealth of Massachusetts:—with a particular account of every Town from its first settlement to the present time; including its ecclesiastical:—together with a Geographical description of the same.—to which is prefixed a Map of the County at large from actual survey, <author statement>

321.
District Court Ledger, 43 MA 33
date of deposit: January 25, eighteenth year of Independence
claimant: A: Foster Waterman
author: . . . AM.
title: The Childs Instructor, being an original spelling book, in two volumes. vol: 1. containing easy words of one & two syllables, is calculated to serve as an introduction to spelling—Vol: II. containing all the primitive words in the English language, with rules for their derivatives & compounds, is capable of being made a complete Test of pronunciation—principally designed for the use of Schools;—but to adults may serve as a substitute for Perry's English Dictionary, whose pronunciation & orthography are generally adopted—<author statement>

322.
District Court Ledger, 43 MA 34
date of deposit: February 18, eighteenth year of Independence
claimant: A: John Nobles
author: . . . Astrologer & Doctor.
title: These are the Predictions of <author statement>

323.
District Court Ledger, 43 MA 34
date of deposit: February 24, eighteenth year of Independence
claimant: P: Isaiah Thomas
author: Caleb Alexander AM. Author of a "Grammatical System of the English language," and "Grammatical Elements."
title: A Grammatical Institute of the latin language; intended for the use of latin Schools in the United States, <author statement>

324.
District Court Ledger, 43 MA 35
date of deposit: March 1, eighteenth year of Independence
claimant: A: Jeremy Belknap
author: . . . D.D.
title: American Biography:—or an historical Account of those persons who have been distinguished in America, as Adventurers, Statesmen, Philosophers, Divines, Warriors, Authors, and other remarkable Characters. comprehending a recital of the events connected with their lives & Actions. VOL. I. <author statement>

325.
District Court Ledger, 43 MA 35
date of deposit: April 29, eighteenth year of Independence
claimant: P: Isaiah Thomas and Ebenezer T. Andrews
author: Samuel Freeman Esquire, Author of the Town Officer & Probate Auxiliary.
title: A valuable assistant to every man: or the American Clerks Magazine.—containing the most useful & necessary forms of writings, which commonly occur between Man and Man under the names of Acquittances, Agreements Assignments, Awards, Bargains, Bills of Sale, Bonds, Conditions, Conveyances, Covenants, Deeds, Feoffments, Fine & Recovery, Gifts and Grants, Indentures, Leases, Lease and Release, Letters of Attorney, Mortgages, Notes, Pleas, Recepts, Releases, Sales, Surrenders, wills, writs & declarations &c &c other Instruments, the whole of which are calculated for the use of the Citizens of the United States and conformable to law <author statement>
note: The clerk has noted in the left-hand margin of the deposit entry in the court ledger: "renewed the 25.th day of January A D 1808."

326.
District Court Ledger, 43 MA 36
date of deposit: May 5, eighteenth year of Independence
claimant: A: Caleb Bingham
author: . . . AM.
title: The American Preceptor;—being a new selection of lessons for reading & speaking designed for the use of Schools <author statement>

327.
District Court Ledger, 43 MA 37
date of deposit: June 9, eighteenth year of Independence

claimant: A: Jedidiah Morse
author: . . . Minister of the Congregation in Charleston near Boston;
title: Geography made easy; being an abridgement of the American universal Geography.—Containing Astronomical Geography; Discovery & general description of America; General view of the United States; particular Accounts of the United States of America, and of all the—Kingdoms, States and Republics in the known world,—in regard to their boundaries, extent, rivers, lakes, mountains, productions, population, character, government, trade manufactures, curiosities, history &c to which is added an improved chronological table of remarkable events from the Creation to the present time. illustrated with maps of the Countries described—calculated particularily for the use & improvement of Schools & Academies in the United States of America. <author statement> Fourth edition, abridged, corrected and enlarged by the Author.

328.
District Court Ledger, 43 MA 38
date of deposit: August 11, nineteenth year of Independence
claimant: A: Elhanan Winchester
title: A Course of Lectures on the Prophecies that remain to be fulfilled.—in four volumes. <author statement>

329.
District Court Ledger, 43 MA 38
date of deposit: August 18, nineteenth year of Independence
claimant: P: John W. Folsom
author: Elhanan Winchester.
title: The universal restoration exhibited in four Dialogues between a Minister & his Friend, comprehending the substance of several Conversations,—which the Author hath had with various persons both in America and Europe, on that interesting subject; chiefly designed fully to state and fairly to answer the most—common objections that are brought against it from the Scriptures.—<author statement> To which is prefixed a brief account of the means & manner of the Author's embracing these sentiments.—Intermixed with Sketches of his life, during four years.

330.
District Court Ledger, 43 MA 39
date of deposit: August 18, nineteenth year of Independence
claimant: A: Abijah Cheever
author: Dr.. . . . —
title: History of a case of incisted—Dropsy;—with a dissection of the several Cysts,—as communicated to the American Academy of Arts and sciences,—Jan. 31. 1787. <author statement> Boston—

331.
District Court Ledger, 43 MA 40
date of deposit: August 26, nineteenth year of Independence
claimant: A: John Norman
title: The American Pilot, containing the navigation of the sea Coast of North America, from the Streights of Belle=Isle to Cayenne, including the Island and Banks of Newfoundland, the West=India=Islands and all the Islands on the Coast;—with particular directions for sailing to and entering the principal harbours, rivers &c—describing also the Capes, head=lands, rivers, bays, roads, havens, harbours, straits, rocks, sands, shoals, banks, depths of water & Anchorage;—shewing the courses & distances from one place to another,—the ebbing of the sea,—the setting of the—tide & currents—&c—with many other things necessary to be known in navigation;—likewise necessary directions for those who are not fully acquainted with the use of Charts.

332.
District Court Ledger, 43 MA 41
date of deposit: November 21, nineteenth year of Independence
claimant: P: Samuel Hall
title: A short and easy guide to Arithmetick, particularly adapted to the use of Farmers and Tradesmen in the United States of—America:—containing all that is necessary to transact common business:—besides other usefull matters—designed for the use of schools and private families.

333.
District Court Ledger, 43 MA 41
date of deposit: November 24, nineteenth year of Independence
claimant: A: Benjamin Dearborn
author: . . . , Member of the American Academy of Arts and—sciences.
title: The Columbian Grammar: or an Essay for reducing a grammatical knowledge of the english language to a degree of simplicity, which will render it easy for the Instructer to teach and for

the Pupil to learn.—accompanied with notes critical & explanatory—for the use of Schools and young Gentlemen and Ladies, Natives or—foreigners, who are desirous of attempting the study without a Tutor.—being designed as part of a general System of Education, in the most useful branches of literature, for—American Youth of both sexes. <author statement>

334.
District Court Ledger, 43 MA 42
date of deposit: November 24, nineteenth year of Independence
claimant: P: Isaiah Thomas
author: Nathan Fiske DD. Pastor of the third Church in Brookfield, Massachusetts.
title: Twenty two Sermons on various and important subjects; chiefly practical. <author statement>

335.
District Court Ledger, 43 MA 42
date of deposit: December 12, nineteenth year of Independence
claimant: A: Elhanan Winchester
title: Ten letters addressed to Mr. Paine, in answer to his pamphlet, intituled the age of Reason.—containing some clear and satisfying evidences of the truth of divine revelation;—and especially of the resurrection & ascention of Jesus. <author statement>

1795

336.
District Court Ledger, 43 MA 43
date of deposit: January 1, nineteenth year of Independence
claimant: P: Joseph Belknap
author: John Clarke, Minister of a Church in Boston.
title: An Answer to the Question, why are you a Christian? <author statement>

337.
District Court Ledger, 43 MA 43
date of deposit: January 20, nineteenth year of Independence
claimant: P: Joseph Belknap
author: Jeremy Belknap, Minister of the Church in Federal Street, Boston—
title: Dissertations on the Character, Death & Resurrection of Jesus Christ, and the evidence of his Gospel;—with remarks on some sentiments advanced in a Book, intitled "The Age of Reason." <author statement>

338.
District Court Ledger, 43 MA 44
date of deposit: February 12, nineteenth year of Independence
claimant: P: Hans Gram, Samuel Holyoke & Oliver Holden
title: The Massachusetts Compiler of Theoretical & Practical Elements of sacred vocal music.—Together with a musical Dictionary, and a variety of Psalm Tunes, Choruses &c chiefly selected & adapted from modern European Publications—

339.
District Court Ledger, 43 MA 44
date of deposit: March 24, nineteenth year of Independence
claimant: P: Isaiah Thomas & Ebenezer T. Andrews
author: James Sullivan;
title: The History of the District of Maine. <author statement> illustrated by a new & correct Map of the District.

340.
District Court Ledger, 43 MA 45
date of deposit: March 24, nineteenth year of Independence
claimant: P: Isaiah Thomas & Ebenezer T. Andrews
author: Samuel Freeman Esquire, Compiler of the Town Officer, Probate Auxiliary, and American Clerk's Magazine.
title: The Massachusetts=Justice;—being a Collection of the laws of the Commonwealth of Massachusetts, relative to the Power & Duty of Justices of the Peace; alphabetically arranged in two parts.—Part I. The Power and Duty of the Justices of the Court of General Sessions of the Peace.—Part II. The Power & Duty of Justices of the Peace in their separate capacity.—To which are added, under the proper heads, a variety of—Forms, grounded on said laws.—the whole intended for the use of those who practise in the Office of a Justice, to assist them in the various duties thereto belonging.—with an Appendix, containing short and concise Rules, for changing, Pounds, Shillings, pence and farthings into—dollars, cents & milles, which a late law has introduced as the money of Account;—also rules for computing interest in such money, and sundry usefull tables respecting the same—to all which an Index is annexed. <author statement>

341.
District Court Ledger, 43 MA 46
date of deposit: April 8, nineteenth year of Independence
claimant: P: Isaiah Thomas
author: Caleb Alexander AM, Author of "A Grammatical System of the English language"—"Grammatical Elements,"—"A Grammatical Institute of the Latin language," and "An Introduction to the speaking and writing of the English language,,"
title: A new introduction to the latin language:—being an Attempt to exemplify the Latin Syntax and render familiar to the mind the grammatical construction of this useful language:—containing critical and explanatory Notes on all the rules of government, and agreement. <author statement>

342.
District Court Ledger, 43 MA 46
date of deposit: May 11, nineteenth year of Independence
claimant: P: Leonard Worcester
title: The Federal ready Reckoner, or Trader's valuable Guide, in purchasing & selling all kinds of Articles, by wholesale and Retail,—calculated in the Federal currency, shewing at one view, the amount of any number or quantity of Articles, Goods &c from one Mill or the tenth part of a Cent to two dollars, in dollars Cents and Mills—to which are added—/ I. A Table, shewing the value of any number of Cents, from one to one hundred, in Shillings, Pence & Farthings—/ 2.—A Table, shewing at one view, the value of foreign Gold, from one grain to twenty penny weights, in dollars and cents, and in pounds, shillings and pence.—/ 3. A Table of Interest at six per cent, calculated in the—Federal Currency, and in pounds shillings &c, for any term of time, from one Month to twelve months and for any sum from one dollar to ten thousand—

343.
District Court Ledger, 43 MA 47
date of deposit: May 26, nineteenth year of Independence
claimant: A: Jeremy Belknap
author: . . . D. D.
title: Sacred Poetry, consisting of Psalms and Hymns, adapted to Christian devotion in public and private, selected from the best Authors, with variations and additions. <author statement>

344.
District Court Ledger, 43 MA 48
date of deposit: June 5, nineteenth year of Independence
claimant: P: Isaiah Thomas
author: <Constantin François Chasseboeuf, comte de Volney>
title: Common Sense, or Natural Ideas opposed to supernatural
note: According to the *National Index of American Imprints* the author is Constantin François Chasseboeuf, comte de Volney.

345.
District Court Ledger, 43 MA 48
date of deposit: June 5, nineteenth year of Independence
claimant: P: Jean Baptiste de la Roche
author: Bernardin de St. Pierre, Author of Paul and Mary &c in French and English,
translator: M & M . . . . . .
title: Voyages of Amasis. <author statement> <translator statement>

346.
District Court Ledger, 43 MA 49
date of deposit: June 30, nineteenth year of Independence
claimant: A: Samuel West
author: . . . D. D. Pastor of the first Church of Christ in New Bedford.
title: Essays on liberty and necessity; in which the true nature of liberty is stated and defended;—And the principal Arguments used by Mr. Edwards and others for necessity, are consider'd.—In two parts. <author statement>

347.
District Court Ledger, 43 MA 50
date of deposit: July 13, twentieth year of Independence
claimant: A: Joseph Chaplin
title: The—Traders best Companion:—containing various Arithmetical Rules, by which simple addition, subtraction, multiplication, division, reduction, practice, interest, loss and gain, bookkeeping &c are applied to the Federal Currency; with several useful Tables:—very necessary in Schools, and for all those who may have occasion to deal in money matters <author statement>

348.
District Court Ledger, 43 MA 50
date of deposit: July 28, twentieth year of Independence

claimant: P: Isaiah Thomas & Ebenezer T. Andrews
author: John Lendrum—
title: A concise and impartial history of the American Revolution.—To which is prefixed, a General History of North & South America.—Together with an account of the discovery & Settlement of North America; and a view of the progress, character and political State of the Colonies, previous to the Revolution.—from the best Authorities. <author statement>

349.
District Court Ledger, 43 MA 51
date of deposit: July 28, twentieth year of Independence
claimant: P: James Reed Hutchins
title: The Gospel Tragedy:—an Epic Poem, in four Books.

350.
District Court Ledger, 43 MA 51
date of deposit: September 30, twentieth year of Independence
claimant: A: Samuel A Ruddock
author: . . . accomptant, Boston
title: Valuable Tables, for the use of American Merchants and Traders, <author statement>

351.
District Court Ledger, 43 MA 52
date of deposit: October 2, twentieth year of Independence
claimant: A: Paul Jewett
author: . . . , of Rowley.
title: The New=England Farrier;—or a compendium of Farriery, in four parts;—wherein most of the diseases to which horses, neat Cattle, Sheep and swine are incident, are treated of; with medical and surgical observations thereon.—The remedies in general are such, as are easily procured, safely applied, and happily successful, being the result of many years experience, and first production of the kind in New=England.—intended for the use of private Gentlemen and Farmers. <author statement>

352.
District Court Ledger, 43 MA 52
date of deposit: October 23, twentieth year of Independence
claimant: P: Thomas & John Fleet
author: Thomas & John Fleet.
title: A Pocket Almanack for the year of our Lord 1796. being a Leap year and Twentieth of American Independence, which began July 4th 1776—calculated chiefly for the use of the Commonwealth of Massachusetts, Boston the Metropolis, being in latitude 42 deg: 23 min: North—longitude 71 deg: 4 min: west from the Royal Observatory at Greenwich;—To which is annexed the Massachusetts Register. <author statement>
note: Numbers 352 and 353 are registered in the same deposit entry in the district court ledger.

353.
District Court Ledger, 43 MA 52
date of deposit: October 23, twentieth year of Independence
claimant: P: Thomas & John Fleet
author: Nathaniel Low.
title: An Astronomical Diary, or Almanack, for the year of Christian AEra 1796.—being Bissextile or Leap year;—and the Twentieth of the Independence of America, which began July 4th,, 1776.—containing all that is usual in an Almanack, and a variety of other matters useful & entertaining.—calculated for the meridian of Boston in America.—latitude 42 deg: 23. min: north. <author statement>
note: See note to entry 352.

354.
District Court Ledger, 43 MA 53
date of deposit: October 24, twentieth year of Independence
claimant: P: William Bradford
title: The Art of Courting, displayed in seven different scenes:—the principal of which are taken from actual life; and published for the—amusement of the American youth.

355.
District Court Ledger, 43 MA 54
date of deposit: October 24, twentieth year of Independence
claimant: P: Joseph Belknap
author: Robert B. Thomas.
title: The Farmer's Almanack, calculated on a new and improved plan, for the year of our Lord 1796. being Bissextile or leap year and twentieth of the Independence of America.—fitted to the town of Boston, but will serve for any of the adjoining States;—containing—besides the large number of Astronomical calculations & the Farmer's Calendar for every month in the year, as—great a variety, as any other Almanack, of new, useful, & entertaining matter. <author statement>

356.
District Court Ledger, 43 MA 54
date of deposit: December 3, twentieth year of Independence
claimant: A: Jedidiah Morse
author: . . . D, D, Minister of the Congregation in Charlestown, Massachusetts.
title: Elements of Geography:—containing a concise and comprehensive view of that useful science, as divided into 1. Astronomical 2. Physical or natural, 3 Political Geography, on a new plan.—adapted to the—capacities of Children and youth;—and designed from it's cheapness, for a reading and classical Book in common Schools, and as a useful winter evening's entertainment for young people in private families.—illustrated with a neat Map of the United States and a beautiful Chart of the whole world.— <author statement>

357.
District Court Ledger, 43 MA 55
date of deposit: November 20, twentieth year of Independence
claimant: A: Jonathan Plummer
author: ,written by himself.
title: Sketch of the history of the life and adventures of Jonathan Plummer Junr̄, <author statement>
note: The clerk has written in the left-hand margin of the entry in the ledger: "This Title having been mislaid was not recorded untill after tho' deposited before the preceding one—."

358.
District Court Ledger, 43 MA 56
date of deposit: December 22, twentieth year of Independence
claimant: A: Samuel Babcock
title: The Middlesex harmony, being an original composition of sacred Music, in three and four parts. <author statement>

1796

359.
District Court Ledger, 43 MA 56
date of deposit: February 16, twentieth year of Independence
claimant: A: Joshua Spalding
author: . . . , Minister of the Gospel, at the Tabernacle in Salem.
title: Sentiments concerning the coming and Kingdom of Christ; collected from the Bible & from the writings of many Antient, and some modern, Believers;—in nine lectures; with an Appendix. <author statement>

360.
District Court Ledger, 43 MA 57
date of deposit: March 12, twentieth year of Independence
claimant: P: John Williamson
title: Oscar & Malvina or the Hall of Fingall.

361.
District Court Ledger, 43 MA 57
date of deposit: April 26, twentieth year of Independence
claimant: A: Hezekiah Packard
author: . . . , Minister of Chelmsford.
title: A Chatechism, containing the first principles of religious and social duties;—adapted to the capacities of Children & youth, and beneficial to heads of families. <author statement>

362.
District Court Ledger, 43 MA 58
date of deposit: May 2, twentieth year of Independence
claimant: P: Edmund March Blunt & Angier March
author: Lawrance Furlong.
title: The Coasting Pilot, for the United States of America, containing directions for sailing into and out of, all the principal Ports & Harbours, from Passamaquady to the Capes of Virginia. <author statement>
note: The clerk has written in the left-hand margin of the entry in the ledger: "This Title alter'd before publishing as in the succeeding Record—." According to the *National Union Catalog* the author is Lawrence Furlong.

363.
District Court Ledger, 43 MA 58
date of deposit: May 2, twentieth year of Independence
claimant: P: Edmund March Blunt & Angier March
author: Capt Laurance Furlong.
title: The American Coast Pilot, containing. the courses and distance from Boston to all the principal Harbours, Capes and Head lands included between Passamaquady and the Capes of Virginia;—with directions for sailing into, and out of, all the principal Ports and Harbours, with the sounding on the Coast Also, A Tide Table, shewing the time of high water at full and Change of the Moon, in all the above places,

<the a in the following word has been crossed out in ms.> toge<a>ther with the Courses and Distance from Cape Cod, and Cape Ann, to the Shoal of Georges, and from said Capes out in the South and East Channell,, and the setting of the Current to the Eastward and Westward, Also the Latitude and Longitude of all the principal Harbours, Capes and Headlands &c. &c. <author statement> Also, Courses, Directions, Distances, &c. &c. from the Capes of Virginia to the River Misissippi, from the latest surveys and Observations. (Approved by experienced Pilots and Coasters).

note: According to the *National Union Catalog* the author is Lawrence Furlong.

364.

District Court Ledger, 43 MA 59

date of deposit: May 12, twentieth year of Independence

claimant: A: Samuel A Ruddock

author: . . . Accomptant Boston.

title: A Geographical view of all the Post Towns in the United States of America, and their distances from each other, according to the establishment of the Post Master General, <author statement>

365.

District Court Ledger, 43 MA 60

date of deposit: May 26, twentieth year of Independence

claimant: P: David West

author: Caleb Alexander AM.

title: The works of Virgil; translated into literal english prose:—with some explanatory Notes. <author statement>

366.

District Court Ledger, 43 MA 60

date of deposit: June 5, twentieth year of Independence

claimant: P: John Dabney

title: An address to Farmers on the following Interesting Subjects: 1 the character of A complete Farmer. 2 the Importance of Manure. 3 Labor. 4 Exchanging Work. 5 The profits of a Nursery. 6 The advantages of an Orchard. 7 The management of Cyder. 8 Keeping a Day Book. 9 Contradicting Debts. 10 Cloathing and Diet. 11 Engaging in Lawsuits 12 Good Neighbourhood. 13 Education. To which is added an Appendix, Containing the most approved methods for the management and Improvement of Tillage, Mowing and Pasture Lands; and for the Practice of the Art of Husbandry in general. (Extracted principally from a variety of Authors, who have written Judiciously on those important subjects")

367.

District Court Ledger, 43 MA 61

date of deposit: July 11, twenty-first year of Independence

claimant: P: Solomon Cotton

title: A Collection of the Speeches of the President of the United States to both Houses of Congress, at the opening of every Session with their Answers, Also the Addresses to the President, with his Answers, from the time of his Election with an Appendix, containing the Circular letter of General Washington to the Govenors of the several States, and his farewell orders to the Armies of America and the Answer Dedicated to the Citizens of the United States of America.

368.

District Court Ledger, 43 MA 62

date of deposit: July 11, twenty-first year of Independence

claimant: <see note> <A: John Clark> P: Samuel Hall

author: John Clark, Minister of a Church in Boston—

title: Letters to a Student in the University of Cambridge, Massachusetts, <author statement>

note: In the claimant entry in the court ledger the name John Clark as author has been crossed out, and the name Samuel Hall as proprietor has been inserted.

369.

District Court Ledger, 43 MA 63

date of deposit: November 4, twenty-first year of Independence

claimant: P: Isaiah Thomas

author: Caleb Alexander, A, M, Author of "a Grammatical system of the Latin language" and "a Grammatical system of the English language" &c, &c—

title: A Grammatical System of the Grecian language. <author statement>

370.

District Court Ledger, 43 MA 63

date of deposit: November 4, twenty-first year of Independence

claimant: P: Isaiah Thomas

author: Joseph Lathrop, D. D. Pastor of the first Church in Westspringfield *title:* Sermons on various subjects, Evangelical, Devotional, and Practical, Adapted to the promotion of Chistian Piety Family Religion, and youthful Virtue, <author statement> in two Volumes—

371.
District Court Ledger, 43 MA 64
date of deposit: November 21, twenty-first year of Independence
claimant: A: John Burk
author: . . . , late of Trinity College, Dublin; now Editor of the Boston Daily Advertizer—
title: Bunker Hill, a Tragedy, in five acts, <author statement>

372.
District Court Ledger, 43 MA 64
date of deposit: December 30, twenty-first year of Independence
claimant: P: David West
title: The American Spectator, or Matrimonial Preceptor.—A Collection, with additions and variations, of Essay, Epistles, Precepts and Examples, relating to the Married State, from the most celebrated Writers ancient and modern;—adapted to the State of Society in the American Republic.

1797

373.
District Court Ledger, 43 MA 65
date of deposit: January 30, twenty-first year of Independence
claimant: P: Francis Marriott
title: The land we live in;—or Death of Major Andre.

374.
District Court Ledger, 43 MA 66
date of deposit: January 31, twenty-first year of Independence
claimant: P: Isaiah Thomas
author: Benjamin Whitman,—Attorney at law.
title: An Index to the laws of Massachusetts:—from the adoption of the Constitution to the year MDCCXCVI. <author statement>

375.
District Court Ledger, 43 MA 66
date of deposit: February 2, twenty-first year of Independence
claimant: A: Daniel Staniford
author: . . . AM—
title: A short—but comprehensive Grammar, rendered simple and easy, by familiar questions and answers;—adapted to the capacity of Youth, and designed for the use of Schools and private families.—To which is added an Appendix, comprehending a list of vulgarisms and grammatical improprieties, used in common conversation, by persons of different Societies, <author statement>

376.
District Court Ledger, 43 MA 67
date of deposit: February 11, twenty-first year of Independence
claimant: P: Isaiah Thomas & Ebenezer T Andrews
author: Samuel Morse, AM.
title: School Dialogues.—A new Collection of Dialogues from a variety of the best plays in the English language: designed for the use of Schools and Academies.—calculated to promote an easy and elegant mode of conversation among the young Masters and Misses of the United States. <author statement>

377.
District Court Ledger, 43 MA 68
date of deposit: February 11, twenty-first year of Independence
claimant: P: Isaiah Thomas and Ebenezer T, Andrews
author: Abner Alden, AM.
title: An Introduction to spelling and reading, in—two volumes—being the first and second parts of a Columbian exercise.—The whole comprising an easy and systematical method of teaching and of learning the english language.—<author statement>

378.
District Court Ledger, 43 MA 68
date of deposit: February 28, twenty-first year of Independence
claimant: A: Benjamin Dearborn
title: The Vocal Instructer, Publish'd in numbers—No. 1. containing the rules of vocal music, by principle in questions & answers;—remarks on the causes of it's decline, and hints for recovering it's respectability.—A morning and an evening Hymn composed and set to Music for this Work;—and a Sliding Music Scale, never before publish'd; in which a moveable Index points out the names and distances of the Notes in all their variations; The other numbers of the Work will contain sacred

moral or Sentimental Psalms, Hymns, Songs &c adapted to particular an general occasions, for the improvement & pleasure of Youth <author statement>

379.
District Court Ledger, 43 MA 69
date of deposit: March 10, twenty-first year of Independence
claimant: P: Margaret Brown
author: William Hill Brown, late of Boston.
title: West Point preserved or the Treason of Arnold, an historical Tragedy in five Acts, <author statement>

380.
District Court Ledger, 43 MA 70
date of deposit : March 18, twenty-first year of Independence
claimant: A: William Charles White
title: Orlando or Parental persecution.—A Tragedy—<author statement> as perform'd at the Theatre Federal Street Boston.

381.
District Court Ledger, 43 MA 70
date of deposit: April 3, twenty-first year of Independence
claimant: A: Osgood Carleton
title: An—accurate Plan of the Town of Boston, and it's—vicinity.

382.
District Court Ledger, 43 MA 71
date of deposit: May 29, twenty-first year of Independence
claimant: A: Jedidiah Morse
author: . . . D. D. Author of the American universal Geography, Fellow of the American Academy of Arts and Sciences & Member of the Massachusetts historical Society—
title: The American Gazateer, exhibiting in Alphabetical Order a much more full & accurate account, than has been given of the States, Provinces, Counties, Cities, Towns, Villages, Rivers, Bays Harbours, Gulfs, Sounds, Capes, Mountains, Forts, Indian Tribes & new Discoveries, on the American Continent also of the West India Islands, and other Islands appendant to the Continent, and those newly discover'd in the Pacific Ocean:—describing the extent, boundaries, population, government, productions, commerce, manufactures curiosities &c of the several Countries, and of their important civil divisions;—and the longitude & latitude, the bearings & distances from noted places of the Cities, Towns & Villages;—with a particular description of the Georgia western Territory.—The whole comprising upwards of seven thousand distinct Articles.—Collected & compiled from the best authorities and arranged with great care by & under the direction of <author statement> illustrated with seven new and neat maps.

383.
District Court Ledger, 43 MA 72
date of deposit: July 22, twenty-second year of Independence
claimant: A: Charles Prentiss
title: A Collection of fugitive Essays, in prose and verse. <author statement>

384.
District Court Ledger, 43 MA 72
date of deposit: August 2, twenty-second year of Independence
claimant: A: Thomas Paine
author: . . . AM.
title: The ruling Passion: an occasional Poem, written by the appointment of the Society of the Φ B K, and spoken on their Anniversary, in the Chapel of the University, Cambridge, July 20.th 1797. <author statement>

385.
District Court Ledger, 43 MA 73
date of deposit: July 31, twenty-second year of Independence
claimant: A: Jonathan Burr
author: . . . AM.
title: A Compendium of English Grammar, for the use of Schools and private Instructers.—To which are annex'd excercises corresponding to the Grammar. <author statement>
note: The clerk has written in the left-hand margin of the entry in the court ledger: "This should have preceded the last."

386.
District Court Ledger, 43 MA 73
date of deposit: August 12, twenty-second year of Independence
claimant: A: David Kendal
author: . . . AM.
title: The young Lady's Arithmetic; containing an Epitome of Definitions, Rules and examples, which explain in a familiar concise and easy manner the first principles & common use of

numbers—calculated in Federal money; and published—by request of several young Ladies desirous of adding to their other mental accomplishments the pleasing and useful Science of Figures. <author statement>

387.
District Court Ledger, 43 MA 74
date of deposit: August 12, twenty-second year of Independence
claimant: A: F. Nichols <Francis Nichols>
title: A Treatise of practical Arithmetic and Book-keeping, containing all the Rules of Arithmetic which are generally useful in transacting business when Arithmetic is requir'd. for the—use of Students—<author statement>
note: According to the *National Index of American Imprints* the author is Francis Nichols.

388.
District Court Ledger, 43 MA 74
date of deposit: August 17, twenty-second year of Independence
claimant: P: Isaiah Thomas
author: Alexander Thomas AM. Orator fit.
title: The Orators Assistant; being a Selection of Dialogues for Schools and Academics, taken from many of the best dramatic Writings in the English language;—to which are added a few highly esteemed pieces for declamation.—intended for Youth of both sexes, to aid in forming an easy, ready & graceful elocution—

389.
District Court Ledger, 43 MA 75
date of deposit: September 1, twenty-second year of Independence
claimant: A: Duncan Mack'Intosh of the said District and his two daughters
title: Essai raisonné sur la Grammaire et la pronunciation Angloise, Á l'usage des Français désirent d' apprendre l'Anglois.—<author statement>

390.
District Court Ledger, 43 MA 75
date of deposit: September 1, twenty-second year of Independence
claimant: A: Duncan Mack'Intosh and his two Daughters
title: A plain, rational Essay on English Grammar: —the main of which is to point out a plain rational and permanent standard of pronunciation, to which is given a Gamut or Key still more simple plain & easy than that given to music, pointing out the quantity & quality of every syllable & word according to the present mode among polite Scholars.—Long syllables are distinguished from short ones, by authority of legal accent;—and the sounds of both clearly pointed out by typographical marks or Characters, and illustrated by such rules & examples as render the whole so very intelligible and easy, even to the weakest capacity, that foreigners as well as natives may learn to read English properly in a few weeks this plan hitherto unattempted is respectfully inscribed to British & American Ladies & Gentlemen, whose generous criticism & assistance is humbly requested by their devoted humble Servants <author statement>

391.
District Court Ledger, 43 MA 76
date of deposit: September 9, twenty-second year of Independence
claimant: P: Perez Morton
title: Beacon Hill.—A local Poem, historical and—descriptive.

392.
District Court Ledger, 43 MA 76
date of deposit: September 11, twenty-second year of Independence
claimant: A: Herman Mann
author: a Citizen of Massachusetts.
title: The Female review:—or memoirs of an American young Lady;—whose—life & Character are peculiarly distinguish'd—being a Continental Soldier for nearly three years in the late American War—during which time she performed her Duties of every department, into which she was called with punctual exactness, fidelity & honor & preserved her chastity inviolate by the most artful concealment of her Sex.—with an Appendix, containing Characteristic Traits, by different hands:—her taste for economy, principles of domestic eduction &c—<author statement>

393.
District Court Ledger, 43 MA 77
date of deposit: September 12, twenty-second year of Independence
claimant: P: Isaiah Thomas & Ebenezer T Andrews
author: Oliver Holden.
title: Laus Deo—the Worcester Collection of sacred harmony—containing I. The Rules of vocal music, in a concise and plain manner—II. A large & choice collection of Psalm tunes, Anthems &c proper for Divine Worship,—many of which

are entirely new—The whole compiled for the use of Schools & singing Societies—the sixth edition alter'd, corrected & revised with additions, <author statement>

394.
District Court Ledger, 43 MA 77
date of deposit: September 19, twenty-second year of Independence
claimant: P: William P and Lemuel Blake
author: Caleb Alexander AM. Author of "A Grammatical System of the English language." the young Gentlemen & Ladies spelling Book" and the works of Virgil translated into literal english Prose."
title: The young Gentlemen and Ladies' Instructor, being a selection of new pieces; designed as a reading Book for the use of Schools and—Academics; containing Subjects historical, geographical, moral,—biographical, anecdotal, instructive and entertaining;—also Dialogues and Orations, with critical remarks on reading, accentuation, emphasis, elements of gestures and oratory. <author statement>

395.
District Court Ledger, 43 MA 78
date of deposit: September 28, twenty-second year of Independence
claimant: P: Edmund M Blunt
author: survey'd by Capt. Paul Pinkham.
title: A Chart of George's Bank, including Cape Cod, Nantucket, and the Shoals lying on their Coast, with directions for sailing over the same &c <author statement>

396.
District Court Ledger, 43 MA 78
date of deposit: October 14, twenty-second year of Independence
claimant: A: Daniel Belknap
composer: Daniel Belknap, Teacher of Music, in Framingham.
title: The Harmonist's Companion;—containing a number of Airs, suitable for Divine Worship:—together with An Anthem for Easter, and a Masonic Ode, never before published, <composer statement>

397.
District Court Ledger, 43 MA 78
date of deposit: November 3, twenty-second year of Independence
claimant: A: Elias Mann
title: The Northampton Collection of sacred Harmony in three parts. containing—I A plain & concise introduction to the Grounds of Music.—II. A large number of Psalm Tunes, selected from the most approved and eminint Authors, adapted to all the different Metres & Keys used in Churches.—III A Number of lengthy pieces of several verses each, many of which are compositions never before published and calculated for the use of Churches and other occasions;—with a number of Universally approved Anthems. <author statement>

398.
District Court Ledger, 43 MA 79
date of deposit: November 11, twenty-second year of Independence
claimant: A: Charles Stearns
author: . . . A. B. since Pastor of the Church and Preceptor of the liberal School in Lincoln.
title: The Ladies' Philosophy of love. A Poem, in four—Cantos, written in 1774—<author statement>

399.
District Court Ledger, 43 MA 79
date of deposit: November 11, twenty-second year of Independence
claimant: A: Charles Stearns
author: . . . AM. Pastor of the Church and Preceptor of the liberal School in Lincoln.
title: Dramatic Dialogues for the use of Schools <author statement>

400.
District Court Ledger, 43 MA 80
date of deposit: November 21, twenty-second year of Independence
claimant: P: Edmund March Blunt
author: Capt. Lawrence Furlong.
title: The American Coast Pilot, containing the courses & distances to all the principal Harbours, Capes & Headlands between—Passamaquady & the mouth of the Missisippi, with directions for sailing into the same, describing the rocks, shoals soundings &c together with the courses & distances from Cape Cod & Cape Ann to George's Bank & through the South & East Channels & the setting of the Currents—with the latitudes & longitudes of the principal Harbours on the Coast,—Together with a Tide Table—<author statement> Also the Merchants & Ship Masters Assistant, containing complete information to Merchants, Masters of Ships & others concerned

in Navigation relative to the mercantile & maritime laws & customs—in the course of which the following Subjects are particularly elucidated;—Disbursements & other Ship Accounts—<the following word has been inserted in the space above the sentence in the ms.> Exchanges Real and imaginary Money of the World & Tables of the agreement which the weights and measures of the principal places of Europe have with each others Owners—Masters—Seamen & Seamens wages—Freight, Charter=Parties & Demurrage—Marine Insurances—Averages—Bottomry & respondentia—Bills of Exchange—Laws of the United States concerning Quarentine, Duties of Import, Registering Vessels &c—manner of transacting business at the Custom houses in the United States &c &c &c—To which is added a practical Treatise on Navigation, with the requisite Tables, which renders this work as useful to learners as to experienced Seamen and precludes the necessity of any other Book—The whole forming a body of information highly useful to all persons in mercantile or maritime employments.

1798

401.

District Court Ledger, 43 MA 81
date of deposit: January 2, twenty-second year of Independence
claimant: P: Isaiah Thomas & Ebenezer T. Andrews
author: Abner Alden AM.
title: An Introduction to spelling & reading, in two volumes.—being the first & second parts of a Columbian exercise.—The whole comprising an easy & systematical method of teaching & of learning the English language. <author statement> VOL. II.

402.

District Court Ledger, 43 MA 81
date of deposit: January 22, twenty-second year of Independence
claimant: P: Angier March
title: A Journal of the captivity & sufferings of John Foss, several years a Prisoner in Algiers:—together with some—account of the Treatment of Christian Slaves when sick;—and observations on the manners and customs of the Algerines

403.

District Court Ledger, 43 MA 82
date of deposit: January 31, twenty-second year of Independence
claimant: A: George Richards Minot
author: . . . , Fellow of the American Academy of Arts & Sciences & Member of the Massachusetts historical—Society—
title: Continuation of the History of—the Provence of Massachusetts Bay from the year 1748.—with an Introductory Sketch of events from its original Settlement. <author statement> VOL. I.

404.

District Court Ledger, 43 MA 82
date of deposit: February 8, twenty-second year of Independence
claimant: A: Asher Benjamin
title: The Country Builder's Assistant, fully explaining the best methods for—striking regular & quirked mouldings:—for drawing and working the Tuscan, Doric, Ionic and Corinthian orders with their Pedestals, Bases, Capitals and Entablatures—Architraves for doors windows & chimnies—Cornices, Bases & Surbase mouldings for rooms Chimney Pieces, Doors & sashes with their mouldings—The Construction of Stairs with their Ramp & Twist Rails—Plan, elevation & section of a Meeting House with a Pulpit at large—Plans & elevations of Houses, Fence posts & railings—The best method of finding the length & backing of Hip Rafters—Also the tracing of Groins, Angle Brackets, circular Soffits in circular walls &c correctly engraved on thirty seven Copper plates with a printed explanation to each. <author statement>

405.

District Court Ledger, 43 MA 83
date of deposit: April 23, twenty-second year of Independence
claimant: P: David West
author: Mrs. Rowson. author of Charlotte, Trials of the Heart, Fille de Chambre &c &c—<Susanna (Haswell) Rowson>
title: Reuben & Rachel or tales of old times, A Novel <author statement>
note: According to the *National Index of American Imprints* the author is Susanna (Haswell) Rowson.

406.

District Court Ledger, 43 MA 83
date of deposit: March 22, twenty-second year of Independence
claimant: A: Judith Sargent Murray
author: Constantia.
title: The Gleaner, a miscellaneous Production, in three Volumes, <author statement>

407.

District Court Ledger, 43 MA 83

date of deposit: May 22, twenty-second year of Independence

claimant: A: John Thayer

author: The Revd . . . .Catholick Missioner,,.

title : A Discourse delivered at the Roman Catholic Church in Boston on the 9th of May 1798, a day recommended by the Presidents for Humiliation & Prayer throughout the United States, <author statement>

408.

District Court Ledger, 43 MA 84

date of deposit: July 11, twenty-second year of Independence

claimant: P: Ebenezer Larkin

author: a lady of Massachusetts; <Hannah (Webster) Foster>

title: The Coquette or the History of Eliza Wharton, a Novel founded on fact <author statement>

note: According to the *National Index of American Imprints* the author is Hannah (Webster) Foster.

409.

District Court Ledger, 43 MA 84

date of deposit: May 17, twenty-first year of Independence

claimant: A: Caleb Bingham

author: . . . A,,M,, Author of the American Preceptor,, Young Lady's Accidence &c,

title: The Columbian Orator, containing a Variety of original & selected peices Together with rules calculated to improve youth and others in the ornamental & usefull art of Eloquence <author statement>

410.

District Court Ledger, 43 MA 85

date of deposit: May 21, twenty-second year of Independence

claimant: A: Peter Oliver

title: the Adopted Son A Comedy in five Acts,

411.

District Court Ledger, 43 MA 85

date of deposit: May 22, twenty-second year of Independence

claimant: P: Edmund March

title: The New theoretic and Practical Navigator, containing later improvements particularly in working Lunar Observations, correcting the watch &c than any book yet extant, Wherin are several Tables and many other important additions never before Published,, The Tables of the Sun's declination are corrected and adapted to the alteration of Stile which takes place in the Year 1800 and the Logarithimic tables of Sines &c have the corresponding times prefixed to the several degrees and minutes of the Sun's Altitude, with the requisite Tables used with the Nautical Almanac in determining the Latitude & Longitude, revised and Corrected by Nicholas Pike Esq Member of the American Academy of Arts and Sciences and Author of the new and complete System of Arithmetic

412.

District Court Ledger, 43 MA 86

date of deposit: June 9, twenty-second year of Independence

claimant: A: Jeremy Belknap

author: . . . D,,D

title: American Biography or an Historical account of those Persons who have been distinguish'd in America, as Adventurers Statesmen, Philosophers, Divines, Warriors, Authors, & other remarkable Characters, comprehending a recital of the events connected with their lives and Actions,, <author statement> Vol. 2

413.

District Court Ledger, 43 MA 86

date of deposit: June 22, twenty-second year of Independence

claimant: P: Edmund March Blunt

author: Capt, Lawrence Furlong

title: the American coast Pilot containing the Courses and distances betwen the Princapal Harbours,,Capes and headlands from Passamaquaddy through the Gulph of Florida with directions for Sailing into the Same describing the Soundings, bearings of the Lighthouses, and beacons from the rocks, shoals, Ledges &c, together with the courses and distances from Cape Cod and Cape Ann to Georges Bank through the South and East Channels, and Setting of the Currents with the Latitudes & Longitudes of the Principal Harbours on the Coast Together with a tide table <author statement> corrected and improved by the most experienced Pilots in the United States,, Also information to Masters of Vessells wherein the manner of Transacting business at the Custom houses is fully elucidated,,

414.

District Court Ledger, 43 MA 87

date of deposit: June 24, twenty-second year of Independence

claimant: P: Jedediah Morse and Thomas & Andrews
author: Jedediah Morse D,D, Author of the American Unevesal Geography, Fellow of the American Academy of Arts & Sciences,, And Member of the <the following word is underlined as well as crossed out in ms.> <American> Massachusetts Historical Society,
title: An Abridgement of the American Gazetteer, exhibiting in Alphabetical order a compendious account of the States,, Provinces Counties, Cities, Towns, Villages, Rivers, Bays, Harbours, Gulphs, Sounds, Capes, Mountains, Forts, Indian tribes, & New Discoveries, on the American Continent And its Appendant Islands; Particularly the West Indies, Describing the extent boundaries, Population, Government, Productions, Commerce, Manufactures Curiosities &c of several Countries and their important Civil Divisions, and the Longitude and Latitude, the bearings & distances from noted places of the Cities, Towns & Villages. to which is Annex'd an Accurate table of all the Post Offices in the United States, <author statement> Illustrated with a Map of North America, abridg'd by the Author,
note: According to the *National Union Catalog* the author is Jedidiah Morse.

415.
District Court Ledger, 43 MA 88
date of deposit: June 25, twenty-second year of Independence
claimant: P: Caleb Bingham
author: a lady of Massachusetts Author of the Coquette, <Hannah (Webster) Foster>
title: The Boarding School or lessons of A Preceptress to her Pupils, consisting of information, instruction, and Advice, calculated to improve the Manners and form the character of Young Ladies to which is Added a Collection of Letters, written by the Pupils to their instructor, their friends & each other, <author statement>
note: According to the *National Index of American Imprints* the author is Hannah (Webster) Foster.

416.
District Court Ledger, 43 MA 88
date of deposit: June 27, twenty-second year of Independence
claimant: A: Abiel Holmes
author: . . . , A.M Pastor of the first Church in Cambridge,
title: The life of Ezra Stiles, D.D.LL.D, A Fellow of the American Philosophical Society; of the American Academy of Arts and Sciences; of the Connecticut Society of Arts and Sciences; A Corresponding member of the Massachusetts Historical Society; Professor of Ecclsiastical History; and President of Yale College, <author statement>

417.
District Court Ledger, 43 MA 89
date of deposit: September 21, twenty-third year of Independence
claimant: P: Isaiah Thomas
compiler: the reverend, Thaddeus Mason Harris AM Member of the Massachusetts Historical Society and Chaplain to the Grand Lodge of Massachusetts.
title: Constitutions of the Antient and Honorable fraternity of Free & Accepted Masons, Collected and Digested from their old records, Faithful Traditions and Lodge books for the use of Lodgers, together with the History & general regulations of the Grand Lodge of Massachusetts. <compiler statement>

418.
District Court Ledger, 43 MA 89
date of deposit: October 4, twenty-third year of Independence
claimant: P: William Spotswood & Caleb P Wayne
title: Amelia or the Faithless Briton, an Original American Novel founded upon recent facts,

419.
District Court Ledger, 43 MA 90
date of deposit: October 17, twenty-third year of Independence
claimant: A: Charles Stearns
author: . . . A. M. Pastor of the Church & Preceptor of the Liberal School in Lincoln,
title: Principles of Religion and Morality in three parts. lst of the evidence of Religion 2d Principles of Religion 3d Principles of Morality, with four Lessons on the Cardinal Virtues, the Whole in Short Lessons, in the form of Dialogues; adapted to Schools, and private instruction in Families, <author statement>

420.
District Court Ledger, 43 MA 90
date of deposit: October 27, twenty-third year of Independence
claimant: P: James Davenport, Francis <the fourth letter in the following word has been crossed out in ms.> Lin<l>ley & John Moore

author: Mr. Davenport, <James Davenport>
composer: Doctor Arne,
title: Columbia and Liberty. a new Patriotic Song <author statement> <composer statement>
note: According to the *National Index of American Imprints* the author is James Davenport.

421.
District Court Ledger, 43 MA 91
date of deposit: October 27, twenty-third year of Independence
claimant: P: Thomas Paine Francis Linley & John Moore
author: Thomas Paine AM,
title: The Green Mountain Farmer, a New Patriotic Song, <author statement> the Music and Accompaniments by the Celebrated Shield, <William Shield>
note: The *National Index of American Imprints* is the authority for William Shield's name.

422.
District Court Ledger, 43 MA 91
date of deposit: November 13, twenty-third year of Independence
claimant: A: Asa Ellis
author: . . . Jun.
title: The Country dier's assistant, <author statement>

423.
District Court Ledger, 43 MA 92
date of deposit: November 15, twenty-third year of Independence
claimant: A: Epaphras Hoyt
author: E Hoyt an Officer in the Cavalry of Massachusetts,
title: A Treatise on the Milatary Art in four parts containing 1st a Comprehensive system of Discipline for the Cavalry of the United States; adapted to the Principles of Baron Steuben's Regulations for the Infantry; and the latest Prussian & English treatises on Cavalry; 2d Regulations concerning the duty of Cavalry in Camp, in time of War. 3d Directions for the conduct of Partizan Corps whether Cavalry or Infantry, in carrying on the Petite Puerre, 4th Maxims relating to the Marching, Encamping & other general operations of an Army, in the feild: Compiled principally from the observations of experienced Officers & the most approved writers of the Art of War. illustrated with Plates <author statement>

424.
District Court Ledger, 43 MA 93
date of deposit: December 17, twenty-third year of Independence
claimant: A: Hañah Adams
title: A summary history of New England from the first settlemens at Plymouth to the acceptance of the Federal Constitution comprehending a general Sketch of the American War <author statement>

425.
District Court Ledger, 43 MA 93
date of deposit: December 20, twenty-third year of Independence
claimant: A: William Heath
author: Major General Heath
title: Memoirs <author statement> Containing, Anecdotes, Details of Skirmishes, Battles & Other Milatary Events during the American War

426.
District Court Ledger, 43 MA 94
date of deposit: December 31, twenty-third year of Independence
claimant: A: Enoch Hale
author: . . . A. M.
title: A Spelling Book or the first part of a Grammar of the english Language as written & spoken in the United States <author statement>

1799

427.
District Court Ledger, 43 MA 94
date of deposit: January 7, twenty-third year of Independence
claimant: A: John Foster Williams
author: their Friend & Brother . . .
title: This chart of Cape Cod & harbour is dedicated to the Boston Marine Society <author statement>
format: chart

428.
District Court Ledger, 43 MA 94
date of deposit: February 1, twenty-third year of Independence
claimant: A: John Miller Russell
author: . . . , A. M.
title: The Pastoral Songs of P, Virgil Maro to which are added Poems sentimental & descriptive <author statement>

429.

District Court Ledger, 43 MA 95

date of deposit: April 2, twenty-third year of Independence

claimant: P: I Thomas & E T Andrews

author: a Lady

title: The new pleasing instructor or young Lady's guide to Virtue & happiness consisting of essays, relations, descriptions, epistles Dialogues & Poetry carefully extracted from the best modern Authors designed principally for the use of Female Schools; but calculated for general instruction and amusement <author statement>

430.

District Court Ledger, 43 MA 95

date of deposit: March 8, twenty-third year of Independence

claimant: A: Josiah Burroughs

title: The Assistant, or a Treatise on the Currency of the United States. Containing—Arithmetical rules to Obtain the pieces of all kinds of commodities in an easy and short way in the federal Currency. also a method of reducing the currencies of a number of States to the Federal, and the Federal to those of the States. Together with an easy method of casting Interest; with many useful Tables.

431.

District Court Ledger, 43 MA 96

date of deposit: March 4, twenty-third year of Independence

claimant: P: Isaiah Thomas

author: David Everett, A. M.—

title: Common sense in Dishabille: or, the Farmer's monitor. containing a variety of Familiar Essays on Subjects moral & economical. To which is added a Perpetual Callendar. or Economical Almanack. <author statement>

432.

District Court Ledger, 43 MA 96

date of deposit: March 5, twenty-third year of Independence

claimant: A: Josiah Goddard

title: A New & Beautiful Collection of Select Hymns & spiritual Songs: Selected from all Authors that are entertaining, Spiritual and Divine; For the use of Churches, religious Societies, and Christian Conferences; and in particular for the Comfort and edification of Private Christians, for which it is mostly designed.

433.

District Court Ledger, 43 MA 97

date of deposit: May 24, twenty-third year of Independence

claimant: P: Edmund M Blunt

author: John Hamilton Moore,

title: The New Practical Navigator; being an Epitome of Navigation, containing The different methods of working the Lunar Observations, and all the requisite tables used with the Nautical Almanac, in determining the Latitude & Longitude and keeping a complete reckoning at sea. Illustrated by proper Rules & Examples. the whole exemplified in a Journal kept from England to the Island of Teneriffe: also, The substance of Information every Candidate for the American Navy ought to be acquainted with, previous to his being appointed: This with the Sea Terms, are particularly recomended to the attention of all young Gentlemen designed for, or belonging to the Sea. The first American from the thirteenth English Edition, <author statement> Improved by the Introduction of several new Tables, and by large additions to the former Tables, and revised & corrected by a Skilful Mathematician & Navigator. Illustrated with copper-plates to which are added, some general Instructions and Information to Merchants, Masters of Vessels, & others concerned in Navigation, relative to the Mercantile & Maritime Laws & Customs.

434.

District Court Ledger, 43 MA 98

date of deposit: June 18, twenty-third year of Independence

claimant: A: Jonathan Grout

title: The Youn Childs Accidence: being a small Spelling Book for little children: containing a selection of words in modern use, arranged in such a manner as will naturally lead the young pupil, step by step, to a right pronunciation. Designed for a cheap book for little children.

435.

District Court Ledger, 43 MA 98

date of deposit: June 24, twenty-third year of Independence

claimant: P: Esther Clarke

author: the late Reverend John Clarke D. D. Minister of the first Church in Boston, Massachusetts.

title: Sermons <author statement>

436.
District Court Ledger, 43 MA 99
date of deposit: July 19, twenty-fourth year of Independence
claimant: P: Perez Morton
author: the Author of the Virtues of Nature. <Sarah Wentworth (Apthorp) Morton>
title: The Virtues of Society. A Tale, founded on fact, <author statement>
note: According to *National Index of American Imprints* the author is Sarah Wentworth (Apthorp) Morton.

437.
District Court Ledger, 43 MA 99
date of deposit: September 6, twenty-fourth year of Independence
claimant: P: Barnard B. Macanulty
author: James Tyler, Compiler of the Medical part of the Encyclopedia Britannica.
title: A Treatise on the Plague and Yellow Fever. with an appendix, containing Histories of the plague at Athens in the time of the Peloponnesian war; at Constantinople in the time of Justinian; at London in 1665; at Marseilles in 1720; &c <author statement>

438.
District Court Ledger, 43 MA 100
date of deposit: October 7, twenty-fourth year of Independence
claimant: P: Joseph Nancrede
title: The Roman in Greece an ancient Tale, descriptive of Modern Events.

439.
District Court Ledger, 43 MA 100
date of deposit: October 10, twenty-fourth year of Independence
claimant: A: William Cobb
title: The Country Traders assistant; or young Clerk's Directory in the art of Book-keeping on a new & approved plan. To which is added A Record of Trade, A Record of Notes & Bills. also a few forms of Notes, Orders, Receipts, Bills &c.

440.
District Court Ledger, 43 MA 101
date of deposit: November 23, twenty-fourth year of Independence
claimant: P: Isaiah Thomas
author: Caleb Alexander, A. M.,
title: The Young Ladies' and Gentlemens Spelling Book: On a new and improved Plan; Containing. a criterion of rightly Spelling and pronouncing the English Language: Interspersed with many in reading, entertaining Fables and collections of moral sentences. Intented for the Use of Schools <author statement>

441.
District Court Ledger, 43 MA 101
date of deposit: December 17, twenty-fourth year of Independence
claimant: A: Benjamin Heaton
author: . . . , A. M.
title: The columbian Spelling Book; being an easy introduction to spelling & reading containing, a selection of words in common use properly arranged & divided in such a manner as to lead the Learner to the right pronunciation: Interspersed with a variety of easy lessons, entertaining fables, and Moral sentences for the use of Schools throughout the United States. <author statement>

1800

442.
District Court Ledger, 43 MA 102
date of deposit: January 14, twenty fourth year of Independence
claimant: A: Thomas Paine
author: . . . A. M—
title: An Eulogy on the Life of General George Washington who died at Mount Vernon, December 14 1799 in the sixty ninth year of his Age. Written at the request of the Citizens of Newburyport & delivered at the first Presbiterian Meeting House in that Town January 2nd,, 1800 <author statement>

443.
District Court Ledger, 43 MA 102
date of deposit: January 18, twenty-fourth year of Independence
claimant: P: Barnard B. Macanulty
author: William Biglow.
title: The Childs Library Part first; containing Lessons for spelling & reading stops & marks, numbers &c <author statement>

444.
District Court Ledger, 43 MA 103
date of deposit: January 21, twenty-fourth year of Independence
claimant: A: Samuel Holyoke
author: . . . A. M.

title: Hark from the Tombs &c & Beneath the Honors &c Adapted from Dr.. Watts and set to music <author statement> Performed at Newburyport 2 January 1800 the day on which the Citizens unitedly expressed their unbounded Veneration for the Memory of our beloved Washington.

445.
District Court Ledger, 43 MA 103
date of deposit: January 25, twenty-fourth year of Independence
claimant: A: Solomon Howe
author: . . . AM.
title: The Worshipper's Assistant containing the rules of Music, & a variety of easy & plain psalm tunes, adapted to the weakest capacities, & designed for extensive utility, as an Introduction to more critical & curious Music. <author statement>

446.
District Court Ledger, 43 MA 104
date of deposit: March 3, twenty-fourth year of Independence
claimant: P: John Russell
title: Washington's Political Legacies. to which is added an Appendix, containing an account of his Illness, Death, and the national tributes of respect paid to his memory, with a Biographical Outline of His Life & Character.

447.
District Court Ledger, 43 MA 104
date of deposit: March 25, twenty-fourth year of Independence
claimant: A: Charles P Sumner
author: Charles Pinkney . . .
title: Eulogy on the Illustrious George Washington pronounced at Milton twenty second of February one thousand Eight hundred <author statement>

448.
District Court Ledger, 43 MA 105
date of deposit: March 21, twenty-fourth year of Independence
claimant: P: Barnard, B. Macanulty
author: William Biglow—
title: The Childs Library Part second containing a selection of Lessons for spelling, reading and speaking <author statement>

449.
District Court Ledger, 43 MA 105
date of deposit: April 17, twenty-fourth year of Independence
claimant: A: Michael Walsh
title: A New System of Mercantile Arithmetic: Adapted to the Commerce of the United States in its Domestic & foreign relations. with forms of Accounts & other writings usually occurring in trade. <author statement>

450.
District Court Ledger, 43 MA 105
date of deposit: May 21, twenty-fourth year of Independence
claimant: A: Joseph Story
title: The Power of Solitude a Poem in two parts <author statement>

451.
District Court Ledger, 43 MA 106
date of deposit: May 26, twenty-fourth year of Independence
claimant: A: Nathaniel Emmons
author: . . . ,D. D. Pastor of the church in Franklin Massachusetts.
title: Sermons on some of the first principles & Doctrines of True Religion <author statement>

452.
District Court Ledger, 43 MA 106
date of deposit: May 31, twenty-fourth year of Independence
claimant: A: Jonathan Leavitt
author: Rev: . . . , AM
title: A concise view of the New Covenant, under the Adamic, Abrahamic or Mosaic, and Christian Institutions, in four Sermons on Phi: 2d, 12th, 13th,—And two Addresses to the Church in Heath:—in which are pointed out the true door of Entrance into the Christian Church;—the Churches duty to all her Members, and the essential & fundamental duties, both of opinion & practice, of pure Christianity: and exposing some Errors, both in faith and practice, which, at this day, are very prevalent among nominal Christians:—and is calculated for the use and benefit of Heads of families, and other pious professors of the Gospel of Christ.—To which will be added a discourse upon 1st. Thess: 5th,, 9th,, shewing Divine Grace to be free, but sovereign. <author statement>

453.
District Court Ledger, 43 MA 107
date of deposit: June 12, twenty-fourth year of Independence
claimant: A: R. Fields <Robert Fields>
author: . . . .Attorney at Law.
title: A Practical Treatise upon the Bankrupt Law of the United States <author statement>
note: According to the *National Index of American Imprints* the author is Robert Fields.

454.
District Court Ledger, 43 MA 107
date of deposit: July 22, twenty-fifth year of Independence
claimant: A: Thomas Pike Lathy
title: Reparation: or the School for Libertines. a Dramatic Piece in three Acts. <author statement>

455.
District Court Ledger, 43 MA 108
date of deposit: August 14, twenty-fifth year of Independence
claimant: P: Isaiah Thomas & Ebenezer T. Andrews
author: Caleb Alexander A. M..
title: The Columbian Dictionary of the English Language: in which many new words peculiar to the United States and many words of general use not found in any other English Dictionary are inserted. The words are divided as they are pronounced, & each word is accented according to the most Approved Authors and Speakers; with Abbreviations used to denote each part of Speech: all the irregular verbs are properly arranged, & made plain to the reader. The whole is calculated to Assist foreigners in acquiring a just pronunciation of the English Language: and to be used as a School Book, by any who wish to study the Language grammatically. To which is prefixed, a Prosodial Grammar, Containing a short Dissertation on Vowels & Consonants. To the whole is added Heathen Mythology: or a Classical pronouncing Dictionary. <author statement>

456.
District Court Ledger , 43 MA 109
date of deposit: August 30, twenty-fifth year of Independence
author: . . . , AM.
title: The Instrumental Assistant containing instructions for the Violin, German-flute, Clarionet, Bass Viol, and Hautboy, compiled from late European publications. Also A selection of favourite Airs, Marches, &c. Progressively arranged, & adapted for the use of learners. <author statement>

457.
District Court Ledger, 43 MA 109
date of deposit: August 30, twenty-fifth year of Independence
claimant: P: Daniel Belknap
author: Daniel Belknap Author of the Harmonist's Companion.
title: The Evangelical Harmony containing. A great variety of Airs, suitable for Divine Worship: besides a number of favourite pieces of music, selected from different Authors, chiefly original. to which is prefixed, A concise Introduction to the grounds of Music. <author statement>

458.
District Court Ledger, 43 MA 110
date of deposit: August 30, twenty-fifth year of Independence
claimant: A: Benjamin Waterhouse
author: . . . .M. D. Fellow of the American Philos. Society; Acad. Arts & Sciences; Mass. Med. & Royal Med. Society London. Physical & Literary Society at Manchester; Philos; & Literary Society at bath; & professor of the Theory & practice of physic in the University of Cambridge.
title: A prospect of exterminating the Small Pox; being the History of the Variolae Vaccinae, or Kine Pox, commonly called the Cow Pox; as it has appeared in England: with an Account of a series of Innoculations performed for the Kine pox, in Massachusetts. <author statement>

459.
District Court Ledger, 43 MA 110
date of deposit: September 9, twenty-fifth year of Independence
claimant: P: Wm. Andrews
title: The rules of Work, of the Carpenters in the town of Boston, formed, & most accurately corrected, by a large number of the first workmen of the Town.

460.
District Court Ledger, 43 MA 111
date of deposit: September 9, twenty-fifth year of Independence
claimant: P: Isaiah Thomas
author: Amasa Smith, Major of Artillery in the Militia of Massachusetts

title: A short compendium of the duty of Artillerists: shewing the method of Exercise with light field peices; of Ascertaining the true line of direction & elevation, corresponding with the bore of a Gun; with a description of the Instruments for the process. also an easy method of finding the distance of an Object, by a plain Table; with its particular description. also observations on experimental Gunnery. <author statement>

461.

District Court Ledger, 43 MA 111

date of deposit: September 20, twenty-fifth year of Independence

claimant: A: George Chipman

title: The American Moralist; containing a variety of Moral & religious lessons. together with Humerous & entertaining pieces. designed principally for the use of schools. <author statement>

462.

District Court Ledger, 43 MA 113

date of deposit: December 4, twenty-fifth year of Independence

claimant: A: Nathaniel Heaton

title: The Columbian Preceptor. containing a variety of new pieces in Prose, Poetry, & Dialogues; with rules for reading. Selected from the most approved Authors. for the use of Schools in the United States <author statement>

New York

1791

463.

District Court Ledger, 130 NY 1
date of deposit: April 30, fifteenth year of Independence
claimant: A: Donald Fraser
author: . . . ,/ School-Master, New-York.
title: The/ Young Gentleman and Lady's/ Assistant;/ Partly Original/ But chiefly Compiled from the Works of/ The most celebrated Modern Authors;/ Calculated/ To instruct Youth in the principles of/ Useful Knowledge:/ In five Parts Viz,/ Geog raphy/ Natural History/ Elocution,/ Poetry—and/ Miscellany/ To which is annexed—A short System of/ Practical Arithmetic;/ Wherein every example is wrought at large,/ and the whole/ Including the Money of the United States,/ rendered easy to the meanest Capacity./ This Work, is divided into small Sections/ for the Convenience of Schools./ <author statement>

464.

District Court Ledger, 130 NY 2
date of deposit: June 1, fifteenth year of Independence
claimant: A: William Linn
author: . . . D. D./ One of the Ministers of the reformed Dutch Church/ In the City of New York
title: Sermons/ Historical/ and/ Characteristical/ <author statement>

465.

District Court Ledger, 130 NY 3
date of deposit: July 13, sixteenth year of Independence
claimant: P: Thomas Greenleaf of the said District Printer,
author: William Linn, D. D.
title: The/ Blessings of America./ <rule>/ A/ Sermon,/ Preached in the Middle Dutch Church,/ On the Fourth July 1791/ Being the Anniversary of the/ Independance of America:/ At the Request of the/ Tammany Society or Columbian Order./ <author statement>

466.

District Court Ledger, 130 NY 4
date of deposit: September 8, sixteenth year of Independence
claimant: A: Samuel Stearns
author: Hon . . . ., Esqr/ Doctor of Physic, and of the Canon and Civil Laws.
title: The/ American Dispensatory./ Containing./ I. The Materia Medica./ II. The Operation of Medicines./ III. The Art and Science of Pharmacy./ IV. The Composition of Medecines./ V. An Index of Diseases and their Remedies./ VI. The Manual Operations and best/ Remedies used in Surgery./ <rule>/ <author statement>/ <double rule>

467.

District Court Ledger, 130 NY 5
date of deposit: September 8, sixteenth year of Independence
claimant: A: Samuel Stearns
author: Hon . . . ., L. L. D./ and Doctor of Physic; Astronomer to the/ Provinces of Quebec, and New Brunswick; also to/ the Commonwealth of Massachusetts and the/ State of Vermont, in America.
title: The/ American Oracle./ Comprehending an Account of Recent/ Discoveries in the Arts and Sciences; with a/ variety of Religious, Political, Physical, and/ Philosophical Subjects, necessary to be known/ in all Families, for the promotion of their/ present felicity, and future Happiness—/ <rule>/ <author statement>/ <rule>/ <quotation in Latin>/ <rule>

468.

District Court Ledger, 130 NY 6
date of deposit: October 27, sixteenth year of Independence
claimant: A: Benjamin Youngprime <Benjamin Youngs Prime>
author: . . . .M. D.
title: Columbia's Glory/ or/ British pride humbled/ A Poem/ on/ The American Revolution/ Some part of it being/ A Parody or an ode/ entitled/ Britain's Glory or Gallic pride humbled/ Composed on the capture of Quebec AD 1759/ <broken rule>/ <author statement>/ <broken rule>/ <quotation in Latin>
note: According to the *National Index of American Imprints* the author is Benjamin Youngs Prime.

469.

District Court Ledger, 130 NY 7
date of deposit: November 22, sixteenth year of Independence
claimant: A: Freeborn Garrettson
title: The/ Experience and Travels/ of/ Mr Freeborn Garrettson/ Minister/ of the/ Methodist-Episcopal Church/ in/ North America—/ <rule>/ <biblical quotation>/ <rule>

470.

District Court Ledger, 130 NY 8

date of deposit: December 30, sixteenth year of Independence

claimant: P: the Minister Elders and Deacons of the reformed protestant Dutch Church in the City of New York

title: The/ Psalms/ of/ David/ with/ Hyms and Spiritual Songs./ also/ The Catechism, Confession/ of faith, and Liturgy,/ of the/ Reformed Church in the Netherlands./ <rule>/ For the use of the Reformed Dutch Church/ in North-America./ <rule>

474.

District Court Ledger, 130 NY 12

date of deposit: October 26, seventeenth year of Independence

claimant: A: Simeon De Witt

title: 1st,, Sheet of DeWitt's State-Map of New York

format: map

Copy Deposit

date of deposit: January 17, 1793

title: *1.st SHEET of* DE WITT'S *STATE-MAP of NEW-YORK*

note: This engraved map is located in the Geography and Map Division (G1201.P2C595 1794).

1792

471.

District Court Ledger, 130 NY 9

date of deposit: January 10, sixteenth year of Independence

claimant: P: Robert Hodge, Thomas Allen and Samuel Campbell

author: Colonel Humphreys.

title: The/ Miscellaneous/ Works/ <author statement>/ <rule>

472.

District Court Ledger, 130 NY 10

date of deposit: June 4, sixteenth year of Independence

claimant: A: Samuel Stearns

author: the Honorable/ . . . —L.LD—

title: The/ Free Masons/ Calender/ and/ Continen tal/ Almanack;/ Containing/ Astronomical Calcu lations./ an account of the ancient and honorable/ Society of Free-Masons,/ with other things neces sary for an Almanack/ Calculated for the benefit of the Inhabitants of/ North America in general and that of free Masons/ in particular—/ <rule>/ <author statement>/ <rule>

473.

District Court Ledger, 130 NY 11

date of deposit: June 11, sixteenth year of Independence

claimant: A: Joel Barlow

author: . . . Esquire

title: Advice/ To—The—/ Privileged, Orders/ —In the—/ Several States of Europe/ Resulting from the/ Necessity and Propriety/ of/ A General Revo lution In the/ Principle of Government/ <rule>/ <author statement>/ <short rule>/ Part. 1.

1793

475.

District Court Ledger, 130 NY 12

date of deposit: March 28, seventeenth year of Independence

claimant: P: the right reverend Samuel Provoost, the reverend Doctor Abraham Beach, the reverend Doctor Benjamin Moore and Doctor Samuel William Johnson

title: The Book of/ Common Prayer/ and Adminis tration of the/ Sacraments/ and other/ Rights and Ceremonies of the Church/ according to the Use of/ The Protestant Episcopal Church/ in The/ United States of America/ Together with the/ Psalter/ or/ Psalms of David./ <rule>

note: The claimants act as proprietors "in Trust for the Convention of the Protestant Episcopal Church."

476.

District Court Ledger, 130 NY 13

date of deposit: September 9, eighteenth year of Independence

claimant: P: John Fellows Junior

author: Joel Barlow, Esq./ Author of Advice to the Priviledged Orders;/ The Vision of Columbus; and the/ Conspiracy of Kings.—/ <short rule>

title: A/ Letter/ To the/ National Convention/ of/ France/ on the/ Defects in the Constitution of 1791,/ and the/ Extent of the Amendments which ought/ to be applied/ <short rule>/ <author statement>/ <short rule>

477.

District Court Ledger, 130 NY 14

date of deposit: September 9, eighteenth year of Independence

claimant: P: John Fellows Junior

author: Joel Barlow
title: The/ Conspiracy of Kings/ A Poem/ <rule>/ <author statement>/ <rule>

478.
District Court Ledger, 130 NY 15
date of deposit: September 19, eighteenth year of Independence
claimant: P: the Ministers Elders and Deacons of the Reformed Protestant Dutch Church in the City of New York
title: The/ Constitution/ of the/ Reformed Dutch Church/ in the/ United States/ of/ America/ <double rule>

479.
District Court Ledger, 130 NY 16
date of deposit: November 2, eighteenth year of Independence
claimant: A: William Wyche Esquire
author: a Gentleman of the Profession
title: Report/ of the/ Trial/ of/ Henry Bedlow/ For committing a rape on Sarah Sawyer/ With the arguments of the Counsel on each side/ At a Court of Oyer and Terminer, and Gaol delivery for/ the City and County of New York held 8th/ October 1793/ <short rule>/ <quotation in Latin>/ <short rule>/ Impartially taken <author statement>/ <rule>

480.
District Court Ledger, 130 NY 18
date of deposit: December 9, eighteenth year of Independence
claimant: A: Samuel Seabury
author: . . . , D.D/ Bishop of Connecticut and Rhode Island
title: Discourses/ on/ Several Subjects/ <short rule>/ <rule>/ <author statement>/ <rule>
note: Page 17 in the New York ledger is blank.

1794

481.
District Court Ledger, 130 NY 19
date of deposit: May 5, eighteenth year of Independence
claimant: P: Jacob Morton Esquire
author: William Wyche/ Of the honorable law Society of Grey's inn London/ and Citizen of the United States of America
title: A/ Treatise/ on the/ Practice/ of the/ Supreme Court of Judicature/ of the/ State of New York/ in/ Civil Actions/ <short rule>/ <author statement>/ <rule>/ <quotation in Latin>/ <rule>

482.
District Court Ledger, 130 NY 20
date of deposit: June 7, eighteenth year of Independence
claimant: A: Christopher Colles
author: . . . of New York.
title: The/ Geographical Ledger/ and/ Systemized Atlas/ being/ An united collection of topographical maps/ projected by one universal principle and laid/ down by one Scale, proposed to be extended to different/ Countries as materials can be procured/ <author statement>/ containing/ 1. Alphabetical references for pointing out the/ situation of lakes, islands, shoals, mills, mines/ churches iron-works, forts, bridges, fords, ferries, coun=/ try seat's, extensive tracts of land, and other remark=/ able objects—/ II. An alphabetical index referring to the different/ parts of the map whereby any City, town, river/ creek, island, lake &ca. can be speedily found by in=/ specting a very small space, without the/ pains of searching over the whole map./ III. An actual survey of a number of roads, specif-/ fying the true situation of every river, creek/ church, mill, bridge, ford, ferry and tavern thereon/ and their distances in miles, exactly engraven/ upon copper—
format: map

483.
District Court Ledger, 130 NY 21
date of deposit: June 17, eighteenth year of Independence
claimant: P: John Fellows Junior
author: Thomas Paine/ Author of works entitled "Common/ Sense, Rights of Man &ca.
title: The/ Age of Reason/ being an/ Investigation/ of/ True and Fabulous/ Theology/ <short rule>/ <author statement>/ <double rule>

484.
District Court Ledger, 130 NY 22
date of deposit: July 19, nineteenth year of Independence
claimant: P: John Goodeve
title: A/ Tribute, &ca/ addressed/ To the Public/ alias/ The Swinish Multitude

485.
District Court Ledger, 130 NY 23
date of deposit: August 27, nineteenth year of Independence

claimant: A: Johan. Daniel Gros
author: . . . .DD./ Minister of the German Reformed Church in the City of/ New York and Professor of moral philosophy, geography/ and chronology in Columbia College.
title: Natural Principles/ of/ Rectitude/ for the/ Conduct of man/ in all/ States and situations of life;/ demonstrated & explained/ in a/ Systematic Treatise/ on/ Moral Philosophy/ comprehending/ The law of nature, ethics, natural jurisprudence/ General economy, politics and the law of nations./ <short rule>/ <author statement>/ <broken double rule>

486.
District Court Ledger, 130 NY 24
date of deposit: September 3, nineteenth year of Independence
claimant: P: George Keatinge
title: The/ Folly of Reason/ being/ Our perfect and unerring/ Guide/ To the Knowledge of/ True Religion/ <rule>/ In answer to the age of reason/ or an/ Investigation of true and of/ Fabulous/ Theology/ By Thomas Paine, author of Works entitled/ ,,Common Sense, Rights of Man'' &ca/ <rule>

487.
District Court Ledger, 130 NY 25
date of deposit: September 26, nineteenth year of Independence
claimant: A: William Linn
author: . . . D. D./ One of the Ministers of the reformed Dutch/ Church, in the City of New York
title: Discourses/ on the/ Signs of the Times/ <short double rule>/ <author statement>

488.
District Court Ledger, 130 NY 26
date of deposit: October 24, nineteenth year of Independence
claimant: A: Donald Fraser
author: . . . author of the Young/ Gentleman's and Lady's Assistant—
title: The/ Columbian Monitor/ being/ A pleasant and easy guide/ to/ Useful Knowledge/ contain ing/ I. A variety of entertaining/ and moral dialouges/ II. Religious dialouges/ III. A short and easy intro-/ duction to English grammar/ <vertical rule>/ IV. A variety of/ useful and/ entertaining/ letters most of/ which are origin/ al together/ with several/ precedents of/ complimen tary/ cards—/ To which is added/ A miscellany of very useful rules for genteel/ behavior and a polite address &ca—/ <rule>/ <six lines of poetry in English>/ <author statement>

489.
District Court Ledger, 130 NY 27
date of deposit: November 21, nineteenth year of Independence
claimant: A: John Prentiss
author: . . . Perfumer
title: The/ Compleat Toilet/ Or Ladies Companion./ A Collection/ Of the most simple and approved methods of/ preparing/ Baths, Essences, Pomalums, Powders, Perfumes/ and sweet scented waters./ with/ Receipts for Cosmetics of every kind that can/ smooth and brighten the skin, give force to beauty and/ take off the appearance of old age./ For the use of the Ladies/ A new Edition/ <author statement>

1795

490.
District Court Ledger, 130 NY 28
date of deposit: April 17, nineteenth year of Independence
claimant: A: Philip Freneau Esquire
author: . . . / of/ New Jersey
title: Poems/ written between the years 1768 & 1794/ <author statement>/ A new edition revised and corrected by the/ Author; including a considerable number/ of pieces never before published/ <quotation in Latin>

491.
District Court Ledger, 130 NY 29
date of deposit: June 26, nineteenth year of Independence
claimant: P: Peter V. Faugeres
author: Margaretta V: Faugeres.
title: Belisarius/ a/ Tragedy/ <author statement>

492.
District Court Ledger, 130 NY 29
date of deposit: June 26, nineteenth year of Independence
claimant: P: Peter V: Faugeres
author: Margaretta V Faugeres
title: Essays/ in/ Prose and Verse/ <author statement>

493.
District Court Ledger, 130 NY 30
date of deposit: July 27, twentieth year of Independence

claimant: A: Anthelme Gay
title: A French Prosodical Grammar/ or/ Reading Book./ Calculated for the use of all those to whom/ the English Language may be a vehicle to/ learn the French pronunciation.

494.
District Court Ledger, 130 NY 31
date of deposit: August 17, twentieth year of Independence
claimant: A: Charles Smith
title: Universal Geography/ Made Easy:/ or,/ A new Geographical/ Pocket Companion:/ Comprehend ing,/ A description of the/ Habitable world.

495.
District Court Ledger, 130 NY 32
date of deposit: August 18, twentieth year of Independence
claimant: A: Phinehas Hedges
title: Strictures/ on the/ Elementa Medecinae/ of/ Doctor Brown,/ <author statement>./ <rule>/ <quotation in Latin>/ <rule>

496.
District Court Ledger, 130 NY 33
date of deposit: September 10, twentieth year of Independence
claimant: A: John Wood
author: . . . ./ Master of the Episcopal Charity School and/ Teacher of English Grammar &c/ in New York
title: Mentor,/ or the/ American Teachers Assistant/ being a selection of/ Essays/ Instructive and enter taining/ from the most approved Authors in the/ English Language/ Intended to diffuse a true taste for/ Elegance in Style and Sentiment/ By exhibit ing to the youth of our/ Schools just Models of Composition/ and with a view to the improve ment/ and amusement of young persons/ at Classicall and other Schools/ and to facilitate the invaluable Arts/ of reading and writing./ <double rule>/ <author statement>/ <four lines of poetry in English>/ <rule>

497.
District Court Ledger, 130 NY 34
date of deposit: December 28, twentieth year of Independence
claimant: A: James Kent
title: Dissertations/ being the/ Preliminary Part/ of/ A course of Law Lectures.

1796

498.
District Court Ledger, 130 NY 35
date of deposit: January 8, twentieth year of Independence
claimant: A: James Rivington
title: Epistles/ Domestic, Confidential,/ And Official,/ From/ General Washington,/ written about the commencement of the/ American contest, when he entered on the/ command of the army of the United States/ With an Interesting series of his letters,/ particularly to the British Admirals, Arbuth-/ not and Digby, to Gen. Sir Henry Clinton,/ Lord Cornwallis, Sir Guy Carleton,/ Marquis de la Fayette &ca. &ca. To Benjamin/ Harrison, Esqr. Speaker of the House/ of Delegates in Virginia, to Admiral/ the Count de Grasse, General Sulli-/ van, respecting an attack of New York; in-/ cluding many applications and addresses/ presented to him with his answers: orders,/ and instructions, on important occasions/ to his Aids de Camp, &ca. &ca. &ca—

499.
District Court Ledger, 130 NY 37
date of deposit: March 25, twentieth year of Independence
claimant: A: William Best
author: . . . , A. B./ Trinity College, Dublin,/ Now Master of a Classical Academy in New York
title: A/ Concise System/ of/ Logics/ In question and answer/ <author statement>

500.
District Court Ledger, 130 MA 38
date of deposit: April 12, twentieth year of Independence
claimant: A: William Dunlap
title: The/ Archers/ or/ Mountaineers of Switzer land;/ An Opera, in Three Acts,/ As performed by/ The old American Company, in New York;/ To which is subjoined/ A Brief/ Historical Account/ of/ Switzerland,/ From the dissolution of the Roman Empire,/ To the final establishment/ Of the Helvetic Confederacy/ By the/ Battle of Sempach

501.
District Court Ledger, 130 NY 39
date of deposit: April 23, twentieth year of Independence
claimant: A: Valentine Seaman
author: . . . M. D./ One of the Physicians of the health Committee/ of New York in 1975

title: An/ Account/ of the/ Epidemic Yellow Fever/ As it appeared/ in the/ City of New York in the year 1795./ Containing/ Besides its History &ca—/ The most probable means of preventing its/ Return, And of avoiding it, in case it/ should again become Epidemic/ <short double rule>/ <author statement>/ <rule>/ <eight lines of poetry in English>

502.
District Court Ledger, 130 NY 41
date of deposit: May 10, twentieth year of Independence
claimant: A: A. Henry De Heusch
author: . . . ,/ Professor of Languages.
title: The/ Teacher;/ or,/ Practical French Gram mar./ On a Plan entirely new;/ A plan, which, while it combines enter-/ tainment with instruc tion, will be/ found to possess another/ desirable property, that/ of being concise/ and explicit./ This Grammar comprehends the nine parts of/ speech, and their construction, so clearly and/ fully stated, with illustrations, as to be under-/ stood at first view, and intelligible to every/ capacity./ <author statement>/ <short rule>/ To be comprised in five parts/ Part 1./ <short rule>

503.
District Court Ledger, 130 NY 42
date of deposit: May 24, twentieth year of Independence
claimant: A: Martel <Michel Martel>
title: .Martel's Elements./ .containing./ I. news essays on education relative especially to/ history moral Philosophy and composition./ II. An intro duction to the French language by means/ of a literal translation of the first hundred pages of/ this Book the conjugation of the verbs and some/ familiar phrases./ III. a selection of delicate bon mots Anecdotes sentences/ sentiments thoughts playon words Anagrams/ witticisms devices puns Jokes Apologues happy application/ of passages in famous writers stories ingenious/ repartees but having nothing of what might alarm/ modesty or excite condemnible laughter upon the/ objects of our duties and of our respect which certainly/ is not the case in the books now in the hands of/ youth to learn French by—
note: There is a blank space preceding the claimant's surname. According to the *National Index of American Imprints* the author is Michel Martel.

504.
District Court Ledger, 130 NY 43
date of deposit: June 21, twentieth year of Independence
claimant: P: Thomas Swords and James Swords
author: Richard Bayley
title: An/ Account/ of the/ Epidemic fever/ which prevailed in the/ City of New.York/ during part of the/ Summer and Fall of/ 1795./ <author statement>/ <short rule>

505.
District Court Ledger, 130 NY 44
date of deposit: July 7, twenty-first year of Independence
claimant: A: John Torrey
title: Scriptural and Alegorical/ Poems/ on the/ Downfall of Superstition/ <author statement>/ <short rule>/ <two lines of poetry in English>/ <short rule>

506.
District Court Ledger, 130 NY 45
date of deposit: July 8, twenty-first year of Independence
claimant: P: Noah Webster
title: A/ Collection of papers/ on the subject of/ Bilious fevers/ Prevalent in the United States for a/ few years past—

507.
District Court Ledger, 130 NY 46
date of deposit: November 16, twenty-first year of Independence
claimant: P: John I Johnson
author: Albert Gallatin
title: A/ Sketch/ of the/ Finances/ of the/ United States/ <author statement>

1797

508.
District Court Ledger, 130 NY 47
date of deposit: January 30, twenty-first year of Independence
claimant: A: William Milns
composer: J. Hewitt
title: Songs &c./ in the/ Comet/ or/ He would be a Philosopher/ a/ Comedy in five Acts—/ as performed by the old American Company/ New York/ <author statement>/ <composer statement>

509.
District Court Ledger, 130 NY 48
date of deposit: February 24, twenty-first year of Independence
claimant: A: Elihu Hubbard Smith
title: Edwin and Angelina;/ or/ The Banditti./ An— Opera in three Acts.—

510.
District Court Ledger, 130 NY 49
date of deposit: March 20, twenty-first year of Independence
claimant: A: Michael Martel
title: Mr Martel's/ Literal Translation—/ of the/ Works of Virgil—/ in which—/ The Order of Con struction to the Latin Text is not only translated/ literally into English, but every Word is com pletely parsed/ explained and illustrated by critical historical, geographical/ mythological and classical notes, in English, from the best/ Commentators both ancient and modern—The English to the/ Latin Word is in Italic, and the Words which have been added/ to render the Sense more intelligible, the English less/ unfashionable, stiff and awkward, and have none to answer/ them in the original, are in a different Character, There is/ in the Beginning of the Work a Sufficiency of Declensions/ and Congugations to enable the Learner to proceed to trans-/ late. After a Couple of Weeks Tuition, a Mother can, with/ this Book, teach Latin to her Child, who will study with/ Advantage and Pleasure, because he can study them, all/ the disheartening Difficulties being removed—/ <rule>/ <quotation in English>/ <rule>

511.
District Court Ledger, 130 NY 50
date of deposit: July 8, twenty-second year of Independence
claimant: A: William Stevens
author: . . . / An Officer in the American Artillery through the/ whole of the late Revolution; and since in the Militia.
title: A/ System/ for/ Discipline/ of the/ Artillery of the United States/ of America./ <rule>/ or the young Artillerist's/ Pocket Companion/ in three Parts—/ <double rule>/ Part I./ Containing— The Formation of the Corps of Artillery/ and the Duty and Practice of light Field Artillery &c/ Part II./ Containing—The Theory and Practice of heavy Artillery/ in Garrison and on Board the Navy: and an Extract/ of a Treatise on the Origin and Principles of/ Court Martials.—/ Part III/ Containing Laboratory Duty—a great Variety/ of Directions for Compositions, and the Method/ of making artificial Fire-Works, with the/ Formation of Ammunition necessary for/ the different Kinds of Ordinance—/ in three Volumes/ <rule>/ <author statement>

512.
District Court Ledger, 130 NY 51
date of deposit: July 29, twenty-second year of Independence
claimant: P: Samuel L. Mitchel, Edward Miller and Elihu Hubbard Smith
title: THE/ MEDICAL REPOSITORY./ <double rule>/ VOL. I.—No I./ <double rule>
note: According to the *National Union Catalog* the editor is Samuel Latham Mitchill.

513.
District Court Ledger, 130 NY 52
date of deposit: August 28, twenty-second year of Independence
claimant: P: Ashbel Stoddard
author: Bildad Barney, A. M.
title: An/ Introduction/ To The/ art/ of/ READING:/ Being a collection of Peices suited to the Capacity of/ Children and designed for the use of Schools./ <rule>/ <author statement>/ <rule>/ <quotation in Latin>

514.
District Court Ledger, 130 NY 53
date of deposit: August 28, twenty-second year of Independence
claimant: A: Chrittopher Flanagan <Christopher Flanagan>
author: . . . , Preacher of the Gospel.
title: The/ Conversation & Conduct,/ of the late Unfortunate/ John Young,/ Who was Executed/ for the/ Murder of Robert Barwick/ (Deputy Sheriff,)/ From the time of Receiving sentence of Death, to that of/ his Execution./ <rule>/ <author statement>/ <rule>/ Who frequently, Visited him, during that Period./ <four lines of poetry in English>/ <short rule>
note: According to the *National Index of American Imprints* the author is Christopher Flanagan.

515.
District Court Ledger, 130 NY 54
date of deposit: September 12, twenty-second year of Independence
claimant: P: Messrs Spencer & Webb <Thomas Spencer and Thomas Smith Webb>

author: a Royal Arch Mason, K. T. K. of M. &c. &c. <Thomas Smith Webb>
title: THE/ FREEMASON'S/ MONITOR;/ OR,/ ILLUSTRATIONS/ OF/ MASONRY:/ In Two Parts./ Part I. Containing—Illustrations of the Degrees of Entered Apprentice;/ Fellow Craft; Master Mason; Master Mark Mason; Passing the Chair;/ Most Excellent Master; Royal Arch Mason; Knights Templars &/ Knights of Malta; with the Charges, &ca. of each Degree. Also a/ Sketch of the History of Masonry in America./ Part II—Containing—An Account of the Ineffable Degrees of/ Masonry, viz. Secret Master; Perfect Master; Illustrious/ secretary; Provost and Judge; Intendants of the Buildings;/ or Master in Israel; Elected Knights; Elected Grand Master;/ Illustri ous Knights; or Sublime Knights Elected; Grand Master/ Architects; Knights of the ninth, or Royal Arch; Grand, Elect,/ Perfect and Sublime, or Ultimate Degree of Masonry:/ together with the History and Charges appertaining to each/ Degree./ <rule>/ <author statement>/ <rule>/ Printed at Albany, for Spencer & Webb, and Sold at their/ Book store, in Market-Street. 1797.
note: According to the *National Index of American Imprints* the author is Thomas Smith Webb.

516.
District Court Ledger, 130 NY 55
date of deposit: September 21, twenty-second year of Independence
claimant: A: William Milns
author: . . . , Member of St, Mary Hall in the University of Oxford;/ Author of the Well-bred Schollar, Penman's Repository, &c. &c.
title: THE/ AMERICAN ACCOUNTANT/ OR,/ A COMPLETE SYSTEM/ OF/ PRACTICAL ARITHMETIC./ CONTAINING./ I. Whole numbers, particularly/ adapted to the American and/ British Commerce./ II. Vulgar Fractions; in which the rules/ are so simple and the contrac tions/ so obvious; as to render the/ Operations remarkably short and easy./ III. Decimals, with concise Methods/ <vertical rule>/ of managing all kinds of simple & Compound/ Repetends; the Extraction of Roots; Interest,/ Annuities &c &c./ IV. Duodecimals; or multiplication of feet and/ inches./ V. Curious useful and Entertaining,/ Questions, with their/ Solutions; &c. &c./ <short rule>/ THE whole calculated to ease the teacher and assist the Pupil; it will be found/ likewise extremely useful to American Merchants, &c. gen eral rules and compact/ tables being given to Change the Currencies, Sterling, French and Dutch Monies into/ each other./ <rule>/ <author statement>/ <rule>/ <quotation in Latin>/ <rule>

517.
District Court Ledger, 130 NY 56
date of deposit: October 2, twenty-second year of Independence
claimant: P: George Foliot Hopkins <George Follet Hopkins>
title: THE TICKLER:/ BEING/ A SERIES OF/ PERIODICAL PAPERS,/ DESCRIPTIVE OF/ LIFE AND MANNERS.
note: According to Roger Pattrell Bristol's *Index of Printers, Publishers, and Booksellers Indicated by Charles Evans in his American Bibliography,* the printer is George Follet Hopkins.

518.
District Court Ledger, 130 NY 57
date of deposit: November 9, twenty-second year of Independence
claimant: P: Messrs Samuel Latham Mitchell Edward Miller & Elihu Hubbard Smith
title: THE/ MEDICAL REPOSITORY.—/ <double rule>/ VOL. I.—No. II/ <double rule>
note: According to the *National Union Catalog* the editor is Samuel Latham Mitchill.

519.
District Court Ledger, 130 NY 58
date of deposit: December 2, twenty-second year of Independence
claimant: A: William Milns
author: . . . ,/ MEMBER of St Mary Hall, in the University of Oxford;/ Author of the American Accountant, Penman's Repository &c. &c.—
title: THE/ WELL-BRED SCHOLAR,/ OR/ PRACTICAL ESSAYS/ ON THE/ Best methods of improving the Taste, and assisting the/ Exertions of Youth in their/ LITERARY PURSUITS./ <rule>/ <author statement>/ <rule>/ <six lines of poetry in English>/ <rule>/ Second Edition, with alterations and revisions./ <rule>

1798
520.
District Court Ledger, 130 NY 59
date of deposit: January 30, twenty-second year of Independence
claimant: P: Messrs..Samuel Latham Mitchell, Edward Miller and Elihu H. Smith

title: THE/ MEDICAL REPOSITORY./ <red double rule>/ VOL. I.<short decorative rule> No. III./ <red double rule>
note: According to the *National Union Catalog* the editor is Samuel Latham Mitchill.

521.
District Court Ledger, 130 NY 60
date of deposit: March 27, twenty-second year of Independence
claimant: P: John C. Robson
author: <John C. Robson>
title: A/ Scriptural/ view/ of the Rise of the/ Heathen, Jewish and Christian/ Monarchies/ in the world;/ with/ An Account of the Dissolution of the present European/ System, according to the prophecies of Isaiah, Daniel and/ John, in the Revelation and others.—/ <double rule>/ <biblical quotation>/ <double rule>/ <biblical quotation>/ <double rule>
note: According to the *National Index of American Imprints* the author is John C. Robson.

522.
District Court Ledger, 130 NY 61
date of deposit: April 6, twenty-second year of Independence
claimant: A: William Dunlap
title: ANDRE;/ A Tragedy, in five Acts/ as performed by the old American Company./ New York March 30th—1798.—/ To which are added/ Authentic documents/ respecting/ Major Andre;/ consisting of/ Letters to Miss Seward,/ The/ Cow Chace,/ Proceedings of the Court Marshal &c.—<rule>

523.
District Court Ledger, 130 NY 62
date of deposit: May 1, twenty-second year of Independence
claimant: P: Elihu H. Smith
author: <Elihu Hubbard Smith>
title: Alcuin;/ a/ Dialogue
note: According to the *National Index of American Imprints* the author is Elihu Hubbard Smith.

524.
District Court Ledger, 130 NY 63
date of deposit: May 1, twenty-second year of Independence
claimant: P: Messrs Samuel Latham Mitchell, Edward Miller and Elihu H. Smith
title: The/ MEDICAL REPOSITORY./ <double rule>/ Vol.—1.—No IV.—/ <decorative double rule>
note: According to the *National Union Catalog* the editor is Samuel Latham Mitchill.

525.
District Court Ledger, 130 NY 64
date of deposit: June 1, twenty-second year of Independence
claimant: P: Thomas Greenleaf
author: a General Officer. <François René Jean, baron de Pommereul>
title: Campaign/ of/ General Buonaparte/ in Italy,/ during the fourth and fifth years of the/ French Republic./ <rule>/ <author statement>/ <rule>
note: According to the *National Index of American Imprints* the author is François René Jean, baron de Pommereul.

526.
District Court Ledger, 130 NY 65
date of deposit: July 17, twenty-third year of Independence
claimant: P: Richard Walker
author: <John Davis>
title: The/ Original/ Letters/ of/ Ferdinand/ and/ Elizabeth./ <double rule>/ <quotation in English>/ <double rule>
note: According to the *National Index of American Imprints* the author is John Davis.

527.
District Court Ledger, 130 NY 66
date of deposit: August 3, twenty-third year of Independence
claimant: P: Messrs.. Samuel Lathem Mitchell, Edward Miller and Elihu H. Smith
title: The/ MEDICAL REPOSITORY./ VOL. II. No,, I.—
note: According to the *National Union Catalog* the editor is Samuel Latham Mitchill.

528.
District Court Ledger, 130 NY 67
date of deposit: August 11, twenty-third year of Independence
claimant: P: James Gibbons
author: James Gibbons./ Teacher of Arithmetic &c. in New York.
title: Dilworth's Assistant:/ adapted to the Commerce/ of the/ Citizens of the United States./ Being a Compendium of Arithmetic/ both

Practical and Theoretical—/ <rule>/ In Five Parts.—/ <rule>/ Containing./ I. Arithmetic in whole Numbers/ wherein all the common Rules/ having each of them a sufficient/ number of Ques tions with their/ answers, are methodically/ and briefly handled.—/ II. Vulgar Fractions, wherein/ several Things, not commonly/ met with are distinctly treated/ of, and laid down in/ the most plain and easy/ manner.—/ III. Decimals, in which among/ other Things are considered/ the extraction of Roots:/ Interest, bothe simple/ and Compound; annuities/ Rebate and Equation/ of Payments.—/ <vertical rule>/ IV. A large Col lection of/ Questions with their Answers,/ Serving to exercise the/ foregoing Rules, together/ with a few others both pleasant/ and diverting.—/ V. Duodecimals, commonly/ called cross multiplica tion/ wherein that sort of arithme/ =tic is thoroughly considered/ and rendered very plain/ and easy; together with/ the method of proving/ all the foregoing Operations/ at once by Division of/ several Denominations/ without reducing them/ into the lowest Terms/ mentioned.—/ The whole being delivered in the most familiar/ way of Question and Answer, is recommended/ by sev eral eminent Mathematicians; Accomptants,/ and schoolmasters, as necessary to be used in schools/ by all Teachers, who would have their Schollars/ thoroughly understand and make a quick/ pro gress in Arithmetic.—/ <double rule>/ Carefully revised, and adapted to the Commerce of/ the Citizens of the United States, with many additions/ in the various Rules;/ <author statement>/ <double rule>

529.

District Court Ledger, 130 NY 69

date of deposit: September 5, twenty-third year of Independence

claimant: P: Hocquet Caritat

author: <Charles Brockden Brown>

title: Wieland/ or the/ TRANSFORMATION./ an/ American Tale./ <short rule>/ <four lines of poetry in English>

note: According to the *National Index of American Imprints* the author is Charles Brockden Brown.

530.

District Court Ledger, 130 NY 70

date of deposit: November 14, twenty-third year of Independence

claimant: P: Messrs.. Daniel S. Dean and Joseph Talcott

compiler: ASA RHOADY.

title: An/ American/ Spelling-Book/ Designed/ For the use of our common Schools; and as an easy/ Introduction to the Art of Spelling and reading the/ English Language with propriety.—/ In two Parts/ PART THE FIRST,/ Containing easy and familiar/ words, divided, accented and/ Methodi cally arranged,/ agreeably to their proper/ Sounds; with Lessons of/ Reading interspersed.—/ <short rule>/ <vertical rule>/ PART SECOND,/ To contain words more difficult and/ irregular; accented; their proper/ Sounds pointed out, and the various/ Significations, ranged (in general)/ in one Line; with instructive &/ enter taining reding Lessons;/ and the most useful parts of Grammar./ <rule>/ <compiler statement>/ <rule>

531.

District Court Ledger, 130 NY 71

date of deposit: November 23, twenty-third year of Independence

claimant: P: Thomas B. Jansen

title: A/ Physical Enquiry/ into the/ Origin and Causes/ of the/ Pestilential Fevers./ <short double rule>/ <four lines of poetry in English>

532.

District Court Ledger, 130 NY 72

date of deposit: December 3, twenty-third year of Independence

claimant: A: Joseph Hamilton

title: Occasional Observations/ on the/ Small-Pox,/ or the/ The Traveller's Pocket-Docter./ <rule>/ <author statement>/ <rule>

533.

District Court Ledger, 130 NY 73

date of deposit: December 4, twenty-third year of Independence

claimant: P: John Murray

author: Lindley Murray.

title: English Exercises/ Adapted to/ The Grammar/ lately published/ By L. Murray;/ Consisting of/ Exemplifications of the Parts of/ Speech; Instances of false Orthography/ Violations of the Rules of Syntax/ <vertical rule>/ Defects in Punctuation; and/ Violations of the Rules/ respecting Perspi cuity and/ Accuracy.—/ Designed for the benefit of/ Private Learners/ as well as for/ the use of Schools./ <double rule>/ <author statement>/ <double rule>

534.
District Court Ledger, 130 NY 74
date of deposit: December 4, twenty-third year of Independence
claimant: P: John Murray Junr..
author: Lindley Murray.
title: English/ Grammar,/ Adapted to the different Classes of/ Learners./ with an/ Appendix,/ con taining/ Rules and Observations for Assisting the more/ advanced Students to write with/ Perspi cuity and Accuracy.—/ <double rule>/ <author statement>/ <double rule>

535.
District Court Ledger, 130 NY 75
date of deposit: December 15, twenty-third year of Independence
claimant: P: Messrs. Samuel Latham Mitchell and Edward Miller
title: The/ Medical Repository.—/ <rule>/ Vol. II. No. II.—/ <rule>
note: According to the *National Union Catalog* the editor is Samuel Latham Mitchill.

536.
District Court Ledger, 130 NY 76
date of deposit: December 28, twenty-third year of Independence
claimant: A: James Hardie
author: . . . , A. M.
title: An/ Account/ of the/ Malignant Fever,/ Lately prevalent in the City/ of New York,/ containing/ I. A. Narrative of its Rise, Progress and Decline with the/ Opinions of some Medical Gentlemen, with respect to its Origin, &c,/ II. The manner in which the poor were releived during this Awful Calamity.—/ III. A List of the Donations, which have been presented to the Health/ Committee for the relief of the Sick and Indigent.—/ IV. A. List of the Names of the Dead, arranged in Alpha betical order,/ with their professions or Occupa tions, and as far as was practicable/ to obtain Information, the Names of the Countries of which they/ were Natives.—/ V. A. Comparative View of the Fever of the year 1798. with that of/ the year 1795.—/ <rule>/ <author statement>/ <rule>

1799

537.
District Court Ledger, 130 NY 77
date of deposit: January 16, twenty-third year of Independence
claimant: P: Hocquet Caritat
author: the Author of Wieland or the/ TRANSFOR MATION. <Charles Brockden Brown>
title: ORMOND;/ or the/ Secret Witness./ <rule>/ <author statement>/ <rule>
note: According to the *National Index of American Imprints,* the author is Charles Brockden Brown.

538.
District Court Ledger, 130 NY 78
date of deposit: February 4, twenty-third year of Independence
claimant: P: Messrs.. Samuel Lathem Mitchel and Edward Miller
title: The/ Medical Repository./ <double rule>/ Vol. II.—No. III./ <double rule>
note: According to the *National Union Catalog* the editor is Samuel Latham Mitchill.

539.
District Court Ledger, 130 NY 79
date of deposit: April 8, twenty-third year of Independence
claimant: A: Peter Tharp
author: . . . Math.
title: A/ New and Complete System/ of/ Federal Arithmetic;/ in three Parts/ with an/ Appendix,/ containing/ Board and Timber measure./ Designed/ for the use of Schools./ <rule>/ <author statement>/ <rule>

540.
District Court Ledger, 130 NY 80
date of deposit: May 9, twenty-third year of Independence
claimant: P: Messrs Samuel Latham Mitchell and Edward Miller
title: The/ Medical Repository/ <double rule>/ Vol. II.—No. IV./ <double rule>
note: According to the *National Union Catalog* the editor is Samuel Latham Mitchill.

541.
District Court Ledger, 130 NY 81
date of deposit: May 11, twenty-third year of Independence
claimant: P: William Torrey
author: a Member of the Bar.
title: An/ Annual History—/ of the/ Legislative Pro ceedings,/ of the/ State of New York:—/ including/ Accurate Copies of the Laws,/ passed in each re spective Session./ <rule>/ <author statement>/ <rule>/ Vol. I./ <rule>/ Containing the proceedings and Laws in 1799./ <double rule>

542.
District Court Ledger, 130 NY 82
date of deposit: May 21, twenty-third year of Independence
claimant: A: Joseph Hamilton
author: . . . , Physician—
title: Occasional Reflections/ on the/ Operations/ of the/ Small Pox,/ or, the/ Traveller's Pocket/ Doc tor/ <rule>/ <author statement>/ <rule>

543.
District Court Ledger, 130 NY 83
date of deposit: August 5, twenty-fourth year of Independence
claimant: P: Messrs Samuel Latham Mitchell and Edward Miller
title: The/ Medical Repository,/ for May, June and July, 1799./ <double rule>/ Vol. III.—No,, I.—/ <double rule>
note: According to the *National Union Catalog* the editor is Samuel Latham Mitchill.

544.
District Court Ledger, 130 NY 84
date of deposit: August 30, twenty-fourth year of Independence
claimant: A: Hocquet Caritat
title: <double rule>/ The feast of Reason and the flow of Soul./ <double rule>/ A New/ Explanatory Catalogue/ of/ H. Caritat's/ General & Increasing/ Circulating Library.

545.
District Court Ledger, 130 NY 85
date of deposit: November 18, twenty-fourth year of Independence
claimant: A: James Church
author: . . . .M. D./ Formerly Pupil to Dr. Dennison, London Hospital.
title: A/ Brief Dissertation/ on the/ VENEREAL DISEASE,/ Seminal Weaknesses,/ Gleets &c. &c./ Including/ The History,/ Cure, and Prevention/ of those Diseases./ By an Approved Method,/ By which persons of both sexes may cure themselves/ with Ease, Certainty, Safety and Secrecy,/ at an easy expence./ <short double rule>/ <author statement>/ <short double rule>/ <quotation in English>/ <short rule>

546.
District Court Ledger, 130 NY 86
date of deposit: December 7, twenty-fourth year of Independence
claimant: P: Messrs. Samuel Latham Mitchell and Edward Miller
title: The/ Medical Repository./ <double rule>/ Vol. III.—No. II./ <double rule>
note: According to the *National Union Catalog* the editor is Samuel Latham Mitchill.

1800

547.
District Court Ledger, 130 NY 87
date of deposit: January 18, twenty-fourth year of Independence
claimant: P: Daniel Phoenix, Chamberlain of the City of New York and assignee of Gouverneur Morris
author: Gouverneur Morris.
title: An/ Oration,/ upon/ The Death of/ General Washington,—/ <author statement>/ <short rule>/ Delivered at the request of the corporation of/ The City of New York, on the 31st./ Day of December 1799./ <short rule>

548.
District Court Ledger, 130 NY 88
date of deposit: January 30, twenty-fourth year of Independence
claimant: A: William Cobbett
title: A/ Concise and Comprehensive/ History/ of/ Prince Suworow's/ Campaign in Italy./ In the Year 1799./ <rule>/ <author statement>./ <rule>
note: The *National Union Catalog* identifies Suworow as Aleksandr Vasil'evich Suvorov.

549.
District Court Ledger, 130 NY 89
date of deposit: February 27, twenty-fourth year of Independence
claimant: P: George F. Hopkins <George Follet Hopkins>
author: John M. Mason, A: M./ Pastor of the associate reformed Church in the/ City of New York—
title: A/ Funeral Oration/ Delivered in the brick Presbeterian Church in the/ City of New York, on the—22d—Day of February, 1800,/ being the Day recommended by Congress to the/ Citizens of the United States, publicly to testify/ their Grief for the/ Death/ of/ Gen. Washington/ By Appointment of a Number of the Clergy of/ New York/ And published at their Request—/ <rule>/ <author statement>/ <rule>

note: According to Roger Bristol's *Index of Printers, Publishers, and Booksellers Indicated by Charles Evans in his American Bibliography,* the printer is George Follet Hopkins.

550.
District Court Ledger, 130 NY 90
date of deposit: February 27, twenty-fourth year of Independence
claimant: P: John Furman, (Assignee of William Linn D. D.)
author: William Linn, D. D.—
title: A/ Funeral/ Eulogy,/ occasioned by the Death of/ General Washington./ Delivered February 22nd,, 1800.—/ Before the/ New=York State Society/ of the/ Cincinnati.—/ <double rule>/ <author statement>/ <double rule>

551.
District Court Ledger, 130 NY 91
date of deposit: March 17, twenty-fourth year of Independence
claimant: A: William Dunlap
translator: <William Dunlap>
title: The/ German Theatre.—/ <rule>/ <author statement>/ <rule>
note: William Dunlap claims the right of the deposit as both author and translator.

552.
District Court Ledger, 130 NY 92
date of deposit: March 22, twenty-fourth year of Independence
claimant: P: Samuel Campbell
author: Tunis Wortman/ counsellor at Law
title: A/ Treatise/ concerning/ Political Enquiry/ and the/ Liberty of the Press/ <author statement>/ <short rule>/ <quotation in Latin>/ <short rule>

553.
District Court Ledger, 130 NY 93
date of deposit: April 2, twenty-fourth year of Independence
claimant: A: Robert G. Wetmore and John Hanmer
author: . . . ,/ Royal Arch Masons/ in the/ State of New York.
title: Observations/ On/ Masonry/ Humbly tendered to the consideration of/ Royal Arch Masons/ in the/ United States of America/ <author statement>

554.
District Court Ledger, 130 NY 94
date of deposit: April 7, twenty-fourth year of Independence
claimant: A: Joseph Hamilton
author: . . . ,/ Author of a Treatise, lately/ Pub lished, called the Trav=/ =eller's Pocket Docker.
title: A certain/ Bar/ Against the/ Approach/ of the/ Yellow Fever/ Written for the Good of the/ Public/ <author statement>

555.
District Court Ledger, 130 NY 95
date of deposit: April 14, twenty-fourth year of Independence
claimant: A: William Coleman
title: Report/ of the/ Trial/ of/ Levi Weeks/ On an Indictment for the Murder/ Of Gulielma Sands/ On Monday the thirty first day of March/ and Tuesday the first day of April 1800/ <short rule>/ Taken in short Hand by the Clerk of the Court/ <short rule>

556.
District Court Ledger, 130 NY 96
date of deposit: May 10, twenty-fourth year of Independence
claimant: A: Samuel Low
title: Poems,/ <author statement>/ <double rule>/ <three lines of poetry in English>/ <double rule>/ In two Volumes.

557.
District Court Ledger, 130 NY 97
date of deposit: May 14, twenty-fourth year of Independence
claimant: P: Samuel L. Mitchill, M. D. Professor of Chemistry in Columbia College, &c and Edward Miller, M. D.
title: The/ Medical Repository./ <short rule>/ con ducted By/ Samuel L. Mitchill, M. D./ Professor of Chemistry in Columbia College, &c./ and/ Edward Miller M. D./ <double rule>/ <quotation in Latin>/ <double rule>/ Vol. III./ <short double rule>
note: According to the *National Union Catalog* the editor is Samuel Latham Mitchill. Page 98 in the New York ledger is blank.

558.
District Court Ledger, 130 NY 99
date of deposit: May 30, twenty-fourth year of Independence
claimant: P: Thomas Hertell

author: Joseph Young, M. D./ of New-York
title: A/ New Physical System/ of/ Astronomy;/ or/ An attempt to explain the operations of the/ Powers which impel the planets and comets to/ Perform eliptical revolutions round the/ Sun, and revolve on their own axis:/ in which,/ The Physi cal System of/ Sir Isaac Newton,/ is examined, and presumed to be refuted./ To which is annexed/ A. Physiological Treatise/ In which the first Stage of Animation is considered, and the means shewn, by/ which circulation is performed in the first Rudiments of the incipient Animal,/ before the Vessels are completely organized, &c. Together with an explanation/ of the general Laws, by which the Animal Economy is gov erned; and/ particularly, the mode whereby the operations of the Vis Medicatrix naturae,/ or the unassisted Powers of nature, are exerted to obviate and cure Disease./ Also/ Successful methods of curing cancerous Ulcers, the/ Quartan Ague, Putrid Fevers, stopping Morti-/ fications, and extracting Frost, so as to leave the/ frozen Member perfectly well./ <short decorative rule>/ <author statement>/ <double rule>

559.
District Court Ledger, 130 NY 100
date of deposit: June 19, twenty-fourth year of Independence
claimant: A: Joseph James and Daniel Moore
title: A/ System of Exchange/ with almost/ All parts of the world/ To which is added,/ The India Directory/ For purchasing the/ Drugs and Spices/ Of the East, Indies, &c

560.
District Court Ledger, 130 NY 101
date of deposit: July 21, twenty-fifth year of Independence
claimant: A: Ezra Sampson
author: . . . , of Hudson (New York)
title: The/ Beauties/ of the/ Bible:/ Being a selection from the/ Old and New Testaments,/ with vari ous/ Remarks and Brief Dissertations,/ Designed for the use of/ Christians/ in General/ And par ticularly for the use of/ Schools,/ and for the/ Improvement of Youth./ <rule>/ <author statement>/ <rule>

561.
District Court Ledger, 130 NY 102
date of deposit: August 13, twenty-fifth year of Independence
claimant: A: John Churchman
author: . . . ,/ Fellow of the Russian Imperial Academy.
title: The/ Magnetic Atlas,/ or/ Variation Charts/ of the whole/ Terraqueous Globe;/ comprising a/ Sys tem/ of the/ Variation & Dip of the Needle,/ By which/ The observations being truly made,/ The Longitude,/ May be ascertained./ <rule>/ The third Edition with additions/ <rule>/ <author statement>/ <rule>

562.
District Court Ledger, 130 NY 103
date of deposit: October 3, twenty-fifth year of Independence
claimant: A: Platt Kennedy
author: . . . , Philo./ And late instructor at Hunting-ton, (L.J.)
title: The/ New Grammatical/ Spelling Book./ Being—/ An easy introduction to the English lan guage—Teaching/ the different parts of speech, and Definitions of all the/ Words contained in the Tables of spelling, from/ Two to Six Syllables./ Also—/ A Synopsis of English grammar, with an easy Praxis on/ some passages in Scripture, to practise the learner;/ The rules of reading and punctuation, &c.—/ The whole adapted to the Capacity of Youth,/ and composed for the use of Schools./ <rule>/ <author statement>/ <rule>

563.
District Court Ledger, 130 NY 104
date of deposit: October 22, twenty-fifth year of Independence
claimant: P: John Lang
author: Alexander Hamilton,
title: Letter/ from/ <author statement>/ concern ing/ The Public conduct and character/ of/ John Adams, Esq./ President of the United States./ <double rule>

564.
District Court Ledger, 130 NY 105
date of deposit: November 3, twenty-fifth year of Independence
claimant: A: Mr. P. Landrin Duport <Pierre Landrin Duport>
composer: . . . / Professor of Dancing from Paris/ & Original Composer of Cadriel's
title: United States/ Country Dances/ with/ Figures/ also/ Accompaniments/ for the/ Piano Forte/ Composed in America/ <composer statement>
note: According to the *National Index of American Imprints* the composer is Pierre Landrin Duport.

565.

District Court Ledger, 130 NY 106

date of deposit: November 10, twenty-fifth year of Independence

claimant: P: P. R Johnson & J. Stryker

author: a Citizen of New York <James Cheetham>

title: An/ Answer/ To/ Alexander Hamilton's/ Letter,/ concerning/ The public conduct and character/ of/ John Adams, Esq./ President of the United States./ <double rule>/ <author statement>/ <double rule>

note: According to the *National Index of American Imprints* the author is James Cheetham. *Longworth's American Almanac, New-York Register and City Directory* for 1801 identifies Paul R. Johnson as a printer in New York City.

566.

District Court Ledger, 130 NY 107

date of deposit: December 17, twenty-fifth year of Independence

claimant: P: Furman and Loudon

author: . . . the Translator of Bounaparte's Campaign, author/ of Ferdinand and Elizabeth &c. &c <John Davis>

title: The/ Farmer of New Jersey;/ or/ A. Picture of Domestic Life./ A. Tale./ <author statement>/ <short rule>/ <four lines of poetry in English>/ <rule>

note: According to the *National Index of American Imprints* the author is John Davis. Roger Bristol's *Index of Printers, Publishers, and Booksellers Indicated by Charles Evans in his American Bibliography* identifies the printers as John Furman and John Loudon.

New Hampshire

1791

567.

Title Page Deposit

date of deposit: July 15

claimant: A: <Samuel Langdon>

author: SAMUEL LANGDON, D. D./ Minister of HAMPTONFALLS, in the State of NEWHAMPSHIRE.

title: OBSERVATIONS/ ON THE/ REVELA TION/ OF/ *JESUS CHRIST to* ST. *JOHN.*/ Which comprehend the most approved SENTI MENTS of the celebrated Mr./ MEDE, Mr. LOWMAN, BISHOP NEWTON, and other noted Writers/ on this Book; and cast much addi tional Light on the more obscure Prophe-/ cies; especially those which point out the Time of/ The RISE and FALL of ANTICHRIST./ IN TWO PARTS./ CONTAINING,/ . . . / <decorative rule>/ <author statement>/ <decorative rule>/ <biblical quotation>/ <double rule>

imprint: <below double rule> PRINTED at WOR CESTER, MASSACHUSETTS,/ BY ISAIAH THOMAS./ <short double rule>/ MDCCXCI.

note: Evans 23486 identifies the claimant. The New Hampshire title pages deposited for copyright are not in the collections of the Library of Congress. Thirty of them are found in Record Group 21 at the National Archives and Records Administration, Federal Archives and Records Center, Waltham, Massachusetts. Some of these lack the clerical notes on the verso that identify claimant and give date of deposit, and others supply the date of deposit but not the identity of the claimant or information about how the work was claimed. Whenever possible, this information has been supplied here from what is recorded in Charles Evans' *American Bibliography.*

Evans' source for the dates of deposit and claimants for New Hampshire imprints is uncertain. It is doubtful that he had access to the collection of title pages but possible that the now lost New Hampshire copyright ledger was available to him. The dates of deposit Evans recorded for New Hampshire titles agree with those appearing on the versos of the thirty extant title pages, and, to provide a chronological order for the entries, Evans' deposit dates and his identification of claimants have therefore been accepted here. Where information has been supplied from a source other than the official copyright records, it is given within brackets in the entry and the authority cited in the note.

1792

568.

Title Page Deposit

date of deposit: February 9

claimant: <P: Eliphalet Ladd>

author: <Richard Burn>

title: *BURN'*s/ ABRIDGMENT,/ OR THE/ AMERICAN JUSTICE/ CONTAINING THE WHOLE/ PRACTICE, AUTHORITY AND DUTY/ OF/ JUSTICES OF THE PEACE;/ WITH CORRECT FORMS OF PRECE DENTS/ RELATING THERETO, AND ADAPTED/ TO THE PRESENT SITUATION/ OF THE/ UNITED STATES./ <double rule>

imprint: <below double rule> *DOVER, (New-hampshire.)*/ PRINTED FOR, AND SOLD BY ELIPHALET LADD, AT/ HIS PRINTING-OFFICE, NEAR THE COURT-HOUSE./ M,DCC,XCII.

note: Evans 24160 identifies the claimant. See the note for entry 567.

569.

Title Page Deposit

date of deposit: <July 9>

claimant: <A: Curtis Coe>

author: CURTIS COE, A. M./ PASTOR OF THE CHURCH AT DURHAM.

title: A/ SERIOUS ADDRESS/ OF A/ MINISTER TO HIS PEOPLE./ THE MEANING OF THE WORD BAPTISM CON-/ SIDERED: SEV ERAL REASONS ASSIGNED/ FOR THE BAP TISM OF INFANTS, AND/ OBJECTIONS ANSWERED./ <double rule>/ <author statement>/ <double rule>/ <biblical quotation>/ <short thick rule>/ *PUBLISHED ACCORDING TO ACT OF CONGRESS.*/ <short thick rule>

imprint: <below short thick rule> PORTSMOUTH (N. H.)/ PRINTED BY JOHN OSBORNE, AT THE/ SPY PRINTING-OFFICE,/ M,DCC,XCII.

note: Evans 24196 identifies the claimant and gives the date of deposit. However, he gives the printer as John Melcher. See the note for entry 567.

570.

Title Page Deposit

date of deposit: <September 15>

claimant: <A: Daniel Humphreys>

author: DANIEL HUMPHREYS, ESQ.

title: THE/ COMPENDIOUS AMERICAN/ GRAMMAR,/ OR/ GRAMMATICAL INSTITUTES IN VERSE;/ DESIGNED FOR THE USE OF SCHOOLS IN THE/ UNITED

STATES./ WITH AN APPENDIX,/ CON TAING RULES FOR THE FORMA-/ TION OF VERBS, AND THE RIGHT USE/ OF THE POINTS AND STOPS./ INSCRIBED TO THE/ AMERICAN INSTRUCTORS OF YOUTH./ <thick rule>/ <author statement>/ <thick rule>/ *PUBLISHED ACCORDING TO ACT OF/ CONGRESS.*/ <short thick rule>/ <quotation in Latin>/ <short thick rule>

imprint: <below short thick rule> PORTS MOUTH, (N. H.)/ PRINTED BY JOHN OS- BORNE, AT THE/ SPY PRINTING- OFFICE,/ (FOR THE AUTHOR.)/ M,DCC,XCII.

note: Evans 24415 identifies the claimant and gives the date of deposit. See the note for entry 567.

571.

Title Page Deposit

date of deposit: <October 5>

claimant: <A,P: Henry Ranlet>

author: HENRY RANLET.

title: THE/ Youths' Instructor;/ OR/ SPELLING- BOOK:/ COMPRISING/ THE FIRST PRINCIPLES/ OF THE/ *English Language.*/ . . . / <rule>/ <author statement>/ <rule>/ <five lines of poetry in English>/ <rule>/ PUBLISHED ACCORDING TO ACT OF CONGRESS./ <double rule>

imprint: <below double rule> EXETER:/ Printed and Sold by HENRY RANLET. M,DCC,XCII.

note: An advertisement is printed on the verso of the title page. Evans 24726 identifies the claimant and gives the date of deposit. See the note for entry 567.

572.

Title Page Deposit

date of deposit: <November 6>

claimant: <A: Thomas Odiorne>

author: <script> Thomas Odiornc.

title: THE/ PROGRESS OF REFINEMENT,/ A/ P O E M,/ IN THREE BOOKS./ TO WHICH ARE ADDED,/ A/ POEM ON FAME,/ AND/ <black letter> MISCELLANIES./ <double rule>/ <author statement>/ <double rule>/ <ornament of ram's head, flowers and vines>/ <double rule>

imprint: <below double rule> BOSTON:/ PRINTED BY YOUNG AND ETHERIDGE,/ Opposite the Entrance of the BRANCH-BANK,/ STATE-STREET./ <short rule>/ MDCCXCII.

note: Evans 24643 identifies the claimant and gives the date of deposit. See the note for entry 567.

1793

573.

Title Page Deposit

date of deposit: April 17

claimant: <A: Phinehas Merrill>

author: PHINEHAS MERRILL.

title: THE/ SCHOLAR's GUIDE/ TO/ ARITHMETIC:/ BEING A COLLECTION OF THE MOST/ USEFUL RULES,/ VIZ./ . . . / TO WHICH IS ADDED, A SHORT TREATISE/ ON MENSURATION OF/ PLANES AND SOLIDS;/ WITH A SUFFICIENT NUMBER OF PRACTICAL/ QUESTIONS AT THE END OF EACH RULE./ *Designed for the Use of Schools.*/ <rule>/ <author statement>/ <rule>/ PUBLISHED ACCORDING TO ACT OF CONGRESS./ <double rule>

imprint: <below double rule> *EXETER:*/ PRINTED AND SOLD BY HENRY RANLET./ 1793.

note: A note on the title page states: "Filed 17th April 1793—Copy given." Evans 25806 identifies the claimant. See the note for entry 567.

574.

Title Page Deposit

date of deposit: <May 14>

claimant: <A: Jonathan Rawson>

author: JONATHAN RAWSON, ESQ./ LATE AID DE CAMP TO GENERAL SULLIVAN.

title: A/ COMPENDIUM/ OF/ MILITARY DUTY,/ ADAPTED FOR THE/ MILITIA OF THE UNITED STATES;/ IN THREE PARTS./ *CONTAINING:*/ . . . / <short thick rule>/ <author statement>/ <rule>/ THE FIRST EDITION./ <rule>/ <quotation in English>/ <double rule>

imprint: <below double rule> PRINTED AT DOVER, (N.H.)/ BY ELIPHALET LADD, FOR THE SUBSCRIBERS./ AND TO BE SOLD IN BOSTON BY DAVID WEST AND/ EBENEZER LARKIN, JR. ALSO, BY THE PRINTER,/ AT HIS OFFICE, NEAR THE COURT-HOUSE./ M,DCC,XCIII.

note: A note on the title page states: "John Rawson's Esqr. Compendium of Military exploits/ Compendium of Military Duty— 1792——/ 1793/ 1793/ united states." Evans 26054 identifies the claimant and gives the date of deposit. See the note for entry 567.

575.
Title Page Deposit
date of deposit: May 27
claimant: <A: Jonathan Rawson>
author: JONATHAN RAWSON, ESQ.
title: THE/ INSTRUCTOR GENERALIS,/ OR/ General Instructor:/ FOR ALL/ TOWN, PARISH AND COUNTY/ OFFICERS./ CONTAINING/ THE DUTY OF EACH, WITH THE/ LAWS OF THE STATE,/ AS IT APPLIES TO THEIR SEVERAL/ OFFICES./ <short thick rule>/ <author statement>/ <thick rule>/ <quotation in English>/ <double rule>
imprint: <below double rule> DOVER:/ PRINTED BY *ELIPHALET LADD,/* M,DCC,XCIII.
note: Evans 26055 identifies the claimant. See the note for entry 567.

576.
Title Page Deposit
date of deposit: May 28
claimant: P: George Hough
author: JOHN COSENS OGDEN, REC-/ TOR of *St. John's* Church, *Portsmouth,/ New Hampshire.*
title: THE/ FEMALE GUIDE:/ OR,/ THOUGHTS/ ON THE/ EDUCATION OF THAT SEX./ ACCOMMODATED/ TO/ The State of Society, Manners,/ and Government, in the/ UNITED STATES./ <thick rule>/ <author statement>/ <double rule>/ *Published according to Act of Congress./* <double rule>
imprint: <below double rule> PRINTED AT *CON CORD,/* BY GEORGE HOUGH, AND SOLD/ AT HIS OFFICE, WHOLESALE/ AND RETAIL./ <short double rule>/ M.DCC.XCIII.
note: With the title page, a separate note written by George Hough on May 23, 1793, to Mr. Silsby states that George Hough is the proprietor of the deposit "by virtue of a written conveyance from the Author."

1794

577.
Title Page Deposit
date of deposit: April 14, eighteenth year of Independence
claimant: <A: Samuel Langdon>
author: SAMUEL LANGDON, D. D.
title: REMARKS/ ON THE/ LEADING SENTI MENTS/ IN THE/ *Rev'd Dr. HOPKINS'/* SYSTEM OF DOCTRINES./ IN A/ LETTER TO A FRIEND,/ FROM/ <author statement>/ *Published according to Act of Congress for the Author./* <ornament and initials HR>
imprint: <below ornament> <first and third words in black letter> Printed AT Exeter,/ BY HENRY RANLET, FOR, AND SOLD BY THE AUTHOR;/ SOLD ALSO BY MOST OF THE BOOKSELLERS IN/ NEWENGLAND, AND BY THE PRINTER HEREOF./ APRIL—1794.
note: Evans 27195 identifies the claimant. See the note for entry 567.

1795

578.
Title Page Deposit
date of deposit: January 19, nineteenth year of Independence
author: Pelatiah Chapin, A. M.
title: <the title page is in ms.> Evangelic Poetry: For the Purposes/ of Devotion, excited by Spiritual Songs:/ And Conviction urged by Gospel Truth./ <author statement>

579.
Title Page Deposit
date of deposit: September 28
claimant: P: Charles Peirce
author: BENJAMIN FRY,/ Who had his education in Astronomy under the tuition of/ Dr. Nathaniel Low, of Berwick.
title: A FRIEND's/ ASTRONOMICAL DIARY:/ OR/ ALMANAC,/ FOR THE YEAR OF CHRISTIAN AERA,/ 1796:/ Being BISSEX TILE or LEAP-YEAR,/ And the Twentieth of the AMERICAN INDEPENDENCE,/ which began the 4th, of the 7th, Month, 1776./ CONTAINING,/ . . . / <rule>/ <author statement>/ <rule>/ <four lines of poetry in English>/ <double rule>
imprint: <below double rule> *PORTSMOUTH, N. H./* PRINTED BY CHARLES PEIRCE, IN COURT-STREET,/ WHERE ALMANACS OF MOST ALL KINDS MAY BE/ HAD BY THE GROCE, DOZEN, OR SINGLE.
note: A preface and part of a poem entitled "Of the Celestial Bodies" are printed on the verso of the title page.

1796

580.

Title Page Deposit

date of deposit: March 2, twentieth year of Independence

claimant: P: Charles Peirce

title: TABLES,/ *SHEWING IN THREE DIF FERENT VIEWS,*/ THE COMPARATIVE VALUE OF/ *THE CURRENCY,*/ OF THE/ States of New-Hampshire, Massachusetts,/ Rhode-Island, Connecticut, Virginia,/ Vermont and Kentucky,/ WITH/ *DOLLARS, CENTS AND MILLS, AND/ STERLING MONEY ;*/ ALSO, OF/ FRENCH CROWNS,/ . . . / <double rule>

imprint: <below double rule> PORTSMOUTH, N. H./ *Printed by CHARLES PEIRCE, Proprietor of the Work.*/ 1796.

note: An index is printed on the verso of the title page.

581.

Title Page Deposit

date of deposit: June 20

claimant: <A: John Young>

author: JOHN YOUNG, Esq./ <black letter> of New=Hampshire, in North=America.

title: A/ *FREE* AND *NATURAL*/ INQUIRY/ INTO THE PROPRIETY OF THE/ CHRISTIAN FAITH./ <author statement>/ VOLUME I./ <short decorative rule>

note: Evans 31679 identifies the claimant. See the note for entry 567.

582.

Title Page Deposit

date of deposit: August 11, twenty-first year of Independence

claimant: P: David Carlisle Jun.

title: THE/ LAY PREACHER;/ OR/ *SHORT SERMONS,*/ FOR/ IDLE READERS./ <double rule>/ <biblical quotation>/ <double rule>/ <rule>/ *Published according to* ACT *of* CONGRESS./ <rule>/ <double rule>

imprint: <below double rule> PRINTED AT *WALPOLE,* NEWHAMPSHIRE,/ BY DAVID CARLISLE, JUN./ And Sold at his BOOK STORE./ <short double rule>/ 1796.

583.

Title Page Deposit

date of deposit: September 16, twenty-first year of Independence

claimant: P: George Kimball

author: <Susannah (Willard) Johnson Hastings>

title: A/ NARRATIVE/ OF THE/ CAPTIVITY/ OF/ MRS. *JOHNSON.*/ CONTAINING/ An ACCOUNT of her SUFFERINGS,/ during *Four Years* with the INDIANS/ and FRENCH./ <rule>/ *Published according to* ACT *of* CONGRESS./ <rule>/ <double rule>

imprint: <below double rule> PRINTED AT *WALPOLE,* NEWHAMPSHIRE,/ BY DAVID CARLISLE, jun./ <short rule>/ 1796.

note: According to the *National Union Catalog* the author is Susannah (Willard) Johnson Hastings.

584.

Title Page Deposit

date of deposit: October 20

claimant: <A: John Young>

author: JOHN YOUNG, ESQ./ *Of* NEWHAMPSHIRE, *in*/ New-England.

title: THE/ POOR MAN'S/ *COMPANION;*/ OR/ *Miscellaneous Observations,*/ CONCERNING PENAL AND SAN-/ GUINARY LAWS, THE MODE/ AND NATURE OF EVIDENCE,/ AND, AN INQUIRY INTO/ THE PROPRIETY AND/ POLICY OF PUNISH-/ MENT./ <short thick rule>/ <author statement>/ <short thick rule>/ <double rule>

imprint: <below double rule> *NEWBURY, (Vermont,)*/ PRINTED BY NATHANIEL COVERLY,/ AND SOLD AT HIS BOOK STORE,/ NEAR THE COURT-HOUSE.

note: Evans 31680 identifies the claimant. See the note for entry 567.

1797

585.

Title Page Deposit

date of deposit: January 24

author: <all except title in black letter> Noah Worcester, A. M./ Minister of the Gospel in Thornton,/ New-Hampshire.

title: THE/ Natural Teacher:/ OR, THE/ <black letter> Best Spelling Book/ FOR/ *LITTLE CHILDREN.*/ <short thick rule>/ <author statement>/ <double rule>/ *Published according to Act of Congress.*/ <double rule>

imprint: <below double rule> PRINTED AT *CONCORD,* AT THE/ <all except first two words in black letter> PRESS OF Geo. Hough,/ *FOR THE AUTHOR.*/ <short thick rule>/ M.DCCXCVI.

586.
Title Page Deposit
date of deposit: June 12, twenty-first year of Independence
author: *JAMES NOYES.*
title: THE/ FEDERAL ARITHMETIC;/ OR,/ A COMPENDIUM/ OF THE/ *Most Useful Rules of that Science,*/ ADAPTED TO THE CURRENCY/ OF THE/ UNITED STATES./ <the second letter of the third word has been crossed out in ms.> *For the U*<u>se of Schools and private Persons./ <short decorative rule>/ <black letter> Published agreeably to Act of Congress./ <short decorative rule>/ <rule>/ <author statement>/ <rule>
imprint: <below rule> PRINTED AT EXETER,/ *BY HENRY RANLET, FOR THE AUTHOR.*/ M,DCC,XCVII.

587.
Title Page Deposit
date of deposit: July 18
claimant: <David Carlisle, Jun.>
author: <Royall Tyler>
title: THE/ ALGERINE CAPTIVE;/ OR, THE/ LIFE AND ADVENTURES/ OF/ DOCTOR *UPDIKE UNDERHILL:*/ SIX YEARS A PRIS ONER AMONG THE ALGE-/ RINES./ <double rule>/ <quotation in English>/ <double rule>/ <short thick rule>/ VOLUME I./ <short thick rule>/ <rule>/ *Published according to* ACT *of* CONGRESS./ <rule>/ <double rule>
imprint: <below double rule> PRINTED AT *WALPOLE,* NEWHAMPSHIRE,/ BY DAVID CARLISLE, JUN./ AND SOLD AT HIS BOOK STORE./ <short double rule>/ 1797.
note: Evans 32945 identifies the claimant. See the note for entry 567. According to the *National Index of American Imprints,* Royall Tyler is the author.

588.
Title Page Deposit
date of deposit: December 9
author: STEPHEN BURROUGHS.
title: MEMOIRS/ OF/ <author statement>/ <thick rule>/ <two lines of poetry in English>/ <short decorative rule>
imprint: <below short decorative rule> PRINTED AT *HANOVER,* NEW-HAMPSHIRE,/ BY BENJAMIN TRUE./ <short double rule>/ MDCCXCVII.

1798

589.
Title Page Deposit
date of deposit: January 2, twenty-second year of Independence
author: A GENTLEMAN OF PORTSMOUTH, N. H. <Jonathan Mitchell Sewall>
title: A/ VERSIFICATION/ OF/ PRESIDENT WASHINGTON's/ EXCELLENT/ FAREWELL-ADDRESS,/ TO THE/ CITIZENS OF THE/ <black letter> United States./ <short thick rule>/ <author statement>/ <short thick rule>/ *PUBLISHED ACCORDING TO ACT OF CONGRESS.*/ <decorative rule>
imprint: <below decorative rule> *PORTSMOUTH, NEW-HAMPSHIRE:*/ Printed and Sold by CHARLES PEIRCE, at the/ Columbian Book store, No. 5, Daniel-Street./ 1798.
note: According to the *National Union Catalog* the author is Jonathan Mitchell Sewall.

590.
Title Page Deposit
date of deposit: May 3
author: Selected by S. Larkin <Samuel Larkin>
title: THE/ COLUMBIAN SONGSTER/ AND/ FREEMASON'*s*/ POCKET COMPANION./ A COLLECTION/ OF THE/ Newest and most celebrated/ . . . / SONGS,/ Being the largest and best collection/ ever published in America./ <decorative rule>/ <author statement>/ <decorative rule>/ <design of flourishes>/ <double rule>
imprint: <below double rule> *PORTSMOUTH:* NEW-HAMPSHIRE,/ PRINTED BY *J. MELCHER,* FOR *S. LARKIN,*/ AT THE PORTSMOUTH BOOK-STORE/ 1798.
note: According to the *National Index of American Imprints* the author is Samuel Larkin.

1799

591.
Title Page Deposit
date of deposit: October 8
author: EZEKIEL LITTLE, A. M.
date of deposit: October 8
title: THE/ USHER./ <black letter> Comprising/ ARITHMETIC IN WHOLE NUMBERS;/ . . . / SURVEYING;/ THE SURVEYOR's POCKET COMPANION, OR/ TRIGONOME TRY MADE EASY, A TABLE OF SINES;/ A TABLE OF TANGENTS; MISCELLANY; TABLES/ OF THE WEIGHT AND VALUE OF

GOLD COINS./ CALCULATED AND DESIGNED FOR YOUTH./ <decorative rule>/ <author statement>/ <decorative rule>/ <black letter> Published agreeably to Act of Congress./ <rule>/ <two lines of poetry in English>/ <double rule>
imprint: <below double rule> <black letter> Exeter:/ Printed by H. RANLET, and Sold at his *Book-Store;* Sold/ also, by the Booksellers in *Boston, Newburyport, Portsmouth,*/ and other places. 1799.

1800

592.
Title Page Deposit
date of deposit: March 11
author: GEORGE RICHARDS,/ Ministering to, the first Universal Society, Portsmouth, New-Hampshire.
title: THE ACCEPTED/ OF/ THE MULTITUDE OF HIS BRETHREN:/ <short thick rule>/ AN/ HISTORICAL DISCOURSE,/ IN TWO PARTS;/ GRATEFULLY COMMEMORAT ING,/ THE/ UNPARALLELED SERVICES,/ AND/ PRE-EMINENT VIRTUES,/ OF/ General George Washington./ <short decorative rule>/ <author statement>/ <short decorative rule>/ <biblical quotation>/ <double rule>
imprint: <below double rule> *PRINTED AND PUBLISHED, AS THE ACT OF CONGRESS DIRECTS,*/ BY CHARLES PEIRCE, AT THE UNITED STATES'/ ORACLE-OFFICE; MARCH, M,DCCC.

593.
Title Page Deposit
date of deposit: June 17
author: A LADY OF MASSACHUSETTS. <Sally Sayward (Barrell) Keating Wood>
title: <black letter> Julia,/ AND THE/ ILLUMI NATED BARON,/ A NOVEL:/ FOUNDED ON RECENT FACTS,/ WHICH/ HAVE TRANSPIRED IN THE COURSE/ OF/ The late Revolution of Moral Principles/ IN/ FRANCE./ <short thick rule>/ <author statement>/ <short thick rule>/ <a note written by hand indicates that the following should be omitted> <six lines of poetry in English>/ <double rule>
imprint: <below double rule> PORTSMOUTH, NEW-HAMPSHIRE,/ PRINTED AT THE UNITED STATES' ORACLE PRESS,/ BY CHARLES PEIRCE, *(Proprietor of the work.)*/ JULY, 1800.
note: A note on the title page states "Copy made out." According to the *National Index of American Imprints* the author is Sally Sayward (Barrell) Keating Wood.

594.
Title Page Deposit
date of deposit: June 17
author: Charles Dennis Rusoe D'Eres,/ A NATIVE OF CANADA;
title: MEMOIRS/ OF/ <author statement>/ . . . / TO WHICH IS ADDED/ AN APPENDIX,/ CONTAINING/ . . . / <rule>/ <black letter> Copy Right Secured./ <double rule>
imprint: <below double rule> PRINTED FOR, AND SOLD BY HENRY RANLET, EXETER./ <short double rule>/ 1800.

595.
Title Page Deposit
date of deposit: June 17
claimant: P: Henry Ranlet
title: <the entire title enclosed by decorative borders> THE/ VILLAGE HARMONY:/ OR,/ <black letter> Youth's Assistant to Sacred Musick./ *CONTAINING,*/ . . . / <decorative rule>/ *DESIGNED PRINCIPALLY FOR THE USE OF SCHOOLS AND SINGING SOCIETIES.*/ <decorative rule>/ <the rest of the title page, including the imprint, has been crossed out in manuscript> <four lines of poetry in English>/ <decorative rule>/ *FOURTH* EDITION, CORRECTED AND IMPROVED./ <decorative rule>
imprint: <below decorative rule> <second word in black letter> PRINTED, Typographically, AT *EXETER,* NEW-HAMPSHIRE,/ *BY* HENRY RANLET, *AND SOLD AT HIS* BOOK-STORE, *BY THE DOZEN OR SINGLE, AND BY MOST OF THE* BOOK-SELLERS *IN*/ TOWN *AND* COUNTRY.—1798. *Price* 10 *dolls per doz.* 1 *doll single.*
note: An advertisement is printed on the verso of the title page.

596.
Title Page Deposit.
date of deposit: September 1
claimant: P: Alexander Thomas
title: THE/ SPIRIT/ OF THE/ FARMERS' MUSEUM,/ AND/ LAY PREACHER's GAZETTE./ Being a judicious selection of the fugitive and valuable produc-/ tions, which have occasionally appeared in that paper, since/ the commencement of its establishment./ Consisting of Amer-/ ican biography, the choicest efforts of the American muse,/ pieces of chaste humour, the easy essays of the Hermit, the/ most valuable part of the weekly summaries, nuts, epigrams,/ and epitaphs, sonnets, criticism, &c.&c.

Rhode Island

1790

597.

District Court Ledger, RI

date of deposit: August 9, fifteenth year of Independence

claimant: A: Enos Hitchcock

author: . . . , D. D.

title: Memoirs of the Bloomsgrove family, in a Series of letters to a respectable citizen of Philadelphia, containing sentiments on a mode of domestic education suited to the present state of society, government and manners, in the United States of America; and on the dignity and importance of the female character—interspersed with a variety of interesting anecdotes, <author statement>

note: The title pages and court ledger for Rhode Island for 1790 to 1800 were never transferred to the Library of Congress. The extant title pages for this period are located in Record Group 21 at the National Archives and Records Administration, Federal Archives and Records Center, Waltham, Massachusetts. The ledger cannot be found, but a transcription made by Howard Wills Preston, "List of Rhode Island Books Entered for Copyright, 1790–1800" was published in the *Rhode Island Historical Society Collections,* 13 (April 1920), 69–72, and 13 (July 1920), 95–101. Preston worked for Preston & Rounds, Booksellers and Stationers, Providence, Rhode Island.

The information in the Rhode Island entries in this work is taken from the title pages in Waltham and the published ledger. Punctuation, spelling, and capitalization from Mr. Preston's transcription have not been changed, but information has been rearranged in the entries to conform to the format used here. For the date given in entry 597, see Preston, p. 69.

(597a)

Title Page Deposit

author: ENOS HITCHCOCK, D. D.

title: MEMOIRS/ OF THE/ BLOOMSGROVE FAMILY./ In a Series of LETTERS to a respectable CITIZEN/ of PHILADELPHIA./ Containing SENTIMENTS on a/ MODE of DOMESTIC EDUCATION,/ Suited to the present State of SOCIETY, GOVERNMENT,/ and MANNERS, in the/ UNITED STATES of AMERICA:/ AND ON/ The DIGNITY and IMPORTANCE of the/ FEMALE CHARAC TER./ INTERSPERSED/ With a Variety of interesting ANECDOTES./ <rule>/ <author statement>/ <double rule>/ <short decorative rule>/ Vol. I./ <short decorative rule>/ <double rule>

imprint: <below double rule> <first and third words in black letter> Printed at Boston,/ BY THOMAS AND ANDREWS,/ At *FAUST's* STATUE, No. 45, NEWBURY STREET./ <short double rule>/ MDCCXC.

note: Except for the volume numbers, the title pages represented by entry numbers 597a and 597b are identical.

(597b)

Title Page Deposit

author: ENOS HITCHCOCK, D. D.

title: MEMOIRS/ OF THE/ BLOOMSGROVE FAMILY./ . . . / <author statement>/ <double rule>/ <short decorative rule>/ VOL. II./ <short decorative rule>/ <double rule>

imprint: <below double rule> <first and third words in black letter> Printed at Boston,/ BY THOMAS AND ANDREWS,/ At *FAUST's* STATUE, No. 45, NEWBURY STREET./ <short double rule>/ MDCCXC.

note: See the notes for entry numbers 597 and 597a.

598.

District Court Ledger, RI

date of deposit: August 26, fifteenth year of Independence

claimant: P: Peter Edes

author: Samuel Buckner.

title: The American Sailor, a treatise on practical seamanship, with hints and remarks relating thereto, designed to contribute towards making navigation in general more perfect, and of consequence, less destructive to health, lives and property, <author statement>

note: See the note for entry number 597 and Preston, p. 69.

Title Page Deposit

author: SAMUEL BUCKNER.

title: THE/ AMERICAN SAILOR:/ A/ TREATISE/ ON/ PRACTICAL SEAMANSHIP,/ WITH/ HINTS AND REMARKS/ RELATING THERETO./ DESIGNED TO CONTRIBUTE TOWARDS MAKING NAVIGATION/ IN GENERAL MORE PERFECT, AND OF CONSEQUENCE, LESS/ DESTRUCTIVE TO HEALTH, LIVES AND PROPERTY./ <short thick rule>/ <author statement>

imprint: NEWPORT (RHODE-ISLAND) PRINTED BY PETER EDES,/ PROPRIETOR OF THE COPY RIGHT.

note: See the note for entry number 597.

1791

599.

District Court Ledger, RI

date of deposit: April 14, fifteenth year of Independence
claimant: P: Robert Adam
author: Alexander M. Donald.
title: The Youth's Assistant; being a plain, easy, comprehensive guide to practical arithmetic, containing all the rules and examples necessary for such a work, viz., numeration, simple addition, subtraction, multiplication and division—division of weights and measures—Reduction of several denominations —The single and double rules of Three—Tare and Trett—practice—simple interest—Assuance—Brokage Commission, discount—Equation of payments—Loss and Gain—single and double fellowship—Reduction, addition—Subtraction, multiplication, and division of vulgar fractions, notation—addition, subtraction, multiplication, division, and reduction of Decimal fractions the Rule of Three, simple and compound Interest in decimal fractions—<author statement>
note: See the note for entry number 597 and Preston, p. 70.

Title Page Deposit

author: ALEXANDER M'DONALD.
title: THE/ YOUTH'S ASSISTANT:/ *Being a plain, easy, and comprehensive/* GUIDE *to* PRACTICAL/ *ARITHMETIC.*/ CONTAINING,/ All the Rules and Examples necessary for/ such a Work, viz./ . . . / The *second* Edition./ <thick rule>/ <author statement>/ <thick rule>
imprint: <below thick rule> LITCHFIELD: *Printed by* T. COLLIER./ M,DCC,LXXXIX.
note: (*With the Priviledge of Copy-Right.*)
See the note for entry number 597.

1792

600.

District Court Ledger, RI

date of deposit: July 22, seventeenth year of Independence
claimant: A: Enos Hitchcock
author: . . . , D. D. Author of Memoirs of the Bloomsgrove Family.
title: The Farmer's Friend or the history of Mr. Charles Worthy, who, from being a poor orphan rose, through various scenes of distress and misfortune to wealth and eminence, by industry, Economy and good conduct, interspersed with many useful and entertaining Narratives, suited to please the fancy, improve the understanding, and mend the heart—<author statement>
note: See the note for entry number 597 and Preston, p. 70.

Title Page Deposit

author: ENOS HITCHCOCK, D. D./ Author of "MEMOIRS OF THE BLOOMSGROVE FAMILY."
title: THE/ FARMER's FRIEND,/ OR THE HISTORY OF/ MR. *CHARLES WORTHY.*/ Who, from being a poor ORPHAN, rose, through va-/ rious Scenes of Distress and Misfor tune, to Wealth/ and Eminence, by INDUSTRY, ECONOMY and GOOD/ CONDUCT./ INTER SPERSED WITH MANY/ USEFUL AND ENTERTAINING NARRA-/ TIVES,/ Suited to please the FANCY, improve the UNDERSTAND ING,/ and mend the HEART./ <double rule>/ <author statement>/ <double rule>/ <ornament of flowers and vines encircles following words> <black letter> Published According to Act of Congress./ <double rule>
imprint: <below double rule> PRINTED AT *BOSTON,*/ BY I. THOMAS AND E. T. ANDREWS,/ FAUST's STATUE, No. 45, Newbury Street./ <short double rule>/ MDCCXCIII.
note: See the note for entry number 597.

1793

601.

District Court Ledger, RI

date of deposit: December 23, eighteenth year of Independence
claimant: P: John Gardner Ladd
author: <Dr. Joseph Brown Ladd>
title: The Poems of Arovet,
note: See the note for entry number 597 and Preston, p. 70. The court ledger entry records two items deposited for copyright, represented here by numbers 601 and 602. According to the *National Index of American Imprints* the author of this work is Joseph Brown Ladd and the title is *The Poems of Arouet.*

602.

District Court Ledger, RI

date of deposit: December 23, eighteenth year of Independence
claimant: P: John Gardner Ladd

author: Dr. Joseph B. Ladd.
title: An Essay on Primitive, latent, and Regenerated Light, <author statement>
note: See the notes for entry numbers 597 and 601 and Preston, p. 70.

1795

603.

District Court Ledger, RI
date of deposit: May 9, nineteenth year of Independence
claimant: A: William Patten
author: . . . , A:M., minister of the second congregational church in Newport.
title: Christianity, the true Theology and only perfect moral system, in answer to the Age of Reason, with an appendix in answer to the Examiners, examined,—<author statement>
note: See the note for entry number 597 and Preston, p. 71.

Title Page Deposit
author: *WILLIAM PATTEN,* A. M./ MINISTER OF THE SECOND CONGREGATIONAL CHURCH/ IN NEWPORT.
title: CHRISTIANITY/ THE TRUE/ THEOLOGY,/ AND/ ONLY PERFECT MORAL SYSTEM/ IN ANSWER TO/ "THE AGE OF REASON:"/ WITH AN/ APPEN DIX,/ IN ANSWER TO/ "THE EXAMINERS EXAMINED."/ <short thick rule>/ <author statement>/ <double rule>
imprint: <below double rule> WARREN (RHODE-ISLAND):/ PRINTED BY NATHANIEL PHILLIPS,/ M,DCC,XCV.
note: See the note for entry number 597.

604.

District Court Ledger, RI
date of deposit: June 24, nineteenth year of Independence
claimant: A: James Ellis
author: . . . , A:M: Attorney at Law.
title: A Narrative of the Rise, progress and Issue of the late law suits, relative to property held and devoted to pious Uses, in the first precinct in Rehoboth, containing the substance of the Records which shew, for whose use and benefit the property was originally intended, together with some observations on certain consitutional principles, which respect the support of public worship, and the equal protection and establishment of all regular denomination of Christians. <author statement>
note: See the note for entry number 597 and Preston, p. 71.

Title Page Deposit
author: JAMES ELLIS, A. M./ ATTORNEY AT LAW.
title: A NARRATIVE/ OF THE/ *RISE, PROGRESS* AND *ISSUE*/ OF THE/ LATE LAW-SUITS/ RELATIVE TO PROPERTY HELD AND DEVOTED TO PIOUS USES,/ IN THE/ FIRST PRECINCT IN *REHOBOTH:*/ CONTAINING/ <. . .>/ <short thick rule>/ <author statement>/ <thick rule>
note: See the note for entry number 597. There is no imprint on the title page.

605.

District Court Ledger, RI
date of deposit: October 10, twentieth year of Independence
claimant: P: John Carter and William Wilkinson, printers and booksellers of Rhode Island
author: William Wilkinson, A:M.
title: The federal calculation and American ready Reckoner; containing federal Arithmetic—The value of any number of yards, pounds, and from 1 to 100, and from 1 mill to 1 dollar, tables of interest, value of Cents in the Currencies of the different States—value of gold, as now established by Law in the United States—<author statement>
note: See the note for entry number 597 and Preston, p. 71. According to the *National Index of American Imprints,* the work is entitled *The Federal Calculator.*

Title Page Deposit
author: WILLIAM WILKINSON, A. M.
title: THE/ <black letter> Federal Calculator,/ AND/ AMERICAN READY RECKONER./ CONTAINING,/ Federal Arithmetic,/ The Value of any Number of Yards, Pounds,/ &c. from 1 to 1000, and from 1 Mill to/ 1 Dollar,/ Tables of Interest,/ Value of Cents in the Currencies of the/ different States,/ Value of Gold, as now established by Law/ in the United States, &c./ <thick rule>/ <author statement>/ <thick rule>/ <ornament>/ <double rule>
imprint: <below double rule> PRINTED AT PROVIDENCE *(R. I.)/ By* CARTER *and* WILKINSON, *and sold at their/ Book and Stationary Store, opposite the Market./* 1795.
note: See the note for entry number 597.

1797

606.

District Court Ledger, RI

date of deposit: February 16, twenty-first year of Independence

claimant: P: John Carter and William Wilkinson, printers and booksellers of Rhode Island

author: Caleb Alexander, A:M: author of "the works of Virgil translated into literal English prose," "A Grammatical Institute of the latin language," "A Grammatical System of the English Language," and "A Grammatical System of the Grecian language."

title: The young ladies and gentlemen's Spelling book; containing a Criterion of rightly spelling and pronouncing the English Language; interspersed with many easy lessons in reading, entertaining fables and Collections of moral sentences; intended for the use of Common Schools, <author statement>

note: See the note for entry number 597 and Preston, p. 71.

Title Page Deposit

author: CALEB ALEXANDER, A. M./ Author of "*The Works of* VIRGIL *translated into literal/ English Prose,*" "*A grammatical Institute of the Latin/* <second word has been crossed out in ms.> *Language,*" <and> "*A grammatical System of the English/* <the comma and title following the first word have been inserted in ms.> *Language,* and "A grammatical System of the Grecian Language."

title: THE/ YOUNG LADIES AND GENTELEMEN's/ SPELLING BOOK:/ CON TAINING/ A CRITERION/ OF RIGHTLY SPELLING AND PRONOUNCING/ <black letter> The English Language;/ INTER SPERSED/ WITH MANY EASY LESSONS IN/ READING, ENTERTAINING FABLES,/ AND COLLECTIONS OF MORAL/ SENTENCES; INTENDED FOR THE/ USE OF COMMON SCHOOLS./ <decorative rule>/ <author statement>/ <decorative rule>

imprint: <below decorative rule> PRINTED AT PROVIDENCE *(Rhode-Island)/* BY CARTER AND WILKINSON,/ And sold, Wholesale and Retail, at their Book Store, opposite the Market/ House.—Sold also by the Author, at *Mendon (Massachusetts)* and by the/ principal Booksellers in the United States./ 1797.

note: See the note for number 597. A note on the verso of the title page states: "Copyright to be in the name of John Carter & Wm. Wilkinson Printers & Booksellers."

607.

District Court Ledger, RI

date of deposit: April 28, twenty-first year of Independence

claimant: P: Samuel Hopkins

compiler: Samuel Hopkins, D. D., pastor of the first Congregational Church in Newport.

title: The life and character of Miss Susanna Anthony, who died in Newport, R. I., June MDCCXCI, in the Sixty-fifth year of her age, consisting chiefly in Extracts from her writings, with some brief observations on them, <compiler statement>

note: See the note for entry number 597 and Preston, p. 72.

Title Page Deposit

compiler: SAMUEL HOPKINS, D. D./ PASTOR OF THE FIRST CONGREGATIONAL CHURCH IN *NEWPORT.*

title: THE/ LIFE AND CHARACTER/ OF/ MISS SUSANNA ANTHONY,/ WHO DIED, IN *NEWPORT,* (R. I.) JUNE 23, MDCCXCI,/ IN THE SIXTY FIFTH YEAR OF HER AGE./ CONSISTING CHIEFLY IN/ EXTRACTS FROM HER WRITINGS,/ WITH SOME BRIEF OBSERVATIONS ON THEM./ <the following line has been crossed out in ms.> <DESIGNED WHOLLY FOR THE BENEFIT OF THE *LIVING.*>/ <short decorative rule>/ <compiler statement>/ <short decorative rule>/ <A line crossed out in ms. is illegible.>/ <double rule>

imprint: <below double rule> PRINTED AT *WORCESTER,* MASSACHUSETTS,/ BY LEONARD WORCESTER./ <short double rule>/ MDCCXCVI.

note: See the note for entry number 597.

608.

District Court Ledger, RI

date of deposit: May 10, twenty-first year of Independence

claimant: P: Nathaniel Phillips

author: Laban Thurber, minister of the Gospel in Attleborough.

title: The Young ladies and Gentlemen's Preceptor, or Eighteen moral Rules, <author statement>

note: See the note for entry number 597 and Preston, p. 72.

Title Page Deposit

author: LABAN THURBER,/ MINISTER OF THE GOSPEL IN ATTLEBOROUGH.

title: THE/ <the second and fifth words have been crossed out in ms.; the third and sixth words been inserted to replace them> *YOUNG* <*GENTLEMAN*> Ladies AND <*LADY'S*> Gentlemens'/ <the colon after the following word has been crossed out in ms.; a semicolon has been inserted> PRECEPTOR<:>;/ <the second word has been crossed out in ms.> OR <THE>/ EIGHTEEN MORAL RULES./ <double rule>/ <author statement>/ <double rule>/ <decorative rule>

imprint: <below decorative rule> *WARREN:*/ <the second and third words have been inserted in ms.; the seventh and eighth words have been crossed out> PRINTED and sold BY NATHANIEL PHILLIPS, <FOR THE>/ <the following word has been crossed out in ms.> <AUTHOR>/ <short rule>/ M,DCC,XCVII.

note: See the note for entry number 597.

609.

District Court Ledger, RI

date of deposit: November 18, twenty-second year of Independence

claimant: A: James Wilson

title: "Apostolic" Church Government, examined and the government "of the Methodist Episcopal Church investigated." <biblical quotation>

note: See the note for entry number 597 and Preston, p. 72.

1798

610.

District Court Ledger, RI

date of deposit: June 15, twenty-second year of Independence

claimant: A: James Wilson

author: . . . , Pastor of the Beneficent Congregational Church in Providence.

title: Apostolic Church Government displayed, and the government and system of the Methodist Episcopal Church investigated, to which is added, an "Appendix, containing a Concise dissertation on the nature and duration of the Apostolic Personal Authority and Office <author statement>" <biblical quotation>

note: See the note for entry number 597 and Preston, p. 72.

Title Page Deposit

author: *JAMES WILSON,*/ PASTOR *of the* BENEFICENT CONGREGATION-/ AL CHURCH *in* PROVIDENCE.

title: APOSTOLIC CHURCH/ GOVERNMENT/ *DISPLAYED;*/ AND THE/ GOVERNMENT AND SYSTEM/ OF THE/ METHODIST EPIS COPAL CHURCH/ *INVESTIGATED.*/ <short thick rule>/ TO WHICH IS ADDED,/ AN APPENDIX,/ CONTAINING/ . . . / <short double rule>/ <author statement>/ <short double rule>/ <biblical quotation>/ <double rule>

imprint: <below double rule> PRINTED *at* PROVIDENCE:/ BY BENNETT WHEELER, AND SOLD AT HIS/ BOOK STORE, NO. 1, WESTMINSTER-/ STREET, 1798.

note: See the note for entry number 597.

1799

611.

District Court Ledger, RI

date of deposit: January 25, twenty-third year of Independence

claimant: P: Samuel Hopkins

author: Samuel Hopkins D. D. pastor of the first Congregational Church in Newport.

title: Memoirs of the life of Mrs. Sarah Osborn, who died at Newport Rhode Island, on the second day of August, 1796, in the eighty-third year of her age, <author statement>

note: See the note for entry number 597 and Preston, p. 95.

Title Page Deposit

author: SAMUEL HOPKINS, D. D./ PASTOR OF THE FIRST CONGREGATIONAL CHURCH IN NEWPORT.

title: *MEMOIRS*/ OF THE/ LIFE/ OF/ MRS. SARAH OSBORN,/ WHO DIED AT/ NEW PORT, RHODEISLAND,/ ON THE SECOND DAY OF AUGUST, 1796./ *IN THE EIGHTY THIRD YEAR OF HER AGE.*/ <decorative rule>/ <author statement>/ <decorative rule>/ <double rule>

imprint: <below double rule> PRINTED AT WORCESTER, MASSACHUSETTS,/ BY LEONARD WORCESTER./ <short double rule>/ 1799.

note: See the note for entry number 597.

Virginia

1790

612.

Title Page Deposit

title: The Life and adventures of Simon Crea McMahon, With Miscellaneous pieces, In prose and verse. Part the first. <quotation in English>

imprint: Richmond: Printed For the author. 1790.

note: There is no district court ledger extant for Virginia. The deposited copyright title pages for Virginia for 1790 to 1800 were never transferred to the Library of Congress. They were published by James Howard Whitty in *A Record of Virginia Copyright Entries (1790–1844)* issued by the Virginia State Library in 1911. Whitty composed his work sometime before 1911 from the original title pages that were in the possession of Judge Robert W. Hughes. Judge Hughes was a newspaperman and unsuccessfully ran as the Republican candidate for the Virginia governorship in 1873 before being appointed United States judge for the Eastern District of Virginia in 1874. There is no information about how he acquired the title pages.

It is clear from State Librarian H. R. McIlwaine's "Letter of Transmittal" in *A Record of Virginia Copyright Entries (1790–1844)* that the original title pages could not be found in 1910, and the editor and compiler of this volume have not been able to improve upon the results of McIlwaine's search. The personal papers of Judge Hughes' son, Robert Morton Hughes, at the College of William and Mary, do not contain the title pages. James Howard Whitty's personal papers at Duke University contain neither the title pages nor the transcripts Whitty made for the Virginia State Library publication. Therefore the entries for Virginia for 1790 to 1800 depend solely on the information provided in *A Record of Virginia Copyright Entries (1790–1844),* reorganized to fit the present volume's format but without any change in capitalization or punctuation. Mr. McIlwaine's "Letter of Transmittal" indicates that some of Whitty's transcriptions were altered to make "a few corrections of evident mistakes in copying." For the data given in entry 612, see Whitty, p. 7.

1791

613.

Title Page Deposit

author: John Asplund.

title: The Annual Register of the Baptist Denomination, in North America, To the First of Novem ber 1790. Containing An account of the churches and their constitutions, Ministers, Members, Associations, their plan and Sentiments, Rule and Order, Proceedings and Correspondence. Also remarks upon practical religion. Humbly offered To the Public. <author statement>

note: See the note for entry number 612 and Whitty, p. 7.

614.

Title Page Deposit

author: John K. Read, present deputy grand master of Virginia, and member of the sublime lodge of perfection, of Charleston, South Carolina.

title: The new Ahiman Rezon, containing the laws and constitution of the grand Lodge of Virginia. To which is added the History of Masonry, from the creation, to the death of Queen Elizabeth. Also illustrations of the royal art; and a variety of other matter relative to that institution. Carefully collated, from the most approved authors, ancient as well as modern. <author statement> <quotation in Latin>

imprint: Richmond: Printed by John Dixon. 1791.

note: See the note for entry number 612 and Whitty, p. 7.

615.

Title Page Deposit

title: A Topographical Analysis of The Commonwealth of Virginia. Compiled for 1790–1 showing the extent and relative situation of the several counties, their distances from the seat of government, population, Force, County Lieutenants, Representatives &c—also the District and County Courts; the civil list of the Commonwealth &c. carefully collected from Public Records, and other authorities. To be continued annually.

note: See the note for entry number 612 and Whitty, p. 7. Whitty has added a question mark after the date of deposit.

1792

616.

Title Page Deposit

date of deposit: March

author: John Pope.

title: A Tour through the Southern and Western territories, of the United States of North America; The Spanish Dominions on the River Mississippi, and the Floridas; The countries of the Creek

Nations; and many uninhabited Parts. <author statement> <quotation in Latin>
imprint: Published for the author and his three children, Alexander D. Pope, Lucinda C. Pope and Anne Pope.
note: See the note for entry number 612 and Whitty, p. 7.

1795

617.

Title Page Deposit
date of deposit: January 6
author: <George Wythe>
claimant: George Wythe
title: Decisions of cases in Virginia. By The High Court of Chancery, with remarks upon Decrees By the Court of Appeals, Reversing some of those decisions.
imprint: Richmond: Printed By Thomas Nicholson. 1795.
note: See the note for entry number 612 and Whitty, p. 8. According to the *National Index of American Imprints,* George Wythe is the author.

1796

618.

Title Page Deposit
date of deposit: September 23
author: Robert F. Palmer.
title: The Prodigal Reformed, By a Virginia Farmer. Contents. The Author's Birth, and Origin, his Education, and Profession, his Travels through England, Ireland, France, Algiers, and America. <author statement>
note: See the note for entry number 612 and Whitty, p. 8.

619.

Title Page Deposit
date of deposit: September 23
author: John Strother.
title: A Treatise on the Distillation of ardent Spirits from materials of the growth of the United States, <author statement>
note: See the note for entry number 612 and Whitty, p. 8.

1797

620.

Title Page Deposit
date of deposit: May 15
author: John Fowler.
title: The Truth of the Bible Fairly put To the Test, by confronting The evidences of its own facts. <author statement>
note: See the note for entry number 612 and Whitty, p. 8.

621.

Title Page Deposit
author: James Wilson, A. M., one of the members of said Presbytery.
title: The Utility of the Scriptures of the old Testament: a Discourse delivered at the opening of a session of the Presbytery of Baltimore, held in Alexandria September 27th 1797. <author statement>
note: See the note for entry number 612 and Whitty, p. 8.

1798

622.

Title Page Deposit
date of deposit: June 29
author: Bushrod Washington.
title: Reports of Cases argued and determined in the Court of appeals of Virginia. <author statement> Vol. 1.
imprint: Richmond: Printed By Thomas Nicholson. 1798.
note: See the note for entry number 612 and Whitty, p. 8.

623.

Title Page Deposit
date of deposit: October 9
author: William Munford, of the County of Mecklenburg, and State of Virginia.
title: Poems, and compositions In prose on several occasions. <author statement> <quotation in English>
imprint: Richmond: Printed By Samuel Pleasants, Jun. 1798.
note: See the note for entry number 612 and Whitty, p. 8.

1799

624.

Title Page Deposit
date of deposit: January 2
claimant: <Theodosius Hansford>
title: Debates In the House of Delegates of Virginia; upon certain resolutions Before the House, Upon

the important subject of the Acts of Congress Passed at their last session, commonly called, The Alien and Sedition Laws.
imprint: Richmond: Printed By Thos. Nicholson. 1798.
note: See the note for entry number 612 and Whitty, p. 8. According to a printed copy of the court ledger entry for this deposit which appears in a copy of the work located at the Virginia State Library (JK 176 1798), the claimant is Theodosius Hansford.

625.
date of deposit: October 1
title: A Plain and Concise Table (particularly calculated for the use of Importing Merchants) of the duties payable by law on all goods, Wares, and Merchandize, imported into the United States after the last day of June 1797.
imprint: Petersburg: Printed By Ross & Douglass. Copy Right Secured By John Potts.
note: See the note for entry number 612 and Whitty, p. 8.

South Carolina

1794

626.

District Court Ledger, SC 1

date of deposit: July 8, nineteenth year of Independence

claimant: William Price Young

author: David Ramsay, M: D: president of the Senate of South Carolina.

title: An Oration, delivered in St. Michaels, Church, before the Inhabitants of Charleston, South Carolina, on the fourth of July, 1794, in commemoration of American Independence, by the appointment of the American Revolution Society, and published at the request of that Society, and also of the South Carolina State Society of Cincinati. <author statement>

note: The South Carolina district court copyright ledger for this period is in the South Caroliniana Library at the University of South Carolina. Its contents have previously been published in a different format with abbreviated titles by William S. Kable in "South Carolina District Copyrights: 1794–1820," *Proof* 1(1971), 180–98.

1795

627.

District Court Ledger, SC 2

date of deposit: March 17, nineteenth year of Independence

claimant: Thomas Mills

author: . . . , Rector of St: Andrews

title: A Compendium of Latin Syntax on a New plan for the use of youth, <author statement> <quotation in Latin>

628.

District Court Ledger, SC 3

date of deposit: July 8, twentieth year of Independence

claimant: Timothy and Mason, printers of the said district <Timothy, Benjamin Franklin and Mason, William>

author: Thomas Tuder Tucker, M: D:

title: An Oration, delivered in St: Michaels Church, before the Inhabitants of Charleston, South Carolina, on the 4:th July, 1795, in Commemoration of American Independence; by the appoint. of the South Carolina State Society of Cincinnati, published at the request of that Society, and also of the American Revolution Society, <author statement>

note: According to Roger Pattrell Bristol's *Index of Printers, Publishers, and Booksellers Indicated by Charles Evans in his American Bibliography* the printers are Benjamin Franklin Timothy and William Mason.

629.

District Court Ledger, SC 4

date of deposit: October 26, twentieth year of Independence

claimant: Charles Lining

author: Reverend George Buist, D. D. Minister of the Presbyterian Church of Charleston

title: An Oration delivered at the Orphan=house of Charleston, South Carolina, October 18th, 1795, being the Sixth Anniversary of the Institution, <author statement>

note: The ledger entry states that the claimant has deposited the work "in Trust for the Orphan=house."

1796

630.

District Court Ledger, SC 5

date of deposit: July 7, twenty-first year of Independence

claimant: P: William Price Young, of the City of Charleston, State aforesaid, Printer and Book=Seller

author: William Smith a Member of the Revolution Society and representative in the Congress of the United States.

title: An Oration, delivered in St: Philips Church, before the Inhabitants of Charleston, So Carolina, on the fourth July, 1796, in Commemoration of American Independence, by appointment of the American Revolution Society, and published at the request of that Society and also of the South Carolina State Society of Cincinnati. <author statement>

631.

District Court Ledger, SC 6

date of deposit: September 6, twenty-first year of Independence

claimant: The honorable Judge John Faucheraud Grimke

title: The Rules and Orders of the Courts of Sessions and Common pleas, of the Court of Equity and the Federal Court, in South Carolina.

1797

632.

District Court Ledger, SC 7

date of deposit: March 20, twenty-first year of Independence

claimant: P: William Parker, druggist of the City of Charleston
title: The domestic Dispensary or complete family and plantation Chest; corresponding with Buchans domestic Medicine and particularly adapted to the diseases of the Southern States;
note: The ledger entry recording this work shows that the claimant deposited "two several books" for copyright, the right of which he claimed as proprietor "in whole and in part." The works are represented by entry numbers 632 and 633.

633.
District Court Ledger, SC 7
date of deposit: March 20, twenty-first year of Independence
claimant: P: William Parker, druggist of the City of Charleston
title: The Seaman's Dispensary; or complete Ship Medicine Chest—
note: See the note for entry 632.

634.
District Court Ledger, SC 8
date of deposit: May 6, twenty-first year of Independence
claimant: A: John Beete
author: . . . Comedian—
title: The Man of the times, or a Scarcity of Cash; a farce, as performed, with universal applause at the Church Street Theatre, Charleston, <author statement>

1798
635.
District Court Ledger, SC 9
date of deposit: January 20, twenty-second year of Independence
claimant: A: John Faucheraud Grimké
author: J. F. Grimke
title: The duty of Executors and Administrators &c—<author statement>

636.
District Court Ledger, SC 10
date of deposit: August 29, twenty-third year of Independence
claimant: A: the Honorable Eilhu Hall Bay
author: . . . / One of the Associate Judges of the said State.
title: Reports/ of/ Cases/ Argued and determined/ in/ The Superior Courts of Law in the/ State of South Carolina/ Since The Revolution/ <author statement>

1799
637.
District Court Ledger, SC 11
date of deposit: March 21, twenty-third year of Independence
claimant: A: Amos Pilsbury
title: The United States/ Sacred Harmony/ The whole containing three hundred Psalm and Hymn Tunes/ To conclude/ With an Appendix/ <author statement>

1800
638.
District Court Ledger, SC 12
date of deposit: January 22, twenty-fourth year of Independence
claimant: A: Doctor David Ramsay
author: . . . M. D.
title: An/ Oration—/ On the Death of Lieutenant General,,—/ George Washington/ Late President of the United States, Who died December/ 14.th 1799, delivered in St,, Michaels Church, January 15.th 1800/ At the Request of/ The Inhabitants of Charleston,/ South Carolina;/ And Published by their Desire—/ <author statement>

639.
District Court Ledger, SC 13
date of deposit: March 25, twenty-fourth year of Independence
claimant: A: John B. Williamson Esquire
author: . . . / Director of the Theatre in Charleston.
title: Preservation;/ or, the/ Hovel of the Rocks:/ A Play, in five Acts:/ Interspersed with part of/ Lillo's Drama,/ In three Acts, called/ Fatal Curiosity./ <author statement>
note: This item is deposited as a "Book or Play." According to the *National Union Catalog,* the author of *Fatal Curiosity* is George Lillo.

Maine

1790

640.

District Court Ledger, 35 ME 1

date of deposit: August 14, fifteenth year of Independence

claimant: A: Samuel Freeman

author: . . . , Esquire.

title: The Columbian Primer, or the School-Mistresses Guide to Children in their first steps to Learning. Part I. Containing Words of one & two Syllables. With an Appendix, containing Sundry Matters which Children may be taught to say by Heart. <author statement>

note: On a separate sheet of paper, the clerk has noted that *The Columbian Primer* was deposited for copyright on August 14, 1790.

1791

641.

District Court Ledger, 35 ME 1

date of deposit: December 6, sixteenth year of Independence

claimant: P: Rev. Elijah Kellogg

author: the Reverend Moses Hemmenway, D. D.

title: A Discourse to Children. <author statement>

Title Page Deposit

author: the Reverend Moses Hemmen-/ way. D. D.

title: A discourse to Children by/ <author statement>

note: An 8 cm x 11 cm piece of paper on which the title is printed is deposited as a title page.

1792

642.

District Court Ledger, 35 ME 2

date of deposit: April 9, sixteenth year of Independence

claimant: A: John Gardiner

title: The Speech of John Gardiner, Esquire, delivered in the House of Representatives on Thursday, the 26. of January, 1792; on the Subject of the Report of the Committee appointed to consider the Expediency of repealing the Law against Theatrical Exhibitions, within this Commonwealth.

643.

District Court Ledger, 35 ME 2

date of deposit: October 25, seventeenth year of Independence

claimant: A: Samuel Freeman

title: The Probate Auxiliary; or a Director & Assistant to Probate Courts, Executors, Administrators & Guardians. Being the Laws of the Commonwealth of Massachusetts, respecting the estates of Testators, Intestates & Wards—Carefully collected: Together with a comprehensive alphabetical Index to the same. To which are added a variety of Forms, for the use of Probate Courts, & such persons as may have business to transact therein.

Title Page Deposit

author: SAMUEL FREEMAN, Esq./ Register of Probate for the County of Cumberland.

title: THE/ PROBATE AUXILIARY;/ OR, A DIRECTOR AND ASSISTANT TO/ Probate Courts, Executors, Admi-/ nistrators and Guardians./ BEING THE LAWS OF THE COMMONWEALTH OF/ MASSACHUSETTS, RESPECTING THE ESTATES/ OF TESTA TORS, INTESTATES AND/ WARDS./ CARE FULLY COLLECTED./ TOGETHER WITH A COMPREHENSIVE ALPHA-/ BETICAL INDEX TO THE SAME./ TO WHICH ARE ADDED,/ A VARIETY OF FORMS, FOR THE USE OF PRO-/ BATE COURTS, AND OF SUCH PERSONS AS/ MAY HAVE BUSINESS TO TRANSACT THEREIN./ <decorative rule>/ <author statement>/ <decorative rule>/ [With the Privelege of Copy Right.]/ <rule>

imprint: <below rule> PORTLAND: (MASSACHUSETTS) PRINTED BY/ BEN JAMIN TITCOMB, JUN./ <short rule>/ 1792.

1796

644.

District Court Ledger, 35 ME 3

date of deposit: May 28, twentieth year of Independence

claimant: A: Abraham Cummings

author: . . . , A. B.

title: A Dissertation upon the Introduction & Glory of the Millennium. To which is prefixed a Sermon on the Two Witnesses. <author statement>

Title Page Deposit

author: ABRAHAM CUMMINGS, A. B.

title: A/ DISSERTATION/ UPON THE/ INTRODUCTION AND GLORY/ OF THE/ *MILLENIUM.*/ TO WHICH IS PREFIXED,/ A SERMON ON THE TWO WITNESSES./ <decorative rule>/ <author statement>/ <decorative rule>

note: A handwritten copy of the ledger entry for copyright is filed with the title page.

1799

645.

District Court Ledger, 35 ME 3

date of deposit: December 9, twenty-fourth year of Independence

claimant: A: Thomas M. Prentiss

author: . . . , Instructor of Union School—Portland.

title: The Maine Spelling Book; containing a variety of Words, divided & accented; with moral & entertaining Lessons for Reading; useful Tables, &c. To which is annexed a concise Geographical Description of the District of Maine. Designed for School, & particularly calculated to be read in Classes. <author statement>

Title Page Deposit

author: THOMAS M. PRENTISS,/ *INSTRUCTOR OF UNION SCHOOL—PORTLAND.*

title: THE/ *MAINE*/ SPELLING BOOK:/ CON TAING A VARIETY/ OF WORDS, DIVIDED AND ACCENTED;/ WITH/ MORAL AND ENTERTAINING LESSONS FOR/ READING; USEFUL TABLES, &c./ TO WHICH IS ANNEXED/ A CONCISE GEOGRAPHICAL DESCRIPTION/ OF THE/ DISTRICT OF MAINE/ DESIGNED FOR SCHOOL, AND PARTICULARLY CALCU-/ LATED TO BE READ IN CLASSES./ <rule>/ <author statement>/ <rule>/ <quotation in English>/ <double rule>

imprint: <below double rule>/ PRINTED AT *PORTLAND,*/ *By* ELEZER A. JENKS.—1800.

note: A handwritten copy of the ledger entry is filed with the title page.

North Carolina

1796

646.

District Court Ledger, NC 1

date of deposit: March 4, twentieth year of Independence
claimant: Jonathan Price and John Strother
author: from Actual Survey by the said Jonathan Price, and John Strother
title: a Chart of the Sea Coasts from Cape Henry to Cape Romayn, and of the Inlets Sounds and Rivers of North Carolina to the Towns of Edenton, Washington New Bern and Wilmington,
format: chart
note: The ledger entry contains two deposits. The first is a chart and the second is a map. According to the court ledger entry, "both" items are from "Actual Survey" by Jonathan Price and John Strother. The North Carolina district court ledger for this period is in Record Group 21 at the National Archives and Records Administration, Federal Archives and Records Center, Atlanta, Georgia.

647.

District Court Ledger, NC 1

date of deposit: March 4, twentieth year of Independence
claimant: Jonathan Price and John Strother
author: from Actual Survey by the said Jonathan Price, and John Strother,
title: a Map of the State of North Carolina, agreeable to its present boundaries <author statement>
format: map
note: See the note for entry 646.

648.

District Court Ledger, NC 1

date of deposit: March 4, twentieth year of Independence
claimant: James H. Green
title: Greens Annual Pocket Ledger—Requisite for the Gentleman Merchant and Planter.

1798

649.

District Court Ledger, NC 1

date of deposit: January 7, twenty-second year of Independence
claimant: Lemuel Sawyer
title: a Journey to Lake Drummond.

Vermont

1793

650.

District Court Ledger, VT 1

date of deposit: January 21, seventeenth year of Independence

claimant: A: the Honourable Nathaniel Chipman of Rutland

author: . . . / Late Chief Justice

title: Reports and Dissertations/ in two parts/ Part 1./ Reports of Cases determined in/ the Supreme Court of the/ State of Vermont, in the year/ 1789, 1790, and 1791./ Part II./ Dissertations on the Statute/ adopting the Common Law/ of England, the Statute of/ Conveyances, the Statute/ of Offsetts, and on the Nego-/ -tiability of notes;—/ with an appendix con-/ -taining forms of special/ pleadings in several cases;/ forms of recognizances; of/ Justices records; and of/ Warrants of Commitment./ <author statement>

note: The Vermont district court copyright ledger for this period is in Record Group 21 at the National Archives and Records Administration, Federal Archives and Records Center, Waltham, Massachusetts.

651.

District Court Ledger, VT 4

date of deposit: May 9, seventeenth year of Independence

claimant: A: the Honourable Nathaniel Chipman of Rutland,

author: . . . / Judge of the Court of the/ United States for the/ District of Vermont.

title: Sketches of the/ Principles of Government/ <author statement>

1794

652.

District Court Ledger, VT 6

date of deposit: August 20, nineteenth year of Independence

claimant: A: Samuel Williams

author: . . . LL. D./ Member of the meteorological/ society in Germany, of the/ Philosophical society in/ Philadelphia, and of the Acad-/ -emy of Arts and sciences in/ Massachusetts.

title: The natural and civil/ history of Vermont./ <author statement>

Kentucky

1800

653.

District Court Ledger, KY 1

date of deposit: September 13, twenty-fifth year of Independence

claimant: A: John Bradford

author: Composed and published, by the said John Bradford, Editor of the Kentucky Gazette, in the Town of Lexington in the State of Kentucky

title: The general Instructor, Or the Office duty and authority of Justices of the peace Sheriffs Coroners, & Constables. in the state of Kentucky with precedents suited to every case that can possibly arrise. in either of those offices under the laws now in force. with references to the laws out of which they do arrise. the whole Alphabetically digested, under the Several letters, with an Index for the ready finding any matter sought. <author statement>

note: The Kentucky district court copyright ledger for this period is in the Clerk's Office of the Federal District Court in Frankfort, Kentucky.

State Department Deposits

1796

654.

State Department Ledger, 324 SD 1

date of deposit: January 19, 1796

depositor: Joseph Crukshank

compiler: John Peirce

title: The new american spelling book, improved &c <compiler statement>

note: Between 1790 and 1831 the Copyright Law required that within six months after a work was registered for copyright in a district court a copy be sent directly to the Secretary of State.

655.

State Department Ledger, 324 SD 2

date of deposit: February 5, 1796

depositor: Elhanan Winchester

author: Elhanan Winchester—

title: a plain political catechism intended for the use of schools in the US. of Am. <author statement>

note: A single entry in the State Department ledger notes two deposits made by Elhanan Winchester, represented here by entry numbers 655 and 656.

656.

State Department Ledger, 324 SD 2

date of deposit: February 5, 1796

depositor: Elhanan Winchester

author: E. W. <Elhanan Winchester>

title: Ten Letters addressed to Mr. Paine, in answer to a pamphlet, intitled the age of reason: <author statement>

note: See the note for entry number 655. According to the *National Index of American Imprints,* the author is Elhanan Winchester.

657.

State Department Ledger, 324 SD 3

date of deposit: February 11, 1796

depositor: Edmund Hogan

title: The Pennsylvania State Trials: &c Vol. 1. printed by F. Bailey at Yorick's Head for E. Hogan—

note: According to Roger Pattrell Bristol's *Index of Printers, Publishers, and Booksellers Indicated by Charles Evans in His American Bibliography,* the printer is Francis Bailey.

658.

State Department Ledger, 324 SD 4

date of deposit: March 5, 1796

depositor: Francis Nichols

title: Analysis of certain parts of a compendious view of natural Philosophy.

note: This State Department ledger entry records two items, represented here by entry numbers 658 and 659.

659.

State Department Ledger, 324 SD 4

date of deposit: March 5, 1796

depositor: Benjn. Dearborn

author: Benjamin Dearborn

title: The Columbian Grammar: or an essay for reducing a grammatical knowledge to a degree of simplicity which will render it easy for the instructer to teach, and for the pupil to learn <author statement>

note: See the note for entry number 658.

660.

State Department Ledger, 324 SD 5

date of deposit: March 15, 1796

depositor: Saml. H. Smith

author: <Edmund Randolph>

title: a vindication of Mr. Randolph's Resignation Phila.: printed by Samuel H. Smith 1795

note: According to the *National Index of American Imprints,* the author is Edmund Randolph.

661.

State Department Ledger, 324 SD 5

date of deposit: March 17, 1796

depositor: Rev. William Duke

author: Rev. William Duke.

title: A Clew to religious truth, &c <author statement>

662.

State Department Ledger, 324 SD 5

date of deposit: March 29, 1796

depositor: Joseph Scott

author: Joseph Scott

title: The United States Gazeteer: &c <author statement>

663.

State Department Ledger, 324 SD 6

date of deposit: April 9, 1796

depositor: William Waller Hening Esq.

author: William Waller Hening attorney at law

title: The new Virginia Justice &c. <author statement>

664.

State Department Ledger, 324 SD 6

date of deposit: April 14, 1796

depositor: Joshua Spalding
author: Joshua Spalding minister of the Gospel at the tabernacle in Salem
title: Sentiments concerning the coming and Kingdom of Christ; &c <author statement>

665.
State Department Ledger, 324 SD 7
date of deposit: April 18, 1796
depositor: Charles Christian
title: The Journeymen cabinet and chair-makers Philadelphia Book of Prices. second edition corrected and enlarged.

666.
State Department Ledger, 324 SD 8
date of deposit: April 26, 1796
depositor: Abraham Bradley Jr.
author: Abraham Bradley Jr.
title: A map of the US. &c. <author statement>
note: The clerk records that Abraham Bradley has deposited only the first sheet of this map.

667.
State Department Ledger, 324 SD 13
date of deposit: May 26, 1796
depositor: Amelia Simmons
author: Amelia Simmons an american Orphan
title: american Cookery, &c <author statement>

668.
State Department Ledger, 324 SD 17
date of deposit: June 10, 1796
author: Zephaniah Swift—
title: A system of the laws of the State of Connecticut <author statement> 2 Volumes in 6 books each—
note: This entry in the State Department ledger specifies that the deposit was received by the Secretary of State "on the 1st instant." No depositor is named.

669.
State Department Ledger, 324 SD 18
date of deposit: June 14, 1796
depositor: David West
author: Caleb Alexander A M.
title: The works of Virgil. translated into literal english prose: with some explanatory notes. <author statement>

670.
State Department Ledger, 324 SD 19
date of deposit: June 21, 1796
depositor: Edmund Hogan
author: E. H. <Edmund Hogan>
title: The prospect of Philadelphia, and Check on the next directory. part 1. <author statement>
note: According to the *National Index of American Imprints,* the author is Edmund Hogan.

671.
State Department Ledger, 324 SD 19
date of deposit: July 9, 1796
depositor: Benjamin Davies
author: Peter Porcupine <William Cobbett>
title: The Bloody Buoy, thrown out as a warning to the political Pilots of America; &c. <author statement>
note: This State Department ledger entry records three deposits, represented here by entry numbers 671, 672, and 673.

672.
State Department Ledger, 324 SD 19
date of deposit: July 9, 1796
depositor: Benjamin Davies
editor: <Baron Honoré Jean Riouffe>
title: Revolutionary Justice displayed &c translated from the french
note: See the note for entry number 671. The *National Union Catalog* gives Baron Honoré Jean Riouffe as the supposed editor.

673.
State Department Ledger, 324 SD 19
date of deposit: July 9, 1796
depositor: Benjamin Davies
author: Peter Porcupine. <William Cobbett>
title: The political Censor &c <author statement>
note: See the note for entry number 671. The *National Index of American Imprints* gives William Cobbett as the author.

674.
State Department Ledger, 324 SD 20
date of deposit: July 13, 1796
depositor: Noah Webster Junior
compiler: Noah Webster, Junr.—
title: A Collection of papers on the subject of Bilious fevers, prevalent in the US for a few years past— <compiler statement>

675.
State Department Ledger, 324 SD 23
date of deposit: October 29, 1796
depositor: William Mitchell
author: William Mitchell.
title: A new and complete system of bookkeeping &c <author statement>

1797

676.

State Department Ledger, 324 SD 28
date of deposit: February 10, 1797
depositor: Edmund M. Blunt
author: <Lawrence Furlong>
title: the American coast Pilot; &c.
note: According to the *National Index of American Imprints,* the author is Lawrence Furlong.

677.

State Department Ledger, 324 SD 33
date of deposit: March 7, 1797
depositor: Andrew Law
author: Andw. Law—
title: The art of singing part 2d. volume 2d. <author statement>

678.

State Department Ledger, 324 SD 34
date of deposit: March 29, 1797
depositor: Isaiah Thomas
author: Benjamin Whitman
title: An Index to the laws of Massachusetts <author statement>
note: This State Department ledger entry records three deposits, represented here by entry numbers 678, 679, and 680.

679.

State Department Ledger, 324 SD 34
date of deposit: March 29, 1797
depositor: Isaiah Thomas
author: Caleb Alexander A. M.
title: A Grammatical System of the Grecian Language—<author statement>
note: See the note for entry number 678.

680.

State Department Ledger, 324 SD 34
date of deposit: March 29, 1797
depositor: Isaiah Thomas
author: Joseph Lathrop D. D.
title: Sermons on various subjects evangelical &c <author statement> in two volumes Vol. II.d
note: See the note for entry number 678.

681.

State Department Ledger, 324 SD 35
date of deposit: May 4, 1797
depositor: Noah Worcester
author: Noah Worcester A. M.
title: The natural Teacher: or the best Spelling Book &c <author statement>

682.

State Department Ledger, 324 SD 35
date of deposit: May 12, 1797
depositor: Thomas and Andrews of Boston
author: Abner Alden A M.
title: An introduction to spelling and reading in two volumes being the first & second parts of a Columbian exercise &c. <author statement> Vol: 1.
note: This entry in the State Department ledger records two deposits made by Thomas and Andrews, represented here by entry numbers 682 and 683.

683.

State Department Ledger, 324 SD 35
date of deposit: May 12, 1797
depositor: Thomas and Andrews
author: Samuel B. Morse A M.
title: School Dialogues. &c <author statement>

684.

State Department Ledger, 324 SD 35
date of deposit: May 15, 1797
depositor: Mr. Freeman <Samuel Freeman of Portland?>
author: <Joseph Dennie>
title: The Lay preacher; &c.
note: According to the *National Index of American Imprints,* the author is Joseph Dennie. This State Department ledger entry records two deposits, represented here by entry numbers 684 and 685. Samuel Freeman of Portland, Maine, who was a publisher and also subscribed to Dennie's *The Spirit of the Farmer's Museum,* may be the Freeman recorded as depositor of this work.

685.

State Department Ledger, 324 SD 35
date of deposit: May 15, 1797
depositor: Mr. Freeman <Samuel Freeman of Portland?>
author: <Susannah (Willard) Johnson Hastings>
title: a narrative of the Captivity of Mrs. Johnson, &c—
note: According to the *National Union Catalog,* the author is Susannah (Willard) Johnson Hastings. See the note for entry number 684.

686.

State Department Ledger, 324 SD 36
date of deposit: May 23, 1797
depositor: E. H. Smith <Elihu Hubbard Smith>
author: <Elihu Hubbard Smith>

title: Edwin and Angelina; or the Banditti An Opera in three acts:
note: According to the *National Index of American Imprints,* the author is Elihu Hubbard Smith.

687.
State Department Ledger, 324 SD 36
date of deposit: May 23, 1797
depositor: Mr Chaplain
compiler: Samuel Hopkins D. D. Pastor of the 1st. Congregational Church in Newport
title: The life and Character of Miss Susanna Anthony &c. <compiler statement>

688.
State Department Ledger, 324 SD 36
date of deposit: June 9, 1797
depositor: Mr. Morse <Jedidiah Morse>
author: <Jedidiah Morse>
title: American Gazetteer
note: According to the *National Index of American Imprints,* the author is Jedidiah Morse. The clerk records that Morse's work was received "about this date."

689.
State Department Ledger, 324 SD 39
date of deposit: July 7, 1797
depositor: Dr. Benjamin Smith Barton
author: <Benjamin Smith Barton>
title: New Views of the origin of the tribes and Nations of America. 1797.
note: According to the *National Index of American Imprints,* the author is Benjamin Smith Barton.

690.
State Department Ledger, 324 SD 42
date of deposit: August 25, 1797
depositor: Thomas Russel
title: The american Spectator or matrimonial preceptor &c. 1 Vol.
note: This State Department ledger entry records five deposits made by Thomas Russel, represented here by entry numbers 690–94.

691.
State Department Ledger, 324 SD 42
date of deposit: August 25, 1797
depositor: Thomas Russel
author: <Caleb Bingham>
title: The Columbian orator &c 1 Vol.
note: See the note for entry number 690. According to the *National Index of American Imprints,* the author is Caleb Bingham.

692.
State Department Ledger, 324 SD 42
date of deposit: August 25, 1797
depositor: Thomas Russel
author: <Thomas Dobson>
title: First Lessons for Children 2 Vols
note: See the note for entry number 690. This item is described in the State Department ledger entry as a pamphlet. According to the *National Index of American Imprints,* the author is Thomas Dobson.

693.
State Department Ledger, 324 SD 42
date of deposit: August 25, 1797
depositor: Thomas Russel
author: <Thomas Dobson>
title: Pleasing instructions for young minds—1 Vol.
note: See the note for entry number 690. This item is described in the State Department ledger entry as a pamphlet. According to the *National Index of American Imprints,* the author is Thomas Dobson.

694.
State Department Ledger, 324 SD 42
date of deposit: August 25, 1797
depositor: Thomas Russel
author: <Thomas Dobson>
title: The Holiday or children's social amusement 1 Vol.
note: See the note for entry number 690. This item is described in the State Department ledger entry as a pamphlet. According to the *National Index of American Imprints,* the author is Thomas Dobson.

695.
State Department Ledger, 324 SD 42
date of deposit: September 27, 1797
depositor: Chauncey Lee
author: Chauncey Lee A. M.
title: The American Accomptant; being a plain practical and systematic compendium of federal Arithmetic in three parts &c. <author statement>

696.
State Department Ledger, 324 SD 43
date of deposit: November 14, 1797
author: a citizen of Massachusetts <Herman Mann>
title: The Female review: &c. <author statement>
note: There is a blank space where the depositor's name should appear in the State Department ledger entry. According to the *National Index of American Imprints,* the author is Herman Mann.

697.
State Department Ledger, 324 SD 43
date of deposit: November 30, 1797
depositor: Thos. McElroy
author: James Wilson Stevens
title: An historical and Geographical account of Algiers &c. <author statement>

698.
State Department Ledger, 324 SD 44
date of deposit: December 4, 1797
depositor: E. H. Smith <Elihu Hubbard Smith>
editors: <Samuel Latham Mitchill>
title: the Medical Repository—
note: This State Department ledger entry records the deposit of the "two first numbers" of this work. Elihu Hubbard Smith is given as one of the editors in the Circular Address in volume 1 of *The Medical Repository*. The *National Union Catalog* establishes Samuel Latham Mitchill and others as editors.

699.
State Department Ledger, 324 SD 45
date of deposit: December 16, 1797
depositor: Messrs. Hudson & Goodwin <Barzillai Hudson and George Goodwin>
author: Nathan Strong,
title: The Doctrine of eternal misery reconcileable with the infinite benevolence of God, &c.— <author statement>
note: According to Roger Pattrell Bristol's *Index of Printers, Publishers, and Booksellers Indicated by Charles Evans in His American Bibliography,* the printers are Barzillai Hudson and George Goodwin.

700.
State Department Ledger, 324 SD 45
date of deposit: December 16, 1797
deposit: Charles Backus A. M.
author: Charles Backus A M.
title: five discourses on the truth and inspiration of the Bible.&c. <author statement>

1798

701.
State Department Ledger, 324 SD 46
date of deposit: January 4, 1798
depositor: Captain Joseph Anthony
author: Duncan Mackintosh and his two Daughters—
title: a plain, rational essay on English Grammar: &c. <author statement> 2 Vols, 1. in French the other in English

702.
State Department Ledger, 324 SD 47
date of deposit: January 10, 1798
depositor: Messrs. Thomas & Andrews
author: Oliver Holden—
title: Laus Deo' &c. <author statement>
note: This entry in the State Department ledger records two deposits, represented here by entry numbers 702 and 703.

703.
State Department Ledger, 324 SD 47
date of deposit: January 10, 1798
depositor: Messrs. Thomas & Andrews
author: Abner Alden A M.
title: an introduction to Spelling and reading. &c Vol. 1 & 2. <author statement>
note: See the note for entry number 702.

704.
State Department Ledger, 324 SD 47
date of deposit: January 11, 1798
depositor: Wm. C. Smith <William Catherwood Smyth>
author: <John Dickinson>
title: The letters of Fabius in 1788 & 1797.
note: According to the *National Index of American Imprints,* the author is John Dickinson. Roger Pattrell Bristol's *Index of Printers, Publishers, and Booksellers Indicated by Charles Evans in His American Bibliography* gives William Catherwood Smyth as the printer.

705.
State Department Ledger, 324 SD 50
date of deposit: February 22, 1798
depositor: E. H. Smith <Elihu Hubbard Smith>
editor: <Samuel Latham Mitchill>
title: the medical repository.
note: This State Department ledger entry records the deposit of the third number of this work. See the note for entry 698.

706.
State Department Ledger, 324 SD 52
date of deposit: March 29, 1798
depositor: Edmund M. Blunt
author: surveyed by Capt. Paul Pinkham.
title: a chart of George's Bank including Cape Cod, Nantucket and the shoals lying on their coast, with directions for sailing over the same &c. <author statement>

707.
State Department Ledger, 324 SD 53
date of deposit: April 14, 1798
depositor: Doctor Benjamin Barton
author: <Benjamin Smith Barton>
title: Collections for an essay towards a materia medica of the United States.
note: According to the *National Index of American Imprints,* the author is Benjamin Smith Barton.

708.
State Department Ledger, 324 SD 54
date of deposit: May 2, 1798
depositor: Wm. P. and L. Blake <William P. Blake and Lemuel Blake>
author: <Caleb Alexander>
title: The Young Gentlemen and Ladies' Instructor, being a selection of New Pieces, designed as a reading book for the use of Schools and Academies &c.
note: According to Roger Pattrell Bristol's *Index of Printers, Publishers, and Booksellers Indicated by Charles Evans in His American Bibliography,* the printers are William P. Blake and Lemuel Blake. According to the *National Index of American Imprints,* the author is Caleb Alexander.

709.
State Department Ledger, 324 SD 56
date of deposit: May 12, 1798
depositor: E. H. Smith <Elihu Hubbard Smith>
editor: <Samuel Latham Mitchill>
title: The Medical Repository.—Vol. I.—No. IV.
note: See the note for entry 698.

710.
State Department Ledger, 324 SD 56
date of deposit: May 16, 1798
depositor: Eben. Larkin
author: <Hannah (Webster) Foster>
title: The Coquette or the History of Eliza Wharton, a novel founded on fact.
note: According to the *National Index of American Imprints,* the author is Hannah (Webster) Foster.

711.
State Department Ledger, 324 SD 59
date of deposit: June 30, 1798
depositor: B. Carr <Benjamin Carr of Philadelphia>
author: J. E. Harwood <John Edmund Harwood>—
composer: B. Carr; <Benjamin Carr>
title: Ellen Arise, A Ballad <author statement> <composer statement>
note: This State Department ledger entry records two deposits made by Benjamin Carr, represented here by entry numbers 711 and 712. The *National Index of American Imprints* gives the author as John Edmund Harwood.

712.
State Department Ledger, 324 SD 59
date of deposit: June 30, 1798
depositor: B. Carr <Benjamin Carr of Philadelphia>
title: The little Sailor Boy, A Ballad &c.
note: See the note for entry number 711.

713.
State Department Ledger, 324 SD 59
date of deposit: June 22, 1798
depositor: Thomas Dobson of Philadelphia
title: Encyclopaedia, or a Dictionary of Arts sciences and Miscellaneous Literature &c. the first American Edition, in eighteen volumes, greatly improved; &c—
note: This entry was written after that of June 30, 1798, in the State Department ledger and the June 22 date recorded in brackets.

714.
State Department Ledger, 324 SD 60
date of deposit: July 2, 1798
depositor: Thomas Greenleaf
author: a General Officer. <François René Jean, Baron de Pommereul>
title: Campaigns of General Buonaparte in Italy, during the 4.th and 5.th years of the French Republic. <author statement>
note: According to the *National Index of American Imprints,* the author is François René Jean, baron de Pommereul.

715.
State Department Ledger, 324 SD 60
date of deposit: July 5, 1798
depositor: Jedidiah Morse, of Charlestown in the State of Massachusetts
author: <Jedidiah Morse>
title: An Abridgment of the American Gazetteer &c.
note: According to the *National Index of American Imprints,* the author is Jedidiah Morse.

716.
State Department Ledger, 324 SD 65
date of deposit: August 9, 1798

depositor: Benjamin Smith Barton
author: <Benjamin Smith Barton>
title: New Views of the Origin of the Tribes and Nations of America.
note: According to the *National Index of American Imprints,* the author is Benjamin Smith Barton.

717.
State Department Ledger, 324 SD 65
date of deposit: September 21, 1798
depositor: P: Edmund M. Blunt of Newbury Port
author: Capt. Lawrence Furlong—
title: The American Coast Pilot, containing the courses and distances between the principal harbours, Capes and Headlands, from Passamaquoddy through the Gulph of Florida &c. &c. <author statement> Second edition:
note: This entry in the State Department ledger states that Edmund Blunt claims the work as proprietor.

718.
State Department Ledger, 324 SD 66
date of deposit: November 2, 1798
depositor: Isaiah Thomas
compiler: Reverend Thaddeus Mason Harris, A. M. &c.
title: Constitutions of the Ancient and Honorable Fraternity of Free and Accepted Masons &c. <compiler statement> Second Edition, revised and corrected &c.

719.
State Department Ledger, 324 SD 67
date of deposit: November 7, 1798
depositor: Enos Weed junr.
title: The American Orthographer,
note: This State Department ledger entry records the deposit of "book 1.st and book 2.d" of this work. These items are described as "two pamphlets."

720.
State Department Ledger, 324 SD 67
date of deposit: November 8, 1798
depositor: Abiel Holmes
author: Abiel Holmes
title: The Life of Ezra Stiles D. D. &c. &c. <author statement>

721.
State Department Ledger, 324 SD 67
date of deposit: November 22, 1798
depositor: Mathew Carey
title: The Columbian spelling and Reading Book, or an easy and alluring guide to spelling and reading &c.

722.
State Department Ledger, 324 SD 67
date of deposit: December 12, 1798
depositor: John Belknap
author: Jeremy Belknap. D. D.
title: American Biography or an historical account of those persons who have been distinguished in America &c. <author statement>

723.
State Department Ledger, 324 SD 68
date of deposit: December 31, 1798
depositor: Oliver D. and I. Cooke of Hartford <Oliver D. Cooke and Isaac Cooke>
author: Nathan Strong
title: Sermons on various subjects, doctrinal, experimental and practical, <author statement> &c.
note: According to Roger Pattrell Bristol's *Index of Printers, Publishers, and Booksellers Indicated by Charles Evans in His American Bibliography,* the printers are Oliver D. Cooke and Isaac Cooke.

1799

724.
State Department Ledger, 324 SD 69
date of deposit: January 24, 1799
depositor: A. J. Dallas
author: <Alexander James Dallas>
title: Reports of cases ruled and adjudged in the several Courts of the United States and of Pennsylvania, held at the seat of the Federal Government: <author statement> Vol. II.
note: According to the *National Index of American Imprints,* the author is Alexander James Dallas.

725.
State Department Ledger, 324 SD 71
date of deposit: February 18, 1799
depositor: Lindley Murray
author: Lindley Murray,
title: English Grammar, adapted to the different classes of learners with an appendix &c. <author statement> the second edition &c.
note: This State Department ledger entry records two deposits made by Lindley Murray, represented here by entry numbers 725 and 726.

726.
State Department Ledger, 324 SD 71
date of deposit: February 18, 1799
depositor: Lindley Murray
author: <Lindley Murray>

title: English exercises, adapted to the Grammar lately published by L. Murray &c.
note: See the note for entry number 725. According to the *National Index of American Imprints,* the author is Lindley Murray.

727.
State Department Ledger, 324 SD 71
date of deposit: February 25, 1799
depositor: Asa Ellis Junr.
author: <Asa Ellis>
title: The Country Dyer's Assistant,
note: According to the *National Index of American Imprints,* the author is Asa Ellis.

728.
State Department Ledger, 324 SD 75
date of deposit: March 21, 1799
depositor: Robert Proud
author: <Robert Proud>
title: The History of Pennsylvania in North America &c.
note: This State Department ledger records that the deposit is a work in two volumes. According to the *National Index of American Imprints,* the author is Robert Proud.

729.
State Department Ledger, 324 SD 75
date of deposit: March 30, 1799
depositor: A: James Ross
title: A plain, short, comprehenisve, practical Latin Grammar &c.
note: This entry in the State Department ledger states that James Ross claims the work as author.

730.
State Department Ledger, 324 SD 76
date of deposit: April 23, 1799
depositor: A: Zachariah Poulson Junior
title: The american Tutors assistant; or, a compendious system of Practical arithmetic &c.
note: This entry in the State Department ledger states that Zachariah Poulson claims the work as author.

731.
State Department Ledger, 324 SD 76
date of deposit: April 24, 1799
depositor: A: Peter Tharp
title: A new and complete system of Federal Arithmetic; in three parts, with an appendix. &c.
note: This entry in the State Department ledger states that Peter Tharp claims the work as author.

732.
State Department Ledger, 324 SD 76
date of deposit: May 16, 1799
depositor: Thomas Dobson
title: Plat of that tract of Country in the Territory northwest of the Ohio appropriated for military services; and described in the Act of Congress, instituted "An Act regulating the Grants of Land appropriated for military services, and for the Society of <the next word is crossed out in ms.> <the> United Brethern for propagating the Gospel among the Heathen" surveyed under the direction of Rufus Putnam Surveyor General to the United States:
note: This State Department ledger entry records two deposits made by Thomas Dobson, represented here by entry numbers 732 and 733.

733.
State Department Ledger, 324 SD 76
date of deposit: May 16, 1799
depositor: Thomas Dobson
title: Letters on the existence and character of the Deity, and on the moral state of Man.
note: See the note for entry number 732.

734.
State Department Ledger, 324 SD 77
date of deposit: May 22, 1799
depositor: Thomas and Andrews, Booksellers of Boston,
author: a lady.
title: The New Pleasing Instructor, or Young Lady's guide to Virtue and Happiness &c. <author statement> &c.

735.
State Department Ledger, 324 SD 77
date of deposit: May 30, 1799
author: Enoch Hale A. M.
title: A spelling Book; or the first part of a grammar of the English Language, as written and spoken in the United States. <author statement> &c.
note: No depositor is named in the State Department ledger entry.

736.
State Department Ledger, 324 SD 77
date of deposit: June 12, 1799
author: himself. <William Heath>
title: Memoirs of Major General Heath, containing anecdotes, details of skirmishes, battles and other military events, during the American war: <author statement>

note: No depositor is named in the State Department ledger entry. According to the *National Index of American Imprints,* the author is William Heath.

737.
State Department Ledger, 324 SD 78
date of deposit: July 3, 1799
depositor: Andrew Law
author: Andrew Law,
title: The Musical magazine, containing a number of favorite pieces, European and American— <author statement> No. 5.th—

738.
State Department Ledger, 324SD 78
date of deposit: July 3, 1799
depositor: Benjamin Smith Barton
author: Benjamin Smith Barton M. D.
title: Fragments of the Natural History of Pennsylvania, <author statement> part 1.st:

739.
State Department Ledger, 324 SD 78
date of deposit: August 5, 1799
depositor: A. J. Dallas
author: <Alexander James Dallas>
title: reports of cases ruled and adjudged &c.
note: According to a note in the State Department ledger, this deposit is the third volume of the work. The *National Index of American Imprints* gives as the author Alexander James Dallas.

740.
State Department Ledger, 324 SD 79
date of deposit: August 23, 1799
depositor: Jonathan Williams
author: <Jonathan Williams>
title: Thermometrical Navigation, being a series of experiments and observations, tending to prove that by ascertaining the relative heat of the sea-water from time to time, the passage of a ship through the Gulph-stream and from Deep Water into soundings, may be discovered in time to avoid danger &c. &c.
note: According to the *National Union Catalog,* the author is Jonathan Williams.

741.
State Department Ledger, 324 SD 79
date of deposit: September 24, 1799
depositor: Edmund M. Blunt
author: John Hamilton Moore
title: John Hamilton Moore's practical navigator, to which are added some general instructions and information to merchants, masters of vessels, and others concerned in navigation, relative to the mercantile and maritime laws and customs;
note: This State Department ledger entry notes that this is a new edition of the work.

742.
State Department Ledger, 324 SD 79
date of deposit: October 5, 1799
depositor: Thomas Herty
author: Thomas Herty
title: A Digest of the laws of Maryland, being an abridgment alphabetically arranged &c. <author statement> &c.

743.
State Department Ledger, 324 SD 80
date of deposit: October 24, 1799
depositor: Seth Williston
title: An address to Parents upon the importance of Religiously educating their children

744.
State Department Ledger, 324 SD 80
date of deposit: October 24, 1799
author: <Joseph Hamilton>
depositor: Joseph Hamilton, Physician
title: occasional reflections on the observation of the Small Pox: or, the Traveller's Pocket Doctor.
note: According to the *National Index of American Imprints,* the title is *Occasional Reflections on the Operations of the Small Pox* and the author is Joseph Hamilton.

745.
State Department Ledger, 324 SD 80
date of deposit: December 5, 1799
depositor: Nathan Grout junr.
author: <Jonathan Grout>
title: The Young Child's accidence &c.
note: According to the *National Index of American Imprints,* the author is Jonathan Grout.

746.
State Department Ledger, 324 SD 80
date of deposit: December 5, 1799
depositor: John H. Ives
title: Twenty four country dances and eight cotillions, for the year 1800

1800
747.
State Department Ledger, 324 SD 82
date of deposit: January 7, 1800

depositor: Enos Weed
title: the Physical Instructor &c.
note: This State Department ledger entry records two deposits made by Enos Weed, represented here by entry numbers 747 and 748.

748.
State Department Ledger, 324 SD 82
date of deposit: January 7, 1800
depositor: Enos Weed
title: An Extract from the first section of the first book of the Common Man's Physical Instructor;
note: See the note for entry number 747.

749.
State Department Ledger, 324 SD 83
date of deposit: January 20, 1800
depositor: Noah Webster junr.
title: A Brief History of Epedemic and pestilential diseases with the principal phenomena of the Physical world which precede and accompany them &c. &c.

750.
State Department Ledger, 324 SD 84
date of deposit: February 20, 1800
depositor: Robert and George Watkins
title: A Digest of the laws of the State of Georgia from its first establishment as a British Province down to the year 1798 inclusive &c.

751.
State Department Ledger, 324 SD 84
date of deposit: February 27, 1800
depositor: Gershom Craft of Trenton New Jersey
author: Reverend Samuel Stanhope Smith D. D.
title: An Oration upon the death of General George Washington, delivered in the State House at Trenton on the 14th of January 1800, <author statement> &c. &c.

752.
State Department Ledger, 324 SD 85
date of deposit: March 12, 1800
depositor: Isaiah Thomas
author: Caleb Alexander A. M.
title: The Young Ladies' and Gentlemens spelling Book: on a new and improved plan; containing a criterion of rightly spelling and pronouncing the English Language &c. &c. <author statement> &c. &c.

753.
State Department Ledger, 324 SD 85
date of deposit: April 2, 1800
author: Thomas M. Prentiss
title: The Maine spelling book, containing a variety of words, accented and divided, with moral and entertaining lessons for reading; useful tables &c. &c. <author statement> &c. &c.
note: This State Department ledger entry notes that the deposit was "Received under a blank cover, supposed from the author."

754.
State Department Ledger, 324 SD 87
date of deposit: April 26, 1800
depositor: David Cook junr.
author: <David Cook, Jr.>
title: Cooks American Arithmetic: being a System of decimal Arithmetic comporting with the federal currency of the United States of America &c. &c.
note: According to the *National Index of American Imprints,* the author is David Cook, Jr.

755.
State Department Ledger, 324 SD 87
date of deposit: April 28, 1800
depositor: William Woodbridge
title: The plain spelling book, and easy guide to reading &c. &c.

756.
State Department Ledger, 324 SD 88
date of deposit: May 1, 1800
depositor: Charles Pinckney Sumner
author: Charles Pinckney Sumner,
title: Eulogy on the illustrious George Washington, pronounced at Milton, 22.nd February 1800, <author statement>

757.
State Department Ledger, 324 SD 88
date of deposit: May 5, 1800
author: the late Reverend John Clarke D. D. Minister of the first church in Boston, Massachusetts
title: Sermons <author statement>
note: In this State Department ledger entry, no depositor is named.

758.
State Department Ledger, 324 SD 91
date of deposit: May 24, 1800
depositor: Richard Alsop
author: Richard Alsop

title: A Poem sacred to the Memory of George Washington, late President of the United States and Commander in Chief of the Armies of the United States—<author statement>

759.
State Department Ledger, 324 SD 91
date of deposit: May 24, 1800
depositor: Benjamin Heaton
author: Benjamin Heaton A. M.
title: The Columbian spelling book &c—<author statement>

760.
State Department Ledger, 324 SD 91
date of deposit: July 1, 1800
depositor: Thomas C. Cushing
author: William Biglow
title: The Child's Library; part first; containing Lessons for spelling and reading, stops and marks, numbers &c. <author statement>
note: This entry in the State Department ledger records two deposits, represented here by entry numbers 760 and 761.

761.
State Department Ledger, 324 SD 91
date of deposit: July 1,1800
depositor: Thomas C. Cushing
author: William Biglow
title: The Child's Library; part second, containing a selection of lessons for spelling, reading and speaking, <author statement> &c
note: See the note for entry number 760.

762.
State Department Ledger, 324 SD 91
date of deposit: July 12, 1800
depositor: Joseph Story
author: Joseph Story
title: The Power of Solitude, A Poem, in two parts, <author statement>

763.
State Department Ledger, 324 SD 91
date of deposit: July 26, 1800
depositor: William Latham
author: William Latham,
title: The political economy of inland navigation, irrigation and drainage &c. &c. <author statement>

764.
State Department Ledger, 324 SD 92
date of deposit: August 7, 1800
depositor: George Rosse
author: Reverend David Ball
title: A Sermon, in consequence of the Proclamation of His Excellency John Adams Esqr. President of the United States of North America, preached on the memorable 9.th day of May 1798, <author statement>

765.
State Department Ledger, 324 SD 92
date of deposit: August 7, 1800
author: <Benjamin Smith Barton>
depositor: Benjamin Smith Barton
title: A memoir concerning the disease of Goitre &c. &c.

766.
State Department Ledger, 324 SD 92
date of deposit: August 14, 1800
depositor: Nathaniel Emmons
author: Nathaniel Emmons
title: Sermons on some of the first principles and doctrines of true religion, <author statement>

767.
State Department Ledger, 324 SD 92
date of deposit: September 8, 1800
depositor: John Churchman
author: John Churchman Fellow of the Russian Imperial Academy,
title: The magnetic atlas, or variation charts of the whole terraqueous globe &c. The Third Edition; with additions, <author statement>

768.
State Department Ledger, 324 SD 92
date of deposit: September 18
depositor: Thomas and Andrews of Boston
author: Caleb Alexander A. M.
title: The Columbian Dictionary of the English Language, in which many new words, peculiar to the United States, and many words of general use, not found in any other English Dictionary, are inserted &c. &c. <author statement>

769.
State Department Ledger, 324 SD 92
date of deposit: September 20, 1800
depositor: Solomon Howe
author: Solomon Howe, A. M.
title: Worshipper's Assistant, containing the rules of music, and a variety of easy and plain Psalm tunes &c. &c. <author statement>

770.
State Department Ledger, 324 SD 93
date of deposit: October 20, 1800
depositor: Samuel Low
author: Samuel Low,
title: Poems <author statement>

771.
State Department Ledger, 324 SD 93
date of deposit: October 30, 1800
depositor: Abel Flint
title: the Connecticut Evangelical Magasine,
note: This State Department ledger entry records the deposit of the first four numbers of this work.

772.
State Department Ledger, 324 SD 93
date of deposit: November 18, 1800
author: Daniel Belknap, Author of the harmonist's companion &c. &c.
title: The Evangelical harmony, containing a great variety of airs suitable for Divine Worship: besides a number of favorite pieces of music, selected from different authors &c. &c. <author statement>
note: No depositor is named in this State Department ledger entry.

773.
State Department Ledger, 324 SD 93
date of deposit: November 18, 1800
composer: Mr. P. Landrin Duport <Pierre Landrin Duport>
title: United States country dances with figures; also accompaniments for the Piano Forte, composed in America <author statement>
note: No depositor is named in this State Department ledger entry. According to the *National Index of American Imprints,* the author is Pierre Landrin Duport.

774.
State Department Ledger, 324 SD 93
date of deposit: December 27, 1800
depositor: Benjamin Waterhouse
author: Benjamin Waterhouse,
title: A prospect of exterminating the small pox, being the history of the Variolae vaccinae or Kine-pox &c. &c. <author statement>

Department of Interior Deposits

1794

775.

receipt in patent office: April 28, 1859
author: Christopher Colles
title: Geographical Ledger (The) & systemized Atlas.
imprint: New York: John Buel, 1794
note: In 1859 Congress passed An Act Providing for Keeping and Distributing All Public Documents, which specified in Section 8 that all books, maps, charts, and other publications that had been deposited in the Department of State would in the future be deposited in the Department of Interior. It also directed that the Department of Interior would henceforth perform the record-keeping duties with respect to the Copyright Law that had been conducted by the Department of State. In complying with this law, the Department of State sent to the Department of Interior some books which had been deposited for copyright long before. These were recorded by the Patent Office, which was the Department of Interior office that assumed this responsibility, as being the first books received for copyright deposit in 1859.

1795

776.

receipt in patent office: April 28, 1859
claimant: Wm Patten
author: William Patten
title: Christianity the true glory.
imprint: Warren, Rhode Island: N. Phillips <Nathaniel Phillips>, 1795
note: According to Roger Pattrell Bristol's *Index of Printers, Publishers, and Booksellers Indicated by Charles Evans in His American Bibliography,* the printer is Nathaniel Phillips.

1800

777.

receipt in patent office: April 28, 1859
author: David Cook
title: American Arithmetic
imprint: New Haven, Ct.: Thos. Green & son, 1800.

778.

receipt in patent office: April 28, 1859
author: D. Staniford <Daniel Staniford>
title: Art of Reading (The).
imprint: Boston: John Russell, 1800.
note: According to the *National Index of American Imprints,* the author is Daniel Staniford.

779.

receipt in patent office: April 28, 1859
author: D. Staniford <Daniel Staniford>
title: Child's first book (The).
imprint: Boston: John Russell, 1800.
note: See the note for entry number 778.

Appendix

It is our hope that the transcription and indexing of the copyright entries for 1790 to 1800 will encourage a future effort to create a database for the records from 1801 through 1870. Though the enormity of such a project—there are approximately 150,000 entries—may never permit a subject file, access by key word should be possible. Though key-word access has limitations, it provides some form of subject control. To simulate computerized key-word retrieval of the records from 1790 to 1800 presented in this volume, the entries have been manually searched by the words listed below and the results given here.

A. music, song(s), ballad(s), anthem(s), Lied(er), Gesang(¨-e), Gesängen: 9, 11, 28, 52, 81, 84, 166, 190, 201, 202, 212, 224, 233, 253, 260, 274, 284, 289, 301, 305, 312, 314, 338, 390, 393, 396, 397, 420, 421, 428, 432, 445, 457, 470, 508, 578, 590, 596, 712, 772.

B. play(s), comedy(ies), tragedy(ies): 2, 81, 84, 112, 349, 371, 379, 380, 491, 508, 522, 639.

C. poetry, poem(s), Poesie(n): 79, 159, 226, 268, 297, 343, 349, 384, 391, 398, 428, 429, 450, 462, 463, 468, 477, 490, 505, 556, 578, 601, 623, 758, 762, 770.

D. map(s), carte(s): 29, 106, 107, 123, 124, 183, 237, 264, 265, 279, 310, 320, 327, 339, 356, 382, 414.

Index

A

B

C

D

E

F

G

H

I

J

K

L

M

N

O

P

Q

R

S

T

U

V

W

Y